ENGLISH LITERARY
PERIODICALS

The Athenian Society, as Pictured in John Dunton's
Young Student's Library, 1692

ENGLISH LITERARY PERIODICALS

by

WALTER GRAHAM

1966

OCTAGON BOOKS, INC.

New York

Reprinted 1966
by special arrangement with Mary W. Graham

OCTAGON BOOKS, INC.
175 FIFTH AVENUE
NEW YORK, N.Y. 10010

LIBRARY OF CONGRESS CATALOG CARD NUMBER: 66-28372

Printed in U.S.A. by
NOBLE OFFSET PRINTERS, INC.
NEW YORK 3, N. Y.

Behind the scenes sit mighty we,
Nor are we known nor will we be;
The world and we exchanging thus,
While we find chat for them they work for us.

—*Young Students Library*, 1692

TABLE OF CONTENTS

FOREWORD

This, the first general survey of English literary periodicals that has ever been written, makes no claim to exhaustiveness or finality. The author does not regard it as a definitive work, nor does he expect it to escape the criticism to which the pioneer in any field is usually subjected. In an undertaking so broad as that which overlooks two and one half centuries of English literature no one can be infallible; and the writer of this book recognizes many weaknesses in his completed work—weaknesses that more concentrated effort on special fields, and the always advancing knowledge of individual investigators, will remedy in later histories of English literary periodicals.

The writer's many obligations are here acknowledged with gratitude, even though, for the most part, this may be done only by a general avowal. In particular, he wishes to thank Mr. Laurence F. Powell, of the Taylor Institution, Oxford, Mr. J. G. Muddiman, of London, Professor David Nichol Smith, of Oxford, and Professor George W. Sherburn, of Chicago, for valuable counsel. He owes much to his colleagues, Professor Jacob Zeitlin, Dr. Caroline F. Tupper, Dr. Clarissa Rinaker, and Dr. Homer Caskey, for critical opinions or aid in collecting material, as well as to the various editors of periodicals now in progress for information of a nature difficult to secure. Notable scholars in the field to whom especial acknowledgment of debt must be made are Professor Chester N. Greenough, Professor Roger P. McCutcheon, and Professors Ronald S. Crane and the late F. B. Kaye, compilers of the *Census of British Newspapers and Periodicals*. To Winifred Gregory and the anonymous compilers of the *Union List of Serials*, the present and all future generations of American scholars are under deepest obligation.

W. G.

University of Illinois
July, 1930

INTRODUCTION

There is no more interesting chapter in the history of England than the story of the newspaper press, involving, as it does, religious persecution, partisan struggle, Royalist or Puritan intrigue, and the various enactments designed to restrict printing. The story of the beginnings of English "literary" periodicals, in the form of book catalogues, abstract serials, and serials devoted to moral instruction and entertainment, is equally interesting, although it does not include the passion of party conflict in more than an incidental way, and religious strife is only to a minor degree one of its factors. But religious opinion, partisan bitterness, and the shadow of press surveillance are never wholly absent from the earlier essay sheets, magazines or reviews; and almost to our own century we find political predilections modifying critical verdicts. Moreover, the history of the English literary periodical during the last two centuries is the story of the English author—his struggle for recognition and reward, his miseries and ambitions, his opinions, ideals and sentiments. What English writers have been interested in or moved by, what they have believed, the dreams they have dreamed—these have gone into the making of the "literary" periodical far more than into the periodical devoted wholly or chiefly to the dissemination of news.

It cannot be denied that before the eighteenth century, periodical literature was produced by inferior pens; nor is it less apparent that from the beginning of this century onward the periodical was the nursery of literary genius. Defoe, Addison, Steele and Swift, on the one hand, elevated the hitherto crude essays in the public journals to a point where they were recognized as writing of permanent value and significance; on the other hand, these writers revealed to the world of letters the importance of the public journals as vehicles of literary enterprise. Since the reign of Queen Anne, English authors have found it advantageous to associate themselves with periodicals.

As time passed, the periodicals of the eighteenth century became, more and more, the repositories of the early works of struggling authors. Collins, Chatterton, Joseph Warton, Christopher Smart, Fielding, Smollett, Johnson, Boswell, and Goldsmith, seized the opportunity offered by the increasing numbers of newspapers, magazines, and reviews, and the consequent multiplication of readers. When the "Golden Age" of political patronage in the reign of Anne gave way to the "Age of Neglect" in the reigns of the Georges, the growth of the periodical presented makers of English literature with a new and glorious prospect—the prospect of a never-ending age of patronage from an ever-increasing body of readers. The decline of the old patronage was followed closely by the rise of the new, of which it was to some extent the cause.

The relations of the public and the men of letters in the eighteenth century have been admirably expounded by Beljame,[1] whose work, however, does not proceed far enough to show the important part played by the periodical in the making of authors and literature. What remains to be demonstrated—and it is a purpose of this work to present it—is the true importance of the periodical in encouraging, supporting, and developing the talent of writers. Even if we confine ourselves to the "literary"

---

[1] *Le public et les hommes de lettres en Angleterre au dix-huitième siécle,* Paris 1881.
See also A. S. Collins, *Authorship in the Days of Johnson,* London 1927.

periodical (the serial that contained in its columns poetry, essays, fiction, and criticism of other literary works, as distinguished from the periodical which disseminated information or partisan opinion), we find that, in constantly increasing ratio, the authors whom posterity has delighted to honor were developed by the rewards of such publication. A roster of names prominent in periodical literature is very nearly an outline of the literary history of the eighteenth and nineteenth centuries. Defoe, Swift, Addison, Steele, Johnson, Christopher Smart, Chatterton, Richardson, Fielding, Smollett, Goldsmith, Scott, Coleridge, Leigh Hunt, Hazlitt, Campbell, Hogg, Macaulay, De Quincey, John Wilson, Lockhart, Lamb, Carlyle, Hood, Dickens, Thackeray, Meredith, Kingsley, George Eliot, Trollope, Tennyson, and Matthew Arnold are notable, either for their management of, or contributions to, essay sheets, magazines, and reviews—to say nothing of a host of writers, not all obscure, whose names now give value to dusty files of half-forgotten periodicals.

That the press laws of England seriously retarded the growth of periodic literature is a fact too obvious to need abundant comment. Under the Star Chamber Court censorship, the Printing Act, and the stamp duties, the literary periodical suffered along with the more offensive journal of news or political propaganda. Until the overthrow of the Star Chamber in 1641, for several years only one serial appeared, and in any year not more than six were published in the British Isles. In 1642 there were no less than fifty-nine periodicals, in contrast with the three that had been published the year before. Periodicals were numerous in the years that followed, until the Puritan censorship with the harsh measures of the Secretary of State in 1655 and 1656 again reduced the number to three. Hopes of publishers rose in the year of the Restoration, 1660, which brought nearly two-score serials into being; but Charles proved as unsympathetic toward letters and freedom of opinion as the Long Parliament and Cromwell. With the enactment of the Printing Act in 1662, and with Roger L'Estrange as Licenser from 1663, the number of published serials dwindled, until in 1674 only the *Term Catalogue* of London booksellers, the official *London Gazette*, and the *Transactions of the Royal Society* were left to represent England's periodical literature. A slight increase during the years 1675-78 preceded an outburst of publishing in 1679 that followed the lapse of the Printing Act. The defiance of the royal will by Shaftsbury's "ignoramus" juries permitted twenty-four serials to appear in 1679; in 1680, twenty-five; and in 1681, forty-one; after which the Court secured the appointment of loyal sheriffs, and therefore of effective juries, at the end of 1682, and the latter gradually reduced the *Mercuries* and other periodical sheets to a total of six in 1686 and seven in 1687. But the Revolution of 1688 once more brought a less rigorous enforcement of the Printing Act, and signs of its end began to appear. Twenty periodicals are now preserved that appeared in 1689. From this point on, the numbers of periodic publications grew steadily from year to year, except for a slight decrease when Anne's stamp duty was imposed in August, 1712;[1] and by the year 1800 a total of two hundred and

---

[1] *Statutes at Large*, 10 Anne, Cap. 19, ci. This statute imposed a tax of ½d on half sheets, 1d on those larger (not more than one whole sheet), and a 12d tax on advertisements, in all "pamphlets, newspapers, or papers containing publick news, intelligence, or occurrences." The tax on advertisements was applied to "any printed paper made publick weekly or oftner." In spite of the contemporary comment (*Spectator* No. 445) "This is the day on which many eminent authors will probably publish their last words," the Statute seems to have made very little difference in the number of new publications (See Crane and Kaye, *A Census of British Newspapers and Periodicals*, Chapel Hill, 1927, p. 183).

sixty-four, of all kinds, were issued for the perusal of British readers.

Literary periodicals of modern times (1850 and following) fall into several rather ill-defined classes or types. There is the "magazine," so-called, really the monthly miscellany of the eighteenth century, the original significance of the term "magazine," as used by Edward Cave, proprietor of the *Gentleman's Magazine*, having been largely lost sight of. We have still with us the reviews, quarterly or monthly, consisting primarily of serious discussion, and in some cases, as in the beginning, consisting of articles purporting to be critical essays upon important books. We have still, as they had in the seventeenth century, the literary features in the daily and weekly newspapers. Of poetry magazines we have a limited number, as well as of theatrical journals. Only one distinct form has virtually passed from the scene— the single essay periodical of the *Spectator* type. This has been absorbed into the more important periodicals as a department or feature—a serial essay, appearing regularly in a certain place in the newspaper or magazine. As a comparatively modern development, we have the weekly journal of criticism, of mixed ancestry, best represented in the *Times Literary Supplement*. It is devoted to the discussion of books, and includes many of the features of the reviews and magazines.

The present work is intended to be a history of literary periodicals in Great Britain, a guide to the literary values of the various types of such periodicals; and a descriptive summary of the form and character of the most notable reviews, miscellanies, essay sheets, weekly critical journals, and specialized serials, which have, during the last two and one half centuries, contributed to the "literary" tradition. The evolution of these various types of periodic publications, the authors associated with them, their influence upon each other and upon English literature since 1665—these constitute the story told in the following pages, a vital phase of the making of modern literature.

I

PERIODICAL LITERATURE BEFORE THE DAYS OF QUEEN ANNE

i

The death of Queen Anne on August 1, 1714, had one far-reaching effect which that unimaginative sovereign could never have foreseen. The political patronage that had made her reign the "Golden Age" for authors of mediocre ability, as well as for the more highly talented, received a blow from which it never recovered. The consequences of her passing were not apparent at first, of course. Addison, and Steele and others who had been loyal to their Whig masters continued to reap for a time the harvest of partisan rewards. But the accession of a king who knew little English, and the gradual emergence of Robert Walpole as the power behind the throne, soon made it clear to men of letters that the golden days were gone. This was to some extent due to Walpole's personal methods and prejudices, but the chief cause for the change was the growth of the newspaper and its influence. Others would have seen, if Walpole had not, that political patronage as a means of support and reward for authors of ability was doomed by the rise of the daily and weekly journal. The appearance of such newspapers as the familiarly-known *Read's*, *Applebee's*, *Mist's*, and *Fog's*, between 1716 and 1728, to say nothing of a score of other more or less successful enterprises of like nature, offered opportunities for the dissemination of political propaganda. It was no longer necessary for political parties to retain writers, as Addison was retained by the Whigs of 1699 with a pension of £300, or as Swift was "bought over" by the Tories in 1710. A poet who could write the *Campaign* and a satirist who could excoriate the Whigs in the *Examiner* were alike superfluous to a Minister who had at his disposal a legion of newspaper hacks to write what he dictated. The beginning of a daily press in London with the *Daily Courant* of 1702, and the rise of the provincial newspaper press in the closing years of Anne's reign, had prepared the way for a breakdown of the old patronage. The Hanoverian Succession and the repeated victories of Walpole over his political enemies completed the disaster. Writers were soon made to realize that political patronage was no longer the royal road to affluence for men of letters.

Thus the death of Anne may be regarded, in one sense, as a milestone in the history of English literature. It marks, vaguely to be sure, the ending of an epoch and the beginning of a new one. From the days of George the First, English authors were obliged to look for other means of support and encouragement. Some like Pope succeeded by a kind of subscription-patronage or "joint-stock patronage," as it has been called. Others looked only to the publishers of their books—Lintot, Tonson, etc., for the financial compensations of literary work. But more and more, as the eighteenth century passed, found their encouragement and reward in the stipends paid by the rapidly increasing numbers of newspapers, essay-serials, magazines and reviews—the periodicals. Periodical publishers gradually attracted to their banners the struggling hosts of poets, essayists, and critics. And toward the end of the eighteenth century more than one must have discerned the future of the *belles-lettres* in the amazing multiplication of periodical enterprises. Although the days of personal and political patronage were gone, writers could look forward hopefully to the new day when an educated reading public should be man's critic and his best patron.

ii

The types of literary periodicals which rapidly developed in the eighteenth century were, almost without exception, foreshadowed in the seventeenth. They first appeared in an atmosphere of theological and political strife, identified with partisan or sectarian controversy. Thus, the book notices of the middle-seventeenth century, earliest ancestors of modern reviews, were frequently condemnations of works subject to Parliamentary investigation, puffs of ecclesiastical or partisan propagandists; or, later, critical censures from the pens of licensers. Even such primitive criticisms were late in appearing. An isolated case of a book "this present day published" has been found in the *Mercurius Britannicus* of 1643; but the suggestions of expressed opinion regarding the merits of a written work began not earlier than 1646, when book notices were appearing in many of the half-sheet folios of the day.[1]

At first, news matter and advertising were ingenuously combined, as in the *Perfect Diurnall of Some Passages in Parliament*, a weekly newsbook edited by Samuel Pecke. A discussion of the victory of Cromwell's Army at Oxford, was interrupted that the writer might recommend to his readers "a booke now in the Presse and ready to be published, entitled *Magnalia Dei Anglicana, or England's Chronicles*, and the most exactest hitherto collected. . . ."[2] Although book publishing and book selling were parts of a single enterprise, few publishers made before 1650 any attempt to advertise their wares other-

---

[1] For a more extended treatment of the history of periodic literature before 1715, see my *Beginnings of English Literary Periodicals*, N. Y. 1926.
[2] *Perfect Diurnall*, No. 156. July 20-27, 1646.

wise than by such an occasional news-reference. The notice was usually written by the publisher of the book, or by a rival publisher perhaps, who, for a religious or political reason, wished to praise or condemn it. During the 1640's the works of Milton,[1] Davenant, Izaak Walton, Browne, and Cowley were "reviewed" in this manner; and not until 1650 or thereabouts did the book notices begin to resemble modern paid advertisements. Soon after 1650, they were grouped on the last page, and printed in smaller type than the news.[2] Advertisements of other things began to appear. Books continued, however, to make up most of the advertising as late as 1655, when Marchamont Nedham, in his *Publick Intelligencer*, separated the notices of books from those of quack medicines and other commodities.

Another ancestor of the modern critical journal, one far more important than the early book notice, was the periodic publication which contained abstracts of books. The success of the *Journal des Sçavans*, established in Paris in 1665, not only gave an impetus to the issuing of periodicals both in Great Britain and on the Continent, but led to the beginning in England of a long line of serials devoted largely to the summarizing of books for

[1] The following notice of Milton's *Eikonoklastes* appeared in 1649:

The Reader may please to take notice of a book published the last weeke intituled IKONOCLASTES, in answer to a late book intituled EIKON BASILIKE, the portrature of his sacred Majesty in his solitudes and sufferings, wherein they who are not willing to be imposed upon, and would be content to be delivered from the danger of that Idolatry which many have committed, may see the gold taken off from that Idol, and that grosse hypocrisie, and incongruity, betweene those specious professions, and the late King's constant practise, sufficiently and clearly laid open by Mr. JOHN MELTON (*A Brief Relation of Some Affairs*, Nov. 20, 1649). See R. P. McCutcheon, "The Beginnings of Book-Reviewing in English Periodicals," *Pub. Mod. Lang. Assn.*, xxxvi (1922), 691-706.

[2] As early as 1615 the black-letter broadside ballad was made an instrument for drawing attention to a book. See Hyder E. Rollins, *Pub. Mod. Lang. Assn.*, xxxiv (1919), 295.

busy or lazy readers, and indirectly led to the critical review.[1] The *Journal des Sçavans* may have been suggested by the Paris *Gazette* and by the reports of Théophraste Renaudot's "Bureau d'adresse" (1633-42). At any rate, in 1663 the historian François de Mézeray obtained a privilege for a literary periodical which came to nothing; and Denis de Sallo, Counsellor of the Parliament of Paris, and a man of some learning, actually set up the first publication of this kind. From Sallo's personal habit of digesting and commenting upon what he read seems to have come the idea of a journal that should contain abstracts of books. As such the *Journal des Sçavans* first appeared.[2]

It was a twelve-page weekly, issued on Mondays. The address of the printer to the reader in the first number (January 5, 1665) shows how much the purpose and content of literary periodicals in England were anticipated.

Le dessein de ce Journal estant de faire sçavoir ce qui se passe de nouveau dans la République des lettres, il sera composé.

Premièrement d'un Catalogue exact des principaux livres qui s'imprimeront dans l'Europe. Et on ne se contentera pas de donner les simples titres, comme ont fait jusques à présent la pluspart des Bibliographes: mais de plus on dira de quoi ils traitent, et à quoi ils peuvent estre utiles.

Secondement, quand il viendra à mourir quelque personne célèbre par sa doctrine et par ses ouvrages, on en fera l'Eloge, et on donnera un

---

[1] Of course, influences may have come indirectly from the *Erbauliche Monatsunterredungen* of Johann Rist, 1663, D. G. Morhof's plans for a history of modern books and learning in Germany, or from Otto Mencke's *Acta eruditorum* (1682-1745) of Leipzig. Likewise, the *Giornale de' letterati* (1668) of M. A. Ricci and Francesco Nazzari, a follower in Italy of the *Journal des Sçavans*, may have had some effect on the earlier English periodicals. Note also the periodicals of Le Clerc and Pierre Bayle. (See E. Hatin, *Bibliographie de la presse périodique française*, Paris, 1866, the *Histoire de la presse en France*, Paris 1859-1861, and Ernest Milberg, *Die Moralischen Wochenschriften des 18. Jahrhunderts, Meissen, n. d.*)

[2] The idea of abstracting books was not original with Denis de Sallo, of course, but may be traced to Photius of Greece, *cir.* 890 A.D., who preserved in his *Myriobiblion* summaries of the works he had perused.

Catalogue de ce qu'il aura mis au jour, avec les principales circonstances de sa vie.

En troisième lieu on fera sçavoir les expériences de Physique et de Chymie, qui peuvent servir à expliquer les effets de la Nature: les nouvelles découvertes qui se font dans les Arts et dans les Sciences, comme les machines et les inventions utiles ou curieuses que peuvent fournir les Mathématiques: les Observations du Ciel, celles des Météores, et ce que l'Anatomie pourra trouver de nouveau dans les animaux.

En quatrième lieu, les principales décisions des Tribunaux Seculiers et Ecclesiastiques, les censures de Sorbonne et des autres Universitez, tant de ce Royaume que des Pays étrangers.

Enfin, on taschera de faire en sorte qu'il ne se passe rien dans l'Europe digne de la curiosité des Gens de lettres, qu'on ne puisse apprendre par ce Journal.

Le seul dénombrement des choses qui le composeront pourroit suffire pour en faire connoistre l'utilité. Mais j'ajoûteray qu'il sera très-avantageux à ceux qui entreprendront quelque ouvrage considerable; puis qu'ils pourront s'en servir pour publier leur dessein, et inviter tout le monde à leur communiquer les manuscripts, et les pièces fugitives qui pourront contribuer à la perfection des choses qu'ils auront entreprises.

De plus, ceux qui n'aimeront pas la qualité d'Auteurs, et qui cependant auront fait quelques observations qui mériteront d'estre communiquées au public, le pourront faire, en m'en envoyant un memoire, que je ne manquerai pas d'inserer dans le Journal.

Je crois qu'il y a peu de personnes qui ne voient que ce Journal sera utile à ceux qui acheptent des livres; puis qu'ils ne le feront point sans les connoistre auparavant: et qu'il ne sera pas inutile à ceux mesme qui ne peuvent faire beaucoup de despense en livres; puis que sans les achepter, ils ne laisseront pas d'en avoir une connoissance generale.

.   .   .

. . . Pour ce qui est du stile, comme plusieurs personnes contribuent à ce Journal, il est impossible qu'il soit fort uniforme. Mais parce que cette inegalité, qui vient tant de la diversité des sujets que des genies de ceux qui les traitent pourroit estre des-agreable; on a prié le Sieur DE HEDOUVILLE de prendre le soin d'ajuster les materiaux, qui viennent de differentes mains, en sorte qu'ils puissent avoir quelque proportion et quelque regularité. Ainsi sans rien changer au jugement d'un chacun, il se donnera seulement la liberté de changer quelquefois l'expression: et il n'épousera aucun party. Cette indifference sans doute sera jugée necessaire, dans un Ouvrage qui ne doit pas estre moins libre de toute sort de préjugez, qu'exempt de passion et de partialité.

Hedouville, who, as Sallo declared, had undertaken to conduct the weekly journal, was said to have been Sallo himself under an assumed name.[1] This incognito gave him a liberty of expression equal to that of Lockhart or Christopher North, a century and a half later. It led him to write in a tone often tart and stinging, and soon brought attention from "authority." Sallo lost his privileges with the thirteenth number (March 30). The enterprise was turned over to another, the Abbé Gallois, in January, 1666. Abbé de la Roque, who had formerly assisted Abbé Gallois, took it up from 1675, President Cousin from 1686, and from 1701 to 1792 it was edited by a commission of men of letters. Suppressed during the Revolution and until Napoleon was defeated, it was again issued in 1816 and following, under government patronage and, later, with the support of the Institute. It is still in progress.

The *Journal des Sçavans* of the seventeenth century was primarily an abstract periodical (i. e., made up of abstracts or summaries of books). This fact deserves emphasis, because of the several English periodicals that followed which were frequently devoted entirely to concise compends of learned works. After the first few numbers of his journal, Sallo included original matter also, in accordance with his plan. Undoubtedly, the appearance of Henry Oldenburg's *Philosophical Transactions of the Royal Society*, which began in March, 1665, had some effect on the Paris journal. The Royal Society had been founded in 1660 (incorporated 1662). Men of letters were included, as is shown by the membership of Dryden and Waller. Oldenburg, who had been Secretary from the beginning, began publishing the *Transactions* in 1665, in an endeavor to give "some account of the present under-

[1] See Isaac D'Israeli, *Curiosities of Literature*, London 1791, p. 5.

takings, studies, and labours of the Ingenious in many considerable parts of the world."

The *Transactions*, which appeared in the form of a sixteen-page monthly serial, contained at first only original articles. In many cases these were signed by the writers, and sometimes accompanied by illustrations inset on folded sheets. The illustrations were probably imitated from the *Journal des Sçavans*, as the abstracts of scientific works which followed later undoubtedly were. The obligation was not one-sided, for, after March, the *Journal des Sçavans* constantly quoted the English serial, usually including translations from it in a section termed *Extraits du Journal d'Angleterre*. After Oldenburg's death in 1677, this publication was edited by various hands until 1752, when a committee of the Society became responsible for it. Only during its early years, while the Printing Act was enforced, was it of any real importance in the history of the literary periodical, or that phase of it concerned with reviewing.

In an age when publishers were booksellers also, it was very natural that the advertisements at the end of newsbooks or "transactions" should sooner or later become catalogues of books, issued as periodicals. The earliest book catalogue in England—Andrew Maunsell's, in 1595 —and an annual catalogue of 1664, are worth noting. But the *Mercurius Librarius*, 1668, the so-called *Term Catalogue* of the London booksellers, was the first real periodical catalogue of books. In a very qualified sense, it is entitled to be regarded as the first literary periodical published in England. The first number appeared in the Michaelmas Term, the projectors announcing that if it found encouragement it should be continued at the end of every term, i. e., four times a year, in February, May, June, and November. It seems to have prospered, for the *Term Catalogue* was issued in this manner until 1709.

Founded and conducted by John Starkey and Robert Clavell,[1] the *Mercurius Librarius* was a trade journal for twenty or more booksellers, whose wares were listed and described. It was not of great importance in the development of periodical literature, although its appearance for so long a time seems to have influenced the form of succeeding publications of a more critical character.[2]

For sixteen years after the Printing Act, no development of literary periodicals is to be noted. The *Transactions* of the Royal Society were published regularly, but did not appeal to a literary public. The *Mercurius Librarius* and other catalogues of books contained no abstracts or criticisms of the works they listed. Then came the Popish Plot and, in June, 1679, the Act of 1662 was allowed to lapse. Licensing was temporarily at an end, the Royal prerogative in the publication of news was defied, and a furious newspaper and pamphlet war broke out. In the midst of it, four early reviews appeared, describing and even containing elementary criticisms of books. In 1679 the *Philosophical Collections*, edited by Robert Hooke, began a precarious existence, and, in 1681, a bookseller named Moses Pitt issued a competing periodical with the same title. *Weekly Memorials for the Ingenious*, which also had a counterfeit, followed in 1682.

The *Philosophical Collections* of Robert Hooke, 1679-82, although otherwise much like the *Transactions of the Royal Society*, had something of the book catalogue character. Hooke had been a colleague of Oldenburg, having

[1] The *Term Catalogue*, ed. Edward Arber, 3 vols., London 1903.
[2] Another *Mercurius Librarius*, or a "faithful account of all books and pamphlets published these last fourteen days," began on Friday, April 16, 1680. According to the prefatory statement, it was started because of the need of a weekly as well as a "term" catalogue, to serve the trade. It was promised to readers every Thursday morning, the contents limited to giving the title and design of each book, and not attempting comment of any sort. The first number contained twenty-six short notices of books, with the name of the seller and the price of each. There are no records regarding its discontinuance, although it seems unlikely that it lasted long.

been appointed curator of experiments for the Royal Society in 1662, and having succeeded Oldenburg as Secretary in 1677. The aim of his periodical work was "a candid commendation of useful discoveries." Each number of the *Philosophical Collections* consisted, on the average, of eight articles, chiefly on scientific subjects and signed by such authors as John Beaumont, Dr. Frederick Slare, or Edmund Halley, the astronomer. These articles were followed, in the first number, by accounts of new books and two advertisements for astronomical apparatus. Later, no distinction was made between book notices and articles or abstracts. The title of a book was quoted in full at the head of each abstract, after the manner of the French journals, and each number was illustrated with a page of woodcuts, similar to that which regularly appeared in the *Journal des Sçavans* or the *Transactions*.[1]

The *Weekly Memorials for the Ingenious*, which had begun in January 1682, was modelled more closely on the *Journal des Sçavans* than any English serial that had preceded it. It began as a small weekly publication of eight pages, printed for Henry Faithorne and John Kersey, and was made up, like its French prototype, of abstracts from foreign books or "transactions" from foreign journals, with now and then an original article. James Petiver probably wrote the numerous papers on botany, but it is not likely that he had any further connection with it. One of the Bodelian copies has "by Mr. Beaumont" written on the title page in faded ink. Probably John Beaumont was meant, a writer on supernatural and scien-

---

[1] John Houghton, with his *Collection of Letters for the Improvement of Husbandry and Trade*, Sept. 8, 1681, anticipated (in a special field and for readers with a special interest) methods which have been generally regarded as of much later origin. Houghton reviewed books like Firmin's *Some Proposals for the Employment of the Poor*, and used books as the subjects of general, practical essays of information. He also recommended books to tradesmen, etc. *Cf. Gentleman's Journal*, of 1692, which recommended books to gentlemen. (See R. P. McCutcheon in *Modern Philology*, XX, 1922-23, p. 255.)

tific subjects. But whether, or by what authority, the work may be assigned to him, has not been determined. *Weekly Memorials* was conducted by the original "author," until the seventh number had appeared. A second *Weekly Memorials* was then set up by this unknown "author," who had quarreled with Faithorne, and attempted to issue the serial himself. The rival publication maintained a bitter competition for only twenty-nine numbers, until September 25. The original *Weekly Memorials* lasted for fifty numbers, until January 15, 1683, and, as far as can be determined, is deserving of more attention from the student; for the author of this periodical proposed an advance over previous works of the same general character—

The bare titles of books yearly printed in our common catalogues are somewhat dry things, scarce able to raise in men that gust and appetite to learning which we may hope these brief accounts will give them. I shall not confine myself in my undertaking only to authors of most books transmitted to us from other parts: and shall transcribe from the Paris *Journal des Sçavans* all that I conceive will be lookt upon here as most valuable, as well in reference to accounts of books, as to other curious novelties contained therein . . .

Like the serials of Hooke and Oldenburg, *Weekly Memorials* quoted fully the titles of books, used occasional wood-cut illustrations, and considered chiefly the works of continental scholars.

After the death of Charles II, in 1685, the Printing Act was renewed, to be allowed to lapse finally in 1695. Much interest, therefore, attaches to the first duly licensed review, issued in 1687 by George Wells, living at the Sign of the Sun, St. Paul's Churchyard. This review was licensed by Robert Midgley, James II's licenser, and was entitled the *Universal Historical Bibliotheque*. The author announced his intention of giving an account of the most considerable books printed in all languages, "wherein a short description is given of the design and scope of almost every book; *and the quality of the author if known.*" This periodical is, therefore, a link which connects the early abstract journal and the later review.

Jean Cornand de la Crose, a Huguenot, was referred to as the author of this serial, in an advertisement for the *Works of the Learned*, which appeared in the *Athenian Mercury*, Feb. 15, 1692. The *Bibliotheque* was a periodical of about seventy pages. That La Crose intended to make a step forward is indicated in the preface where he promised an account of books printed in England and asked for contributions. This is notable as the first case on record of the author of an English periodical inviting aid from contributors. The author also designed to publish some entire pieces that were thought worthy to be known to the world, yet were too short to be printed alone. His preface contains some interesting comment on the necessity of criticism at that time and the difficulty of finding it owing to "the divided state of Christendom." An original feature was the double title sometimes used at the head of abstracts—the foreign language of the original title on one side and the English equivalent on the other.

By 1688 the interest in learned periodicals had reached the Scotch capital. John Cockburn, a minister at Ormiston, East Lothian, was the author, in January of that year, of a monthly serial, the *Bibliotheca Universalis*, "an Historical Accompt of Books and Transactions of the Learned World." That it was the earliest work of such a nature, in Scotland, is now generally agreed. The one number extant consists of material borrowed from two continental journals, the *Bibliothèque universelle et historique* and the *Journal des Sçavans*, from the former of which Cockburn apparently adapted his title.[1]

---

[1] For accounts of this and other Edinburgh periodicals, see W. J. Couper, *The Edinburgh Periodical Press*, Stirling, 1908.

Another *Weekly Memorials* began in London, January 19, 1688, "an account of books lately set forth, with other accounts relating to learning." The two numbers available are dated Wednesday and Saturday of the same week, in spite of the title. This is probably the first and the last periodical to devote each of its numbers entirely to an abstract of one book. In the initial number, the author pointed out the advantages of his method, the easy access it gave to the information to be found in long treatises, here made accessible to the busy reader in a single folio half-sheet. At the end of each abstract, the author employed a new device—an announcement of the contents of the following number—used by La Crose and Dunton thereafter, and suggesting the elaborate announcements of forthcoming features by periodical editors of our own day.

A similar two-page folio half-sheet, the *Mercurius Eruditorum*, August 5, 1691, is even more important as an anticipation of later forms. It is a genuine offspring of the *Term Catalogue, Philosophical Transactions*, and the early half-sheet of party propaganda; its purpose, a discussion of books and authors, presented in dialogue form. A sub-title, "News from the Learned World," at the head of the page, was followed by a brief synopsis of the contents, and the names "Alexis, Philemon, Theodore"—*dramatis personae*, who gave each other, at the time of meeting, supposedly Tuesday, an account of the books they had read. They then discussed the books, and not only the authors of the books but "their journalists themselves"—meaning the authors of other journals which noticed the books. They planned to limit their critical discussion to "what is most remarkable for Beauty or Defects in what comes out."

Successive numbers of the *Mercurius Eruditorum* contained some excellent general observations, and favorable comment on such well known works as Wood's *Athenae Oxonienses*. In addition, the club or "society of gentlemen" idea was very clearly anticipated—the idea which developed into the Spectator Club of Addison and Steele, the "Monastery" group of the *Lay Monk*, 1713-14, and, much later, into the "Noctes Ambrosianae" of *Blackwood's Magazine*.

Meanwhile, the less rigorous enforcement of the licensing restrictions, and the general and increasing desire for knowledge, conspired to produce another form, which is related to the serious periodicals already considered. John Dunton, a bookseller at the Black Raven in Princes Street, began to scatter abroad miscellaneous information in a much more popular way than his contemporaries, by means of a question and answer paper called the *Athenian Gazette*. The first rude hint of it, so he tells us in his *Life and Errors*, "was the idea of concealing the querist and answering the question," but it is no doubt true that Dunton received helpful suggestions from Renaudot and the "Bureau d'adresse."[1] Perhaps he was led to it by the dialogue form of many early political papers, notably, L'Estrange's *Observator* of 1681. The result was the real progenitor, in method, at least, of the modern *Notes and Queries*.

Dunton's *Athenian Gazette, or Casuistical Mercury*, "resolving the nice and curious questions proposed by the Ingenious,"[2] has, however, a greater importance than that in the history of literary periodicals. It was begun

---

[1] *Life and Errors of John Dunton*, London 1818, i, 189.

[2] Charles Gildon, in his *History of the Athenian Society* (London 1728), later pointed out a remote predecessor in the *Sphinx Theologica Philosophica*, 1636 (Cantabrigiae). See *A Supplement to the Athenian Oracle*, Lon. 1710, pp. 1-76. The "Athenian" was derived from *Acts* xvii, 21, according to Dunton. It is well to note, however, a passage in the *Mercurius Bifrons*, No. 1, 1681, "People of late have all turned Athenians, and there is much inquiry after news," and a similar use of the word in *The Times Anatomized*, by T. Ford, 1647. In fact, John Taylor's pamphlet, *A Letter Sent from London*, contains the word used in this sense as early as 1643. Probably the term was commonly thus used in Dunton's day.

March 17, 1691. The author was soon "obliged by authority" (see No. 12) to change his title; so it became thereafter the *Athenian Mercury*, under which name it appeared until February, 1696. It was later revived for ten numbers, in 1697. Richard Sault, a teacher of mathematics, and Dunton were, for one number, the entire staff of the little periodical. They were soon overwhelmed with correspondence, for the "ingenious" were curious beyond their most extravagant anticipations. Sault procured the aid of John Norris, who gave his services gratis, wishing apparently to assume no responsibility. After the second number had appeared, Samuel Wesley, a Church of England divine, small poet, and father of the famous John and Charles Wesley, became a partner in the undertaking. On the tenth of April, Dunton, Sault, and Wesley signed articles of agreement by which the first was to have freedom of editorial management. Sault and Wesley were to be paid ten shillings a week for a regular amount of material. They also agreed to meet Dunton regularly one day a week for consultation.[1]

The impression seems to have been general that a considerable group composed the "Athenian Society." But it is probable that Dunton and his three helpers constituted, for a time, almost the whole staff, and answered all the questions. Confidently claiming all knowledge as their province, these men were often obliged to give answers that were little better than evasions. Other answers seem absurd to modern readers, just as the questions which provoked them are absurd. But humor and common sense frequently saved the "Athenians," when faced with much of the superstition and false-science of the period. A few typical questions and answers show their rationalizing abilities on occasion:

[1] Rawlinson MSS. vol. 72, no. 65. Bodleian Library.

Ques. Why rats, toads, ravens, screech-owls, etc., are ominous, and how they come to foreknow fatal events?

Ans. If the querist had said *unlucky* instead of *ominous*, he might easily have met with satisfaction. A rat is so because he destroys good Cheshire cheese, and makes dreadful ravages on a good flitch of bacon. A toad is unlucky because it is poisonous. As for ravens and screech-owls, they are just as unlucky as cats, when about their courtship, because they make an ugly noise which disturbs the neighborhood. The instinct of rats leaving an old ship, is because they cannot be dry in it, an old house because they want victuals. A raven is such a prophet as our almanack makers, foretelling things after they are come to pass. . . . They follow armies for the dead men, dogs, and horses that must be left behind. . .

Ques. When had angels their first existence?

Ans. Who but an angel knows?

Ques. Whether a public or private courtship is better?

Ans. The private is more safe and pleasant.

Occasional queries indicated a desire for guidance in matters literary. "Which is the best poem ever made?" asks one reader. The reply considers "Grandsire" Chaucer, "Father Ben," Shakespeare, Spenser, Davenant, and Cowley. The replier asserted that Milton's *Paradise Lost* would never be equalled, and that Waller was the "most correct poet."

Often the Athenian Society was called upon to answer such queries as these:

Whether it is more easy to resist pain or pleasure? Whether it was a sin for Noah to curse his son Ham for his nakedness? Whether or no fishes think? Which is greater, the hurt or profit that cometh of love? What is colour? Where is the likeliest place to get a husband in? Whether virtue does not consist in intention? Whether Adam was a giant? Whether negroes shall rise at the last day? Where extinguished fire goes? Whither went the ten tribes?

Aristotle and holy writ frequently helped out the answerers of such questions, and many a querist was referred to these two authorities. It is notable, moreover, that both questions and answers often took the form of letters, as in the following:

Ques. I have by promise of marriage engaged myself to a young lady, and not long after my circumstances obliged me to travel, before which I conjured my mistress to be mindful of her contract with me; she at that time gave as great testimonies of her fidelity as I could desire; but it was not long 'ere she entertained another gentleman, and so successful was my Rival, that doubtless he had married her, but being discovered the very night before it was to be put into execution, all their measures were irrecoverably broke, her Relations being bitterly averse thereto. At first knowledge thereof, I did not resolve what to do, but since (after mature consideration) I so resent her Behavior, as I believe I should be as willingly hanged as married to her, therefore I have secured a Discharge in writing, wherein we mutually and voluntarily acquit each other from all the Obligation of matrimony. *Whether my unhappy contract is not void, or how far it obliges me?*

Ans. Void, Yes: we should be very unhappy creatures, if our vows must be of force whether the women proved constant or no, for they have their share of Fickleness as well as we; and since your Reason has had the conquest, all you have to do is to pay it such a deference, as to follow its advice in a second engagement.[1]

The *Athenian Mercury* consisted of a single half-sheet folio, published, after No. 3, on Tuesdays and Saturdays. Discontinued on February 8, 1696, after 570 numbers and five supplements had been issued, it was resumed on May 14, 1697, for a run of five weeks. Its popularity may be judged by the fact that the great Marquis of Halifax read it—as Dunton proudly tells us in his *Life and Errors*—while Poet Laureate Tate, Peter Motteux, Defoe, Charles Richardson, and Swift sent the proprietor poems praising the "Athenian Society," and pointing out the benefits it was conferring upon mankind. Sir William Temple wrote frequent inquiries, and Sir Thomas Blount, Sir

[1] *Athenian Mercury*, Dec. 30, 1693.

William Hedges, Sir Peter Pratt, and others commended the *Mercury* highly to Dunton.

The *Athenian Mercury* may appear absurd to readers of our day, but there can be no question about its prestige in the years 1691-96. Dunton's purpose to have it "lye for common chatt and entertainment in every coffee-house board," was probably realized at nearly all the resorts of London.[1] The large numbers of queries in all languages, the wide range of subjects appealing to all classes of society, the semi-weekly frequency with which it made its appearance for five years—a long time for a periodical in those days—the honest tributes of imitators, as well as the high regard in which it seems to have been held by contemporaries; all these combine to give it an important place among the serials of this time. In addition to this, the *Athenian Mercury* contained much verse; and because of its serious nature and its popularity did much to counteract the Puritan objections. The *Mercury* showed that poetry was not always associated with flippancy and vice—a view expressed by La Crose, about this time—but could be a medium for "virtuous and serious thought."

No predecessors of this question and answer periodical have been pointed out.[2] But a score of other publishers, in the two decades which followed, were glad to employ, in some form, Dunton's popular device to engage the reading public. Even Defoe's *Review*, the *Tatler*, and the *Gentleman's Magazine* were the debtors of the *Athenian*

---

[1] A suggestion for both Dunton and Steele (see *Tatler*) may have been derived from the *Coffee-House Mercury* of 1690, a weekly news sheet. It was in the half-sheet folio form, and was made up principally of foreign news.

[2] L'Estrange's *Observator* of 1681 differed from the *Athenian Mercury* in that the questions were obviously proposed by the author for the sake of the point he wished to make, whereas Dunton actually undertook to answer the queries sent to him. It is well to notice, however, that the *Observator* contained questions and answers in the form of letters.

Mercury in this particular—alone sufficient to give Dunton's publication an assured place in the history of English literary periodicals.[1]

The remarkable success of the *Athenian Mercury* was soon challenged. On February 1, 1692, Thomas Brown set up his *London Mercury* on similar lines (with No. 9, the title was changed to *Lacedemonian Mercury*). William Pate, "the learned woollen-draper," was Brown's partner in this "aping" undertaking—so Dunton relates. The proprietor of the *Athenian Mercury* met this damaging competition with characteristic firmness and dispatch. He advertised that all questions answered in Brown's paper should be answered again in his own—"with amendments." In addition, the life of Brown was to be "exposed." The threat of the last was evidently too much for Brown. We are informed by Dunton that the two staffs met at the Three Cranes, and under some pressure Brown agreed to stop his paper.[2] The last issue was that of May 30.

Another short-lived imitator was the *Jovial Mercury* of 1693. The few copies available show that it was a weekly, begun on March 3. It is distinguished by the fact that it employed the question and answer as a vehicle for amusement, since the *Athenian Mercury* was primarily a serious publication. Among its questions are found: "Whether women have rational souls? Whether at the skip of a flea the earth moves out of its center? Whether poets, musicians, and painters are half crackt?" Although its purpose was primarily to entertain, the *Jovial Mer-*

[1] "By the Athenian Society" became a kind of trade name for Dunton, the publisher and bookseller. The *Athenian Library*, the *Athenian Oracle* in various editions, the *Young Students Library*, 1692, a translation of Lucian, 1695, and *Athenian Sport*, 1707, were all advertised and sold by him, as "By the Athenian Society" or "By a member of the Athenian Society." *Cf.* Roger P. McCutcheon, "John Dunton's Connection with Book-Reviewing," *Studies in Philology*, XXV (1928), 346.

[2] *Life and Errors of John Dunton.* London 1818, i, 190.

cury was not entirely devoted to such material as the foregoing. Several "characters" were included, and, in the
last two numbers, "moral paradoxes"—"An Atheist, if
not a fool, is the most pernicious creature in the world,"
and "Duelling, a kind of Madness"—show an interest in
the reform of manners and morals.

A few numbers, likewise, are all that we have of the
Ladies Mercury (beginning February 18, 1694), a semi-
weekly, half-sheet folio, differing at this time from the
Athenian Mercury only in the length of the questions, of
which there were sometimes only three or four in the two
pages. Yet questions and answers in the form of letters
are to be found occasionally in L'Estrange's *Observator*
of 1681; and the tendency toward the letter form has been
remarked in the *Athenian Mercury*. This lengthening of
questions and answers in these early periodicals is significant, for it led directly to the letters of correspondents
answered by Steele in the *Tatler*. The name, *Ladies Mercury*, was a misnomer. Gentlemen as well as ladies were
"desired" to send their questions relating to love, etc., to
the Latin Coffee-House. The author appears to have been
a pioneer in advice to our lovelorn ancestors.

The *Athenian Mercury* and its imitators represent attempts to satisfy in a popular way the general desire for
knowledge. While such serials were dispensing information in palatable form, the less popular *genre*, the
"learned" periodical, was continuing its unbroken line of
progress, under the energetic La Crose. The Huguenot
proposed in his *History of Learning* (July, 1691) to give
English readers of foreign journals—what they had not
possessed before—an abstract serial of their own, treating
chiefly new works published at home, but (and this is a
characteristic of La Crose's work from first to last)
considering only such works as deserved the perusal of the

"studious and serious reader."[1] He asked in the preface of the first number to be excused from giving critical judgments, yet by his proposed plan actually assumed the office of censor. With a characteristic lack of humor, he writes:

The reader must excuse me, if I omit giving a Judgment upon the style and language of authors; which I shall avoid, and chuse rather to give an account of things than words. I shall, also, as little as possible, take any side in the disputes of learned men; or if it should happen that I adhere to one party in such disputes, I hope the ingenious reader will believe it to be the force of reason and truth that draws me to its side.

La Crose exhibited further inconsistency by promising to "mark out the most considerable passages, and the places best writ of every author." He did this by comment and by the occasional use of italics.

The *History of Learning* made its initial appearance in July. The public response was a disappointment to the projector, as he intimates in a later preface, blaming the bookseller with whom he was engaged. A change of booksellers was one result, therefore. Another was the appearance in August of not a second number but an entirely new periodical, the *Works of the Learned*, which was continued until April, 1692. For convenience, the two periodicals may be considered as one, for only very slight changes were apparent in the form and plan of the second. A catalogue of books for the following month was added, and at the end, in later numbers, a department entitled "the News of Learning," which included items from France, Italy, Holland, and other countries, after

---

[1] The idea of such a work as the title implies is an old one. It has been traced to Apollodorus of Athens, 240 B.C., and Diodorus of Sicily, in the reign of Augustus. But the student of periodicals need go no further back than the *Journal des Sçavans* to find La Crose's inspiration.

See D. C. A. Agnew, *Protestant Exiles from France*, Edin. 1871, ii, 148, and *Nouvelle Biographie Générale*, xxviii, 610.

the manner of Bayle's *Nouvelles de la République des Lettres* (Amsterdam) of 1684.[1] In some degree the author intended his new work to take the place of the *Philosophical Transactions*, which he thought about to be given up, and many of its pages are occupied with scientific discussions.

As has been noted, the articles in the *History of Learning* and the *Works of the Learned*, although mainly composed of abstract or translation, approach later reviews in character, in that they do contain an element of criticism, however simple it may seem when compared with the periodical criticism of a century later. Such articles are those dealing with L'Estrange's *Fables*, Raleigh's *Arts of Empire*, Sir William Temple's *Memoirs*, and Wood's *Athenae Oxonienses*. The majority of the articles, however, have to do with such non-literary topics as a "Project of a Method for the Reform of Men's Morals," a "Defense of Pluralities," or "A New Explication of the Deluge." La Crose gave a reason for this when he indicated his moral purpose. He declared he could not mention works of a light nature, "plays, satyrs, romances, and the like," since they were "fitter to corrupt men's morals, and to shake the grounds of natural religion, than to promote learning and piety"—an illuminating comment, in view of the later corrective efforts of Defoe and Steele.

The last item in the articles signed by Dunton, Sault and Wesley was an agreement that Dunton should get translated by other hands the *Acta Eruditorum*, the *Journal des Sçavans*, *Bibliothéque universelle et historique*,

---

[1] L. P. Betz, *Pierre Bayle und die "Nouvelles de la République des Lettres,"* Zurich 1896.

Bayle's influence upon the *Works of the Learned* and other early English critical journals was unquestionably great. His *Nouvelles de la République des Lettres* was the first thorough-going attempt to popularize literature; and it brought into prominence the wide fields of opportunity in other countries which the literary periodical was soon to take for its own.

and *Giornali de'letterati*, or any other periodicals, and add to the *Athenian Mercury* as many numbers as he pleased, thus invading the proper field of the "learned" periodicals.[1] Accordingly the first volume of the *Mercury* was closed with the thirtieth number, and the first supplement issued. This was in May, 1691. It will be remembered that La Crose's *History of Learning* did not appear until July. Dunton's later reference to this periodical as based upon an idea of his own has been regarded with skepticism. But the articles referred to show that there was justice in his assertion; for the first, as well as later supplements of the *Mercury*, was made up entirely of just such material as La Crose later used in the *History*—abstracts of books from foreign periodicals, and translated excerpts from "A new book entitled *Entretiens sérieuses et galantes*." In the preface to the fourth volume it was declared—"These Supplements will be continued constantly by several learned persons, and comprehend a brief idea of all the valuable books published from time to time." But in the fifth (Jan. 30, 1692) Dunton mentioned La Crose's useful design, which he declares his *Supplement* will not in the future supplant. Indeed, he had become financially interested in La Crose's work, which was licensed for him and registered by the Stationer's Company on February 22, 1692, although the Huguenot remained "editor" of it until it was stopped.[2] Accordingly, in the preface to the sixth volume of the *Athenian Mercury*, Dunton advertised that he had bought the rights of the *Works of the Learned*, which would now be carried on "by a London Divine." Nevertheless, the last issue of this serial, consisting of March and April numbers in one, bore La Crose's name.

[1] Rawlinson MSS. vol. 72, No. 65, Bodleian Library.
[2] Roger P. McCutcheon, "John Dunton's Connection with Book Reviewing," *Studies in Philology*, XXV (July, 1928) 355.

In May appeared a virtual continuation of it, the *Compleat Library; or, News for the Ingenious*, printed monthly for John Dunton and conducted by him, although Richard Wooley was named as author.[1] Its nine sheets (thirty-six pages) Dunton planned to divide thus: three for original pieces, four for historical accounts of books in English and in foreign journals, two for "notes on memorable passages happening monthly, as well as the state of learning in the world." Although this original plan of contents was followed pretty well up to May, 1693, after that the monthly became a quarterly, and consisted only of a long catalogue of books, and a short section of "news from the learned world." It was stopped in April, 1694. The original articles, while they lasted, were invariably concerned with matters of scriptural interpretation and controversy, and have little relation to literature. The criticisms of the catalogue, on the other hand—some of them very short, but others running to a length of five or six pages—furnished further interesting illustrations of the near approach to reviews of a later day.

During the later years of the seventeenth century, isolated cases of criticism appear now and then, usually more or less envenomed. Such a case is to be found, as we have seen, in the *Mercurius Eruditorum* of 1691. An even more remarkable example was furnished in 1692 by the *Moderator*, a half-sheet folio concerned mainly with political controversy. This serial began with little enough distinction, but the third number (June 9) was given over to an attack on Langbaine's account of the dramatic poets, especially his criticism of Dryden. The

---

[1] It is well to note here that the term "editor," as used to indicate the conductor of a periodical publication, did not come into common use until the middle of the eighteenth century, although it was used as early as 1712 (see *Spectator* 470) for one who prepares the literary work of another for publication. It will be used hereafter where needed for convenience, however.

unknown journalist champions Dryden, berating Langbaine in language worthy of Lockhart or John Wilson
Croker. Of Langbaine's book, *An Account of English
Dramatic Poets* (Oxford 1691) he says, "Never was a
noble design worse managed." He then proceeds to defend Dryden from the critic's attack. Some of his remarks
are worth repeating:

> In your accounts of men confessedly great, you only tell us their
> memory will be dear to all lovers of poetry; or else their memory to all
> posterity, etc., without ever pointing out their beauties and defects,
> which make up the character of every author and distinguish him from
> all others. . . . There is nothing, for example, so courtly writ, or which
> expresses so much of the conversation of a gentleman, as Sir John Suck-
> ling, nothing so sweet and flowing, as Mr. Waller, nothing so majestick,
> so correct as Sir John Denham, nothing so elevated, so copious and full
> of spirit as Mr. Cowley. . . . They have each their proper graces; and
> which makes every one appear the individual poet he is.

The author of the *Moderator* quoted derisively from
Langbaine's lives of the poets, to illustrate the error of his
method. Returning to Dryden, he then made an effort to
free him from Langbaine's imputation of plagiarism, by
showing many examples (Beaumont, Fletcher, Ben Jonson, etc.) of the wholesale borrowing of plots—to justify
Dryden's practice. *Moderator* number four was filled
with adverse criticism of the verse which occasionally appeared in the contemporary *Athenian Mercury*. In evident imitation of the *Yeekly Memorials* of 1688, the
author announced at the end of each *Moderator* his subject for the next week.

In *Memoirs for the Ingenious* (January-December,
1693) La Crose continued the progress of the serious
type of periodical with which his name is associated. This
author, who had expressed contempt for anonymity,
signed himself, in this case, "J. De la Crose, E. A. P."
The new form indicated in the sub-heading, "In Miscellaneous Letters," showed that La Crose was not

uninfluenced by the less serious *Gentleman's Journal* of Motteux, which had been started the preceding year (see below, p. 55). Each number of the thirty-two page monthly *Memoirs* consisted of letters, written to eminent scholars of the day like Sir Robert Southwell, President of the Royal Society, or Richard Sault, the mathematician, or Dr. Samuel Garth, the famous physician. Again, as in the *Works of the Learned*, La Crose remarked that few papers of the Royal Society had appeared since Oldenburg's death. The *Memoirs* were to take the place of the *Transactions*, in some degree, and to contain "all that is new and short and rare, and may make men more learned and good." La Crose's serial appeared for only one full year.[1]

The *Memoirs for the Ingenious* was followed immediately by *Miscellaneous Letters*, a weekly serial, during the closing months of 1694. In January, 1695, it became a monthly publication, continuing in this form until March, 1696, with a total of twenty-five numbers. *Miscellaneous Letters* is distinguished as the first serious English periodical to contain discussion of the stage. Although in letter form, and only as translations from the French, yet the long *Dissertation* in condemnation of the stage and players (No. 10) and the *Refutation* (No. 11) represent new material for this sort of publication. Letters were destined to be common ingredients of the social

---

[1] *Memoirs for the Ingenious*, or "the Universal Mercury" (January 1694) was designed as a monthly of the same type, except that the "several hands" who professed to conduct it made an effort to popularize their erudition. The authors imitated La Crose in attempting to convey their learning in letters . . . "whatever is curious in all sorts of learning . . . not contrary to religion, good manners, or government." The announcement of contents included "Philology and all its known criticisms"—a fact worth noting. The six letters of the single number show the effort made by the authors to avoid "raw and undigested ideas," as they put it in the preface, and to present information in a form more acceptable to the reader.

Another *History of Learning* appeared in May, 1694, a feeble imitation of La Crose's earlier work. It was a quarto, licensed by D. Poplar. Only one number survives, and it seems unlikely that more were published.

periodical; few magazines of the eighteenth century were without them, and occasionally—as in the *Tatler*—each number of a serial consisted of a single letter.

Still another *History of the Works of the Learned*, or "an impartial account of books printed in all parts of Europe, with a particular relation to the state of learning in each country," was issued from January, 1699, to March, 1712, as a sixty-page monthly serial, "done by several hands." Conducted on the same general plan as the *Works of the Learned* of 1691, its reviews were fuller, and the contributed articles were sometimes as long as sixteen pages. Good examples of reviews are the articles on Collier's *Second Defence of the Short View*, etc. (January 1700) and that on the *Privileges of the House of Commons* (October 1701). Like the earlier serials of La Crose, this one avoided the "trifling" books—did not even mention their titles (see introduction to No. 1). The authors designed to hold the middle course "between tedious extracts and superficial catalogues made up only of title and preface, the former being tiresome to the reader as well as injurious to the sale of books; and the latter being a mere imposition on the Publick." Several pages of each number were devoted to the "State of Learning"—a catalogue of recently published works. According to his biographer, George Ridpath, who was later the conductor of the *Flying Post*, "assisted" on the staff of the periodical, although there is probably no reason for calling him editor.[1]

---

[1] The first number of the *History of the Works of the Learned* was reprinted in April, 1699, by James Watson of Edinburgh, and sold to readers for sevenpence, a lower price than it brought in London. His promise to continue the publication of a Scottish edition was kept for eight numbers at least.

James Baldwin, a London publisher, brought out in 1701 another *Memoirs for the Curious*, "an account of that which is Rare, Secret, Extraordinary, Prodigious, or Miraculous . . . in Nature, Art, Learning, Policy, or Religion." This monthly serial is worth noting as an example of the effort to satisfy public interest in the strange and extraordinary—an effort that

Many of the periodicals that followed included the question and answer among other features, but the best later example of the type was the *British Apollo* (1708-1711) "Perform'd by a Society of Gentlemen."[1] A four-page folio, published on Wednesdays and Fridays until No. 79, and then thrice a week, for a total of 410 issues, it differed from the earlier *Athenian Mercury* in containing much more verse—not always decent—exchange and treasury reports, and "the most material occurrences foreign and domestic." It differed also in the undisguised obscenity of many of the questions and answers, inasmuch as the "Athenians" had always consistently refused to print or answer lewd inquiries. On the other hand, the pious cant of many of the answers reminds one of Dunton's serial. Many of the queries were answered in rime. As in the *Ladies Mercury*, questions or answers were often so long as to approach closely the letters of the *Tatler*. They covered a very wide range of subjects—from mathematics to gallantry and theology—and became so numerous that twenty-one twelve-page monthly supplements and five twelve-page quarterly supplements were issued. The news space diminished, as time passed, and the quality of the verse could hardly permit it to have a wide appeal; the *British Apollo's* success must be laid partly to the "noble" subscribers, who subsidized the publication, and partly to the questions and answers. In March, 1710, it was announced that the *Apollo* would henceforth

---

connects it with the earlier *Athenian Mercury* and the later miscellany form, although the table of contents would hardly remind one of the *Gentlemen's Magazine* or *Blackwood's*. As a matter of fact, it was an unsuccessful attempt to turn the "learned" periodical into one of entertainment.

The *Censura Temporum* (January, 1708-November, 1710), a thirty-two page monthly, was concerned with the "good or ill tendencies of books, sermons, pamphlets, etc., in a dialogue between Eubulus and Sophronius." The author proposed to discuss only those books which promoted or opposed the interests of religion or virtue.

[1] See note on authorship, *Notes and Queries*, Ninth Ser., viii (Aug. 3, 1901), 97, 158. The *British Apollo* was probably a work of William Smith, an antiquary.

be published independent of subscribers. The independence was enjoyed for only a year, when the serial became defunct, in May, 1711.

The youthful Aaron Hill was a contributor to the *Apollo*. A dozen or more of his poems, unsigned, which are listed in Dorothy Brewster's *Aaron Hill* appear in the early numbers.[1] Hill later became, with William Bond, a co-author of the *Plain Dealer*, one of the best of the followers of the *Spectator*. Other possible contributors were Dr. Samuel Garth and John Arbuthnot.

Competition may have been the chief cause of the discontinuance of the *British Apollo*. Dunton had re-entered the field on March 7, 1710, with his *Athenian News; or, Dunton's Oracle*, a four-page, twice-a-week paper, largely consisting of questions and answers. It was avowedly antagonistic to the *British Apollo*, which Dunton called "dull, ignorant, and stupid." For twenty-seven numbers, until June 6, it satirized the *British Apollo* whenever that was possible, and copied certain features of the contemporary *Tatler*, among them the long letter or essay. One department was called regularly the "Casuistical Post, or Athenian Mercury," another made up of sappy letters, the "Love-Post" or the "Sibil-Post." Occasional departments were also a "Miser's Post" and a "Rhiming Post"—the latter a head for several columns of verse.

Such, with some chronological coherence, are the beginnings of what may be termed the "learned" periodical, the obvious response to the demand for information on all sorts of subjects. Advertisements, book catalogues, and abstract-serials became the abstract-reviews of 1700. Such development involves the beginnings of criticism in periodicals and the impulse to reform, although neither is limited to the serious type of publication we have been

[1] See Dorothy Brewster, *Aaron Hill*, N. Y., 1913, p. 18.

discussing, but is to be found quite as frequently in periodicals which were designed for entertainment.

iii

The effort to furnish diversion caused a profound change in the character of periodicals in the second half of the seventeenth century. In the early pamphlets and corantos, in the caustic satire and ribald jests of political controversialists, the seeds of this change were sown. The derisive tone of many small political half-sheets easily led to the development of periodicals published for the sole purpose of amusing. There were, moreover, popular amusing tracts such as the pamphlets of John Taylor, the Elizabethan "water poet," and his contemporaries. In fact, the *Harleian Miscellany* contains tracts dated as far back as 1608 which might be cited.[1] The effort to gain and hold the attention of readers by amusing them led, further, to the issuing of such serials as the *News from Hell*, 1647, the *Man in the Moon*, 1649, the *Mercurius Democritus*, 1652 (eight pages of doggerel verse "published for the right understanding of all the mad-merry people of great-Bedlam"), the *Mercurius Jocosus*, 1654, and the *Mercurius Fumigosus*, 1654-5. Written in a Hudibrastic style, often containing scraps of ribald verse, full of pointed and obscene personal allusions, and of mordacious wit—these news and political sheets are hard to classify. It is difficult to tell when and to what extent the author endeavors to entertain his readers. There is a limited kind of entertainment in them even today; but one can never be quite sure the authors intended them for amusement.

By 1680, however, it is evident that writers have discovered a reading public for papers with little or no

---

[1] See the *Pennyless Parliament of Threadbare Poets; or, All Mirth and Witty Conceits, Harleian Miscellany*, i, 180.

party or cause. *News from Parnassus* (from No. 2 called *Advice from Parnassus*), which began February 2, 1681, gave the proceedings of the "Grand Council of Virtuoso and Literati," in a highly allegorical treatment of social and political affairs, written in a sort of burlesque of the *Sueños* of Quevedo, which Roger L'Estrange had translated a dozen years before. The *Strange and Wonderful News from Norwich*, also of 1681, is another representative of a class of serials in which the modern reader can discern little propaganda. *Heraclitus Ridens; or, A discourse between Jest and Earnest* (1681), by Thomas Flatman, an authorized comic weekly, may be regarded as a remote predecessor of our London *Punch*. The *Weekly Discovery, Weekly Discoverer Stripp'd Naked, Mercurius Bifrons, News from the Land of Chivalry*, and the *Democritus Ridens*, "a new jest and earnest prattling concerning the times," of 1681, are some of the many which may be cited as examples of a transition state. The controversies, religious or political, which brought most of these small publications into being, do not concern us here. But the ribaldry, the burlesque news and mock advertisements, the fact that an effort was made by authors to attract and entertain readers as well as persuade them —all point the way toward the magazine of literary entertainment of a later day. In this progress, books had a great influence, of course. Such early works as William Winstanley's *Muses' Cabinet*, 1655, or the *Sportive Wit, or Muses' Merriment*, 1656, contain exactly the sort of entertainment that soon came to be provided in serial form; while such foreign publications of amusement as Jean Loret's *Muse Historique* (1650) or his rimed *Gazette*, 1650-1665, and *Le Mercure Galant* of 1672 ff., exerted an influence on English publishers and authors, impossible now to estimate, but unquestionably great.

This increasing effort to amuse as well as to instruct or

persuade may be seen also in journals like L'Estrange's *Observator* of 1681. This assailant of Dissenters and Whigs had, in later numbers, a synopsis of the contents of each number printed below the title, and obviously employed to catch the reader. The effort to amuse is especially apparent in the *Mercurius Bifrons, or the English Janus* of 1681. This was a half-sheet folio, having the "True and Serious Intelligencer" on one side and the "Jocular Intelligencer" on the other. In 1688 appeared William Winstanley's *Poor Robin's Publick and Private Occurrances and Remarks*, written "for the sake of merriment and harmless recreation," and anticipating Defoe's *Review* and the *Tatler*, with its advices—"From Moabitish quarters it is advised," "From Huffing Row," "From Swift-Street." The next year saw the publication of *A Ramble around the World, or the travels of Kainophilos, a lover of novelties*, a weekly folio. *Momus Ridens*, 1690, in form much like the *Tatler* of Steele, contained verse along with its "comical remarks on the weekly reports," and sections of jocose news matter dated "From the Hague," "From Westminster," or "From Whitehall." All such serials, because of their evident design for entertainment, whatever the actual purpose, are in a sense remote ancestors of the entertaining miscellanies and essay sheets of the eighteenth century.

This effort to amuse the reader resulted during the last decade of the seventeenth century in the development of two types of entertaining serials. The one is valuable for its employment of "character" and for the light it throws on taverns and coffee-houses and social life of the period, yet may be given scant consideration in literature because of its obsession with filth and obscenity. The *Mercurius Fumigosus, or the Smoaking Nocturnall* (1654), represents a great many such serials of the century. Its eight pages were filled with coarse amusement of no literary and little other value.

The best known and most able author of this sort of periodical was Edward Ward. His *London Spy* (1698-1700), a sixteen-page folio, presented the character of a countryman guided about London by a city acquaintance, a notable anticipation, though not the only one by any means, of Sir Roger de Coverley. The monthly numbers of the *Spy* are full of well-drawn sketches of London life, showing the author's keen observation. The *Spy* contains much that is filthy, and much that is unintelligible patter to the present-day reader. The style of Ward now presents difficulties. But it is worth noticing that the essay form was used, that Ward wrote from the first-person point of view, and that sometimes he was allegorical in the moral manner of Steele and Addison.[1]

Another publication of the less reputable type, likewise valuable as a precursor of the *Tatler*, was the *English Lucian* (January 18-April 18, 1698). In its form and make-up, it closely approximated the work of Steele. It was filled with facetious news, often lewd, dated from different places—"White-chapel, Lincoln-Inn-Fields, Old Baly, Drury-Lane, Lombard Street, St. James," and "From my Lodgings in Kent Street." The last two suggest the "St. James' Coffee-House" and "From My Own Apartment" of Steele. The dating thus of news from well-known places anticipates the datings of the *Tatler*; and the considerable space given to satirical comment on "Partridge John, a foreteller of things," anticipates Swift, and suggests the entertainment that Bickerstaff derived from abuse of the same astrologer, John Partridge. That it was published like the *Tatler*, three times a week, is suggestive but not important. The *English Lucian*,

[1] See *London Spy* . . . Ed., with notes, by Arthur L. Hayward, Lon. 1927.

printed for John Harris, who had lately returned from America, was continued for at least fifteen numbers—that being the number in the Burney Collection at the British Museum.

A small periodical called the *Weekly Comedy*, "as it is dayly acted at most coffee-houses in London," deserves special note because of its originality. *Dramatis personae* were announced at the head of the title page, namely:

Snarl, a disbanded Captain	Squabble, a lawyer
Truck, a merchant	Whim, a projector
Scribble, a newswriter	Log, a marriner
All-craft, a turncoat	Scan-all, a poet
Cant, a precision	Plush, a quack
Snap, a sharper	Prim, a beau

Five of these anticipate very distantly the characters of the notable *Spectator* group. Ned Ward was probably the author of this weekly half-sheet folio; for it carried only one advertisement—that for Ward's *London Spy*, which was published by J. How, the printer of the *Weekly Comedy*. It appeared May 10, 1699, and ran for at least ten numbers, to July 12. The characters were not all intended to speak on one occasion; the author used them to suit his mood or convenience. The average number of speakers in each copy was three or four. The "club" idea was suggested, but not definitely brought out. Some of the figures may be considered well delineated "characters," although in most cases traits were poorly developed.

The *Infallible Astrologer*, October 16, 1700, of one who called himself "Sylvester" Partridge (probably another thrust at John Partridge, the butt of various periodical journalists) must certainly be included in this category, for its "Prophecie and prediction of what shall infallibly happen in, and about the Cities of London and Westminster," periodically regaled a section of the reading public with undisguised salacity. Likewise, the *Merry*

Mercury, or a Farce of Fools, of the same year, because of its matter, is bedamned to inclusion in this group. Its form deserves some attention, however, for the contents were presented, like those of *Momus Ridens* and the *English Lucian*, as advices, facetious and lewd, dated from various well-known places in and out of England. This division of the journal into parts suggesting the early numbers of the *Tatler* is further seen in the *Secret Mercury*, September 1702, which took the form of seven "rambles" on the seven days of the week. In design, it was much like Dunton's *Night Walker*[1] of 1696, turned, however, to less pious uses. The *Secret Mercury* is noteworthy only for its form, "characters," and entertaining aim.

The *Diverting Post* of Henry Playford was designed for the entertainment of "those only, whose understanding and judgment have been refined, by liberal education and genteel conversation, from the heavy dross which clogs the reason of the vulgar; who take delight in the pleasing paths of poetry, not in the rugged ways of business; who had rather line their heads than their pockets. . . ." He promised to publish all manuscripts sent in, provided they were free from scurrilous language and immodest reflections. In spite of the author's expressed aim, the *Diverting Post* had a rather brief and ignoble career (October 28, 1704 to June 30, 1705, as a half-sheet weekly; then during January and February 1706, as a ten-page monthly). It began well enough, filled with occasional verse, news matter, and dialogues. By January 1705, the news matter had disappeared, as well as the dialogues. From this point on the *Diverting Post* was made up entirely of verse—prologues for Wilkes, Booth,

---

[1] A monthly periodical of twenty-six pages, published for the avowed purpose of reforming fallen women. Seven extant numbers preserve this curious effort to exploit the reform urge of the time. *Cf. The Wandering Whore*, a pamphlet of 1660.

and Betterton, riddles, limericks, and long poems. Like many of its predecessors, it became, as it progressed, more unequivocally indecent.[1] Meanwhile, in January, such unpublished poems as had been found too concretely carnal for even the *Diverting Post*, were issued by Samuel Philips in the weekly *Poetical Courant*.[2]

Almost identical in design with the *Weekly Comedy* of 1699 was Ward's weekly four-page sheet of 1707. It was first entitled *The Humours of a Coffee-House, A Comedy*, "as it is daily acted by

Levy, a recruiting officer	Querpo, a quack
Hazard, a gamester	Trick, a lawyer
Bate, a sharper	Horoscope, an astrologer
Nice, a beau	Shuffle, a time server
Blunt, a plain dealer	Bays, a poet
Whim, a projector	Compass, a sailor
Venture, a merchant	Harlem, a news-writer
Talley, a stock jobber	Bohee, the coffee man"

With the ninth number, the title was changed to *Weekly Comedy; or the Humours of the Age*, and with the nineteenth number, it became simply the *Weekly Comedy*. Like its predecessor, this serial was written in dramatic dialogue, introducing several of the sixteen characters in each number. Eight of the *dramatis personae*, it may be noted, correspond with those of the earlier publication. In the later numbers, the description was changed to read —"as it is acted by town and country," the list of characters being omitted. *The Humours of a Coffee-House* ap-

---

[1] Playford had been, in 1699-1702, one of the two conductors of the *Mercurius Musicus*, a twelve-page monthly folio, made up of songs with music. This serial is noteworthy as the first real musical journal in English, although several had used sheet music as a feature.

[2] Although it was published anonymously, the Bodleian copy of No. 1 has, written in faded ink, "by Samuel Philips, Gent., late of St. John's Coll., Oxon. See note to number 12." The note referred to is of such a nature that it seems certain the annotator must have identified the author from personal allusions in the poems. The *Poetical Courant* was issued for a total of thirty numbers.

peared weekly on Fridays, from June 25, as a four-page serial, for a total of at least nineteen numbers; and was printed "for the benefit of Bohee, the coffee man."

The *Wandering Spy*, a four-page sheet of 1705, and finally Ward's own *London Terrae Filius or Satyrical Reformer*, 1707-8, represent the logical end of this line of development toward filth and ribaldry. Both periodicals were short-lived. Of the former, only a few issues are now to be found, while the latter appeared as a thirty-two page monthly for six numbers. Some merit may be found in the *Wandering Spy*, in that the successive issues were filled with single essays, written in allegorical narrative suggestive of the later *Tatler*. The reforming trend of the times is suggested by this publication, however perverted the reform may appear to the modern reader.

By 1709 the service of such works in the evolution of the literary periodical had been accomplished. Ward's publications, especially, reflected, to some extent, the rising tide of reform respecting men's manners and morals. These periodicals had also helped to develop the "character," as a device for securing concreteness. But what is more important, they had given the public much entertainment in serial form, making more urgent the subsequent necessity for amusing readers.

The other line of development was best illustrated before 1700 by the *Gentleman's Journal* of Peter Anthony Motteux, which appeared first in January 1692. A Huguenot who had come to England at the revocation of the Edict of Nantes, Motteux was a man of letters, not a scholar, ecclesiastic, or politician. This is important, for it meant that in 1692, for the first time, the literary periodical was in the hands of professional writers.

Motteux modeled his *Journal* on the famous *Mercure Galant*, of Paris, which owed much of its popularity to the prominence it gave court news and gossip. The French publication was designed for the perusal of the "smart set," who made many contributions to it.[1] Each number was in the form of a letter to a lady who had left Paris for the provinces, but wanted to keep in touch with her friends of fashion. Motteux acknowledged his debt, in that he employed the letter device in his *Journal*—this time to a gentleman in the country rather than a lady.[2] Although his model was in reality a newspaper, Motteux, with considerable originality, set up a miscellany, such a miscellany as had never been issued before and has seldom been seen since. He included in the sixty-four octavo pages of his first few numbers every kind of material that had ever been proved of value in attracting and interesting readers—news, foreign and domestic, history, philosophy, questions and answers, letters, poetry, music, translations, items of the learned world, "novels," essays, fables, and book notices. Even wood-cuts were not omitted. Verses by Prior, Sedley, Mrs. Behn, Oldmixon, Dennis, D'Urfey, and Tate jostled for a place beside learned disquisitions on "The Nature of Dryness and Moisture," or "A Description of the Kingdom of Poetry." More or less original features included a "Lover's Gazette," made up of advices from the City of Beauty, the Town of Pride, or the Commonwealth of Enjoyment.

But so many diverse elements did not at this time necessarily make for long-continued success, although Cave and other later "magazine" editors made variety the foundation stone of their popularity. The news dwin-

[1] Established (1672) and conducted by Donneau de Vizé and Thomas Corneille, *Le Mercure Galant* sought to combine grave and gay qualities. Like the *Gazette de France*, it contained permitted state news and court circulars, and like Loret's rimed *Gazette*, it amused its readers with satirical verses and personal sketches of spicy nature.

[2] See the excellent article on "The Earliest Precursor of Our Present-Day Monthly Miscellanies" (*Pub. Mod. Lang. Ass.* xxxii, 22-58), by Professor Dorothy Foster, who makes much of the conditions in London at this time as explanation of the rise of such a journal in England.

dled to a perfunctory paragraph in the seventh number, and disappeared altogether—as it later disappeared from the *Tatler*—with a kind of apology by Motteux for his ever having tried to compete with the newspapers. Other sorts of material appeared less frequently; and the *Journal* became smaller, until it was less than half its original thickness. The last number was published in November 1694.

As a literary periodical, the *Gentleman's Journal* was the most important serial publication of the seventeenth century. Up to this time there had been among readers a strong prejudice against fiction and poetry, as we gather from the statements of writers like La Crose. Verses or works of "romantick" nature had been considered unfit for the perusal of the "serious reader." Literary appreciation could not begin, nor could criticism develop, until such a prejudice was overcome. The *Gentleman's Journal* and its contemporary, the *Athenian Mercury*, exerted more influence than any previous publications in effecting the change. To what extent this is true of Motteux's *Journal* is shown by a reading of the tables of contents during the first few months. In the January number (1692) we find verses by Tate, imitations of Horace, a description of the Kingdom of Poetry, enigmas and an article on enigmas, dramatic criticisms, and songs with music. The February number contains verses by Prior, an article on *Cleomenes*, "a new Dryden tragedy," a notice of Dryden's *Juvenal and Persius*, an essay on the "friendly cheat," and a critical discussion of Perrault's *Parallèle des anciens et des modernes*. Similar were the contents of each monthly number. Beginning with the third month, each number contained a story, called a "novel," while the interest in critical discussion is made evident by papers on Boileau, on new books and plays, and on the need of an academy in England. The first

number of the *Gentleman's Magazine* (1731) which has
been generally referred to as the first magazine of a modern type in England, contained only one form of contribution that is not to be found in this work of Motteux's. Even
the title is reminiscent of the *Gentleman's Journal*. And
other miscellanies between 1692 and 1731 were, without
exception, obvious imitations of this pioneer.

The first important periodical of this sort was entitled
Miscellanies over Claret, "or the Friends to the Tavern
the best friends to Poetry." Appearing in 1697, it consisted of a twenty-page, monthly collection of poems. The
author admitted his debt to the *Gentleman's Journal*, from
which his own serial differed in being made up entirely
of verse. In fact, it was the first real journal of poetry.[1]
A second imitator of the *Gentleman's Journal* appeared
in 1701, when Dunton first published his *Post Angel*, a
monthly serial of about seventy pages. The one feature
of the *Gentleman's Magazine* omitted in Motteux's
Journal is here supplied in short biographies of dead or
living persons. In the moral tone of the *Post Angel* is
seen the influence of the *Mercurius Theologicus* of the
previous year—a corrective temper that anticipated Defoe and Steele—while the variety of its contents allies
this periodical with the miscellany form. At the beginning, the projector divided the *Post Angel* into five parts,

---

[1] The *Weekly Entertainment* (October 24, 1700) not only supplies a
further illustration of this tendency to wholesome amusement, but—what
is more important—in form and content is one of the best anticipations of
the later *Tatler* or *Spectator*. It was a large half-sheet folio, filled with a
single essay—a dream narrative, not greatly different from those of Steele
and Addison.

The *Mercurius Theologicus; or The Monthly Instructor* (January to
December, 1700) belongs here only because of its influence on a later
miscellany. "Briefly explaining and applying all the doctrines and duties of
the Christian religion that are necessary to be believ'd and practis'd in order
to Salvation," it was devoted to religious propaganda, but the general idea
of reform and its essay style connect it with the *Weekly Entertainment*, as
another predecessor of Steele's *Tatler*.

to each of which was added a "spiritual observator" in marginal comments. A new part was added for original poetry, in July 1702, and another section devoted to original essays "on all manner of diverting subjects." Among these subjects we find sympathy of souls, disobedient children, divine titles, and the Tower of Babel. In spite of the religious bent of the *Post Angel*, the mingling of such elements as obituary notices, questions and answers, moral essays, and a catalogue of books, gives it a prominent place in the history of English literary periodicals.[1]

Defoe's *Weekly Review*, the most celebrated periodical before the *Tatler*, was not to any great degree a "literary" periodical. In this study, only the numbers between its beginning, February 19, 1704, and the issue of May 17, 1705, concern us; for these contained the *Mercure Scandale*, "Advice from the Scandalous Club, being a weekly history of nonsense, impertinence, vice, and debauchery." The idea of an imaginary club was unquestionably borrowed from the Athenian Society; while the term "Advice" had been used in the same sense by many predecessors of Defoe.[2] The Scandalous Club answered the questions of correspondents, and, in the words of Defoe, generally "censured the actions of men." After the eighteenth number, Defoe dropped the title, which was an obvious reminiscence of the French *Le Mercure Galant*, and the department appeared as "Advice from the Scandalous Club" (after the forty-sixth number, "Advice from the Scandal Club"). As its popularity increased, this department tended more and more to monopolize the space of the *Review*. In fact, its success spoiled the plan Dunton had cherished of issuing another "question-project," and forced Defoe to put out a twenty-eight

[1] The *Pacquet from Parnassus* (1702) appeared as a thirty-two page miscellany of verse, with a slight admixture of prose.

[2] Certainly as early as 1678—see *A Pacquet of Advice from Rome*.

page monthly supplement of "Advice from the Scandal Club." On May 15, 1706, he announced that this feature would thereafter be omitted from the *Review*, and would proceed by itself, as a Wednesday and Friday *Little Review*. The "Advice" had been omitted for several issues before this announcement was made—evidently crowded out by what Defoe considered of greater importance.

The *Little Review; or, An Inquisition of Scandal*, "consisting in answers of questions and doubts, remarks, observation, and reflection," was begun June 6, 1705, as a small four-page periodical. The contents of the twenty-three numbers issued were similar to those of the earlier *Athenian Mercury*. It is the best example after Dunton of the pure question-answer serial. As it lengthened the queries into letters and the answers into essays, it was an important link between the *Athenian Mercury* and the *Tatler*. The *Little Review* was a continuation, not so much of Defoe's "Advice from the Scandal Club" as of the monthly supplements that accompanied his *Review*, which consisted of questions and answers almost entirely. Defoe's prefaces show that originally he had no thought of becoming a successor to Dunton as a dispenser of wisdom, but the volume of queries submitted to the Club forced him to issue, first supplements and then a separate publication. Defoe's reforming prose is nowhere better exhibited than in the answers of the *Little Review*. Although this serial must have been a profitable venture, since it carried from two to three columns of advertisements, Defoe's interest was apparently soon claimed for other things. It has been justly observed that Defoe's original *Review* was superior to the periodicals it derived from, both in the kind of entertainment it furnished and the style in which its contents were presented. More than anything else, the club idea, and the spirit with which it made war on the vices and follies of the time, connect it with the works of Steele and Addison.[1]

An excellent example of the influence of the *Gentleman's Journal* was set up by John Oldmixon, in the *Muses Mercury* (January 1707–January 1708). The initial number of twenty-four pages contained poems by Tate, Manning, the Earl of Roscommon, and Steele, as well as Dryden's prologue for the *Prophetess*, Garth's and Dennis's prologues for *Tamerlane* and *Julius Caesar* respectively, an account of the stage, comment upon new operas and plays, a hostile discussion of Collier's attack on the stage, and notices of new books, including Congreve's *Poems* (then "in preparation") and Prior's works. Some criticisms of contemporary works are notable ingredients in this miscellany—for example, that of Addison's opera:

The *Opera of Rosamund* was performed on Tuesday, the Fourth of March; and the Town has by its applause justified the character we presumed to give it from our own judgment. The Harmony of numbers and the Beauty of the sentiments are universally admired. It has been disputed, whether the music is as good as that of *Arsinoe*; but, without entering into any comparisons, it must be confessed, that the airs of *Rosamund* are fine, the Passions well touched, and there being such a vast difference between the merit of the poems, the Dispute, 'tis probable, when decided, will be determined in favor of *Rosamund*.

It has been elsewhere shown that Addison's imitation of Horace (*Ode* iii, *lib.*, iii) appeared anonymously in this periodical, with a commendatory notice that would seem to establish Addison as a friend of Oldmixon. Moreover, it is significant that *Chevy Chase* was commended in the *Muses Mercury* long before Addison called attention

[1] Defoe, when he announced the separate publication of "Advice from the Scandalous Club," promised readers of the *Review* a little diversion at the end of the paper. This was provided in the "Miscellanea," usually a discussion of some question of trade, theology, or popular controversy. The "Miscellanea" can be of little interest here, except as evidence that this periodical writer had accepted it as part of his task to entertain readers as well as admonish and inform them.

to it in the *Spectator*.[1] Addison's connection with this earlier periodical, although almost completely overlooked by scholars, is significant, in view of his later contributions to the *Tatler*.

A rival of the *Muses Mercury* soon appeared in the *Monthly Miscellany; or, Memoirs for the Curious*, "by several hands," which continued as a thirty-two page monthly from March, 1707, to September, 1710. The desire to know, stimulated by the several serials of La Crose and Dunton, and the desire for entertainment, fostered by lighter periodicals, were here exploited together, although the entertainment furnished was made to conform to a very strict decorum. "The amusements of poetry will refine the conversations of the sullen and morose, and polish such a conversation as wants a mixture of gallantry and complaisance," declared the projector. A section of the *Miscellany* was, therefore, devoted to the muse; but most of the columns were occupied with learned subjects or the inevitable controversial divinity—either in the analysis and abstracting of books or in original articles. The *Monthly Miscellany* deserves emphasis here, because it was primarily a literary periodical. An essay on wit and humor, a treatise on poetry, dialogues upon literature and "critick," articles on books that had grown scarce, on the lives of philosophers, orators, poets, letters concerning tragedy, the academies of Paris, the "character" of Bayle's *Dictionary*, a dissertation on pastoral poetry, Dr. Bentley's emendations, a vindication of the ancients against Perrault, a new method of cataloguing libraries, a new edition of Longinus, the best method of reading the classics—these are representative of the subjects treated. It was easily the foremost literary journal of its time in anything like a modern sense. The character of popular

[1] E. K. Broadus, "Addison's Influence on the Development of Interest in Folk-Poetry in the Eighteenth Century," *Mod. Phil.* VIII, 123-134 (see p. 124, note).

miscellany was preserved by lighter matter, such as "Advice to husbands of bad wives," a descriptive essay on the Amazon River, "characters," and travels in Persia.

Captain John Tutchin, an aggressive Whig pamphleteer, whose *Foreigners* had called forth Defoe's *True-Born Englishman*, first issued in 1702 his *Observator*, a folio half-sheet, appearing Wednesday and Saturday. With a title obviously derived from L'Estrange's *Observator* of 1681, it was mainly concerned with attacks on the Tories, like so many serials of the time. The trenchant observations on plays and players in numbers 40, 57, 59, 78, 90, and 91, and the frequent employment of verse, usually of a political nature, give it some title to attention here. Between 1703 and 1704 it took the form of a series of dialogues between a countryman and the "Observator." Throughout Tutchin's life (he died in September 1707, and the paper was continued by other hands until 1712, when it fell before Queen Anne's stamp duty) the reforming tone is constantly present. Somewhat wrong-headed but always tart and arresting, Tutchin made continual onslaughts on the immorality of the stage, a fact which makes his critical observations of very little value. As a predecessor of the *Tatler*, however, the *Observator* cannot be ignored.

By 1707 criticism had become a common ingredient of the social periodical, as the "Advice from the Scandalous Club" and the pages of the *Monthly Miscellany* or *Muses Mercury* well illustrate, although literature was not yet evaluated by critics without religious or moral reservations. It remained for the early periodicals of entertainment to justify the reading of poetry, fiction, drama, and other forms of light literature. Motteux's *Gentleman's Journal*, Dunton's *Post Angel*, and Oldmixon's *Muses Mercury* included practically every sort of material that is later found in the "magazines" of the eighteenth century

—news, letters, poetry, articles of historical or philosophical interest, music, translations, stories, biographies,
fables and book notices. The seventeenth century and first
decade of the eighteenth saw the beginnings of what was
to be eventually a complete and more or less permanent dissociation of the *belles-lettres* from piety and
partisanship.

II

THE *TATLER, SPECTATOR,* AND *GUARDIAN*

The *Tatler*, with which periodical writing of a "literary" quality is generally agreed to have begun, was the inheritor of the devices and methods and tone of many predecessors.[1] In fact, there was only one original thing about Steele's project. His plan to have "accounts of gallantry, pleasure, and entertainment" come from White's Chocolate House, poetry from Will's Coffee House, learning from the Grecian, foreign and domestic news from St. James's, and whatever else he had to offer on any subject from "My Own Apartment," was an attractive and rather novel idea. Steele proposed, in other words, to fix definitely the kind of matter dated from four of the best known resorts of readers in London. The importance of these datings has never hitherto been pointed out, but is plainly apparent to any one who observes them carefully. White's Chocolate House was the most fashionable and famous gaming resort of the city, situated in the new and aristocratic West End of London. It later became White's Club.[2] Will's had long been known as the coffee house most frequented by Dryden and other "wits," and was actually referred to at this time as the "Wit's Coffee House."[3] The Grecian Coffee House, one of the oldest in London, was the haunt of barristers from the Temple near by, and of members of the Royal Society, who are known to have often adjourned their

[1] See my "Some Predecessors of the *Tatler*," *Jour. of Eng. and Germanic Philology*, XXIV (1925), 548-554.
[2] See Hogarth's *Rake's Progress* and Algernon Bourke's *A History of White's*, 1892, i, 19.
[3] *London Spy*, No. 10.

meetings at Gresham College in favor of its more congenial atmosphere.[1] St. James's Coffee House was not
only a notable gathering place of the Whig politicians,
which undoubtedly tended to make it a center of news
gossip, but was also situated close to the royal residence,
St. James's Palace, and was, therefore, to some extent frequented by army officers and soldiers of the Guard, who
could be relied upon for the latest gossip of foreign
affairs.[2]

That Steele did not adhere to this plan for any length
of time, is well known. News later appeared in other
sections than that dated from "St. James's," and entertainment was not by any means limited to the letter from
"White's."[3] Steele's plan must have been suggested, however, by the old device of dating from familiar places.
As early as 1688 we find it used in *Poor Robin's Publick
and Private Occurrances*, while *Momus Ridens* contained
sections of facetious news, dated from the Hague, from
Westminster, and from Whitehall. For this reason these
half-sheet folios were much like the *Tatler* in appearance.
The *English Lucian*, 1698, "with reflections on the vices
and vanities of the times" approximated the work of
Steele even more closely in form and make-up. It was
filled with travesties of the day's news, dated from White-
chapel, Lincoln-Inn-Fields, Old Baly (*sic*), Drury-Lane,
Lombard Street, St. James, and My Lodgings in Kent
Street. The *Merry Mercury, or the Farce of Fools*, a
paper published the next year, dated its "advices" from
similar well known places.

The *Athenian Mercury* of Dunton was undoubtedly
the earliest periodical in which the questions of corre-

---

[1] Ralph Thoresby, *Diary*, London, 1830 (May 22, 29, 1712).
[2] Edward Hatton, *New View of London*, London, 1708; *Daily Courant*,
Jan. 4, 1703; Joseph Spence, *Anecdotes*, 1820, p. 113.
[3] See, for example, a letter full of war news from a "Camp before Mons,"
in the section dated from Will's Coffee House (*Tatler* No. 87).

spondents were answered, although the question-and-answer as a periodical device is earlier seen in L'Estrange's *Observator* of 1681. In the *Athenian Mercury*, the questions and answers were frequently as long as letters. Between this serial of 1691-7 and the *Tatler* of 1709 were several others, in whose columns the usually short questions and answers of Dunton gradually expanded into the essay-like letters of Steele. William Smith's *British Apollo*, of 1708-11, should not be overlooked, if only because of its contemporaneity. It was a notably successful publication begun a year before Steele's undertaking, combining news and miscellaneous entertainment with questions and answers that were virtually letters. When the *Tatler* appeared, the *Athenian Mercury* had been stopped for a decade and Defoe's *Little Review* had not been published for four years, while the *British Apollo* was Steele's to read at least twice a week. It has been already pointed out that any suggestions Steele derived from the question and answer periodical must have come from his contemporary.

The idea of a "club" or group of friends appears in *Tatler* No. 132, dated from "Sheer-Lane." It is interesting simply as an anticipation of the much more famous coterie of characters in the later *Spectator*. According to Steele, the group of "heavy, honest men" at the Trumpet consisted of Sir Geoffrey Notch, Major Matchlock, Dick Reptile, a bencher at the inn, and the author—only five members. This club idea was certainly one of the least original devices of Steele. The contemporary *British Apollo* was published as "By a Society of Gentlemen." This, in turn, was foreshadowed by Defoe's "Scandalous Club" in the *Review*, the "Athenian Society," and the trio of critics in the *Mercurius Eruditorum* of 1691.

Important prototypes of some of the various "characters" to be found in the *Tatler*, were those of the *Weekly*

Comedy, the *Diverting Post*, and the *Humours of a Coffee-house*. Several writers have pointed out Steele's possible indebtedness to Edward Ward's *London Spy*, 1698, which contained sketches of London types. Little or nothing has been said about the *Weekly Comedy*, "as it is daily acted at the Coffee Houses in London" (1699) also credited to Ward. Its possible relation to the "characters" of Steele is obvious. Five years later, the *Diverting Post* of Henry Playford contained dialogues spoken by such "characters" as Mr. Blunt and Mr. Grumbleton, or Mr. Stingy and Mr. Freeman. It is reasonable to suppose that Steele was familiar with these periodicals. He may have been influenced by them, as well as by Ward's *Humours of a Coffee-House*, "A Comedy" of 1707, which employed a *dramatis personae* of sixteen characters. Steele, in including verse in the columns of the *Tatler*, was merely doing what many periodical writers had done before him. In now and then venturing to comment on a book or author, in the *Tatler* or *Spectator*, he was following the broad path laid out by such serials as La Crose's *Universal Historical Bibliotheque* of 1687, the *Mercurius Eruditorum* of 1691, and the *Moderator* of 1692. John Dunton declared his purpose to have the *Athenian Mercury* "lye for common chatt and entertainment in every coffee-house board." With this early suggestion, and with the additional examples of two periodicals designed to relate the "humours" of the coffee-houses, in 1699 and 1707, it is easy to guess why Steele wished to make his *Tatler* a coffee-house and tavern oracle.[1]

The superiority of the *Tatler* and *Spectator* over all preceding English periodicals is beyond question. Although unoriginal in form and tone and in the nature of their contents, the periodicals of Steele and Addison re-

---

[1] By 1710 there were two thousand coffee-houses in London and Westminster. (See Roger North's *Examen*, London 1740.)

vealed to English readers a better quality of literary journalism. It is now understood that they gradually developed the periodical essay out of the section of the *Tatler* entitled "From My Own Apartment." They thus produced in its highest form the essay serial, to be sure, but it is not wholly true that they created a new type of periodical—the single-essay type. Some of the earlier half sheet folios consisted of crude essays. Probably the best early example is the *Weekly Entertainment* of 1700. The one extant number is filled with an essay containing a moral dream narrative, not very different from many to be found in numbers of the *Spectator*—or in the later numbers of the *Tatler*. Thomas Baker's *Female Tatler*, which was set up three months after Steele began the *Tatler*, consisted from the beginning of a single essay, dated "From My Own Apartment." This *Female Tatler* was undoubtedly the most serious rival of Steele's publication. It is surely significant that Steele, soon after the appearance of Baker's publication, gradually abandoned all other departments, until—a few months before the end—most of the numbers of the *Tatler* consisted of single essays, under the heading "From My Own Apartment."

Steele was a good journalist. He gave his readers what he knew they liked to read. It is reasonable to believe that before entering upon this new enterprise he made himself intimately acquainted with all the methods and devices of Motteux, Dunton, Defoe, and others of his more successful predecessors. Moreover, there could have been no uncertainty in his mind as to the tone of his publication or the kind of matter that should fill his columns. La Crose, Dunton, and Defoe had popularized reform. Manners and morals, matters of human conduct and social relations, had long been the subjects of discussion by writers of periodicals. For example, the genial observations of Steele regarding the worth of family ties and the delights of conjugal felicity find certain anticipation in the *Ladies Mercury* of 1694 and the *Memoirs for the Curious* of 1701. In its subject matter, the *Tatler* shows constantly the influence of Ned Ward's wit and comment on London life, the reforming urge of Dunton, Defoe, and Tutchin, Motteux's miscellaneous entertainment, and the increasing tendency to comment on books and writers illustrated in the *History of Learning*, 1691, the *Compleat Library*, 1692, and the *Monthly Miscellany* of 1707-8. In short, it may be said that everything in the evolution of the literary periodical in England leads up to the *Tatler*. Steele not only produced the first periodical criticism of lasting value; he was the first journalist to reveal the possibilities of the periodical as a medium for literature.

Steele began to publish the *Tatler* on April 12, 1709, as a thrice-a-week folio half-sheet, selling, after gratuitous circulation of the initial numbers, for one penny. For another half-penny, Steele's readers could secure also a blank-sheet for transmission by post, so that any scraps of gossip or other messages which one might care to send to his friends could be included. By the close of the year 1709 the *Tatler* was probably more popular and more widely read than any other English periodical of that time. After considerable miscellaneous literary work, Steele seems to have made this periodical venture chiefly in hope of financial gain, although he had had little or no experience as a journalist, except as official gazetteer—of dubious value for the undertaking now in hand. Like Dunton, seventeen years before, he planned to have his publication read in the coffee house. Henry Morley pointed out Steele's main ambition—a "widely diffused influence for good." Yet there is no great evidence of this in the contents of the first few numbers of the *Tatler*.[1]

[1] *Spectator*, ed. 1891, i (Introduction), xxxvi.

Female Tatler.

By Mrs Crackenthorpe, *a Lady that knows every thing.*

From **Monday** October 17, to **Wednesday** October 19, 1709.

THERE are a sort of Whimsical People in the World call'd *Poets*, whose Delight, whose Transport, nay, generally speaking, whole Livelyhoods proceed from *Satyr* and *Invective*, from malitiously observing the little failings of the rest of Mankind, and from an unhappy *Genius*, turn'd to Scandal, improving 'em into the groffest *Ridicule*; Some do it in *Comedy*, others by *Paraphrastical Transitions*; some by downright *Libel*, and others more by *Panegyrick*. Lady *Fancy-ful*, who had the Vanity to think herself expos'd in the *Memoirs from the New Atalantis*, started the Question, What kind of Creatures are these People? They must be *unparalell'd* in *Religion, Loyalty, Chastity, Sobriety*, all *Moral Virtue*, and *Correct Qualifications*, as nice *Dress* and *Address*, a just and proper *Decorum*, in different Companies and Conversations, but above all in —— *prompt Payment*: That they seem to take an affur'd Freedom in lathing not only the impin'd Vices of the Town, but the pretty, pleasing, harmless Affectations of our Sex, which divert our selves, and give Offence to no body. *Colonel Florid*, who so judiciously penetrates into Mankind, and with so much Modest Ease and Musical Eloquence, delineates not only particular Persons, but any Sect of People, that he bewitches our Attention, enter'd upon the Subject. This Notion of Poets was, that they are a *Chymerical Tribe*, but few Degrees remov'd from *Madmen*, who ought not be trusted with themselves, but like headless, rambling *School-boys*, have ev'ry thing provided for 'em, their *Bounds* let 'em, and their *Pocket Money* paid 'em ev'ry Day; they have no more Concern about their passing thro' the *World*, than if they were not in it; yet have a more refin'd *Taste* of Dress, Equipage, *Buildings, Furniture* and *Entertainments*, than all the World besides; they have Cloaths, regardless of what Price they buy 'em, and as regardless of discharging it; ride in *Great* Men's Charriots, are at *Great* Men's Seats, and as their Wit and Humour are the Spirit of the *Table*, think the *Greatest* Men are oblig'd to 'em for their Company.——Stepping out of the Room to give some Directions, I happen'd to hear Mrs. *Lovelefs*, my Intimate Acquaintance, and as I thought my Friend, sneeringly cry,——Why, what is *Crackenthorpe* but a *Poetess?* The Company was alarm'd at the *Aspersion*, and Mrs. *Wiseman* wonder'd, how a Serious, Reforming Paper, tho' larded with Jests, Epigrams and pleasant Tales, cou'd bring me under that Denomination; but when I found the Dispute growing high, I belted smilingly into the Room, and told em Supper was just ready.——The Collonel proceeded, That *Poets* having a finer thread of Understanding, a quicker Apprehension, and more noble Ideas of Things than the Generality; they

are intoxicated with *Sublime Conceptions*, fancy their Bodies, where their Imaginations Soar, and in the heat of their Poetical Flights, discover the Lunatick in all his Shapes and Postures; a *Poem* well finish'd is to them beyond teaching a mere Act of Parliament, they have no *Plots* but in *Plays*, and seldom any there, and a *Comedy* once brought to a full Third Night, is to them coming to a vast Estate: They have no Notion of Honour, but in the Hero of a *Tragedy*, Friendship but for those who lend 'em Money, Sobriety after a hard Debauch, nor Regularity either in Thought, Deed, Time, or Habitation; therefore when their Patrons bestow Preferments on 'em, knowing their Disposition for Business, they generally take Care they shall be *Sine Cures*. And are these Creatures, says *Lady Fancy-ful*, that set up for *Observators*, that won't let one be a little particular in Publick Places to be taken notice of, but one's Character is in the next *New Comedy*, which perhaps is so Beastly a thing, one is n't able to sit it out; but Mrs. *Tire-quill*, who has the *Indiscretion* of Scribling herself, wou'd n't allow *Poets* to be so Contemptibly treated; she said, they were rather *Demi Gods* than *Men*; that their Thoughts were *Supernatural*, and tho' their Mortal Clay over-animated for so small a Tenement, oblig'd 'em sometimes to *Terrestial* Confabulation, yet they more frequently convers'd with *Dieties*; *Jupiter* gave 'em *Majestick Notions*, *Mars* show'd 'em a *Specimen* of War, *Venus* told 'em pretty *Love-Tales*, and they had rather be inebriated with *Bacchus* in Imagination, than be really so with the most distinguish'd *Animal* below the *Spheres*: That such Persons, whose Writings make Mortals as Immortal as themselves, ought not to grovel about Worldly Cares, nor subject their Fancies, which are always upon the Wing to any manner of Constraint: That little thought Conversing with an *Author*, and perusing his *Works*, before they were blown upon by the Ingrateful World, was, next to happy Conceptions of her own, the greatest Felicity upon Earth. Mrs. *Tire-quill* was so Zealous for the Reputation of the *Here* and *Thereians Tribe*, and grew to inspir'd upon the Subject, that she wou'd immediately have talk'd in Verse, had not Collonel *Florid* turn'd the Discourse upon a sort of miserable Creatures, call'd *Wou'd-be-Poets*; Wretches! that are in Business, *Tradesmen, Petty-foggers* and *Notary Publicks*, that might plod on in their Thoughtless Vocation, grow Rich, keep Coaches, and never think of the next World, yet fancying they have a Genius, leave their prosperous Knavery to write Songs, Madrigals and damn'd Plays, till they starve indeed, being shunn'd by their own Tribe, and laugh'd at by the *Kit-Kat Club*. There are an Incorrigible Crew, who, tho' they are punish'd with Poverty, and the utmost Contempt, ye

h

In "The Lucubrations of Isaac Bickerstaff, Esq.,"
Steele made use of a name which was already well known
throughout England as Swift's nom de plume in several
pamphlets of 1708 which prophesied the death of John
Partridge, the infamous almanac maker and astrologer.
Steele gave Swift such credit as was due him, and for
some time carried on the jest at Partridge's expense.
Steele's Bickerstaff was "an old man, a philosopher, an
humorist, an astrologer, and a censor"—a happy creation
that grew to proportions his creator did not dream of in
the beginning. Bickerstaff took the center of the stage,
supported by a numerous family of Staffs. These furnished a thread of narrative interest that served to unify
the diverse elements of the new periodical.

The *Tatler* began its career with contents not very different from those of the *Gentleman's Journal*, "Advice
from the Scandalous Club," the *Monthly Miscellany*, or
Muse's Mercury. Yet it had two distinct advantages over
its predecessors. One was the attractiveness of its plan.
Different sections were dated from popular resorts of
readers, as has been remarked. The five departments were
not intended to be used in each number of the *Tatler*, but
rather to be employed as occasion or convenience dictated.
An important advantage of the plan was its flexibility—
the author's privilege of including miscellaneous matter
of all sorts under the heading "From My Own Apartment."

A second distinct advantage which set the *Tatler* apart
from all publications which preceded it was its superior
style. Steele and Addison were its authors, to say nothing
of other able pens among its contributors. The English
periodical had at last acquired "literary" quality. Nathan
Drake and others declared that the world owes Addison
to Steele. The latter himself said, "I claim to myself the

merit of having extorted excellent productions from a person of the greatest abilities, who would not have let them appear by any other means."[1] Although it is now reasonably certain that Steele furnished most of the popular tact for the enterprise, Addison's help to Steele is probably of greater importance than critics are accustomed to admit. He wrote alone probably not more than forty-two out of 188 papers,[2] and it is probably true, as alleged, that Addison usually elaborated the hints he received from Steele, who was the creative genius of both *Tatler* and *Spectator*. Addison's first paper is believed to have been in No. 18, although not until the autumn of the year did Steele receive substantial aid from him. Yet this darling of the Whigs added appreciably to the prestige of Steele's publication. Moreover, he brought to it what Steele lacked—an exceptional classical training. He contributed, in his treatment of men and manners, the philosophy and wit and observation of the ancients, impressing a public long familiar with the heavier serials of De la Crose and the works of classical authors.[3]

Little by little, the *Tatler* took the world of manners and conduct for its theme, dropping one after another of the departments less congenial to its conductor. Its tone was simple, almost conversational. Its air was that of persuasive authority, free from dogma—influential in a day when men gave attention to any self-constituted referee in their debates who could speak to their convictions or point out their weaknesses with sympathy and tact. So much has already been written about this aspect of the

[1] *Spectator*, 532.

[2] Profesor C. N. Greenough grants Addison forty-five, although he questions some. ("The Development of the *Tatler*, Particularly in Regard to News," *Pub. Mod. Lang. Assoc.*, 1916, XXI, 639-649.)

[3] *Cf.* W. Ricken, *Bemerkungen über Anlage und Erfolg der wichtigsten Zeitschriften Steele's und den Einfluss Addison auf die Entwicklung derselben* (Elberfield), 1885.

Tatler that it would be folly to add more here. A contemporary said more in a few paragraphs than have all the commentators since. John Gay, in 1711, wrote of Bickerstaff in the *Present State of Wit*:

To give you my own thoughts of this Gentleman's Writings, I shall, in the first place, observe, that there is a noble difference between him and all the rest of our polite and gallant Authors. The latter have endeavoured to please the Age by falling in with them, and encouraging them in their fashionable vices and false notions of things. It would have been a jest, some time since, for a man to have asserted that anything witty could be said in praise of a married state, or that Devotion and Virtue were any way necessary to the character of a Fine Gentleman. *Bickerstaff* ventured to tell the Town that they were a parcel of fops, fools, and coquettes; but in such a manner as even pleased them, and made them more than half inclined to believe that he spoke truth.

Instead of complying with the false sentiments or vicious tastes of the Age—either in morality, criticism, or good breeding—he has boldly assured them that they were altogether in the wrong; and commanded them, with an authority which perfectly well became him, to surrender themselves to his arguments for Virtue and Good Sense.

It is incredible to conceive the effect his writings have had on the Town; how many thousand follies they have either quite banished or given a very great check to! how much countenance they have added to Virtue and Religion! how many people they have rendered happy, by shewing them it was their own fault if they were not so! and, lastly, how entirely they have convinced our young fops and young fellows of the value and advantages of Learning!

He has indeed rescued it out of the hands of pedants and fools, and discovered the true method of making it amiable and lovely to all mankind. In the dress he gives it, it is a most welcome guest at tea-tables and assemblies, and is relished and caressed by the merchants on the Change. Accordingly there is not a Lady at Court, nor a Banker in Lombard Street, who is not verily persuaded that Captain *Steele* is the greatest scholar and best Casuist of any man in England.

Lastly, his writings have set all our Wits and Men of Letters on a new way of Thinking, of which they had little or no notion before: and, although we cannot say that any of them have come up to the beauties of the original, I think we may venture to affirm, that every one of them writes and thinks much more justly than they did some time since.[1]

Isaac Bickerstaff, an eloquent and versatile mouthpiece for Steele and Addison, uttered "lucubrations" on a wide variety of subjects. The pride of the rich, the simple virtues of the poor, the fads of fashion, women in love, the deaths of friends, social prejudices, and the inconveniences of travel were not beyond the observation of Bickerstaff; nor did he fail to find in them lessons for the average reader of the *Tatler*. Yet convictions were not pressed insistently upon readers, in the dogmatic manner of Dunton refuting Anabaptists, or with the pedantic argument of La Crose. Readers were allowed to glean what they would. Steele's Puritan seriousness was humanized by good taste and disarming humor. He found it his greatest pleasure "to trace human life through all its mazes and recesses, and show much shorter methods than men ordinarily practise, to be happy, agreeable, and great."

On January 2, 1711, the *Tatler* was abruptly discontinued. The projector had tired of his original plan, to which —it has been pointed out—he had always adhered very carelessly. The contents of the letter from Will's were by no means limited to poetry and drama, nor were these included only in this department. From the first numbers, there was no hard and fast classification of material. Actually—whether writing from White's, the Grecian, or Will's—Steele and Addison touched men and things discursively, with no apparent limitations of subject. Clearly, Steele and Addison, as well as other contributors, gradually found it more congenial to write from the less restricted "My Own Apartment." In fact, Professor Greenough has shown that nearly one-half the let-

[1] Reprinted in *An English Garner: Critical Essays and Literary Fragments*, ed. J. C. Collins, N. Y., n. d. pp. 201-210.

ters in the *Tatler* were thus dated.[1] From Number 100 to the end, other departments headings were used infrequently—White's five times, Will's four times, the Grecian, which had never been much employed, only three times, and St. James's six times. "From My Own Apartment," on the other hand, was used steadily more and more—eighty-five times before the hundredth number, and one hundred and twenty times thereafter. Moreover, from the one hundredth, there was a noticeable tendency to devote each number to a single letter, whatever the place of dating. In other words, most of the later numbers of the *Tatler* consisted of single essays by single authors. The earliest containing a single essay is No. 28; the last divided number is 176. "Sheer-Lane," a new place of dating, appeared in the one hundredth number, to be used with increasing frequency as time passed.[2] Nearly always these "Sheer-Lane" papers occupy an entire number. In short, the *Tatler*, under the influence of Baker's *Female Tatler*, perhaps, had gradually dropped those features least congenial to the author.

In the *Tatler* and *Spectator*, the single-essay periodical, a literary phenomenon unique in the eighteenth century, was developed and popularized. The *Tatler* established it as a type; in the *Spectator* it was perfected. The success of the *Tatler* was marked, but was evidently felt by Steele to have little relation to the original purpose of the periodical, which seems to have been hurried to a close. Steele had evidently envisioned the possibilities of a daily essay. He was probably glad to end the *Tatler*, and thus free himself from whatever obligations to readers he had assumed under the old plan. On March 1, the first number of the *Spectator* appeared, little different in appearance from the later *Tatler*. It appeared on each day except

[1] C. N. Greenough, "The Development of the *Tatler* Particularly in Regard to News," *Pub. Mod. Lang. Assn.* (1916), XXI, 633-662.

[2] "Sheer-Lane" is used as dating of a letter in No. 27.

Sunday, to "grow into the life of the reader like an intimate friend." It was concerned chiefly with morals and manners, each number developing a single theme—a clean-cut homily enlivened with inimitable humor. Bickerstaff, who had scorned to be an inquisitor, although he admitted he was a reformer, was here succeeded by Mr. Spectator, who stepped into the foreground and furnished the daily essay with a concrete character. Later came other characters, now too famous to need description, who summarized in themselves all the worthy traits of the literary characters of the past—the lively curosity, the profound learning, the wit, or sentiment or homely piety.

The change from a thrice-a-week *Tatler* to a daily *Spectator* was justified by the prosperity of the latter. At first, three thousand copies were printed. Later, the circulation rose to four thousand, probably—far from the extravagant estimates of some commentators, yet impressive enough if one keeps in mind the conditions in 1712, when, as Mr. Spectator put it, "an average copy was read by a score of disciples." When the tax on newspapers went into effect on August 1, the *Spectator* increased its price and survived, although many other periodicals gave up the ghost. It was greatly handicapped, however, and only a large amount of advertising enabled it to continue until Dec. 6, 1712. Steele seems to have been a very good business man, without too many scruples, securing for his columns paid notices for every sort of commodity. Theatrical performances, books, Canary wines, quack medicines, barber's supplies, perfumes, shoe blacking, and manor houses, were impartially advertised in the *Spectator*.[1]

---

[1] See L. Lewis, *The Advertisements of the Spectator*, N. Y. 1909, p. 64. Lewis thinks the short career of the later thrice-a-week *Spectator* (June 18 to September 29, 1714), issued by Addison without Steele's help, was due to its inability to compete with newspapers for the advertising market.

Among their varied and agreeable contents, the criticism of the *Tatler* and *Spectator* is notable. It had little likeness to the heavy discussions of the earlier abstract serials. Rather it savored of the familiar criticism of nineteenth-century essayists. Steele was informal and impressionistic, with no enunciated theory or critical principles. When he attempted to set forth his views, he used reason and good sense, the shibboleths of the age. He was impatient of formalism. At his best he allowed his individual taste to be its own justification. Addison had something in common with Steele. Like the latter, he opposed a narrow rationalism. A classicist by training, he was much more than a strictly classical critic, and was led, to a great extent, by his own tastes. He enjoyed revealing the object of his own admiration to others, although his criticism was somewhat more analytical than that of his colleague. There is nothing among Steele's papers similar to Addison's essays on *Paradise Lost*, *Chevy Chase*, or those on the pleasures of the imagination. It has been said that in so far as they can be pigeon-holed at all, Steele and Addison belong with the early Romanticists. Be that as it may, their principles as well as their methods were well adapted to popularize literary criticism among the readers of the *Tatler, Spectator*, and *Guardian*.[1]

Of the writers who contributed to the *Tatler* we may name with some certainty Swift, John Hughes, Samuel Fuller of Petersfield (Steele's friend, a youth of sixteen at this time, of whom Steele afterward wrote in the *Theatre*), Heneage Twisden, William Congreve, E. W. Mon-

---

Probably the death of Anne on August 1, and the subsequent change in Addison's fortunes, had something to do with the ending of it. See No. 632 for Addison's playful explanation of the origin of the later *Spectator*.

[1] "It is not too much to say that in the suggestive papers on the imagination Addison laid the foundation of the whole romantic aesthetics in England" (J. G. Robertson, *The Genesis of Romantic Theory in the Eighteenth Century*, Cambridge, 1923, p. 241).

tagu, and Anthony Henley. Charles Dartiquenave, Arthur Maynwaring, Pope, Gay, and Temple Stanyon were possibly collaborators. The contributors to the original *Spectator* are less easy to be certain of than those of the *Tatler*, especially as little attempt has yet been made to distinguish between the *Spectator* of Steele and the *Spectator* of Addison and Budgell. In *Spectator* No. 555, which concluded the original series, Steele acknowledged the assistance of Addison, Henry Martyn, Pope, John Hughes, Walter Carey, Thomas Tickell, Thomas Parnell, and Laurence Eusden. Later—in the first reprinted edition—he added his acknowledgment of the contributions of Richard Ince. Others, whose names have been conjecturally associated with the earlier or the later *Spectators*, were Dr. George Smallridge, Thomas Burnet, Bishop Francis Atterbury, Mrs. Oldfield, the actress, Dr. Samuel Garth, Rev. William Asplin, James Greenwood, and William Harrison. The later *Spectator* of Addison and Eustace Budgell was reprinted as Volume VIII in the collected edition.

The *Tatler* and *Spectator* were the supreme examples of the essay-periodical type. Many such serials followed, but none could compare with them in consistent moral instruction, simple yet finished style, genial humor, or influence and popularity with contemporary readers. None could compare with them in presenting cross-sections of contemporary life—pictures of the age—revealing English men and manners, professions, theatres, trades, and homes. They record the prevailing sentiments regarding education, religion, politics, and literature. Almost every condition of life, pursuit, pastime, conversation, taste, fashion, vice, folly, and virtue appears. Little of consequence in the Age of Anne seems to be left out of the picture.

The original *Spectator* came to an end on December

6, 1712. In the following March, Steele came forward with the *Guardian*, which, however, had been planned before the *Spectator* was concluded. Steele introduced a new plan and a fresh set of characters. Nestor Ironside, Esq., the fictitious conductor, announced his plan in the initial number:

My Design upon the whole is no less, than to make the Pulpit, the Bar, and the Stage, all act in Concert in the Care of Piety, Justice, and Virtue. For I am past all the Regards of this Life, and have nothing to manage with any Person or Party, but to deliver myself as becomes an Old Man, with one Foot in the Grave, and one who thinks he is passing to Eternity. All Sorrows which can arrive at me are comprehended in the sense of Guilt and Pain; if I can keep clear of these two Evils, I shall not be apprehensive of any other. Ambition, Lust, Envy, and Revenge, are Excrescences of the Mind which I have cut off long ago: But as they are excrescences which do not only deform, but also torment those on whom they grow, I shall do all I can to persuade all others to take the same Measures for their Cure which I have.

With this apparent profession of freedom from politics, the new serial began agreeably, and appeared daily for 175 numbers. Addison is now credited with fifty-two papers of the total number. Fourteen papers are included in the collected works of George Berkeley. Pope, Thomas Tickell, Eustace Budgell, John Hughes, John Gay, Ambrose Philips, William Wotton, John Carey, Richard Ince, Thomas Parnell, Henry Martyn, and Laurence Eusden were occasional contributors. In spite of early professions, Steele was drawn into political controversy, and on October 1, 1713, this essay periodical was brought to an end, to make way for another, avowedly political— the *Englishman*.

The *Guardian*, while it continued, was a periodical not unworthy to take its place beside the *Tatler* and *Spectator*, although its contents lack the freshness and novelty of those earlier essays. Some idea of its popularity may be gained from the fact that by 1797 twenty-six editions had been published. Its design, "to make the Pulpit, the Bar, and the Stage, all act in Concert in the care of Piety, Justice, and Virtue," was promoted, for a time at least, by essays on such subjects as "The Excellency and Superiority of the Scriptures," "Grounds to expect a Future State Proved," "On Sacred Poetry," "On the Conduct of Certain old Fellows in Gray's Inn Gardens," and "On the Tragedy *Othello*." Criticism of home and family, that staple of his stock, Steele pleasantly introduced through the medium of the Lizards, clearly related to the Staffs in the *Tatler*. They are described in the early numbers of the *Guardian*—the widow of Sir Marmaduke, Lady Lizard, her daughters, Jane, Annabella, Cornelia, Betty, and Mary, Sir Harry, the son and heir, with other minor characters, their friends and relatives. In the capacity of executor and guardian, Nestor Ironside acted as an intimate friend—having as much anxiety for the successful issue of the Lizard's affairs as the father might have had. His manner of educating the son and his conduct toward the numerous members of the family were woven into a criticism of common life. The chief entertainment arose from what passed at the tea table of Lady Lizard, as "Aspasia." Items about the members of the family, their cares, passions, interests, and diversions, were presented, from time to time, as news from Lady Lizard's drawing room, a source undoubtedly suggested by the tea-table gossip of Mrs. Crackenthorpe in the *Female Tatler*.

For its general criticism, particularly, is the *Guardian* valuable. Steele's plea for tolerant and catholic criticism (12), his wise advice about the difficulties of easy writing (15), Tickell's various animadversions on pastoral poetry, Hughes's praise of Othello (37), Pope's sly essay contrasting Philips's pastorals with his own (40), the several essays on *Cato*, Pope's satirical receipt for an epic poem (78), to say nothing of references to Prior and Congreve, to Boileau and Longinus, and to various dramas then on the stage—all these make up a not inconsiderable body of critical literature, and give the *Guardian* a distinguished place in the history of critical periodicals.

The *Tatler, Spectator* and *Guardian*, which established the essay periodical as a type, represent in themselves the best examples we have of it in the first half of the eighteenth century. Their success gave rise to a long line of imitations, among which the essay of morals and manners was adapted to a variety of uses almost as wide as the diversity of human interests. The popularity of the essay as a separate periodical virtually died with the end of the century. It will be shown that essays were appropriated to the newspapers and magazines as "features," and ceased to have distinct periodic identity. But even in the age of Anne and political patronage, Steele and Addison demonstrated that periodical writing was a new and dependable means of reward for authors. They were in a sense the prophets and leaders who pointed the way to future generations of literary journalists. It is more important to students of literature, perhaps, that the *Tatler, Spectator,* and *Guardian* differed from all the periodicals which had preceded them and from many of those which followed, in that they were the receptacles of literature of permanent value. Before they appeared, periodical literature had received few contributions of any merit. It was produced by writers of mediocre talent. It suffered from the ills of partisan truculence, rampant sectarianism, crude taste, and personal rancor. What we now call journalism was regarded with contempt by authors of repute. The stigma attached to it actually remained in newspaper writing until the days of Walter Scott; it is not entirely absent even today. Thanks to Steele and Addison, the "literary" periodical became respectable, and with essay writing, journalism began to lose its stigma. Unlike all their predecessors and most of their followers, Steele and Addison earned their niche in the halls of literary fame solely by their periodical writing. In the *Tatler, Spectator*, and *Guardian*, journalism and literature were first brought into happy union.

III

IMITATORS OF THE *TATLER* AND *SPECTATOR*
BEFORE 1750

The success of Addison and Steele as authors of periodical essays is attested by the extraordinary number of
imitators which sprang into existence before the middle
of the eighteenth century. Most of these are now forgotten; but it should not be thought that all were without
merit. Some, by their original devices, and by their
slightly different application of old features, deserve mention in any history of English literary periodicals. Such
essay serials as are considered in the following pages to a
greater or less degree exemplify the remarkable adaptability of this type of publication when employed for the
conveyance of instruction, persuasion, or entertainment.[1]
Unscrupulous efforts to capitalize the popularity of
Steele's and Addison's work appeared in several publications, whose authors pretended (in some cases, at least)
their folio half-sheets to be continuations of either the
Tatler or the *Spectator*. On January 4, two days after the
last of Steele's *Tatlers* was issued, another *Tatler*, printed
and sold by J. Baker, began as No. 272, "with the character of Mr. Steele, alias Isaac Bickerstaff." This short-
lived publication (only two numbers survive) may or
may not have been an attempt to dupe readers. But there
is no doubt about the object of another, started within
two days, as Nos. 272, 273, and printed for Morphew, the
printer of the original *Tatler*. Under the title was the

---

[1] See George S. Marr, *Periodical Essayists of the 18th Century*, N. Y.
1924; Nathan Drake, *Essays . . . Illustrative of the Tatler, Spectator, and
Guardian*, Lon. 1805; and my *Beginnings of English Literary Periodicals*,
N. Y. 1926.

statement, "This paper, which was not published on Thursday last, is now, upon better thoughts, resolved to be continued as usual, By Isaac Bickerstaff, Esq." The first number contained what purported to be a further installment of the "Court of Honour," continued from December 19, just as the installment of that date was continued from December 5. A faithful follower of Steele's *Tatler*, the imitator survived until May 19, overshadowed and finally eliminated by the rivalry of still another *Tatler*. This third serial appeared January 13, 1711, printed for Mrs. A. Baldwin, and with William Harrison for its conductor. Swift helped "little Harrison" to set it up,[1] and Congreve and "Anthony Henley, lately dead," were among its contributors.[2] New characters were introduced, such as "Humphrey Wagstaff, kinsman to Bickerstaff." Letters were dated from the "Young Men's Coffee-House" and "Channel Row," as well as from resorts already familiar to readers. Many of the papers are from the pens of Swift and Harrison, the former's sketch of Steele in No. 28 being most important. But except for a defence of the theatre in No. 31, and advice to dramatic writers in No. 36, little critical effort is shown, to give this periodical literary value.

In a similar way the reputation of the *Spectator* was exploited. The later *Spectator* of Addison was discontinued December 20, 1714. On January 3, 1715, another volume was begun by William Bond. The initial issue appeared as No. 636, and the form and manner of the original *Spectator* were closely followed. The work con-

---

[1] See *Journal to Stella*, 11 Jan., 1711.

[2] On Feb. 3, . . . in consequence of a quarrel with his printer, Harrison shifted to Morphew, took over Morphew's numbering, and continued to publish through Morphew to the end of the series; so that from No. 285, Feb. 3, to No. 330, May 19, Harrison's continuation and Morphew's were one and the same paper. As reprinted in volume, Harrison's *Tatler* included Nos. 1-6, printed for Mrs. Baldwin, and Nos. 285-330, printed for Morphew, the whole renumbered 1-52. (Crane and Kaye's *Census of British Newspapers and Periodicals*, 1620-1800, Chapel Hill, N. C., 1927, p. 102.)

tains much that is sheer parody of Addison and Steele, including a burlesque of the former's poem, *The Campaign*. This *Spectator* appeared twice a week, for fifty-nine numbers. The last number is made up entirely of pastorals, evidently parodies of those of Pope and Ambrose Philips. In its reprinted form, it appeared as the rare ninth volume of the *Spectator*.[1]

The first number of the original *Tatler* was not yet three months old when the *Female Tatler* appeared, "by Mrs. Crackenthorpe, a lady that knows everything." Phoebe Crackenthorpe, the fictitious conductor, really Thomas Baker, proposed to give the town another paper of this sort on Monday, Wednesday, and Friday, "since Tatling was ever adjudged peculiar to our Sex. . . ." Baker declared in his preface, "More ridiculous things are done every day in London than ten such journals can relate." Mrs. Crackenthorpe was a great lady, who had twice a week an assembly of both sexes, "from his grace, My Lord Duke, to Mr. Sagathie, the spruce merchant . . . from the Duchess to Mrs. Top Sail, the sea captain's wife at Wapping . . . I shall date all my advices from my own apartment." These advices recounted the conversation of "Grave Statesmen, Airy Beaus, Lawyers, Citts, Poets, Parsons, and Ladies of all Degrees," ranging over books, removals at court, disputed law cases, prices of stocks, and new fashions.

[1] An interesting *Tatler Reviv'd* appeared in 1727 (Oct. 16—Jan. 15, 1728) as "by Isaac Bickerstaff." It was in appearance a perfect imitation of Steele's later *Tatler*, even to the single-essay dated "From My Own Apartment." Readers were requested to give help—"Mr. Bickerstaff hopes that all his Old Friends, who are in the land of the living, will renew their correspondence with him as before; and also invites all others, of whatever Age, Sex, or Degree soever, who have any Wit or Time to spare for the Public Good, in promoting an innocent and useful Entertainment, to convey their thoughts to him on Morality, Wit, Oeconomy, Friendship, Conversation, Love, Poetry, or any other subject whatsoever, except scandal and politics. . . ." Altogether, the *Tatler Reviv'd* appears to be one more clever effort to dupe readers. Another *Tatler Revived* (1750) was referred to by Johnson in the *Rambler*. A *Tatler* of 1753-4 was unimportant.

The competition of a rival which started with such a plan, and one with such success as is indicated by the column and a half of advertisements which Baker carried from the beginning, is obvious. But it need only to be remarked here that Steele must have been stimulated to his greatest editorial ingenuity by the rivalry of Baker. In particular, the expressed intention of dating all advices in the *Female Tatler* from "My Own Apartment" seems to have been very suggestive; for soon after the initial publication of Baker's serial, Steele began to use his similar dating more and more, finally making the *Tatler*, as we have seen, virtually a single essay—as Baker's essay sheet had been practically from the first.

The *Female Tatler* is the only one of these early imitators that appears to have influenced Steele, or to have achieved to any degree the manner and tone of the authors of the original *Tatler* or *Spectator*. A few paragraphs from the *Female Tatler* (No. 22) show how well Baker approximated the style of his great contemporaries:

Amongst all the different Degrees, Ranks and Orders of Humane Species, there can be no greater object of Compassion, nor any one more worthy the regard of the sensible part of mankind, than he that in spite of Natural Simplicity, and amidst the frowns of an unaccountable Fortune, has the additional Curse of imagining himself to be a Wit. . . . Whether he is or not, is little to the purpose, 'tis enough that he thinks so, and the very Notion imperceptibly hurries him into all those Inconveniences, Expectations and Disquietudes that usually attend on Persons under that unhappy Circumstance . . . 'Tis a Condition the more to be lamented, because not to be prevented, and generally seizes on a Man's most sensible Part, disorders his Reason, and carries him out of the World before he has the Opportunity of knowing himself to be a Fool.

Thus it is with my Friend *Tom Careless*, who, tho' really an Ingenious Man and fit for Business, (has no Estate, nor ever like to have any) yet thinks himself above it. His head is always full of Chymerical Ideas of Merit, he is continually disquieting himself with the fancy'd prospect of what he is never like to attain to, and at the least Interruption of Providence in the Prosperity of his Life, blames his Fortune, curses his Stars, and rails at the degeneracy of Mankind; tho' at the same time he sees not his own Error in indulging such notions, that will (if not in time prevented) be his Ruin. As I know him to be a Man worthy of a better Fate, I have by an application of Argument, endeavoured to reclaim him, but in vain. All the answer he gives me, is, *That he is sensible of the Truth of what I say, but that the Superior Madness is so rooted in his Soul, that he cannot shake it off, tho' at the same time he sees his Ruin in too visible Characters before him.*

Even if the *Female Tatler* influenced him, Steele and his work prospered while Baker's serial declined. On November 4, 1709, Baker announced a change of plan. Mrs. Crackenthorpe gave way to a "Society of young ladies." Each number, from this time on, was Lucinda's Day or Artesia's Day, etc., until 111 numbers had been published. On March 31, 1710, the first important rival of the *Tatler* gave up the competition. Evidently, the deserved popularity of Steele's *Tatler* was by this time too much for Baker. It is worth noting that the inferiority of the *Female Tatler* to its greater model is apparently due to the coarseness of its language and the suggestiveness of much of its contents. Like the work it imitated, it was made up of letters, narrative, and allegorical lessons of various sorts; but the corrosively ironical tone and the questionable taste in which it was often written reveal, perhaps, why this periodical, and many other rivals of Steele's work, failed to divide seriously the reading public of the *Tatler*.[1]

[1] The *Tatler* was reprinted in Edinburgh by James Watson, beginning with Steele's No. 130, apparently. Soon after the conclusion of the London work, in 1711, Watson put out a *Tatler* of his own, as by "Donald Mac-Staff of the North." The real conductor of the essay sheet was Robert Hepburn, a twenty-one-year-old advocate. It was written with some force and wit (see A. F. Tytler, *Memoirs of the Life and Writings of Henry Home of Kames*, 2nd ed. Edin. 1814, i, 228n). A *North Tatler* is referred to by George Chalmers in his *Life of Thomas Ruddiman*, 1794, p. 121, and appears to have been issued from April 1, 1710, although no copies are now known to exist. Two copies are all that are now known of the *Mercury*,

A group of immediate followers of the *Tatler* and *Spectator* deserve but a few words. Swift's jest, carried out by Steele in the *Tatler*, became a boomerang when one who signed himself "Jo. Partridge, Esq." issued his *Titt for Tatt*—for at least five numbers (March 2-11, 1710)—and announced that Steele was dead and buried in Lincoln's Inn. The *Gazette-a-la-Mode, or, Tom Brown's Ghost*, denounced in *Tatler* 299 as one of the unscrupulous followers of Steele, began May 12, 1709. On August 22, 1709, appeared the *Tatling Harlot*, "in a dialog between Bes 'o Bedlam and her brother Tom . . . by Mother Baudy-coat." Another imitator, the *Whisperer*, October 11, 1709, was evidently inspired by *Tatler* No. 10, for it was conducted by "Mrs. Jenny Distaff, half-sister to Isaac Bickerstaff," a character created by Steele. Still another, *The Grouler; or, Diogenes Robb'd of his Tub*, January 27, 1711, is more interesting than either the *Whisperer* or *Gazette-a-la-Mode*, for it will be remembered, with the later *Grumbler* and *Prater*, as an example of the adaptation of the essay serial to the development of a single trait or the correction of a single vice.

Other ephemeral followers of the great models include the *Rambler* (chiefly notable for its anticipation of Johnson's famous title), only one number of which is preserved, No. 4, dated March 19, 1712; the *Miscellany*, the seventh number of which is dated June 9, 1711; the *Restorer*, August 17, 1711; the *Inquisitor*, June 26; and the *Surprize*, "by Humphrey Armstrong, formerly fellow of the Ancient and Renowned Society of Seven Sleepers" (No. 4, dated September 6, 1711). All were short-lived and, in form, closely modeled on the *Tatler*. The *Freethinker*, on the other hand, five numbers of which survive, seems to be an imitation of the *Spectator*, for it con-

---

or the *Northern Reformer*, "by Duncan Tatler, Esq.," of 1717, a professed imitator of Steele's *Tatler*.

tains well developed essays on manners. It appeared Tuesdays and Saturdays, from November 13, 1711. Important, in that they show the adaptation of this form to purely religious purposes, were *Serious Thoughts* (August 15, 1710) and the *Silent Monitor* (March 3, 1711).

The *Examiner* (August 3, 1710–July 26, 1714), inspired by the political aspects of the *Tatler*, and opposed to the Whiggish politics of Addison and Steele, was the work of Dr. William King, Mrs. Manley, William Oldisworth, Bolingbroke, Prior, Bishop Atterbury, Dr. Robert Freind, and Swift, the last of whom wrote thirty-three essays for it and made it his great weapon for attacks on the Whig ministers.[1] Like the spurious *Tatlers*, it throws much light on the activities of Steele and Addison. A critical comparison of the styles of these two essayists, in an early number, is especially interesting. On the whole, however, the *Examiner* has little value today outside the field of political journalism. But it gave rise to the *Whig Examiner* of Addison (September 14–October 12, 1710), the *Medley* of Arthur Maynwaring and John Oldmixon (October 5, 1710–August 6, 1711; revived March 3–August 1, 1712), the *Englishman* of Steele (October 6, 1713–February 15, 1714; July 11–November 21, 1715), and the *Reader* of Steele (April 22–May 10, 1714). Of these, the *Medley* was not wholly devoted to politics. It employed fable, narrative, and other forms of writing common to the moral essay, but its contents possessed little literary distinction.

The *Visions of Sir Heister Ryley* (August 21, 1710–February 20, 1711) has been attributed on scanty evidence to Defoe, but was probably conducted by Charles Povey, a miscellaneous writer and projector. For eighty numbers it appeared thrice-a-week, a four-page serial, consisting of "Two Hundred Discourses and Letters representing,

---

[1] The *Examiner* was reprinted in Dublin by C. Carter of Fishamble St.

by way of Image and Description, the Characters of Ver-
tue, Beauty, Affectation, Love and Passion; the Agree-
ableness of Wit, Truth, and Honour, made conspicuous
by Morals. As also Scenes of the Birth of Nature, the
sudden Turns of Fortune, the Madness of Domestick
Contests, the Humours of the Town, and the False Arts
of Life, both of Human and Irrational Beings, trac'd
thro' all their Intricate Mazes." Just as the last phrase of
the projector suggests the works of Steele, so the plan of
the *Visions* reveals it to be a close imitator of the *Tatler*.
Essays, letters, and the other usual ingredients were included in departments dated from Will's Coffee House,
From My House in St. James's Square, From the Strand,
From Tower Hill, From Eutopia, etc. The manifest effort to go Steele one better—apparent in other imitators
—is here very pronounced. But like many other essay periodicals, the *Visions* failed in its content. Its matter
tended too generally toward the salacious and disreputable.

The author of the *Tory Tatler* (November 27, 1710)
assured readers at the start that his title was only a term
of distinction and did not indicate any intention of entering into party disputes. He was going to confine himself
to subjects of pleasantry, humor, and morality—"at once
to divert and instruct my countrymen . . . and if I can
get money into the bargain. . . ." His impudent frankness
was at least novel. The *Tory Tatler*, issued three times
a week for sixteen numbers, was one of the closest imitators of the original *Tatler*, dating its letters from the
familiar White's, the Grecian, and "My Own Apartment," with additional datings such as "Drury Lane."
Its essays, however, approximated the tone of the *Tatler*
much less closely than those of the *Hermit* (August 4,
1711–February 23, 1712) or "view of the world by a person retired from it." The thirty available numbers of the

Hermit consist of single essays with such titles as On the
Old Cavaliers, On Burying in Churches, On Discipline,
On Good Husbandry, On the Abuse of Scripture to Per-
petuate War, On Liberty of Printing. Their author
achieved, in a striking degree, the manner of Steele and
Addison.

The *Rhapsody* (January 1–March 8, 1712) deserves notice, in that the author's expressed purpose was to make
antiquity live again. In a long preface, he presented the
"landskip" of classic days, asserting that the reader, by
acquainting himself with the ancients, might improve his
judgment and his morals. The loose essays which filled
the folio half-sheet were, therefore, devoted almost exclusively to classical subjects. The *Rhapsody* was published thrice-a-week for thirty numbers. Along with
considerable superficial criticism of contemporaries, it
carried matter concerning problems of education. To
parents interested in the education of children, Ascham's
Scholemaster was once recommended. Occasionally, the
author resorted to filling up his two pages with translations from Plato or Sophocles. Altogether, the *Rhapsody* is an excellent example of the wide variety of uses
to which the essay periodical was adapted by the imitators of Steele.

Before the death of Anne, the essay serial had a well
established vogue. A host of minor writers had seized
upon the opportunity offered by this popular form, and
were helping to mould public opinion, to entertain readers with poetry and prose, or to improve literary taste.
Politics appropriated the form for its own uses—which
are not our concern here—and a majority of the essay
serials of the century were probably of political importance only. But a survey of literary periodicals cannot be
written without reference to the periodic essays of many
writers whose names have a permanent place in the rec-

ords of English literature. To name them all would be unnecessary and impossible within the limits of this study. Nathan Drake enumerated two hundred and twenty-one followers of the *Tatler*, while Aitken in the standard biography of Steele furnished the titles of one hundred and twenty-one English and foreign imitators.[1] Those considered in the following pages appear to have some literary merit or other interest for the modern student that should justify their inclusion in this survey.

The *Lay Monk* (November 16, 1713–February 15, 1714) a thrice-a-week essay serial, was one of the best imitators of the *Spectator*. It was the work of Sir Richard Blackmore, physician to Queen Anne, and John Hughes, a writer who had served his apprenticeship with the masters of the periodical essay type. Upon the Club of the *Spectator* they modeled their Monastery, which was conceived as a "voluntary" fraternity of gentlemen, disengaged from business and zealous in the interest of learning and morality, who took turns writing essays. These essays were presented on nights of meeting, a custom reminiscent of the *Mercurius Eruditorum*. "Laws and orders" were propounded by their secretary, "Jacob Ravencraft." The members are described in the second number of the *Lay Monk*—Mr. Johnson, critic; Dr. Lacon, lover of classical learning; Sir Eustace Lockar, metaphysician and theologian; Sir Arthur Wimbleton, a kind of Sir Roger de Coverley; and finally, a Ned Freeman, the Mr. Spectator of the group. The "Monastery" is a remarkably close, early anticipation of the "Noctes Ambrosianae" idea, as well as an imitation of the Spectator Club. Readers were invited to contribute subjects for discussion. Stories, letters, and verse supplied matter for the single essay. A "lay

---

[1] Nathan Drake, *Essays . . . Illustrative of the Tatler*, etc., Lon. 1805; and *Essays . . . Illustrative of the Rambler, Adventurer and Idler*, Lon. 1809-10; G. A. Aitken, *Life of Richard Steele*, Lon. 1889, ii, App. V, pp. 424-428.

nunnery" was created to give them a constant object for wit and banter. With the fortieth number, this serial came to an end, and the essays were reprinted in 1714 with the title, *The Lay Monastery.*

Another attempt was made by Steele to repeat the success of the *Tatler* in the *Lover*, which appeared February 25–May 27, 1714. Marmaduke Myrtle, who had made his debut in the former serial, and combined in himself qualities of both Cynthio and Sir Roger de Coverley, was the center of interest here, on the model—as Steele conceived him—of "judicious ambition, correct love, and elegant desire." Mr. Severn, the lover, and the members of his club carried on the tradition of Steele's earlier publications. Since the author's project was to trace the passion of love through all its joys and inquietudes, the *Lover* naturally contains far more of interest to women than any of its predecessors. The moral aim of the *Lover* was somewhat broader than that implies, however. It aimed to do more than "kill monsters and relieve virgins." The *Lover* was not without its politics; in fact, toward the end, many papers were quite out of harmony with the general plan. When the fortieth number had been issued, it was abandoned for the *Reader*, which Steele had already started on April 22, "to disabuse those readers who are imposed upon by the licentious writers of this degenerate age" (the Tories of the *Examiner*).

An excellent periodical, too likely to be overlooked by the student because of its rarity today, is the *Grumbler* (February 24–July 15, 1715). Conducted by Thomas Burnet, who had, perhaps, been a contributor to Steele's *Tatler*, the *Grumbler*, like the *Prater* of years later, is distinguished by the originality of the conception that made it. It attacked one particular foible of humanity, grumbling, and concentrated its effort upon this universal fault of men and women. "Anthony Gizzard" was the chief mouthpiece of Burnet and his aids. A family of Gizzards, several of whom died of the grumbles, undoubtedly suggested by the Lizard family of the *Guardian*, performed for the author the same service, in mildly criticising the vanities and imperfections of the average English home. Like its great prototypes, the *Grumbler* is filled with visions, letters, and other entertaining and corrective matter. Unprecedented features are logical developments from the title, i. e., the family, all except Tom, infested with the grumbles to some degree, the recipe for the curing of grumbles, and the cleverly written "Rules of the Grumble Book." The essays are still moderately interesting; and they are all clean and well written.

Thirty-four numbers of this weekly half-sheet folio were published. Burnet's letters to George Duckett, who on insufficient evidence has been credited with *Pasquin* (1722-4), a political paper, make clear some of the details.[1] Burnet several times mentioned the aid he received from a "helpful genius" who wrote every other number. Clearly, Duckett was not the genius referred to, although he probably wrote the letter on the Law of Treasons in No. 13 and shares in Nos. 5 and 6. Many contemporaries believed Addison to be the unknown correspondent, but Ambrose Philips is a more likely conjecture, because of the personal animus displayed in the allusions to Pope.[2]

Meanwhile, other variants of the essay periodical were demonstrating its manifold uses. The *Muscovite* (started May 5, 1714) was written by one who held the theory that the "intricacies" of human nature might be better understood by a comparison of nationalities. In consequence, a Frenchman, a Dutchman, an Italian, and a Spaniard were among the *dramatis personae* of this unique half sheet.

[1] See D. Nichol Smith's edition of the Burnet-Duckett correspondence, *Publications of the Roxburghe Club*, Oxford, 1914.

[2] Whoever he was, he signed his letters with O, T, I, U, or M—numbers 10, 11, 14, 16, 18, 19, 22, 29, 30.

Available records of the experiment are limited to one number in the Bodleian Library. The *Town Talk* of Steele, "in a letter to a lady in the country," (December 17, 1715–February 13, 1716) was published weekly for nine numbers as an eight-page quarto, selling for threepence. The editor of the 1790 collected edition (Dublin) believed that the letters were genuine, written by Steele to his Lady, who was actually in the country, and printed to meet some pressing exigency. Be that as it may, the letters contain nothing of critical interest. They are valuable chiefly as another possible instance of the multifarious periodical activity of Steele. The same may be said for *Chit-Chat* (March 1716) which was advertised in *Town Talk* as a continuation, by "Humphrey Philroye." A small twelve-page pamphlet, priced at 3d, and issued on Saturdays, it contained in its weekly "letter to a lady in the country" much personal propaganda for Steele. He was probably the author, although there is no conclusive evidence to prove this. Only three numbers were issued.[1]

"William Smith, Gent.," one time undertaker of the *British Apollo*, had come forward, in the meantime, with a fresh venture, a four-page single sheet called the *Daily Oracle* (August 1, 1715). The title was not the only thing about it reminiscent of Dunton, for it set out to answer all questions, "in every art and science, either serious, comical, or humorous, both in prose and poetry, with other amusements...." Like the *Athenian Mercury*, it also had spiritual kinship with the *Tatler*, for it proposed to include "satyrs against the vices and follies of the age." With No. 11, it became the *Oracle*, a thrice-a-week serial

[1] A four-page *Medley, or Daily Tatler*, by one who called himself "Jeremy Quick" (begun April 21, 1715) was a further departure from the original type. Much poetry appeared in its pages; sometimes it was made up of verse. Fifteen numbers were issued, when it was announced that in the future the *Medley* would appear thrice a week. But no later numbers give evidence of further vitality.

instead of a daily. The last known number is that of August 26.

The *Censor* of Lewis Theobald was made of more enduring stuff. The author opened with a sentiment endorsed by modern scholars of the period when he declared that the age following the *Tatler* should be called the "age of counsellors," for every blockhead who could write his name attempted to inform and admonish and amuse the public. Theobald hoped the *Censor* might help to "mend the taste of the age," however, and delineated the character of the *Censor* himself on the lines of Ben Jonson. Thirty numbers appeared between April 11 and June 17, 1715. Abandoned for a year and a half, the *Censor* was then resumed on January 1, 1717, as a thrice-a-week publication. By June 1 it had reached in this form a total of sixty-six numbers. It was stopped "because the bookseller had enough to complete the third volume."

The *Censor* was a far more substantial periodical than most of its predecessors in the essay form, although it was published as a single sheet folio, selling for only twopence. The large amount of criticism it contained warrants our considering it one of the most important literary journals of the early eighteenth century. Critical writing —chiefly Theobald's own—in the *Censor* ranged from Greek drama to Dryden, from Horace to the contemporary stage. The seven papers on Shakespeare and the four or more on contemporary players and plays are undoubtedly the most valuable. After Shakespeare, the most common critical subject in the *Censor* was Greek drama. Theobald professed to be a lover of antiquity, and liked to see his contemporaries busy retrieving sacred monuments "from obscurity and oblivion." For issue No. 60, he translated a long passage from Aeschylus's *Prometheus*. But living authors were not neglected. He abused Dennis persistently in the *Censor* papers, and gave some praise to Pope. The latter rewarded him in the *Dunciad* for this and for *Shakespear Restor'd* (1726). Pope called Theobald a dunce, and dunce he has remained to many readers, who know the *Dunciad* but little else of the period. Yet in spite of Pope, discerning students have found values in Theobald's work much above those of the average eighteenth-century critic. And it is worth noting that some of his other contemporaries appreciated Theobald's taste and learning, if Pope did not.

A revival of the dialogue form is found in the *Weekly Observator* (No. 5 is dated May 26, 1716), wherein we have the political and social reflections of Honest Ralph, another of the stock countryman characters, and another Observator, who is akin to Mr. Spectator. The rambles of Honest Ralph, as recounted to the Observator, give the paper a touch of originality. There is nothing distinctive in the weekly *Wanderer* (February 9–August 1, 1717) of John Fox and Daniel Hanchet, except perhaps the fact that the authors took no particular pains to conceal their indentity. By March, the sheet was almost entirely made up of letters—sentimental, frothy stuff in the guise of admonition. A serial of more intrinsic worth was the *Entertainer* (November 6, 1717–August 27, 1718). Up to No. 40, it was published as a half-sheet, then for three numbers as a six-page paper. "Diversion and edification" were the objects of the authors, who made a great deal of fun at the expense of quacks by describing a wonderful necklace which cured the desire to yawn in company, the infirmities of love, melancholy, etc. This original apparatus of the *Entertainer* was embodied in single essays of the *Spectator* type. The news and manners of the day were discussed with undisguised sarcasm and with some religious and partisan heat. Another close imitator of the *Spectator* was the *Honest Gentleman* (November

5, 1718–April 22, 1719), which, however, was not otherwise distinguished.

The *Critick for the Year MDCCXVIII* (later called
the *Critick*), which was continued for only twenty-one
numbers (January 6–May 28, 1718), certainly merits
more attention. This weekly half-sheet folio, appearing on
Mondays, was the first serial that deliberately set out to
be a critical publication in the modern sense. As a matter
of fact, only eight of its numbers have to do with literature. At the beginning, Thomas Brereton, the author,
declared:

> Criticism is sound judgment applied to the information of mankind,
> being that leven which equally runs through all, and without which all
> would be equally jejune and insipid.

Brereton pointed out that criticism in the past had been
too often inspired by ill-nature or prejudice. He referred
to the *Spectator* with the highest praise, and esteemed the
Censor of Theobald for what the author attempted to
do. Moreover, he saw "exquisite judgment and modest
freedom" in the "author" of *Memoirs of Literature*.
Numbers 1, 7, 9, 10, 18, 20, and 21 of the *Critick* are concerned with literature, though not always with English
literature. Tasso was lauded at the expense of Homer in
an interesting paper; a general defence of poetry is found
in another essay, of which an excerpt shows well the attitude of the author:

> But poetry, indeed, is so far from being a trifling concern, that I see
> no reason why it should be distinguished from the useful and severe
> studies; except it be the extreme freedom, which has of late been taken
> with it by its own professors; who, to give them their due, have most
> successfully wrought it out of vogue, and put wit in the mouth of fools,
> that they may laugh wise men out of countenance.

That the writer of these lines had Congreve and Dryden
in mind when he wrote, is demonstrated by his concluding
paragraphs.

One of the best of the followers of the *Spectator* was the *Freethinker* of Ambrose Philips, published for 350 numbers (March 24, 1718–July 28, 1721). It was a semi-weekly half-sheet folio, each number consisting of a single essay. Probably the title had more than a little to do with the popularity of the paper, for the author humorously comments on his courage in using it—a synonym for "atheist"—and in the first number emphasizes its application to the most intelligent minds of the age. "All the ways of men and women fall under the cognizance of the *Freethinker*. He is by nature curious and inquisitive, tied to no party, nor place, nor profession—neither rich nor poor, nor old nor young."

In his undertaking, Philips had able assistants. Dr. Hugh Boulter, Dean of Christ Church, Oxford, wrote on education and learning; Richard West, later Lord Chancellor of Ireland, treated politics; Dr. Gilbert Burnet, son of the great Bishop, and himself chaplain to George I, was author of papers on superstition and enthusiasm as enemies of religion; the Rev. Henry Steevens is credited with Nos. 6, 106, 149, 157, and 158; most of the others were by Philips or one or two minor contributors. The *Freethinker* was well written; superior, in fact, to most of the imitators of the *Tatler* and *Spectator*. Each paper was a well arranged essay, adapted with care to the season, or events of the day, and having a timely appeal to readers. Thus No. 5 was about Holy Week; No. 8, on James Shepheard (recently executed at Tyburn). No less than seventeen numbers contained poetry; others, letters on love, criticisms of the classics, discussion of the evils of ignorance, the benefits of conversation, and true notions of honor. There was also considerable fiction. A constant increase in the last ingredient is seen in later numbers, especially in the form of the popular eastern tales.

Steele made his final appearance as a periodical essay-
ist, in the *Theatre* (January 2–April 5, 1720) by "Sir John
Edgar." By the title one would naturally suppose the first
theatrical magazine had evolved. Such was not the case,
however. The *Theatre* was a semi-weekly half-sheet folio,
composed of single essays, like scores of its predecessors.
In this case, Sir John Edgar, his son Harry (a projection
of Steele's own son), Sophronia, their elderly lady friend,
Flavia and Lysetta, friends of Sophronia, and Sophonisba,
a dependent relative, were the "characters" who engaged
the interest of readers. Sir John explains prefatorily that
because of the generous concern of Sophronia he was pre-
vailed upon to undertake in this public manner the
preservation and improvement of the English stage. His
interest was not critical but reformatory. Steele set out to
free actors from the tyranny of the ill-mannered audi-
ences of those days. Thus, almost from the first, we find
him conducting a periodical of general uplift—concerned
with manners—and, after the first few numbers, with no
particular reference to the drama. In its twenty-eight
numbers, the *Theatre* contained several prologues, one
signed by Mrs. Manley. By the tenth, however, Steele was
drawn into an ignoble controversy with Cibber, on which
he wasted most of the space in the numbers which followed.[1] Steele was attacked in *Applebee's Journal* by
"Andrew Artlove," who defended the French stage
against the *Theatre* (February 13, 20, 27). General moral
essays, and, toward the end, several articles directed at the
evils of stock-jobbing, brought the *Theatre* to a close on
the fifth of April. Among the best essays are those on the
whimsical man, on the death of Hughes, and on the Siege
of Damascus.[2]

---

[1] The Nichols copies of the *Theatre* in the Bodleian Library have some
annotations which must interest students of Cibber.

[2] The *Anti-Theatre*, "by Sir John Falstaffe," began on February 15, and
was continued for fifteen semi-weekly numbers, stopping apparently one

The device used in Steele's *Town Talk* and in *Chit-Chat*, i. e., a series of letters to a lady in the country, was once more employed in the *Tea Table* (February 12–June 22, 1724), a work of Mrs. Eliza Haywood. The author desired to "vindicate the true Briton," and to tell whatever passed in the great metropolis, whether of public or private nature. In truth, she professed to be nothing more or less than a scandal monger. Many essays were of a political nature, and allusions were frequently made to theatrical entertainments and to the masquerades of the celebrated Heydegger.

The *Plain Dealer* (March 23, 1724–May 7, 1725) of Aaron Hill and William Bond was announced as a periodical of select essays on several curious subjects and polite literature. Richard Savage was a contributor to this undertaking, if not a partner in it, and the three men, with the possible aid of Edward Young,[1] seem to have written all the essays. Hill was undoubtedly the best of the group, and it is likely that the prosperity of the *Plain Dealer* was most pronounced during the periods of which Hill's pen was employed, the individual quality of his papers giving the periodical a deservedly higher standing than nine-tenths of such serials. The main purpose of the *Plain Dealer* was social rather than political. Frequent essays on manners and morals, and occasional papers, such as that on the unfortunate young gentleman of No. 28, in which Savage's unhappy life is depicted, give it a right to

---

day before the *Theatre* did. It was put out for the apparent purpose of invalidating as much as possible the sentiments and opinions of Steele. As a periodical, it was inferior to the *Theatre*.

Nicholas Amhurst's *Terrae Filius* may be called a periodical of Oxford morals and manners, although Cambridge came in for a share of correction, too. With much flippant verse, and some ribald allusion, this serial lasted for a total of fifty-two semi-weekly numbers, an example of the type that attempts to deal with one sort of life only—in this case, academic life. The fact that Amhurst was expelled from Oxford lessens the value of its criticism of the University. It was published from January 11–July 12, 1721.

[1] But see Dorothy Brewster's *Aaron Hill*, N. Y. 1913, p. 163.

inclusion in this survey. Obvious imitation of the *Spectator* may be discerned in the group of characters—Patty Amble, Sir Portly Rufus, Ned Volatile, Major Stedfast, etc. Some criticism of real value is to be found. Hill's notice of Pope's *Homer* was one of the "offences" that caused him to be included among the heroes of the *Dunciad*. The *Plain Dealer* appeared Monday and Friday, for a total of 117 numbers.

A pretentious beginning was made in 1728 by the *Intelligencer*, published in Dublin, a weekly of the single-essay type. Dr. Thomas Sheridan was the chief author, and Swift gave occasional aid. The periodical seems to have ended with the nineteenth number, for lack of public support, although it was well written and of greater value than many a longer-lived publication. Swift admitted the authorship of Nos. 1, 3, 5, 7, and 9, and the verses in 8 and 10. The 15th, 18th, and 19th numbers were filled with praise for the "Drapier," and arguments aimed to create further opposition to the English law. No. 18 was written by Sheridan and the other two by Swift. The latter's criticism in No. 3 is a notable defense of the *Beggar's Opera*, which alone should save this periodical from oblivion. Propaganda by Swift himself is found in No. 15, which exploits his own work—

My countrymen, I hope, will forgive, if I complain there has been so little notice taken of a small but most excellent pamphlet, written by the Drapier. It is entitled *A Short View of the State of Ireland*. There never was any Treatise yet published with a zeal more generous for the universal Good of a nation, or a Design more seasonable, considering our present lamentable condition; Yet we listen not to the voice of the Charmer.

Swift described his share in this enterprise in letters to Pope on March 6, 1729 and June 12, 1731.[1]

The *Intelligencer* appears to have been published from

[1] Pope's *Correspondence*, ed. Lon. 1871, ii, 270, 271 (*Works*, ed. Elwin and Courthope, vol. vii.)

May 11 to September 21, 1728, although a twentieth number, which is preserved in the Trinity College Library in
Dublin and in the reprinted volumes, is dated 1729. This
last may or may not have been one of the periodic issues
of the regular run. The journal apparently served as "a
vehicle of Satire against the Dean's political and literary
enemies," in particular, against those who criticised the
patriotic zeal of the "Drapier."

Mrs. Eliza Haywood, the prolific writer who has already been mentioned in several places, is credited with
a folio half-sheet which began as a weekly on September
25, 1728—the *Parrott*, by "Mrs. Prattle, the relict of
Peter Prattle, late of London." A mixture of politics and
social matters, this serial well deserves its suggestive title.
It is thought that Mrs. Haywood's identity was revealed
in the zeal of Kitty Magpies, who, with Fanny Flutter
and other *dramatis personae*, furnished the entertainment.
When the *Parrott* stopped is uncertain, but it apparently
did not last long. It should not be confused with a later
periodical of the same name.[1]

Two minor developments of the essay periodical—the
newspaper which carried regularly an essay department,
and the essay sheet conducted by a fictitious Bickerstaff
or Sir John Edgar—led by an easy advance to a newspaper edited by a "character" and carrying entertaining
essays and poems as amusement features. The first really
notable example of this hybrid was the *Universal Spectator and Weekly Journal*, "by Henry Stonecastle, of
Northumberland, Esq." Henry Baker was the conductor
—a son-in-law of Defoe, who, writing the initial number,
helped his less-experienced relative to get his enterprise
well started. Baker's own set of the papers is preserved
in bound form at the Bodleian, with the names of con-

---

[1] See also the *Echo, or Edinburgh Weekly Journal*, January 10, 1729-
April 10, 1734 (Couper, *op. cit.*, ii, 62).

tributors noted in the editor's handwriting. Within the front cover is written: "Having for above four years and a half been the chief manager of the *Universal Spectator*, and all my essays during that time being collected together here, I desire that, after my death, this book may be preserved in my family, since the printing of them together may perhaps sometime hereafter be of use. Baker."

Unfortunately, Baker's marking is only carried out well until No. 149, after which, with one exception, he marks none but his own. But we are thus enabled to ascertain with some certainty the work of individuals employed with him, and his own part up to that point. Baker credits himself with seventy-eight numbers. Of the others, Duncan Campbell, John Kelley, and William Levin were the most prolific contributors, while Defoe, Henry Carey, Thomas Warton the elder, and Ambrose Philips are credited with single numbers. William Oldys and Sir John Hawkins, who have been named as contributors by various authorities, may have assisted with later numbers.[1] In general, the earlier numbers of the *Universal Spectator* were in half-sheet folio form. From October 12, 1728, it ran until December 15, 1746. Its contents place it among the best half dozen publications which were inspired during the eighteenth century by the *Tatler* and *Spectator*. "Stonecastle" took a place in the front rank of the characters who followed in the train of Bickerstaff and Mr. Spectator. A leader in the form of an essay from "My Chambers, Lincoln's Inn," discussed manners and

[1] From Baker's copy it is ascertained that Campbell wrote 14, 16, 18, 20, 22, 46, 47, 50, 84, 88, 92, 94; Kelley, 24, 26, 28, 30, 32, 34, 36, 40, 42, 44, 51, 56, 60, 61, 65-67, 70, 72, 74, 79, 81, 99, 102; Levin, 96, 98, 106, 108, 113-115, 117, 119, 120, 122, 124, 126, 130, 131, 133, 137, 139, 140, 142, 144-146, 149; Defoe, 1; Carey, 4; Warton, 6; and Baker himself all the others before 149, except 11, which is marked "anonymous, from Oxford." After this number, Baker credits himself with 168, 171-174, 186, 213, 218, 225, 227-229, 232, 234-236, 239, 241. Over the title of 241 is written "This is the last I wrote." No. 247 is assigned to Philips.

morals. Selections from the *Universal Spectator* were published in 1736, 1747, and 1756, adding not a little to the fame of "Stonecastle" and the profits of the owners of the work.

The *Grub Street Journal*, which was begun January 8, 1730, has usually been included in lists of serials of the essay periodical type. It should rather be regarded, perhaps, as a newspaper with entertaining features, like *Applebee's, Fog's* and the *London Journal*. Yet it was evidently designed as a "literary" journal, and remotely anticipates the weekly literary journals of the nineteenth century. Pope confided to Gay, on October 23, 1713, what appears to be the germ of the project—a monthly journal, to be called "The Works of the Unlearned, . . . in which whatever book appears that deserves praise, shall be depreciated ironically."[1] The *Journal* actually appeared, however, as a small four-page weekly, was enlarged in size with the seventh number, as advertisements increased, and continued in this form until the 418th number, December 29, 1737. Its plan was entirely original. The news was, from the first, quoted with sometimes satirical embellishments, from contemporary newspapers. News items were furnished, then the authority for them given. Much news matter was appropriated, in this way, from the four *Evening Posts*. This general plan of borrowing material from other periodicals was taken up with a more serious purpose by the *Gentleman's Magazine* of the next year, when Cave adapted the idea to his own needs. Budgell followed this practice in the *Bee* (1733), and many other serials soon adopted the idea of preying upon their contemporaries. Before the middle of

[1] *Correspondence*, ed. Elwin, Lon. 1871, ii, 412 (*Works*, ed. Elwin and Courthope, vii). See also Arbuthnot's *Art of Political Lying*, 1712, and an anonymous pamphlet, *The Critical Specimen*, 1711. It should be noted that the *Journal* was not a burlesque of "learned" works, as the reference of Pope would suggest that the projected work was intended to be.

the century practically every periodical of a miscellaneous nature pirated its matter—or at least a good part of it. Apparently, this practice was initiated by the *Grub Street Journal*, although Hillhouse does not mention it.[1]

One purpose of the *Grub Street Journal* was made clear from the beginning by a motto from the *Dunciad*, as well as by the introductory paper which described the "Society." Letters to "Bavius," the Secretary of the Society (Dr. Richard Russel), papers, verses, and other forms of entertainment, always permeated with satire, filled several columns. But at the beginning, news took up the major part of the space. This is to be noted with care. These news elements were never dropped, although as advertising increased they were given less and less room. By the one hundredth number, advertisements filled the last page; by the two hundredth, they had very nearly filled the third page also. A department was introduced early, called "From the Pegasus of Grub Street." It was on and of poetry. As advertisements dwindled in the last one hundred numbers, the news was not increased, but the satirical and amusing matter was given greater space.

Dr. Richard Russel as "Bavius" had a coadjutor in Dr. John Martyn ("Mavius"), and with the assistance of other writers—even Pope, perhaps—passed judgment on the literature of the day—ironically depreciated Pope and his friends and heaped ridiculous praises on the "dunces." Pope himself may have written epigrams and inscriptions for the *Journal*, although he professed to have nothing to do with it and to know nothing about it.[2] The news from other papers was signed by "Mr. Quidnunc," and the verse features appeared over the nom de plume "Mr. Poppy."

[1] See James T. Hillhouse, *The Grub Street Journal*, Durham, N. C. 1928, for an extended study of this periodical and its editors.

[2] Hillhouse made an effort to establish and define Pope's connection with the *Journal*, but confessed his failure, *op. cit.*, p. iii.

As has been said, one object of the *Grub Street Journal* was satire of contemporary periodicals and persons. Among those who came in for especially vicious attack were Fog's *Journal*, the *London Journal*, the *Gentleman's Magazine*, the *London Magazine*, the *Weekly Register*, the *Hyp-Doctor*, the *Bee*, and the *Prompter*; and the individuals, Bentley, Theobald, Cibber, Edmund Curll, John Dennis, "Orator" Henley, James Ralph, William Arnall, Laurence Eusden, Henry Fielding, and Leonard Welsted. Pope's enemies were called "Theobaldians," "Grubeans," and "Knights of the Bathos"; his friends, "Popeans" and "Parnassians."

When John Nichols, in 1821, in an essay on the "Rise and Progress of the (Gentleman's) Magazine," referred to the *Grub Street Journal* as an "enemy of all works of merit,"[1] he expressed a view that was probably general in the eighteenth century. It should be noted, however, that the *Grub Street Journal* was a weekly literary periodical remotely anticipating such nineteenth-century journals as the *Academy*. It was the avowed champion of good writing, and, in pretence at least, regarded itself as the defender of certain Augustan literary ideals. Especially for its literary and dramatic criticism, the *Grub Street Journal* is valuable, in this sketch of the growth of literary periodicals.

At the end of 1737, the form and the title of the periodical were changed. A four-page periodical, the *Literary Courier of Grub Street* (January 5-July 27, 1738), was virtually a continuation, but not in a strict sense, as the remarks in the closing numbers of the *Grub Street Journal* indicate. News space shrank to one and one-half columns, with one page of advertisements. The *Literary Courier of Grub Street* has been called a "miscellany,"

---

[1] *General Index to the Gentleman's Magazine, from the Year 1787 to 1818*, iii, (Introduction) xxii note.

but can hardly be thus classified. It was really a newspaper still, of very original plan and purpose to be sure,
but far from the type of the *Gentleman's Magazine* or the
London Magazine of the same period. Two apparently
unauthorized volumes of selections from the *Grub Street
Journal* were published about 1731. The first was known
as *Essays, Letters, and Other Occasional Pieces Relating
to the War of the Dunces*; the second, as the *Grub Street
Miscellany in prose and verse, by Mr. Bavius Jr., F. G. S.*,
a brochure of fifty-four pages. Selected verse was published in one volume in 1732. It was referred to as
"Grubiana," and given the title *Grub Street Miscellany,
printed for Mr. Bavius*, and later reprinted as *Faithful
Memoirs of the Grub-Street Society*. The *Select Memoirs*,
an "authorized" compilation from the *Grub Street
Journal*, issued in 1737, is chiefly valuable for the long
preface, which throws much light on the history of the
Journal.

A good example of an essay-sheet turned to purely religious purposes may be seen in the Rev. William Webster's *Miscellany* (December 16, 1732–June 27, 1741;
from No. 3, as *Monthly Miscellany*), of which 444 numbers were published. Its title notwithstanding, it was a
follower of the *Spectator*, and appeared on Saturdays as
a single essay. It purposed to defend religion and the
Church of England. Although mainly interesting as a
variant of the *Tatler-Spectator* type, the *Miscellany* has
a claim to notice because of a single paper on the theatre
(87); for the moral controversy of the day, Webster took
a middle ground between the extremists of either camp.
"It is better to reform than abolish," expressed his attitude. In conclusion, he recalled that plays had done and
still might do much good as vehicles of instruction. "How
glorious would be the attempt to reverse the infamy of

the theatre, and make it not only innocent but useful—the elegant school of human life!"

The *Prompter* (November 12, 1734–July 2, 1736) by Aaron Hill, with assistance from Budgell and Popple, deserves notice here, not only because of its superiority to many direct descendants of the *Tatler* and *Spectator*, but because of its contents, which were largely concerned with drama and the stage. The Prompter, a character derived from the stage, was an original and admirable conception—one who stands behind the scenes and prompts the players. Yet the motto of the first number, "All the world's a stage," indicated accurately that the actors to and of whom the Prompter spoke were not necessarily actors in the narrow sense. Morals in general, as well as stage matters, were subjects of discussion in this semi-weekly, half-sheet folio. The drama and the theatre, however, were so frequently the themes that the *Prompter* may fairly be looked upon as one of the earliest theatrical journals. Besides the usual letters, poetry, dialogues, and "characters" of such an essay serial, criticism of *Hamlet* may be found in the *Prompter*, articles on Congreve's works, Wycherley's *Country Wife*, Dryden's plays, Voltaire's *Brutus*, and on contemporary plays such as Hill's *Zara*, Popple's *Double Deceit*, and Miller's *Man of Taste*, as well as strictures upon players like Mrs. Cibber, and upon contemporary managers and theatres. Excerpts of dramas were also published from time to time. The Bodleian Library has 173 numbers, the only complete set of the *Prompter* that seems to have been preserved.

After the beginning of the *Gentleman's Magazine* in 1731 (see Chapter V) there was a very natural tendency for many serial essay sheets to become more like the miscellany in character. In fact, some are difficult to classify, for this reason. A good illustration is the *Weekly Oracle* (1733-34), a folio half-sheet, of which only No. 68 (May

15) is available. This copy was published with the words "By a Society of Gentlemen," under the sub-title, "Universal History." It contains an essay on constancy, songs, epigrams, and an imitation of Martial, to indicate the variety aimed at by the authors. Other examples are to be seen in the *Medley* of Corke, 1738, a four-page paper consisting of essays and news, and the *Medler* of Dublin, 1744, also a four-page paper of news and essays, which ran to twenty-six numbers.

Another and better known example of this mixed character is Mrs. Eliza Haywood's *Female Spectator*, a monthly publication appearing in London, April, 1744. It should be compared with the *Female Tatler* of 1709, for its title and plan are reminiscent of the earlier ones of Baker. The essays were supposed to be the products of a club composed of four women, a staff not greatly different from Mrs. Crackenthorpe's "modest young ladies" in the *Female Tatler*. The *Female Spectator* has some claims to attention for its critical efforts. Essays on Shakespeare, on true and false taste, and on Akenside's *Pleasures of the Imagination* indicated an interest in literature, however superficial. When issued in four volumes, in 1771, the *Female Spectator* had reached its seventh edition, indication of an unusual popularity.[1]

The last number of the *Female Spectator* came out in April, 1746. On August 2 appeared a new undertaking by the same prolific author, the *Parrot*, "with a Compendium of the Times." It was an interesting attempt to combine the weekly periodical essay with the newsletter. The device made famous by Motteux and Steele—a letter to a friend in the country—was employed, the matter of the whole serial being written in a rather disjointed comment on things going on, with moralizing and not a little

---

[1] The *Reveur* of Edinburgh, November 18, 1737–May 19, 1738, likewise illustrates this essay-miscellany character. Dr. Robert Wallace was author of most of the essays. See W. J. Couper, *op. cit.*, ii, 67.

THE
ENTERTAINER.

By *CHARLES MERCURY*, Esq;

NUMBER I.

To be continued every TUESDAY.

TUESDAY, *September* 3, 1754.

From my own APARTMENT.

Virtute me involvo, probamque
Pauperiem fine dote quæro. HOR.

—— *Me biremis præfidio fcaphæ*
Tutum per Ægeos tumultus
Aura ferat, geminufque pollux. HOR.

RAISE and renown are two paffions which naturally fpring in the human breaft, and make a certain effect upon our minds, according to our different tempers.

Renown is twofold, either true or falfe; virtue is the parent of the former, and vice that of the latter. A virtuous man endow'd with feveral aimiable qualities will eafily attain a high degree of true renown, and raife himfelf up to the efteem and regard of all mankind.

ON

A FOLLOWER OF THE *Rambler*, WHICH ILLUSTRATES ALSO THE "ISAAC BICKERSTAFF" TRADITION

of the flavor of politics. The whole has been accurately analyzed as of two parts commonly: moralizings on life and manners by a human sort of parrot, and a digest of whatever the author could get—stale information and vague surmises, so long as they had news value.[1] But the author's style is not without distinction, and the contents frequently recommend the *Parrot* to more than passing interest. Mrs. Haywood was probably the only writer concerned in the nine numbers—all that appeared—in spite of her efforts to give a contrary impression.

Like the earlier *Universal Spectator*, the *Champion* appeared (November 15, 1739) with a fictitious editor, one "Captain Hercules Vinegar," whose name was taken from a bear-garden hero of that decade. The influence of the *Craftsman* (December 5, 1726–1747) is apparent in the form and material. Henry Fielding, the real projector and chief author of the *Champion*, could hardly have been unaffected by this earlier periodical, for it will be observed that the same general plan of publication and nature of contents is found in both. In Fielding's use of the well known device of a family lies the real difference between the periodicals. Eight Vinegars were thus characters, not unlike the groups of Staffs, Lizards, and Gizzards now familiar to students of essay periodicals. An original minor feature of the *Champion* was the attractive catch-title, which the publisher put at the head of each paragraph of news.

The *Champion* was a political organ, like the *Craftsman*. Its purpose was to make war on the Walpole administration. But under the guidance of Fielding, and with the help of James Ralph, it became more than that. Published thrice a week for seven or eight booksellers, it took the mantle of the *Tatler* and *Spectator* upon itself.

[1] George F. Whicher, *The Life and Romances of Mrs. Eliza Haywood*, N. Y. 1918.

Captain Hercules Vinegar, with his ostentatious humility, his contempt for those who caviled at his works, his marvellous club which gave point and emphasis to his dogmatic pronouncements, was a character after the heart of Mr. Spectator, if a little more blustering in manner than that Addisonian gentleman. The Captain's personality was set off by those of the seven other Vinegars, the Duke, Nehemiah, the Counsellor, Dr. John, Joan his wife, and his boys, Tom and Jack. Different in personal characteristics, their function, as a group, was very much like that of the Spectator Club.

Nevertheless, the contents of the *Champion* really distinguished it from other newspapers, on the one hand, and from most of the followers of the *Tatler* and *Spectator* on the other. It contained criticism of real value. General papers on writers and fame, on wit, on the perverted uses of words, on poetry and criticism, and particular critiques on Steele and the *Tatler*, on the *Spectator*, on Pope's works, on Massinger's plays, on the *Freethinker*, on imitation of Spenser, on Somerville's *Chase*, and on Dyer's *Ruins of Rome*, added not unworthily to the beginnings of criticism already seen in other periodicals. Little but praise is found, however. The critics of the *Champion* seem interested only in approving—as compared with those of the *Prompter*, who often condemned. The last number of the *Champion* was issued on September 15, 1743.

Fielding's *Jacobite's Journal* (December 5, 1747– November 5, 1748) was also a newspaper. More or less like the *Grub Street Journal* in that it borrowed its news contents from other papers, it was nevertheless a kind of throw-back to Defoe's *Review*, with its Court of Criticism, in which the "Censor of Great Britain" administered justice in the "Republic of Literature." The Censor here is the same Fielding who, as censorial Champion of a few years before had essayed to keep rogues in fear of his famous club, inherited from Hercules of old. The *Journal* consisted of a four-page sheet appearing weekly on Saturdays. "John Trottplaid, Esq." was the Bicker-staffian conductor of this serial. The humorous situation of the Jacobites in England gave pertinence to the wit of Fielding, as expressed in this novel publication.

It should be noticed that this *Journal* was much like the later *Rolliad* and *Anti-Jacobin* in tone. Like them also it was a real work of ingenuity. The essays which regularly occupied the first space are excuse for including it among the followers of the *Tatler*. But the observations in the Court of Criticism are, like the findings of Defoe's earlier Scandalous Club in his *Review*, all that give it a permanent value in literature. The well merited castigation of Foote, and the puff of *Clarissa Harlow* (March 3, No. 14) have been mentioned elsewhere; but the sentences of "grubbing" passed on obscure novelists, the remarks on Addison, and observations on theatrical performers of the day—Mrs. Clive, Mrs. Woffington, Mrs. Cibber, Garrick, and Quin—are also worth recalling. The appreciation of Thomson's *Castle of Indolence*, in the decision of the Court for June 2, 1748 (No. 27) should certainly not be overlooked:

> The Court delivered the following Opinions concerning the Castle of Indolence, lately published by Mr. Thomson: "This "is a noble allegorical Poem, and truly breathes the Spirit of "that Author which it professes to imitate.
>
> "The Description of the Castle is truly poetical, and contains "every Image which can be drawn from Nature, suitable to "the Occasion. The Author hath, with wonderful Art, brought "together all the Inducements to Slumber; and at the same "time hath taken sufficient care that they shall have no Effect "on his Reader.
>
> "No less Genius appears in the Wizard's Speech. The Epi-"curean System is here enforced with Arguments of such

"seeming Solidity, that we cannot wonder if it captivated the
"Hearers. Their Entrance into the Castle is finely described in
"the 28th Stanza, and illustrated with a beautiful Simile.

"The Inside of the Castle is described with wonderful
"Power of Fancy. The Subjects of Paintings are happily chose,
"and in the exact Spirit of the Antients. The Music likewise
"is adapted with much Knowledge and Judgment."

After July 16 (No. 33) the Court of Criticism was
omitted.[1]

The *Jacobite's Journal* was not, in form, at least, a very
faithful imitator of the *Tatler, Spectator*, or *Guardian*;
but in its contents and devices it was unquestionably an
offspring of the tradition that produced Isaac Bickerstaff,
Mr. Spectator, and Nestor Ironside.

[1] Perhaps suggested by such things as Boccalini's *Advices from Parnassus.*
See also Brett's *Miscellany*, Dublin 1748, consisting of a number of quaint
serial essays, and *The Tickler*, of Dublin, the same year, containing the
essays of Dr. Paul Hiffernan.

IV

THE *RAMBLER* AND THE DECLINE OF THE SINGLE-ESSAY PERIODICAL

Essay periodicals fall naturally into two groups; those appearing before 1750, led by the *Tatler, Spectator* and *Guardian*, and those appearing later, headed by the *Rambler*. Johnson's famous essay publication may be regarded as the immediate inspiration of many others, after the middle of the eighteenth century, when new periodicals were numerous. There had come, since the days of the *Tatler* and *Spectator*, a considerable change in the form of such publications. The half-sheet folio had developed into the four- or six-page serial. The former's two or three columns of matter had generally given way to the single column to a page, thus emphasizing typographically the importance of the single essay. Finally, the lightly moralizing note struck so admirably by Steele and Addison had very gradually changed either to a heavier didacticism or a gaily bantering tone with little or no moralizing at all.

The *Rambler* is the most famous example of this later serial-type—a six-page, single-column paper, containing a single essay. It differed from most of its predecessors in the more serious and philosophical nature of its contents—its dignity and ethical precept. The truest imitators of the *Rambler* are the *Mirror*, 1779, and *Periodical Essays*, 1780,—serials which followed the tone as well as the form of Johnson's work. The *Rambler* began on March 20, 1750, and appeared until March 14, 1752, on Tuesdays and Saturdays, for a total of 208 numbers. It sold for twopence, reaching a circulation of little more than five hundred copies. Payne, the bookseller of Paternoster Row, paid Johnson two guineas for each paper, and admitted him to a share in the profits of the work as subsequently reprinted, an interest which Johnson afterwards sold. It has been said that No. 97, written by Samuel Richardson, had a larger circulation than any other single number. On the whole, the *Rambler* was not widely popular. It was not designed to appeal to any large number of people. But it elevated Johnson in the opinions of his contemporaries, as an author and moral philosopher, and made its way slowly to a secure place in the world of letters. No less than twenty editions had been printed by 1817.

Johnson, in his last number, acknowledged his obligations to contributors. They were very few. Richardson, Miss Mulso (afterwards Mrs. Hester Chapone), Miss Catherine Talbot, and Mrs. Elizabeth Carter wrote one or two papers each. In other words, Johnson, in spite of his labor on the *Dictionary* during the same period, was responsible for all but five numbers of the *Rambler*. Naturally, he wrote the original papers in haste often, and under great pressure. But in the book editions during his lifetime, he made many alterations. By the time the third edition was published, he had practically rewritten the *Rambler*; for he felt that in large measure his subsequent fame would rest on these "moral essays."[1]

In respect to its contents, the *Rambler* was especially original. Although it seemed as if every subject under the sun had already been written about, Johnson brought to his task a scholarly mind and broad understanding of human nature which made all things new. Without the exquisite talent for throwing ridicule upon the minute improprieties of life which gave Addison his fame, he

---

[1] See David Nichol Smith, *Johnson and Boswell Revised*, Oxford 1928, p. 12.

still found in his own time endless texts for commentary and timely admonition. In particular, Johnson was attracted by subjects pertaining to the personal concerns of men of letters, the miseries and dangers of literary ambition, the relations of authors with the public in the years when declining patronage of literary genius made the profession of writing a hazardous one. No periodical author before him so often dwelt upon the literary profession, its disappointments, anxieties, and rewards. No previous essay sheet devoted so much space to general observations upon criticism. Unlike the *Tatler* and *Spectator*, the *Rambler* contains little humor, although Nos. 46, 51, 59, 82, 101, 117, and 138 may be cited as evidence that this quality was not entirely lacking. True to the tradition of the essay sheet, the *Rambler* made concrete its lessons by means of "characters," sometimes drawn from life. But such elements were limited to a few numbers. On the whole, this periodical is distinguished from its predecessors chiefly by the elevation of its language— by which it affected perceptibly many subsequent periodicals. It was further distinguished by the sheer dominating strength of the mind of Johnson, which here found expression in serious discussion of the follies and vanities of life, in the exposition of the advantages of virtue and sincerity and honor, in a range of subjects that included such various topics as the Effect of Sudden Wealth upon the Manners, the History of a Legacy Hunter, the Art of Living at the Cost of Others, the Narrowness of Fame, the Folly of Annual Retreats into the Country, Remedies for Bashfulness, the Vanity of Stoicism, and Sententious Rules of Frugality.

After the *Spectator*, the *Rambler* is easily the outstanding single-essay periodical of the century. Undoubtedly, Johnson was the man of highest talents to devote himself to the arduous labor of such periodical authorship. Posterity has confirmed emphatically his own opinion that in the *Rambler* essays he was writing for enduring fame. The unique personality of Johnson is bountifully expressed in the *Rambler*—in content, if not in form, the unique essay periodical of the later eighteenth century.

Not the *Rambler*, but the *Universal Spectator* and *Champion* were the models of the *Covent-Garden Journal*, undertaken by Fielding as a possible new source of income.[1] It appeared Tuesday and Saturday as a four-page paper, from January 4 to July 4, 1752, and then until November 25 as a weekly, with a total of seventy-two numbers. "Sir Alexander Drawcansir, Knt. . . . Censor of Great Britain" was, in this case, the successor of Stonecastle and Vinegar. Like the preceding serials named, the *Journal* was made up of an essay or other features, followed by news. The essays on many topics are what give it value today, especially the essays of Fielding. Arthur Murphy's copies are preserved at the Bodleian, in which he indicated the numbers he assigned to Fielding—essays in Nos. 1, 4, 8-10, 17, 21, 23-4, 33-5, 37, 42, 44, 47-9, 51, 59, 60-61. Of other helpers, Joshua Brogden, Fielding's clerk, and Rev. William Young may be regarded as certain. Professor Cross believes Murphy was associated with them for a time.[2] The relation of the *Journal* to the paper war between Fielding and the "Army of Grub Street" is now well known.

On January 16, 1752, the young Bonnell Thornton, whose journalistic labors were to win him an important place in the subsequent history of periodicals, founded his *Have at You All, or, Drury Lane Journal*, in opposi-

[1] The title was apparently suggested by the *Convent Garden Journal* of 1749, an ephemeral political sheet directed at Lord Trentham.

[2] Wilbur L. Cross, *History of Henry Fielding*, New Haven, 1918, ii, 371-373.

The *Convent-Garden Journal* was reprinted entire by Gerard E. Jensen, Yale Univ. Press, 2 vols., 1912. See the discussion of authorship, i, 99-118.

tion to the work of Fielding. "Drawcansir, Knt." was addressed by "Madam Roxana Termagant," upon the subject, "The Present Paper War." This *Journal* was a weekly, and made no pretence of dispensing news. Its contents were satirical and frothy—with parody advertisements of "Shamelia" and similar works. In the third number began a series of very amusing parodies of other journals—the *Midwife* of Smart, the *Rambler* of Johnson, the *Gentleman's Magazine*, the *London Magazine*, and the *Universal Spectator*, to say nothing of the *Covent-Garden Journal*, of which the serial of Thornton was a general parody. A department known as the "Covent-Garden Journal Extraordinary" ran through four numbers, from January 16 to April 9, 1752. The *Drury Lane Journal* contains much entertainment that may be enjoyed even today. It appeared on Thursdays, for a total of twelve issues.

A few months later, on November 16, another and very similar periodical appeared, supposed to be also the work of Thornton. The *Spring-Garden Journal* was conducted by "Mrs. Priscilla Termagant," a near relation of Mrs. Roxana, and represented as an eighteen-year-old lady. Addressed to "Alexander Drawcansir," like its predecessor, it was issued on Thursdays, professing an endeavor to be "delicate in sentiment and polite in expressions." The contents of the *Spring-Garden Journal* are of critical interest, for the first number began with a review of a contemporary production of Johnson's *Epicene*. Other notices of plays then on the London stage occupied considerable space in subsequent numbers. A weekly catalogue of books was run on the last page, while book advertisements, "Domestic News"—a short paragraph—and some burlesque advertisements appeared. A "new Female Spectator" and a "Covent-Garden Journal Extraordinary" (see November 30) were entertaining features.[1] Its life was limited to four numbers, the last on December 7, 1752.

Of more vitality was the *Gray's-Inn Journal* by "Charles Ranger," a six-page newspaper conducted by Arthur Murphy (September 29, 1753–September 21, 1754). Murphy had been engaged sometime before this in the *Craftsman*, with essays somewhat similar to those which he made the most prominent parts of the new periodical. He began to number the new journal from No. 50, issuing the next two as 51 and 52. With the fourth he changed the number to 4, and thereafter numbered them seriatim. Primarily an essay sheet, the *Gray's-Inn Journal* made no pretence of publishing news. It can hardly be regarded as a newspaper like the *Covent-Garden Journal*, but rather, like the *Drury-Lane Journal* or *Spring-Garden Journal*, as an essay serial tending towards the miscellany in form. Murphy was one of the latest of the many followers of the *Tatler* tradition to employ the datings, "White's Chocolate House" and "St. James's Coffee-House." The *Journal* contains some notable criticism, which distinguishes it. On Macbeth (8), Shakespeare Vindicated in a Letter to Voltaire (12), King Lear (16, 17), On Tragedy (48), On Comedy (49), and On the Burlesque Style (50), are essays which lift the *Gray's-Inn Journal* above the general level of its contemporaries. Some, but not all, of these criticisms had already been published in a slightly different form in the *Craftsman*.

After the close of this work with the fifty-second number, Murphy, in 1756, got out two volumes of essays, 104 in all, including some of the revised material of the

---

[1] There were no less than three works in which the latter title was used. The *Drury Lane Journal* contained a "Covent-Garden Journal Extraordinary," as has been noted; while there is extant (in the Dickinson collection at Yale University) a single copy of what appears to be a separate periodical with this title.

Craftsman, with the title, *Gray's-Inn Journal*. In his prefatory remarks he failed to indicate the source of so many essays in the two volumes. He also failed to explain that the matter had been rearranged, and to indicate why it covered a period from 1752-4, as announced. This has led to a doubt of Murphy's integrity. Probably Murphy, like Dr. Johnson and other essayists of this century, was much interested in the profits of a collected edition, and his only thought was to fill well the volumes. He undoubtedly took some of the material of his old *Craftsman* essays (which, however, are chiefly political), adapted it to suit himself, and republished with an eye only to the salability of the volumes. This seems the most plausible way to account for the additional essays in the published volumes of 1756.

Eight months after the decease of the *Rambler*, John Hawkesworth, a friend of Johnson, set on foot an essay serial somewhat less famous, as literary fame goes, but certainly more popular in its day. Like its predecessor, the *Adventurer* contained criticism—more of it than any other serial up to this time. It might have developed into a full-blown critical periodical, except for the attitude interestingly expressed by Hawkesworth in his preface— the fear of making it appear too pedantic. Writers of the day, who courted popularity with the general reading public, were afraid to be critical. Hawkesworth referred to Swift's *Polite Conversation*, declaring that where Swift had plucked up a weed, the staff of the *Adventurer* should plant a flower. "With this in view," he said, criticism had in this paper been "intermixed with subjects of greater importance." An astute editor, Hawkesworth saw the folly of forcing too much criticism on a public among whom the "tinsel of a burletta had more admirers than the gold of Shakespeare."

Hawkesworth was responsible for the name, design,

and conduct of the *Adventurer* (November 7, 1752–March 9, 1754), and himself wrote nearly half of the 140 numbers. Published as a half-sheet folio, appearing on Tuesday and Saturday, the *Adventurer* had a wide circulation, and when republished, sold four large editions in eight years. It established Hawkesworth's literary character, and brought the proprietor, Thomas Payne, a comfortable profit.

Among the contributions which enhanced the general popularity of the *Adventurer*, Hawkesworth's own allegorical, oriental, and domestic tales easily rank first. By their number and merit they distinguished the periodical from every preceding essay serial. Johnson contributed twenty-nine numbers, beginning with April 10. He marked his papers "T." When papers have the signature "Mysargus," it was the theory of Boswell that Richard Bathhurst, Johnson's friend, had a hand in them. It has been recently shown, however, that the last two of the "Mysargus" papers were by Johnson himself.[1] After No. 49, Joseph Warton's first contribution, an arrangement seems to have been made by which Hawkesworth should be responsible for forty-six papers, and Johnson and Warton for twenty-three each. Warton signed his essays "Z." Of Warton's twenty-four essays, ten contain notable criticism. His papers were numbers 49, 51, 57, 63, 71, 75, 76, 80, 83, 87, 89, 93, 97, 101, 109, 113, 116, 122, 127, 129, 133, and 139. Among other subjects, Johnson wrote on modern criticism in 58, and on Virgil in 92. Miss Mulso ("Y") wrote the story of Fidelia (77-79), George Colman, the "Vision" (40), Rev. Richard Jago, a friend of Shenstone, the fine "Elegy" (37), while various writers have assigned papers to William Hamilton, John Boyle, and Bonnell Thornton.

[1] L. F. Powell, "Johnson's Part in *The Adventurer*," *Review of English Studies*, III (Oct., 1927), 420-429.

The publishers of the *Adventurer*, we may note, had their eyes on the book value of bound editions, as was the case with the proprietors of the *Rambler* and the *Gray's-Inn Journal*. Hawkesworth, in No. 140, described the original plan for the periodical. When they began, he and his associates intended definitely to publish four volumes and no more. When the four volumes were complete, the *Adventurer* was stopped. This is interesting and important. It further illustrates the fact that many of the so-called "short-lived" essay sheets of the eighteenth century were never intended to be published indefinitely. Writers have generally failed to take this into account when commenting on the periodicals of this century. Some attempts were made to put out essays by the volume, but these do not seem to have been very successful. Authors and publishers had come, by Hawkesworth's day, to realize that a series of essays must make itself popular with the reading public first, if any wide sale was to be expected for it in book form, just as today producers of moving pictures find it more profitable to exploit the reputation of a popular novel than to picturize an unknown story.

The tales of Hawkesworth and Miss Mulso have had their day and no longer greatly entertain readers; but the papers of Johnson and the criticism of Warton still give the *Adventurer* a high rank among essay serials. The critical views of Johnson are well known, and his *Adventurer* essays need not be dwelt upon here. Joseph Warton's periodical criticism, on the other hand, has never been fully appreciated. Elsewhere, it may some day have the consideration it deserves. Here, we can only note that in essays for the *Adventurer* he reviewed Pope, anticipating his *Essay on the Writings and Genius of Pope* (1756–82), wrote three papers on the *Odyssey*, two on the *Tempest*, one on Jewish poetry, one on *Paradise Lost*, one on the fragments of Menander, and two on *King Lear*. He thus helped to give the *Adventurer* a critical volume in excess of either the *Spectator* or the *Rambler*.

The *World* by "Adam Fitz-Adam" (Edward Moore) was a less meritorious essay journal. The author was employed by Robert Dodsley, in behalf of a large group of collaborators, nearly all of them men of wealth and fashion. Johnson declared the *World* "wanting in matter," a stricture undoubtedly justified, although the serial was gay and entertaining, and is even to-day amusing. Moore himself referred to it as a weekly paper of entertainment. . . . "My design is to ridicule, with novelty and good humor, that part of the known species which calls itself the World, and to trace it through all its business, its pleasures, and its amusements." He rejected religion and politics—or at least made a pretence of doing so. The *World* was to be made mildly corrective of manners by means of irony and gentle ridicule.

Moore, the author of the *Gamester* and other popular dramas, was given his opportunity in this periodical undertaking chiefly through the interest of Lord Lyttelton. The editor wrote sixty of the 209 essays, which covered a period of four years (January 4, 1753–December 30, 1756). Joseph Warton has been credited with No. 26; Lord Chesterfield (Stanhope) wrote twenty-four, including Nos. 90, 91, 100, 101, 189, and 196 (two of which have to do with Johnson's *Dictionary* project); Horace Walpole, nine; Soame Jenyns, at least four; R. O. Cambridge, some twenty-one; John Tilson, five; Edward Lovibond, five; Hamilton Boyle, two; and John, Earl of Cork, four. Robert Dodsley, John and William Duncombe, the Earl of Bath, Thomas Cole, John Gilbert Cooper, Hon. Francis Coventry, Thomas Gataker, David Dalrymple, James Marriott, Walter Moyle, Thomas Mulso, James Ridley, William Hayward Roberts, James Scott, John Whitaker, and Sir Charles Hanbury Williams were other contributors.

Appearing weekly on Thursdays, the *World* seems to have been even more popular than the *Adventurer*. It is said on slender authority that twenty-five hundred copies were sold each week. The large group of aristocrats interested in the undertaking should have given it success under any circumstances. Toward the end of 1756, however, they planned to discontinue it; and—the story goes —for a final joke, Horace Walpole wrote a *World Extraordinary* (signed "Vandyke") describing the imaginary death of the author, i. e., Edward Moore. The last number of the *World*, conducted by Mary Cooper (widow of T. Cooper, the bookseller) gave a facetious account of a fearful accident which befell "Adam Fitz-Adam," the overturning of his new chaise, and contained long quotations from the dying man about the folly of the social ambition which had thus undone him. A tragic turn was given to the jest by the sudden death of Moore soon after this.

Another essay periodical which Johnson criticised for want of matter was published by George Colman and Bonnell Thornton, both of whom became popular writers of their generation. The *Connoisseur*, their six-page serial, issued on Thursdays, was an excellent example of the type, with its single entertaining essay, aimed at the vices and follies of the community, and its fictitious editor—"Mr. Town, Critic and Censor-General." The *Connoisseur* began January 31, 1754, and lasted until September 30, 1756, for a total of 140 numbers. It was often poor in style and lacking in substance, faults that may fairly be attributed to the inexperience of its authors (Coleman was twenty-two and Thornton thirty) and their youthful predilection to satire. In the final number of the *Connoisseur*, they—like other authors of similar

periodicals—revealed vaguely the identity of their contributors. "A. B." was a "gentleman of Cambridge";
"G. K." was unknown to them, as was also the author of
letters in 82, 98, 112, and 130; "a friend in law" wrote
75, 78, 87, and 104 (in part); "a gentleman of the Temple" (William Cowper) was assigned Nos. 111, 115, and
119;[1] a member of Trinity College, Cambridge (Robert
Lloyd) was responsible for verses in 67, 90, 125, 135, and
a song in 72. In addition to these, a Methodist preacher,
a mechanic, and Orator Henley each wrote one.[2]

Like the *Grumbler* of Burnet, the *Prater* (March 13–
November 6, 1756) was distinguished by the originality
of its conception and the high quality of its matter,
throughout the thirty-five numbers of its life. "Nicholas
Babble, Esq." was the successor of Squire Gizzard. His
motto was, "Thou, Novelty, art my *goddess*." That he
was conscious of his lineage is indicated by his references
to Bickerstaff and Nestor Ironside. But the *Prater* carried
on the tradition of the *Grumbler*, in confining itself to
the correction of one human foible—in this case, that of
talking too much—and practically all the essays which
make up the volume deal with aspects of this general
theme. Its humorous possibilities are obvious. They are
well illustrated in the lengthy genealogy of the Babble
family:

> The Babbles are not only remarkable for their antiquity, but for
> their alliances with the greatest families of all kingdoms; nay, we boast
> of being nearly related to crowned heads. A certain British monarch,
> noted for the prolixity of his speeches from the throne, was undoubtedly
> descended from a female branch of the family . . . My grandfather,

[1] William Hayley, *Life and Letters of William Cowper*, Chichester, 1809,
i, 92 and iv, 414, attributes to him Nos. 119, 134, and 138. Southey, *Works
of William Cowper*, London, 1836-7, v. 261 ff., assigns him Nos. 111, 115,
119, 134, and 138.

[2] An excellent if undistinguished example of the *Rambler* type is the
Entertainer, 1754, "by Charles Mercy, Esq.," issued on Tuesdays for
twelve numbers. The *Dublin Spy* "by Roger Spy, Esq." (1753-54) employed
the family device, in the persons of Sir Telescope Spy, Laetitia Spy, etc.

Sir Gregory Babble, was so delighted with the music of his own voice, and so obstinately prepossessed in favor of his oratorical talents, that he would scarce permit his auditors to utter a syllable.

Epistles from Miss Chatter, love queries from Rose Plump, Jack Tattle's remarks on brokers and physicians, and the observations of Sir Politic Query, a newsmonger who neglected his own business, were some of the elements of entertainment and mild satire that went into this interesting sheet.

The *Friend*, a neat little six-page Sunday paper, was issued for at least ten numbers (January 5-March 9, 1755), and is worth remark, if only because its title anticipated that of Coleridge's nineteenth-century serial. It is not impossible that Coleridge may have seen a copy of it, of course, although there is no record of such an occurrence. "Characters" and the single-essay form ally it with other followers of the original *Tatler*. It is readable today, even though it is chiefly devoted to moral and religious instruction.

The *Old Maid* (November 15, 1755-July 24, 1756), a weekly six-page sheet conducted by "Mary Singleton, Spinster," was composed of letters, tales, and verse, and attacks on "Mr. Town" of the *Connoisseur*. It was distinguished by nothing, however, except its feeble criticism, of which the praise of Johnson and his *Rambler*, the discussion of Dryden, and the high regard expressed for the songs of Beaumont and Fletcher are most important.[1]

[1] As a variant of the type, the *Crab-Tree* (April 26-July 26, 1757) deserves mention. It was a six-page weekly, published for fourteen numbers. Its single-column essay contained a burlesque history of Bruit-land or Anger-Land, the latter name said to be derived from the passionate temper of its inhabitants. For the purposes of the author, this fictitious country (representing Great Britain, of course) was located on two beautiful islands in one of the largest lakes of North America. Only the original design gives this periodical interest here, although the essays were very well written. The substance of the essays was propaganda entirely, called

Out of the swarm of such periodicals that followed the *Rambler*, Goldsmith's "ephemeridal" *Bee* emerges, notable to students of literature, in spite of its very brief career of eight weekly numbers (October 6-November 24, 1759). Since its essays are most often reprinted, the *Bee* is usually thought of as an essay serial. It should not be so classified, however, for it is quite as much a miscellany or review. It began as a thirty-two page serial, whereas the genuine follower of the *Spectator* or *Rambler* form consisted of from two to eight pages. The first number of the *Bee* was divided into six parts, roughly distinguished as (1) an essay, (2) verse, (3) remarks on the theatres, (4) fiction—a story or translation—(5) letters, (6) biography. Evidently, Goldsmith modeled his *Bee* quite as much on the *Gentleman's Magazine* as on the *Rambler* or *Tatler*. After a few numbers, through a tendency to do the thing most congenial, he dropped one or more of the departments. The *Bee* became smaller in volume and more like a single-essay sheet as it advanced, reminiscent of the change in the *Tatler*. The last number contains only an essay and fiction. The remarks on the theatres, the essays on the use of language, and the contribution of Voltaire on wit, sum up the criticism of the *Bee*.

Of the *Spendthrift* (March 29-August 9, 1766) Henry Fox, Lord Holland, was probably the conductor, or at least that was the opinion of Isaac Reed (a copy is now in the British Museum Library, with marginal notes in Reed's handwriting). A six-page, single-column essay

into being by the crisis between England and France, with reference to the struggle then going on for supremacy in the continent of America.

The *Centinel* of 1757 was another interesting, although not very important, follower of the *Rambler*, with its six-page, single-essay form. It appeared every Thursday from January 6 to July 6, and sold for twopence. The Burney set of this serial contains a note dated 1780, by Isaac Reed, in which he assigns the work to Dr. Thomas Francklin. He indicates also that George Steevens wrote some of the essays. including Nos. 5, 12 and 18.

filled the serial each Saturday of its brief career; and while many of these essays are not concerned with matters of lasting importance, that on modern comedy (1) and one in praise of Burke's *On the Sublime and Beautiful* (17) are notable. From manuscript letters, it is learned that John Hawkesworth wrote at least two numbers—"On Taste" (8) and "On Painting" (13).

The *Templar and Literary Gazette*, published Wednesday and Saturday (November 6-December 22, 1773) in a six-page form, was chiefly concerned with the intolerant spirit, licentiousness, and absurdity of contemporary newswriters and "magazine mongers." Samuel Paterson, the famous cataloguer, was its projector and editor. "Mr. Templar" filled an office similar to that of Mr. Spectator, while a "triumvirate of whimsical philosophers," Francis Fairley (Honest Frank), Miles Saunter, the happy indolent, and Sir Walter Wag, were the "Club." Paterson was capable of straight thinking, as is indicated by his interesting proposal to tax magazines as well as newspapers. "Every newspaper, nowadays, is a magazine," he says; "so every magazine is a newspaper: the former comprehending (besides a jumble of mixed, and, generally, improper matter for a newspaper) all the intelligence of the day; the latter an incoherent assemblage of joco-serious bits and scraps . . . together with an exact register of all the news and falsehoods of the week, or of the month . . . " Notwithstanding his criticism, Paterson concluded his *Templar* with a department of literary intelligence and book notices.

A few years later there arose in the Scottish capital a coterie of writers, led by Henry Mackenzie, who were responsible for two periodicals of literary importance. The first was the *Mirror*, begun January 23, 1779, and continued for 110 numbers, until May 27 of the next year. It appeared Tuesday and Saturday, and contained contributions from well known men of the day. Like many a predecessor, the *Mirror* had its "Society of Gentlemen," —in this case, however, a genuine group rather than an individual. The "Society" really consisted of six young advocates, who wrote most of the papers. Drake, who should be more trustworthy here than in matters of earlier date, assigned thirty-nine essays to Mackenzie, and thought he assisted in ten others.[1] The best of his criticism is evidently in numbers 12, 25, 42-4, 49, 53, 72, 99, 100, 108, and 109. William Craig, who is said to have suggested the *Mirror*, alone wrote sixteen, and had a hand in three others. His essays, 10, 19, and 36, are critical. Alexander Abercromby probably contributed eleven, of which 87 and 90 have to do with literature. George Horne, a clerk in the Court of Session, was responsible for sixteen, 39, 70, and 71 being the most interesting here. William McLeod Bannatyne contributed five—6, 28, 33, 58, and 76; and Robert Cullen three—13, 27, and 48, the first, on *Ossian*, being the best. Correspondents of the "Society" included Professor William Richardson of Glasgow, who wrote five critical essays; Lord Hailes, who contributed six of a humorous sort; Dr. William Beattie (73, 74); David Hume, nephew of the historian (50, 103); Professor Frazer Tytler of Edinburgh University (59); Alexander Craig (52); and Baron Jordan of the Exchange of Scotland (82).

The *Mirror's* popularity in book form was so great that by 1783 five editions had been published. By 1813 the work had reached the eleventh edition. Moreover, the *Mirror* was reprinted twice in America—in Boston, 1792, and in Philadelphia the following year. Conducted by

[1] Nathan Drake, *Essays, Illustrative of the Rambler, Adventurer, etc.* Lon., 1810, ii, 369. J. Kluge, *Henry Mackenzie, sein Leben und seine Werke*, Halle A. S. 1910, p. 32, assigns him forty-two. *The Works of Henry Mackenzie*, Edinburgh, 1808, contain forty-one complete essays and parts of two others.

"the Scottish Addison," as Scott called Mackenzie, the *Mirror* was, undoubtedly, one of the best later imitators of the *Spectator*, so much so that a charge of plagiarism was preferred against Mackenzie.[1] Much of its matter is of perennial interest to students of literature. The essays were, for the most part, serious and well written, and one of the authors, Mackenzie, has a secure, if not very distinguished, place in English letters.

The essay type of serial, so long popular in London and Edinburgh, found many provincial imitators as the century advanced. The *Yorkshire Freeholder*, published in York on Thursdays, beginning January 20, 1780, is an excellent example. "Lancelot Lackrent, Esq." was the somewhat original fictitious editor, who admitted frankly his kinship with Isaac Bickerstaff and Adam Fitz-Adam. Admitting also that he had principles perfectly Shandean, he introduced a family of Lackrents; and with their help he handled York affairs in a manner worthy of Tristram Shandy himself. The foibles and opinions and activities of the Lackrents are mixed with narrative and occasional verse in a way which gives the *Yorkshire Freeholder* a title to some notice. It lasted until March 28.[2]

Periodical Essays (December 2, 1780–March 3, 1781) was one of the most carefully written and excellently planned of the essay serials of the century. Appearing weekly for fourteen numbers, it contained only the work of Archdeacon Robert Nares. In the initial number, the author declared that he was going to deviate from the tracks of the *Spectator* and all other predecessors;

1. By making greater excursions into the region of pure philosophy and religion,
2. By soliciting no favors from correspondents,

---

[1] *Notes and Queries*, 5th Ser., II, 325.
[2] See also the *Remembrancer* of Bath, 1771; the *Weekly Miscellany*, 1773-83, and *Weekly Entertainer*, 1784-1818, of Sherborne; and the *Loiterer* of Oxford, 1789-90, other provincial essay serials of this period.

3. By not confining himself to fixing a motto to every number (a well established practice).

And he boldly declared it his purpose to make the work "not an entertainment for an hour, but a treasure never to be relinquished." The most original thing about the *Periodical Essays* was the design. Through successive numbers, Nares built up an elaborately organized government for a Monarchy of Letters, with a Literary Majesty, a Privy Counsellor, Laws, and a Court of Classical Authority. But he was not a great writer, nor did he have much to say. Consequently, the *Periodical Essays* are no longer read. The very cleverness and originality of the plan alienated Nares' work from the general reader, by whose judgment a periodical essay must stand or fall.

Five years after the discontinuance of the *Mirror*, the "Society of Gentlemen" in Edinburgh, which had by this time developed into the "Mirror Club," began to issue the *Lounger*. Like its predecessor, it was a four-page, single-column folio, but appeared only once a week, on Saturdays. Like it, the *Lounger* also consisted of the single essay, varied with letters and verse. Beginning February 5, 1785, it was issued until there were enough papers for two neat volumes, 101 numbers. It was then concluded on January 6, 1787. The "Scottish Addison," Henry Mackenzie, was again the editor and chief writer, furnishing fifty-four numbers, of which 20, 27, 28, 50, 68, 69, and 97 contain criticism of value, on novel writing, on Shakespeare's characters, on tragedy and comedy, and on the poetry of Burns—the last a very notable critique of the "Ayrshire ploughman," as Mackenzie called him, and one of the earliest appreciations of Burns's genius. William Craig wrote fifteen papers, of which 37 and 49 are critical. Abercromby contributed nine, Cullen three, Fraser Tytler seven, and McLeod Bannatyne two, 13 and 39. Although in reality a continuation of the *Mirror*, the

Lounger is admittedly inferior, both in general style and in the permanent interest of its essays.[1]

A thrice-a-week essay serial called the *Busy Body* (January 2, 1787-February 26, 1788), by Walley C. Oulton, the historian of the London theatre and defender of Ireland's *Vortigern*, deserves little notice except as another example of attention paid to one human foible—this time the common one of prying into everybody's affairs. It is distinguished, however, by a few papers on matters pertaining to literature, the best being No. 3, on grammatical precision, 11, on critics, and 22, on how to write a comedy. Considering Oulton's interest in the theatre, it is surprising to find so little about drama in these essays. It ought to be noticed, in passing, that the title was first employed in Ben Franklin's "Busy Body" papers in the *American Mercury* of 1729.[2]

The nature of *Olla Podrida* of Oxford and London (March 17, 1787-January 12, 1788) is well indicated by its title. There is little among its widely varied contents, however, which may be called criticism. Number 13 contains a good paper on the character of Johnson, written by Bishop Horne of Norwich. Henry Headley, also of Norwich, contributed a paper on tragedy in No. 16. Thomas Monro of Magdalen College, Oxford, wrote

[1] Other Scottish followers of the *Spectator* tradition were the *Gleaner*, 1795 (only one number); the *Trifler*, December 19, 1795-August 1, 1796; and the *Ghost*, April 25-November 16, 1796. Neither their matter nor their manner entitle them to much notice here.

Among student publications of this time, the *Microcosm*, published by Etonians, stands high. It appeared (November 6, 1786-July 30, 1787) for forty numbers. Contributors included Lord Henry Spencer, Capel Lofft, George Canning and John Hookham Frere. The early satire and burlesque from the last two is doubly interesting in view of their later work on the *Anti-Jacobin*. Two other famous school papers not mentioned elsewhere were the *Trifler* (1788-9) of St. Peter's College, Westminster, and the *Flagellant* (1792) of Westminster, edited by Robert Southey. For later examples see *Camb. Hist. of English Lit.* xiv, Chap. V, pp. 226-233.

[2] A *Busybody* was issued for a few numbers in 1742, while another to which Goldsmith contributed in 1759 was published by one Pottinger. The latter is distinguished only by Goldsmith's two essays and two poems. See *Works of Oliver Goldsmith*, ed. P. Cunningham, London, 1854, iii, 138n.

twenty of the forty-four numbers and appears to have been the projector and editor. Rev. Henry Kett of Trinity College supplied Nos. 4, 22, 27, 39, and 42; Rev. Richard Graves of Cloverton, 30; Francis Grose, the antiquarian, 20; while Rev. Joseph Holden Pott, George Monck Berkeley, and William Agutter of Magdalen, and other Oxford men, contributed papers.

An admirable series of essays on literature and manners is to be found in the *Lounger's Miscellany*, or the "Lucubrations of Abel Slug, Esq." (Charles Gower, M. D.), who described the "Lounger" in No. 1 as a relict of the "Epicurean sect"—whose business in life was "nothing to do." The twenty numbers (May 31, 1788-March 7, 1789) are, with three exceptions, all the work of the one writer (See Preface). The characteristic single essay is varied with original features, such as a witty comparison of ancient and modern manners, presented in parallel columns. Some good criticism is to be found in this six-page folio weekly. On the poet Thomson (Nos. 4 and 5), *On Julius Caesar* (12 and 13), and an article on the poet Nicholas Breton (18) are excellent papers. An interesting, if not valuable, anticipation of romantic criticism appears in No. 17—on the hardships of dramatic poets when obliged to conform to the so-called Aristotelian rules.

The perennial effort to reform each successive age was derided by the author, Nathan Drake, in his introduction to the *Speculator*, which appeared twice a week, from March 22 to June 22, 1790—a serial of literary significance far out of proportion to the length of its career or the prominence of its authors. Only one was on the editorial staff besides Drake, and that one anonymously, although several friends contributed. Disclaiming any interest in the reform of manners, Drake declared life and letters to be the subjects of the *Speculator*, and pointed out the opportunity then existing for criticism of contemporary German literature. Considering the great influence being exerted by German literature upon English at this time, and the importance of this influence upon the Romantic Movement, it must be acknowledged that the *Speculator* has an unusual value to students. Indeed, it deserves to be called the first organ of the Germanophile romanticists in England. Articles on *Werther* (5) Lessing and German drama (6) German tragedy (9), Goethe (13), Schiller and the terror plays (19), and translated parts of Schiller's *Kabale und Liebe* (20, 21) connect it with the flood of German influence that later affected Scott and Coleridge; while essays on the Gothic imagination and *Ossian* (4), an ode to fancy (3), an ode to superstition (7), one on sensibility (18), and a "Romantic description of the Lake Region" (23) show how much it deserves notice in the literature of the late eighteenth century.[1]

Only a feeble effort to preserve the *Spectator* or *Rambler* form is evinced in the *Looker-On* (March 10, 1792-January 11, 1794) by the "Rev. Simon Olive-Branch," i. e., William Roberts of Corpus Christi College, Oxford, who was later the editor of the *British Review* (1811-22). The *Looker-On* contained eight folio pages of essays and poems, twice a week. No elaborate machinery was employed, although the characters of Mr. Blount and the Projector are familiar types. At least a dozen numbers contained narratives, poems by a lady occasionally appeared, while considerable religious propaganda was mingled with other matters. James Beresford, a fellow of Merton College, wrote clever parodies of sentimental

---

[1] Of course, earlier periodicals had called attention to German literature, especially from 1774, with the outpouring of enthusiasm in England for *Werther*. But no preceding publication devoted so much of itself to the subject as the *Speculator*. Note the later influence of William Taylor in the *Monthly Magazine* and *Monthly Review*.

tours, poetry, history, novels, and biography. Among his contributions are parodies of Boswell's *Johnson* and Milton's *L'Allegro*. Alexander Chalmers wrote two papers for this serial.

After the *Yorkshire Freeholder* of 1780, the first important essay periodical published in England, outside of London, was the *Country Spectator* (October 9, 1792-May 21, 1793). It was a six-page weekly, published on Tuesdays in Gainsborough, for thirty-three numbers. Although its life was short, it was a serial of real merit; and it was edited by Thomas Fanshaw Middleton, who believed there had too long been a neglect of "provincial" readers. Some general criticism appeared, as in the essay "On Egotism in Writing"; but the *Country Spectator* is really distinguished for its treatment of the life of rural England, in contrast to that of the city. Written in loose, single-essay style, imitative of the *Rambler* rather than the *Spectator*, its contents are remarkably interesting, even today. The most notable papers are those on country imitation of London manners, domestic economy in the country disturbed by London visitors, and the so-called simplicity of rural life. "Wilson and Mary: a tale" is told in the manner of Johnson; and original features are common, such as the creeds of the aristocrat and democrat respectively (No. 5). The editor indicated in the concluding essay that he, unaided, was the author of most of the numbers. Rev. D. H. Urquhart who signed himself "Z," James Stovin of Yorkshire, who signed "Y" to his articles, and George Smith of Sheffield ("A") were contributors. Middleton later became an editor of the *British Critic* and Bishop of Calcutta.

A curious variant of the essay type is the *Sylph* (September 22, 1795-April 30, 1796), a weekly whose author in the preface of the bound volume admitted that only "visionaries, old maids, Methodists, and country girls" believed in the existence of the "Sylph." This suggestive introduction prepares the reader for the unique vehicle of the author's ideas, namely, Ariel, who descends to him and promises to dictate observations upon men and manners. Throughout the forty numbers of the *Sylph*, the visions of the author, inspired by Ariel, fill the pages. Original apparatus was employed in the Court of the Fan, the Court of Passion, and the several "Proclamations" issued—mainly on matters of love. A serious poem —an elegy—is found in No. 21, while the later numbers are occupied with pseudo-eastern tales. Perhaps the most illuminating paper to the student is the attack on novel reading (No. 5) as pernicious to morals.

The *Flapper* of Dublin (February 2, 1796-September 10, 1799) is a very interesting essay serial, generally overlooked by students. Its title, taken from *Gulliver's Travels*, suggests a kind of stinging reminder. After some initial irregularity, it appeared Tuesday and Saturday as a four-page folio. Moral purpose was evident in its table of contents. "Useful" reading was commended, novels were condemned, biography was praised. An essay on the danger of making vicious characters popular cited as examples Joseph and Charles Surface, Blifil, and Tom Jones. Really important contemporary criticism appeared in three essays on the poetry of Cowper (34, 38 and 40). The author of these, who signed himself "L," later reviewed Collins' *Ode on the Passions* (47).

The *Quiz* of 1797-8, which lasted for thirty-eight numbers, was another puny scion of the now run out *Tatler-Spectator* family. It purported to be the work of a "Society of Gentlemen," whose biographies were sketched under the names "Anthony Serious," Major Stienkirk, J. Hubert, Sir Arthur Hildebrand, and Isaac Fitzhakory. Really, it was the work of the youthful Charles Dibdin, Sir Robert Porter, his sister, Jane Porter, and others.

The usual apparatus of letters is used—from "Charles Chickenheart" or "Sophonisba Vellum." In one of these, Goldsmith is accused of plagiarizing in his poem "Edwin and Angelina," from a poem in a novel entitled *Les deux habitants de Lozanne.* The *Quiz* contains nothing else of value, except some remarkably incompetent imitations of Shakespeare's verse and Dr. Johnson's prose. But it should be noticed that Jane Porter's first published works appeared in it.

Of the essay periodicals issued after 1800, only one needs to claim attention. Leigh Hunt's *Reflector,* 1810, a 200-page quarterly periodical of literature and politics, had the sub-title "a collection of essays." Each number contained about twenty-five articles. Obviously, the form of the *Reflector* was influenced by the form of the Review. Leigh Hunt in his autobiography says that most of the contributions came from persons educated at Christ's Hospital.[1] Fortunately, there has been preserved in the British Museum Library an "office copy," which contains indications of the authorship of articles. From this we learn that George Dyer, Barron Field, Dr. John Aikin, Thomas Barnes, O. G. Gilchrist, and Charles Lamb were, with Hunt, the principal contributors. Lamb wrote seven out of twenty-four essays in the first number, and at least eight others before the end of the year. Gilchrist as well as Lamb wrote on drama, Aikin on biography, and others on subjects of general interest. Of course the most famous of the contributions were Lamb's essays—"On Garrick and Acting," "A Bachelor's Complaint of the Behavior of Married People," "Farewell to Tobacco," "Edax on Appetite," "Hospita on the Modern Indulgence of the Pleasures of the Palate," "The Good Clerk," "On Hogarth," "On Burial Societies," and "On the Inconveniences Resulting from being Hanged."

[1] *Autobiography*, Oxford Press, 1928, p. 260-1.

Such were the chief developments in the later history of the essay serial. Anticipated by the half sheets of the seventeenth century, its form was established and given an extraordinary vogue by the popularity of the *Tatler* and *Spectator*. It really began as a news sheet, which gradually popularized the literary essay as a department, and then became a single essay purely, as illustrated in the *Spectator* or the *Rambler*. Imitators of Steele and Addison adapted the single-essay serial to political uses. Then it became a vehicle for amusement of all sorts, for instruction in the arts and sciences, and for criticism of literature. Its usefulness as a separate publication practically ended with the close of the century. In fact, its later history before 1800 is one of decline, as it became absorbed into the newspapers and magazines, appeared less and less often as a separate publication, and virtually disappeared at the beginning of the nineteenth century.

Like other "literary" periodicals of the eighteenth century, the essay serial was distinctly a class publication, in that the general public was little touched by it.[1] Its readers belonged exclusively to the leisure classes. It reached its highest level and its most distinctive function in gently ironic comment on the morals and manners of the time, and was perfectly adapted for that purpose. Partly because the period was an intensely analytical one, the essay form persisted throughout it with great vitality. The list of eighteenth century writers who made use of it is a list of the century's great names—Steele, Addison, Pope, Swift, Theobald, Fielding, Joseph Warton, Johnson, Goldsmith, Mackenzie, Cowper, and many others. Some authors worked in it to the exclusion of other forms, but more found it a fertile seeding ground for other growths, of which the novel is perhaps the finest fruit.

[1] See G. S. Marr, *The Periodical Essayists of the 18th Century*, N. Y. 1924, p. 253.

Moreover, the periodical essay determined to a great extent the familiar and intimate prose style of the future. The influence of the single-essay serial on the later form of the essay was unquestionably profound. It is hardly too much to say that because of its popularity, and through the influence it had on other forms, the essay periodical determined, to a great degree, the literary history of the eighteenth century.

V

THE *GENTLEMAN'S MAGAZINE* AND ITS PRECURSORS

While the essay periodical of Addison and Steele was rising to the height of its popularity, as a form, and gradually declining to a minor status, other important developments were taking place. The main stream of tendency in the various and widely different periodicals of the late seventeenth century had been, after all, toward the miscellany form. The *Gentleman's Journal* was the first genuine miscellany, and the only example of the type before 1700. It combined in itself all the features of proved value which had been used by the publishers of other serials. The *Post Angel, Muses Mercury*, and *Monthly Miscellany* continued this development, although adding little to the pioneer efforts of Motteux. By 1710 the ingredients of the eighteenth-century miscellany were pretty well determined. Instructive or moral essays, entertainment in the form of poetry, fiction, epigrams, riddles, etc., biographical notices, feature articles on scientific subjects of interest to the curious, information on a variety of the world's affairs, and, for a long time, news matter—all these miscellaneous elements were common in the periodicals that later came to be known as "magazines," and most of them continue to make up the major part of the letterpress in the popular periodic miscellanies of our own day.

Fiction, which had been for several years among the contents of entertaining periodicals, became in 1710, for the first time, the entire substance of one. *Records of Love; or Weekly Amusements for the Fair Sex* (January

7-March 25) supplied female readers with sixteen pages
of sentimental romance every Saturday, for a total of
twelve weeks. Here the "continued" novel first appears,
in stories called the *Fashionable Quaker*, the *Romantick
Lady*, the *Generous Heiress*, or the *Wandering Dancing
Master*—usually in three installments. Two of the tales
named are translations from the French, but the others
appear to be "original." Although the publisher offered
the serial at "one and six" the quarter, delivered to the
houses of subscribers, it cannot be said to have foreshadowed the great later success of the *Novelist's Magazine*. It is noteworthy, however, as the first genuine periodical for women, the first magazine devoted entirely to
fiction, and the first to contain stories in installments.

Throughout the year 1711, John Tipper, the almanac
maker, conducted *Delights for the Ingenious; or,
Monthly Entertainment for both Sexes* . . . containing
a vast variety of pleasant enigmas, delightful arithmetical
questions, curious stories, witty epigrams, surprising adventures, and amazing paradoxes, together with songs,
anagrams, emblems, dialogues, elegies, epitaphs, and
other useful and diverting subjects, both in prose and
verse." The fulness of Tipper's design is significant. He
combined all the appeals of his predecessors, from Dunton and Motteux to Steele, in an effort to attract readers.
The use of mathematics as an entertaining element seems
incongruous to the reader of today, but is to be found
likewise in the *Gentleman's Magazine* and several other
periodicals of the eighteenth century. "Poetry" included
verse by George Herbert, Henry Walker, and Thomas
Dod. Richard Bentley was among the answerers of questions. An essay on "Neat and Elegant Behavior" connects
this publication with the *Tatler* and its kind. Moreover,
fiction with an aggressively moral tone was included. But

THE
Gentleman's Journal:
OR THE
MONTHLY
MISCELLANY.
By Way of
LETTER
TO A
Gentleman in the COUNTRY.

Confifting of

*News, Hiftory, Philofophy, Poetry,
Mufick, Tranflations, &c.*

DECEMBER 1692.

Carmina feceffum fcribentis & otia quærunt.   Ovid.

*Non ego meorum præmium libellorum
(Quid enim merentur?) Apulos velim campos.
Quid concupifcam, quæris ergo? dormire.*   Martial.

LONDON Printed, For *Rich. Parker* ; And are to be Sold by
R. *Baldwin*, near the *Oxford Arms* in *Warwick-lane*, and at the
Black Lyon in *Fleet-ftreet*, between the *Two Temple-Gates.* 1692.

Where are to be had Compleat Sets for the whole Year.

THE EARLIEST ANCESTOR OF MODERN LITERARY MAGAZINES

the extreme variety of its contents did not prolong the life of the *Delights for the Ingenious* beyond the eighth number.[1]

The *News from the Dead*, or "A Monthly Packet of True Intelligence from the Other World, written by Mercury," appeared, somewhat irregularly, for seven numbers. The first was that for October 1714, and the last that for July 1715. It contained about forty pages, chiefly occupied by mild attempts at fiction of a highly extravagant sort. Quite a feature was made of enigmas, answered the following month. *News from the Dead* seems to have been designed purely for entertainment. The character of the fiction in it suggests that the author may have been attempting to capitalize the popularity of Defoe's *Apparition of Mrs. Veal* (1706).

That other parts of Great Britain than London were not wholly lacking in serials of the miscellany type is demonstrated by the *Northampton Miscellany* (January-June 1721), a forty-page monthly, "calculated for the diversion of the countryside and the profit of the printer." Robert Raikes and W. Dicey were the proprietors of it. They had earlier, in 1721, founded a newspaper, the *Northampton Mercury*. The *Miscellany* was issued from January 1721, as a companion publication to the newspaper, which had hitherto contained some entertaining matter. Although the table of contents varied with each of the six numbers, that of the first gives an idea of the *Miscellany's* contents. Three Merry South Sea Tales, and A Curious Diversity of Ingenious Enigmas, Alge-

[1] The last number was dated "October-December."

The *Miscellanea Curiosae* of York (1734-5) was obviously modelled on Tipper's serial, and like it is interesting only as an off-shoot of the learned periodical. The contents of its six numbers are similar to those of the *Delights*, except that No. 3 is almost entirely devoted to mathematics, which seems to have furnished the idle with amusement in the eighteenth century as cross-word puzzles have done in our own generation.

braic Problems, and Paradoxes, are all in verse; in prose
are the Political Journal for the Month of January, and
the Abstract of the Act for Restraining the Directors of
the South Sea Company from going beyond the Sea., etc.
The last two numbers contain Virgil's *Art of Husbandry*,
as translated by Dryden.

No other miscellany of importance in Great Britain
appeared before the *Gentleman's Magazine* was established in 1731. It has already been shown that this work
of Edward Cave was not the first miscellany in English,
but was preceded by several like the *Gentleman's Journal*
and the *Muses Mercury*. Equally certain it is that the
Gentleman's was not the first magazine or miscellany *in
the modern sense*, although it was different in character
from any that had preceded it. Writing in 1821, John
Nichols described it as the invention of a new periodical
form, i. e., "treasuring up as in a magazine the most remarkable pieces from the various journals and half-
sheets." Neither the publisher Cave nor the later editor
Nichols conceived of the *Gentleman's Magazine* as a
publication, like the magazine of our day, principally of
original matter. Cave's main purpose seems to have been
to furnish in his "magazine" a summary of news, along
with the best of the entertaining features to be found in
the daily or weekly sheets. In his introduction to the first
volume, he sets forth the idea he had in founding it. There
were so many half-sheets and other serials appearing each
month in London that no man could read them; therefore
Cave proposed to reprint the best from all of them.[1] His
idea survives today, in modified form, in a few periodicals

---

[1] See Dr. Johnson's *Memoir* of Cave, in the *General Index of the
"Gentleman's Magazine," 1731-1786*. It first appeared in the *Gentleman's
Magazine*, XXIV (Feb. 1754), 55-58.

The "Sylvanus Urban" on the title page was probably derived from an
early newspaper, the *Urbanicus and Rusticus, or, the City and Country
Mercury*, 1691 (Nichols, *Literary Anecdotes*, Lon. 1812, iv, 75).

like the American *Review of Reviews* and *Literary Digest*.[1]

Yet beyond this main purpose, which gave its sole claim to originality, the *Gentleman's Magazine* was a miscellany—such a miscellany as Motteux had published forty years before. Cave, like Motteux, combined all the popular and desirable elements of other serials, and put out a forty-eight page monthly, in an effort to appeal to all classes of readers at once. For years he advertised on the title page "containing more than any book of the kind or price," or a similar slogan. From his predecessors, he borrowed the idea of a fictitious editor, a "society," the original essays of the moral sort, the questions and answers, the letters on love matters and other subjects, the learned discussion of recondite themes, poetry, epigrams, enigmas, the summaries of foreign and domestic affairs, the lists of births, deaths, promotions, stocks, the obituary articles, the occasional illustrations, and the register of books. Every one of these components had appeared in earlier

[1] " . . . our present undertaking, which in the first place is to give monthly a View of all the Pieces of Wit, Humor, or Intelligence daily offer'd to the Publick in the Newspapers (which are of late so multiplied as to render it impossible, unless a man makes it a business, to consult them all) and in the next place we shall join therewith some other matters of Use or Amusement that will be communicated to us."

John Nichols, at the age of seventy-four, writing in the Preface to the *Index*, 1787-1818 (ii, iii, and vi), put it thus: "Not to enter too deeply into the arcana of a miscellaneous publication, the very nature of which depends on a sort of Masonic secrecy . . . This consideration (the ephemeral nature of journals of news) induced several gentlemen to promote a monthly collection, to treasure up, as in a *Magazine* the most remarkable pieces . . . or at least impartial abridgements thereof, as a method much better calculated to preserve those things that are curious, than that of transcribing."

Upon receiving some congratulatory verses from Samuel Richardson (*Gentlemen's Magazine*, VI, 51) Cave wrote in reply
"Blest be the Bounties of the Nine;
I've stores of verse, a *Magazine*."

The first number of the Gentlemen's contained extracts from the *Craftsman*, the *London Journal*, *Fog's Journal*, *Grub Street Journal*, *Weekly Register*, *Universal Spectator*, *Free Briton*, *British Journal*, *Daily Courant*, and *Read's*—filling a total of seventeen pages, or more than one-third of the magazine. Five editions of the first number of the *Gentleman's Magazine* were sold immediately.

serials, most of them prior to 1700.[1] As time passed, original features came—most notable among them, the debates in Parliament and the later "Debates in the Senate of Magna Lilliputia." But earlier numbers of the *Gentleman's* show, except for the greater amount of borrowing from other journals, not a single advance over its predecessors. The truth is, Cave had the secret of all successful publishers of serials—he gave the public what he knew it wanted, and much for its money.

Edward Cave (1691-1754) first attracted notice as a periodical journalist when he conducted a newspaper, the provincial *Norwich Courant*, for his then employer, one Collins. Later, as a Tory pen, he wrote for Mist's *Weekly Journal*. Still later he changed his political principles somewhat, or rather returned to older liberal, though moderate, views, and after his appointment to a small place in the post office, made the most of his opportunities by supplying the London papers with country news, and the country papers with London intelligence, including some account of the proceedings in Parliament (the written minutes of Parliament which were regularly circulated in the coffee houses). He was taken into custody and reprimanded for this. Later, by his extension of the offence in the *Gentleman's Magazine*, he helped to secure important reforms.[2]

Opening a small printing office of his own, Cave began to print the *Gentleman's Magazine* in 1731. The story of the launching of this periodical and its remarkable success has been told in detail by one of its editors, John Nichols, who has given a fairly complete list of the earlier

[1] W. J. Couper (*Edinburgh Periodical Press*, ii, 73) makes the erroneous statement that most of these features were original with the *Scots Magazine* (1739 ff.) and from it adopted by later magazines.
[2] See H. R. Fox Bourne, *English Newspapers*, London 1887, i, 126, and Nichols, *Literary Anecdotes*, v, 1 ff.

contributors.[1] All that is necessary here is to present the more salient features of this most notably successful of all the eighteenth-century literary miscellanies. Johnson wrote in 1754 that the *Gentleman's*, which had then existed for twenty-three years, was still one of the most lucrative publications. After ninety years, Nichols testified that the same thing was true of it. Published until 1907, it enjoyed a longer life than any other English periodical of a miscellaneous and literary nature.

Altogether, the most important single feature of the *Magazine* was that known as "Debates in the Senate of Lilliput." Although Johnson, the great contributor, was responsible for the character of these, Cave himself deserves the credit for the course of events which brought them into being. From the time of his work on the *Norwich Courant*, Cave had considered the utility of publishing Parliamentary debates; and, as has been said, had an opportunity to develop the idea while employed in the post office at London. He acted contrary to the orders of the House, and in 1728 was penalized somewhat because he had supplied his friend, Robert Raikes, with the Minutes for use in his *Gloucester Journal*. Yet after starting the *Gentleman's Magazine*, he continued to cherish his idea, not daring to put it in practice until January 1732, when he began by printing only the King's speech. In

---

[1] "Correspondents" of the *Magazine*, 1731-1818, included Moses Browne, John Duick, Foster Webb, John Smith, John Canton, William Rider, Richard Savage, Samuel Boyse, Adam Calamy, John Eames, Samuel Pegge the elder (*Gentleman's Magazine*, 1796, June-December), Mark Akenside, Henry Price, Richard Yate, John Bancks, John Lockman, William Guthrie, Sir John Hill, Christopher Smart, Ephraim Chambers, John Newbery, John Hawkesworth, Thomas Percy, nephew of the Bishop, John Duncombe, Samuel Ayscough, Richard Gough, James Boswell, Charles Burney, Richard Farmer, Benjamin Franklin, William Gilpin, Richard Glover, James Grainger, Edward Jerningham, Andrew Kippis, Bennet Langdon, William Mason, Arthur Murphy, Joseph Priestly, Charlotte Smith, Gilbert Wakefield, Joseph and Thomas Warton, Gilbert White, and Arthur Young. (John Nichols, "The Rise and Progress of the Magazine," in Preface to vol. iii of *Index, 1787 to 1818*, Lon. 1821.)

June he published two protests of the Lords; and from
the speeches in the Commons, the Speaker's thanks to
Lord Viscount Gage, May 31, with Lord Gage's reply.
But in the July number, Parliament then being pro-
rogued, he ventured to introduce the "Proceedings and
Debates of the Last Session of Parliament."

The laborious manner in which Cave obtained his copy
is told by John Hawkins. Cave got himself and a friend
admitted to the Houses, where in some concealed stations
they took notes of the speeches. Later they compared
these, and finally they turned them over to William Guthrie, who, with the help of Thomas Birch, doctored them
up for publication. For a time all went well enough, and
the "proceedings" proved to be a feature popular with
readers. Other magazines, imitating the *Gentleman's*,
likewise printed Parliamentary debates. But as their popularity increased, the offense to the government grew in
proportion, until in April 1738, the Speaker of the House
of Commons declared it was high time to put a stop to
this practice of publishers. The Prime Minister, Walpole,
and others of the members considered means of ending it.
Meanwhile, in 1734, Johnson had offered his services to
Cave, in a letter dated November 25. His assistance was
not accepted, however, until after he had made another
offer, and had, in March 1738, contributed flattering
Latin verses—"Ad Urbanum"—addressed to the proprietor. Then he was made a member of the staff, and began
in June that series of "debates" which gave great popularity, for a time at least, to the *Gentleman's*.

In April 1738, when Parliament resolved that "any account" of debates and proceedings was subject to punish-
ment, Johnson was ready with his subterfuge. In the June
number of the *Magazine*, the debates were prefaced with
what was called "An Appendix to Captain Lemuel Gulliver's Account of the famous Empire of Lilliput." The

THE 250.10.16

LONDON MAGAZINE:

O R,

GENTLEMAN's *Monthly Intelligencer.*

MDCCXXXII.

I. Pine Sculp

MULTUM IN PARVO.

LONDON: Printed by C. ACKERS in St. *John's-Street,*
For J. WILFORD, behind the *Chapter-House* in St. *Paul's Church-Yard;* T.
COX at the *Lamb* under the *Royal-Exchange;* J. CLARKE at the *Golden-
Ball* in *Duck-Lane;* and T. ASTLEY at the *Rose* over-against the *North
Door* of St. *Paul's.*

THE CHIEF RIVAL OF THE *Gentleman's Magazine*

proceedings were given, thinly veiled, as "Debates in the Senate of Lilliput," sometimes with fictitious designations of the several speakers, sometimes with denominations formed of the letters of their real names in an anagram. To further secure himself, Cave published his *Magazine* as by "Edward Cave, Jr."

The following excerpts from the *Gentleman's Magazine* (February, 1740, pp. 43-5) illustrate the manner of reporting Parliamentary debates:

PROCEEDINGS AND DEBATES IN THE SENATE OF LILLIPUT

On the 124th Day of the Session, the House of Hurgoes being met, the Order of the Day was read for taking into Consideration the State of the Nation, and the Hurgo Quodrert spoke to the following purpose. My Lords,

We are now met to consider of the State of the Nation, a State more fit for Meditation than Discourse; a State whereof none of our Forefathers has seen the Parallel, and which requires all your Lordships attention to prevent our Posterity from feeling its Consequences.

As your Lordships have already found, that the Obligations which *Iberia* had entered into by the later Convention, are on her Part unfulfilled, the House I hope, will pardon me if I now treat that Measure as no longer existing, and lay before your Lordships a Detail of what Prudence, Honour, and a just Regard for the Interest of this Nation, ought to have dictated to those, who negotiated that Convention, as the proper Measures to be pursued, instead of that Ruinous Treaty . . .

The Hurgo Stordraff spoke next, and was of Opinion that the Question should be put upon the Motion; but the Hurgo Hickrad saying that any Peer might move for a previous Question, the House Seemed to acquiesce in his Opinion, and Hurgo Castroflet spoke next in Substance as follows. . . .

By 1752, the increasing number of contributors had made it possible and desirable to discontinue gradually the "week essays" from other periodicals. So by degrees the *Gentleman's* became a publication made up of original material—a magazine in the more modern sense. On Cave's death in 1754, a new era began under the guidance of David Henry, brother-in-law of Cave, and Richard Cave, a nephew of the publisher. By them, the *Magazine* was edited, published, and printed at St. John's Gate. Johnson, whose *Rambler* had been printed by Cave in 1750, was still an occasional contributor.[1] Other important writers at this time were Sir John Hill, Christopher Smart, Ephraim Chambers, John Hawkesworth, who succeeded Johnson as "compiler" of debates, and John Newbery, who purchased a share in the periodical, and whose son's name appeared on the title page after the death of Richard Cave, in 1766. When this son, Francis Newbery, died in 1780, his widow carried the *Magazine* on to the end of the century.

The "Review of Books," an important department, was conducted for years by John Hawkins. It was later taken over by John Duncombe, poet and antiquarian, whose contributions were signed "Crito." Duncombe also appears to have been editor of the *Magazine* for a time. On his death in 1786, Richard Gough, the antiquary, who had been since 1767 a regular correspondent, took charge of the literary department.[2] Gough and William Beloe wrote the prefaces (1780–1820). John Nichols, who had assisted in the management of the *Gentleman's* from 1778, became in 1792 solely responsible for it, and continued to edit the publication until his death in 1826. His son, John Bowyer Nichols, became part editor upon his father's death, and sole proprietor in 1833. His son, in turn, John Gough Nichols, was an assistant editor from 1828 to 1851, after which he occupied the editorial chair for a period of five years.

The special antiquarian, biographical, and historical

[1] See Courtney and Smith, *A Johnson Bibliography*, Oxford 1915, for Johnson's contributions; and F. A. Pottle, *The Literary Career of James Boswell*, Oxford 1929, for the many contributions of Boswell, 1767-1794.

[2] *Gentleman's Magazine*, lvi (June 1786), 451-2; lxxix (March, April 1809), 195-197, 317-322,

features which make the *Gentleman's Magazine* so valuable a storehouse of information for the period it covers, were dropped in 1868. In an "entirely new series" it appeared until 1907 as a miscellany of light literature, successively edited by Joseph Hatton, Richard Gowing and Joseph Knight. Since the latter date, copies have been periodically filed at the British Museum—that is, the covers are printed and numbered, with a few pages of letterpress, of any sort whatever—to prevent the title from expiring. Thus, legally, the *Gentleman's Magazine* is still in progress at the end of exactly two hundred years.

The last fifty years of the *Magazine's* career were years of declining prosperity, as competition increased, and are of little consequence in the history of literary periodicals. In fact, the status of the *Gentleman's Magazine* as early as 1823 was thus excellently expressed by William Hazlitt in the *Edinburgh Review*:

Of the *Magazines*, which are a sort of *cater-cousins* to ourselves, we would wish to speak with tenderness and respect. There is the *Gentleman's Magazine*, at one extremity of the Series, and Mr. Blackwood's at the other. . . . For the *Gentleman's Magazine* we profess an affection. We like the name, we like the title of the Editor, (Mr. Sylvanus Urban—what rustic civility is there in it!)—we like the frontispiece of St. John's Gate—a well-preserved piece of useless antiquity, an emblem of the work—we like the table of contents, which promises no more than it performs—There we are sure of finding the last lingering remains of a former age, with the embryo productions of the new—some nine day's wonder, some forlorn *hic jacet*—all that is forgotten, or soon to be so—an alligator stuffed, a mermaid, an Egyptian mummy—Southsea inventions, or the last improvement on the spinning-jenny—an Epitaph in Pancras Church-yard, the head of Memnon, Lord Byron's Farewell, a Charade by a Young Lady, and Dr. Johnson's dispute with Osborn the bookseller! Oh! happy mixture of indolence and study, of order and disorder! Who, with the *Gentleman's Magazine* held carelessly in his hand, has not passed minutes, hours, days, in *lackadaisical* triumph over ennui! Who has not ran it slightly through in reading rooms? If it has its faults, they are those of an agreeable old age, and we could almost wish some ill to those who can say any harm of it.[1]

The *Gentleman's Magazine*, this "well-preserved piece of useless antiquity," was for one hundred and fifty years —and its files remain to this day—the greatest storehouse or "magazine" we have of eighteenth and nineteenth-century science, genealogy, biography, of the antiquities of city or church or ruined castle, of topography, laws, criticism, poetry, Parliamentary proceedings, and news summaries.[2] Moreover, the *Gentleman's* was a sort of literary clearing house, and for many generations performed the functions of the later *Athenaeum, Academy, Notes and Queries*, and the specialized periodicals of travel, biography, and science, as well.[3] To students of literature it is of importance—beyond most periodicals of the time —for its critical articles and reprinted poems and essays; and it is an invaluable source of information regarding obscure authors. "O happy mixture of indolence and study!"

[1] "The Periodical Press," *Edinburgh Review*, XXXVIII (May 1823), 369.
[2] The *Monthly Chronicle* (1728-32) was a twenty-six page miscellany, twenty pages of which were filled with the foreign and domestic news of the month, and the remainder of its space given to a long catalogue of books. Undoubtedly, the great success of Cave's more comprehensive project had a good deal to do with the discontinuance of the *Monthly Chronicle*. It should be noted, however, that summaries of news were common departments in the magazines of the century.
[3] John Nichols published a list of 522 correspondents, at the end of the eighteenth century (Preface to vol. iii, *General Index of Gentleman's Magazine, 1787-1818*, 1821). An *Index to the Plates*, etc., was published in 1818; and in 1781 an *Index to Biographical and Obituary Notices, 1731-1780*.

VI

LATER MAGAZINES OF THE EIGHTEENTH CENTURY

For several years previous to 1731, Edward Cave talked of his plan to booksellers and printers, but none of them thought it worth a trial. Yet the *Gentleman's Magazine* had plenty of rivals as soon as it began to prosper. Like the *Tatler*, it initiated a movement, and determined to a great degree the course of periodical evolution. As was true in the case of the essay periodical of Addison and Steele, not every follower of Cave's *Magazine* can be taken into account in this survey. But in a similar way, it is valuable to notice the variations of the type, and the diverse uses these variants served in the literary history of the century which followed.

Johnson, who wrote the preface of the *Gentleman's* for the year 1738, enumerated twenty imitators which the success of this miscellany had given rise to. He reserved the least complimentary of his observations for the *London Magazine*, which had begun to give its model the keenest kind of competition, and continued to do so until it finally ceased publication in 1785. Page for page, the *London Magazine* of 1732 was an almost exact imitation of the *Gentleman's*. Whereas Cave's subtitle was "Monthly Intelligencer," the *London's* was "Gentleman's Monthly Intelligencer." Its motto, after his own, was "Multum in Parvo." Even a similar "Society" was suggested on the title page. In make-up, the *London* perfectly matched its prototype. The "View of Weekly Essays and Disputes this Month," quoting long extracts from the *Universal Spectator, Craftsman*, etc., ran to thirty-six pages in No. 1, longer than the same department in the

Gentleman's for the same month. True to its model, the *London* had pages of "poetical essays," a department of current news, as well as columns of births, deaths, stocks, and the concluding catalogues of books.

To trace the rivalry of these two miscellanies through the long period of their success would be impossible within the limits of this work. It is only necessary to notice that as often as the *Gentleman's* added a feature, the *London* copied it, a point neatly illustrated in the introduction of Parliamentary debates and biographical sketches. Published by a powerful association of booksellers, the *London* was a not unworthy, if sometimes unscrupulous, rival of the *Gentleman's*. That the original had greater vitality than its imitator must certainly be accounted for, in the main, by the pens of Johnson and the more able of his colleagues and successors. Notable among the later contributors to the *London Magazine* was Boswell, whose seventy "Hypochondriack" essays appeared in it between 1777 and 1783. Boswell was intimately connected with its management for a time, as part owner perhaps. Between 1767 and 1783 he gave it a large share of his literary industry.[1]

The booksellers who projected the *London Magazine* must have felt that Cave's great success was partly due to the wide variety of the appeals he made—the large

[1] See F. A. Pottle, *The Literary Career of James Boswell*, Oxford Press, 1929, pp. 221-228.

An interesting example of a serial influenced equally by essay sheet and miscellany, is the *Comedian; or, Philosophical Enquirer* (1732-33) of "Hesiod" Cooke, a monthly pamphlet of twenty-five to forty pages, although its intrinsic merit is not great. Each of the eight extant numbers is made up of three or four papers, a "History of the Times" with occurrences from Spain, the Hague, Corsica, Ratisbon, etc., occasional translations, and reflections on "some modern plays." The last are sweeping condemnations of almost everything contemporary, even George Lillo's work. A defense of Fielding's *Modern Husband* against the *Grub Street Journal*, a letter to Pope, and "London, An Ode" are interesting features.

The *London and Dublin Magazine* (issued January-June 1734) was a reprint of the *London Magazine*. A later and more successful reprint in Dublin was Exshaw's *London Magazine and Monthly Chronicle* (1742-83).

amount of entertaining and informing matter the reader received for a small price—for they advertised, "This work may boast greater variety in less compass than any other kind of performance." But the real point of imitation in the followers of the *Gentleman's Magazine* was the selection of the best material from the thrice-a-week or weekly journals, a certain evidence that the journalists of the day regarded that feature, adapted from the *Grub Street Journal*, as the most important. Eustace Budgell, whose name is enrolled among the contributors to the *Spectator*, put more emphasis on this point than others did. In fact, he devoted the first number of his *Bee*, 1733, to a description of his most important sources of material —politics from the *Craftsman, Fog's Journal*, etc., amusement from the *Grub Street Journal, Weekly Register, Universal Spectator*, etc. "By sucking out the quintessence of every publick paper," the *Bee* was to get "something to hit every man's taste and principles." Evidently Budgell's project was more successful than many of those in this period, in spite of his troubles with the stamp taxes, for the *Bee* continued to flourish until 1735, for a total of 118 numbers of forty-eight pages, and was bound up in nine volumes.[1]

Another *Gentleman's Magazine (and Monthly Oracle)* appeared in September 1736, issued by "Merlin the Second," the cover adorned with a wood-cut of Merlin's cave. These, however, were the only original features, for its barefaced claim, "More in quantity, and greater variety than anything of the kind," had now by repetition lost its force. The sixty pages of contents were like those of Cave's *Magazine*, and included letters, mathematical

---

[1] With the tenth number, the *Bee* was suppressed by the stamp taxers, and was published thereafter as the *Bee Reviv'd*.

Another *Bee Revived* was published in 1750. It was a compilation from other periodicals for the sake of a prisoner in Whitechapel.

problems, a journal of the Proceedings and Debates of Parliament, weekly essays from the more frequently published journals, poetry, news—all the ingredients of the earlier miscellanies.

Partly "that the Caledonian Muse might not be restrained by want of a public echo to her song," the *Scots Magazine*, a close imitator of Cave's serial, was set on foot in Edinburgh in January 1739. Its primary object, however, was to give Scotch readers an impartial view of affairs in Europe. To this end, each of the earlier numbers began with a "Summary of the State of Europe." Then came the usual quoted matter from the *Craftsman, Daily Gazetteer, Common Sense, Weekly Miscellany,* or *Universal Spectator,* under the head, "Weekly Essays." On occasion, entire issues of such papers as the *Edinburgh Lounger* were included in its columns. Space was found in the poetry section for Young's *Night Thoughts.* The other departments were not different from those of other imitators of the *Gentleman's Magazine.*

The *Scots Magazine* has had a long and interesting career. The original authors and projectors are now unknown. William Smellie was employed on the staff from 1759-1765, under contract to supply "abstracts, extracts or transcripts of such pieces as we may have occasion for."[1] Dr. James Browne, later editor of the *Caledonian Mercury,* is known to have been a correspondent, James Beattie's first published poem appeared in it, and Boswell contributed to it steadily from 1758 to 1793. John Leyden, Hugh Murray, and Hector Macneil were later editors. With some variations of title, the *Scots Magazine* continued until July 1817, when it became, in a new series, the *Edinburgh Magazine and Literary Miscellany.* As such, it contained much more literary matter and less of

[1] Robert Kerr, *Memoirs of William Smellie,* Edin. 1811, i, 33.

a general nature. It was concluded in June 1826, with the fall of the house of Constable.[1]

Sixty-one years later, a revived *Scots Magazine* was set up in Perth, to last for thirteen years. In April 1924, the respected title was again used for an eighty-page popular periodical now in progress—the *Scots Magazine*, "a Monthly Miscellany of Scottish Life and Letters." It is described on the title page as "First published 1739." This latest resuscitation, published at Dundee by the St. Andrew Society, is the official organ of Scottish Societies throughout the world. But it is of more importance than that fact implies. Its columns are filled with fiction by such writers as A. S. Neill, D. Wilson MacArthur, Neil M. Gunn, James Rhynd, Alex. S. Macdonald, A. Maitland Murray, Victoria M. Gaul, Elizabeth Emslie, and John Sillars; with plays of Scotch life by Donald Carswell, G. R. Malloch, Nannie K. Wells, and John Corrie; with poetry by R. J. M'Leish, T. S. Cairncross, D. C. Thomson, Arthur W. Ball, Nan Shepherd, Pittendrigh Macgillivray, and others; as well as criticism and general articles. A roster of its contributors shows that it is indeed a magazine of Scottish life and letters, written for and by Scotch people. The present *Scots Magazine* is an excellent example of the literary periodical with sharply drawn boundaries of interest, and a reading public limited by national sentiment and predilections.[2]

Robert Dodsley, the well-known man of letters of this period made a rather notable attempt to issue a weekly magazine of the type of Cave's monthly when, on Jan-

[1] The *Scots Magazine* became in 1794 the *Scots Magazine and General Repository*; in 1804, the *Scots Magazine and Literary Miscellany*; and in 1817, the *Edinburgh Magazine and Literary Miscellany*.
[2] The *Universal Spy* (April 13, 1739) began as a four-page weekly newspaper, and later adopted a twelve-page miscellany form. "Timothy Truepenny, Gent." conducted it. Its ingredients were "characters," letters, Robert Drury's *History of Madagascar*, Sir Isaac Newton's *Creed*, and similar pieces. It sold for a penny.

uary 3, 1741, he began the *Publick Register*, a sixteen-page octavo. It was dedicated to novelty, and each number began with an essay—on laughter, castle-building, education, humor, vanity, flattery, taste, etc. Gay contributed a poem, and Lords Chesterfield and Peterborough sent in essays and verse. Excepting biography, all the features of the *Gentleman's Magazine* were used, even to the accounts of Parliamentary debates. After twenty-four numbers, the *Register* was discontinued, on June 13, partly because of the Stamp Duty, and partly because of its inability to attract advertisers.[1]

The *Publick Register* was obviously a victim of competition—for by this time the *Gentleman's* and the *London* were magazines well established. Dodsley, however, was not discouraged. In January 1746, he entered into an agreement with Mark Akenside to publish the *Museum; or, the Literary and Historical Register*, the forerunner of his *Annual Register*. Akenside supplied an essay for each issue of the *Museum* and acted as editor. Orthodox miscellany materials were supplied by Joseph Warton, William Collins, William Whitehead, Stephen Duck, David Garrick, Soame Jenyns, and others. After a career of thirty-nine numbers, the *Museum* ceased publication on September 12, 1747. Thus ended Dodsley's second ambitious effort to publish a literary journal. In its fortnightly periodicity it shows the influence of the *Publisher* of 1745, and is an interesting anticipation of the attempt made in the *Fortnightly Review* of a century later.

A worthy effort to give readers instruction and amusement at less expense was made in 1746, when the *Penny*

---

[1] See Ralph Straus, *Robert Dodsley*, London, 1927, pp. 68-72.

The *Publisher* (1745) was one of the first of many fortnightly periodicals. Three numbers exist, showing it to have been a not very meritorious mixture of heavy learning and frivolous amusement, collected by J. Crockatt, bookseller.

Medley; or Weekly Entertainer was issued for twelve numbers of sixteen pages each, each twelve numbers to sell for a shilling, the usual price for each copy of a monthly magazine. Stories, travels, adventures, "wonderful productions of nature, shipwrecks, etc.," conquests and revolutions, strange and amusing curiosities, were among the diverting materials advertised on the title page. In reality, each number contained much less than was there suggested; but contents worth remark are a *History of England* and the *Travels of a Shilling*, both in parts, as well as a life of Becket, and *Travels* of Mandeville and Drake.

In the *British Magazine* is to be found the first distinct improvement upon the *Gentleman's*. It was begun in March 1746 (continuing until December 1750), and increased in size from month to month, to forty-eight pages, under the editorship of Sir John Hill. It was more elaborately illustrated than its predecessors, and its contents were of a more generally entertaining nature, although instruction as well as amusement was one of its objects. An "Occasional Spectator" essay occupied the first pages of earlier numbers—later changed to a "Moralist." Parody of the magazines which borrowed essays and news, occasional travesties of Shakespeare and other classics, were mingled with serious and scholarly articles. Altogether, the *British Magazine* was more like modern magazines than any of its forerunners. An imitator of this serial, in the Scotch capital, was the *British Magazine; or the London and Edinburgh Intelligencer* (1747-48), an almost exclusively political undertaking, which seems to have been soon killed by the competition of the *Scots Magazine*.

Other parts of Great Britain were not without imitators of the *Gentleman's Magazine*. For example, the *Newcastle General Magazine*, begun in January 1747, used the "Debates of the Political Club" (really borrowed from the *London Magazine*). It also reprinted the most valuable periodical essays that had appeared within the month; but it asked for and received essays from country correspondents as well. To the usual department of verse, the chronicle of the times, and catalogues of books, were added articles from the *Philosophical Transactions*.

A pretentious monthly periodical was the *Universal Magazine of Knowledge and Pleasure* (1747-1803; as *Universal Magazine* until 1814; as *New Universal Magazine* until 1815). It had little in common with the *Gentleman's* and *London* magazines, for its fifty-four pages were filled with experiments in the more popular phases of science, facts of husbandry—a "Farmer's Companion" and a "Gardener's Calendar"—a department called "the Compleat English Housewife," replete with culinary information, chapters on local history, mathematics, and sport in a department called "The Angler and Sportsman." Its literary value is found in a section devoted to poetry and its occasional biography of an author (for example, the life of Pope, which began in the issue of October, 1747, and ran through several numbers). It was, in fact, a "popular" magazine in the modern sense.

Borrowing something, perhaps, from the rare *Lady's Weekly Magazine* of 1747, the *Ladies Magazine; or, the Universal Entertainer* (November 18, 1749-November 10, 1753) by "Jasper Goodwill of Oxford, Esq.," also derived more than the notion of a fictitious editor from the periodicals that preceded Cave's. The "History of England in Question and Answer," which was a feature of many numbers, finds an ultimate source in L'Estrange's *Observator* of 1681. The extracts of books on popular subjects connect it with the learned seventeenth century serials, while the sentimental fiction, sometimes printed serially, as in the case of Mrs. Behn's *Royal Slave*, reminds one of the "novels" in the *Gentleman's Journal* and *Monthly Miscellany*. The *Ladies Magazine* appeared fortnightly on Saturday, like the *Museum* of a few years before, although it was much smaller in size. It is chiefly valuable as an early magazine primarily for female readers.

The interest in travel, indicated in the contents of several previous publications, finally brought out a *Traveller's Magazine* in 1749 (January–December) "or Gentleman's and Lady's Agreeable Companion." The contents are of a most superficial sort, aimed at a diversity of interests—history, novels such as *Zulima, or the Force of Pure Love*, geography, travel, dialogues giving elementary instruction regarding historic places, voyages, letters, mathematical problems, much poetry, songs, and abstracts of dramas—Johnson's *Mahomet and Irene*, and Aaron Hill's *Merope*—as well as a criticism of Thomson's *Coriolanus*, then on the stage.

Promising that all political disputes and whatever was offensive to good manners should be avoided, the *Student; or, Oxford Monthly Miscellany* (January 1750–July 1751) appeared, under the ægis of Christopher Smart, for twenty numbers—its purpose "to comprehend all the branches of polite literature." Poems (mostly reprinted) of Pope, of Thomas Warton the younger, Smart, Somerville, and Congreve; essays on many moral themes, scientific experiments, modern history; articles on tradesmen and servants in Oxford, on the abuse of scripture, advertisements for wives, a "panegyrick" on ale, and occasional criticism made up its heterogeneous matter. It was, in truth, a miscellany of great merit and not a little originality. Bonnell Thornton and George Colman were the chief contributors, the former commencing here his literary career with an "elegy" on the comforts of a retired

life. Johnson, whose contemporary *Rambler* was praised
by the *Student* (October 1750) as equal, if not superior,
to the *Spectator*, contributed the "Life of Cheynel."[1]
Smart's own important contributions are listed in the
Transactions of the Bibliographical Society.[2]

An extraordinary variation of the miscellany type appeared in 1750, in the *Kapelion; or, Poetical Ordinary*,
by "Archimagirus Metaphoricus," i. e., William Kenrick.
Its forty-six pages were devoted to entertainment purely,
as the introduction "by Whimsy Banter, Esq." indicates.
As a forty-six-page miscellany, selling for sixpence, it
was continued for six numbers, made up chiefly of *vers
de société* and parody, prose fiction and songs. For the
predecessors of this journal, which consisted chiefly of
verse, we must go back to some of the half-sheet folios of
the seventeenth century. These early serials, as well as the
Kapelion, prepared the way for more important works
like the *Poetical Magazine* of 1764 (January to June), a
monthly of forty-four small pages, which was filled with
contributed verse by Charles Hanbury Williams, Garrick, and many writers now forgotten. And all, in turn,
led to the publication of the *British Poetical Weekly* of
1799 (Huddersfield), which ran for thirty numbers, as
an eight-page folio, and included poems by dead and living authors—Southey, Coleridge, Bürger, Monk Lewis,
Mrs. Piozzi, Cowper, Collins, Mrs. Barbauld, Miss Seward, Sheridan, Thomson, Burns, Gray, and Goldsmith.[3]

The *Magazine of Magazines*, which began in July
1750, carried Cave's method to its logical end by turning
to the other monthly periodicals like the *Gentleman's*
and *London* for a large part of its material. It skimmed
the cream from the cream. The purpose of its founders

---

[1] Boswell, *Life of Johnson*, Hill ed., i, 243.
[2] Vol. vi, 275.
[3] See Chapter XII, Sect. 3, for a sketch of the poetry magazines.

was no less than that of giving a "compleat library and historical account of the period." Illustrated with maps and cuts, with many original articles, especially on scientific subjects, with extracts of books, and each number introduced by some "agreeable moral piece to enlighten the mind," the *Magazine of Magazines* was an obvious attempt to beat Cave and his kind at their own game. This monthly contains, however, little to interest the student of literature. We may note that it forced Gray's *Elegy* into print by the threat of publishing it, and later reprinted it in the February number, 1751. The predatory principle was carried to a further extreme by the *Grand Magazine of Magazines*, 1758-9, in which the proprietor, viewing "the other compilations" about him, attempted to select material for one grand compilation that would defy competition. He showed excellent critical sense in reprinting some of Johnson's *Rambler* essays. It is interesting and important to note that in his preface, he refers to the conductors of other magazines as "compilers."

Such parasites among magazines have little to recommend them and may be easily dismissed. The most prominent later examples of this vicious compiling tendency, started by the *Grub Street Journal* and Cave, were the *Aberdeen Magazine* (1761), the Newcastle *Literary Register* (1769-1772), the *Caledonian Weekly Magazine* (1773), the *Monthly Ledger* (1773-75), the *Monthly Miscellany* of 1774, and the *Edinburgh Eighth-Day Magazine* of 1779.

In contrast with the predatory nature of the *Grand Magazine of Magazines*, the *Midwife, or Old Woman's Magazine* (1750-53), by Christopher Smart and John Newbery, part owner of the *Gentleman's*, was an original and notable miscellany. Announced as by "Mary Midnight, with a preface by Ferdinando Foot," it was a fifty-page monthly, selling for threepence; and was a more definite effort in the direction of humor than any preceding periodical. No. 1 contains an essay from the *Rambler*, with a note below, advertising Johnson's essay serial as "a paper . . . worthy the patronage of all gentlemen of taste and genius." Each of the successive numbers contained an essay from the *Rambler*, followed by original features, prologues, a parody of a funeral service, or letters from Mary Midnight to David Garrick, telling him that he excels Betterton, Booth, and Wilkes, in spite of what people who remember them say. There is much interesting matter on the stage and drama, and condemnation expressed of current plays. In a section called "Midwife's Politicks or a Gossip's Chronicle of the Affairs of Europe," fun is made of political events; while verses, essays, letters, epigrams, and ballads enliven the pages—all written in a comic or mock-serious tone. A "Letter from a Country Squire to his Papa," a "Letter from an Eminent Undertaker in Town to an Eminent Physician in the Country," a parody of *Gulliver's Travels*, and a "Panegyrick on Loquacity," are especially amusing contributions. Perhaps the best bit of fooling is the solemn "Letter from Mary Midnight to the Royal Society . . ." "containing some new and curious improvements of the cat-organ." Criticism of the critics is another original theme. Altogether, the *Midwife* was an admirably conceived and well executed performance, with little or no objectionable matter. It alone is enough to give Smart a place with the foremost humorists of the century.[1]

By the middle of the century, it is seen, the miscellany had been adapted to many uses—husbandry, humor,

---

[1] For the *Dramatic Censor*, 1751, the first English periodical devoted wholly to the stage and drama, see Chapter XII, Section 1.

travel, science, general information, as well as literature. From this point on, matters of genuine literary interest become less commonly ingredients of the magazine type, as periodicals become more and more highly specialized. Consequently, only a comparatively small number need to be considered. Among these few, however, is the *Universal Visitor and Memorialist,* 1756, a monthly magazine selling for sixpence. Boswell told the story (quoting Dr. Johnson) of Gardner's extraordinary contract with Christopher Smart and Richard Rolt, by which they were to receive one third of the profits of the magazine, but were to write exclusively for it for ninety-nine years.[1] Johnson's story, as recorded by Boswell, has long been regarded as incredible; but Mr. Stuart Piggot's recent discovery of the actual contract between Allen, Gardner, and the two "hacks" has set the matter at rest.[2] The con-

[1] James Boswell, *Life of Samuel Johnson,* ed. Hill, 1887, ii, 345.
[2] Articles of Agreement between
  Mr. Smart
  Mr. Rolt
  Mr. Allen &
  Mr. Gardner
Articles of Agreement quadrupartite made November 11, 1755, "BE-TWEEN Christopher Smart, of the parish of Saint Mary, Islington, in the county of Middlesex, Gentleman, of the first part; Richard Rolt, of the Liberty of the Rolls, in the same county, Gentleman, of the second part; Edmund Allen, of the parish of Saint Dunstans, in the West London, Printer, of the third part, and Thomas Gardner, of the parish of Saint Clements Danes, in the said county of Middlesex, Stationer, of the fourth part."
The parties agree to publish "a certain periodical work to be entitled or called the Visitor or Monthly Memorialist," to contain six demy half sheets octavo and to consist of various writings, and to be published at sixpence, with the usual trade allowance. Commencing on February 1, 1756, and continuing monthly, Smart and Rolt are to supply the material and the whole expense of the undertaking is to be borne by Gardner and Allen. Each of the writers is to supply "as much Copy as will make two of the above-mentioned half-sheets at least and Deliver the same to the said Edmund Allen on or before the first day of January next," and the same for each month. On their part, Allen agrees to print the paper and Gardner to publish it, and they are to pay all expenses. The accounts are to be carefully kept by Gardner, but Smart, Rolt, and Allen can "inspect the same and take Copys as they shall have Occasion."
As regards the payment, Smart and Rolt are each to have "one full fourth part of the clear profits" which might be left when Allen's and

tract did exist, extraordinary as it was, but was soon cancelled by the failure of the enterprise with the twelfth number. In the meantime Johnson had contributed several essays, to help "poor Smart," whose mental aberrations made the fulfilling of his part of the contract a difficult matter.

Smart and Rolt apparently divided the labor of the magazine, the former conducting the literary department and correspondence, while Rolt took care of the politics. The British Museum Library now possesses Anne Gardner's copy of the *Universal Visitor*, in which are indicated the names of the contributors. Among other things, Smart is credited with "Some Thoughts on the English Language," "Literary Observations," and a "Brief In-

---

Gardner's expenses were paid. These fourth parts are to be paid "within one month after the expiration of every three succeeding months."

Then follows a prohibition "that neither of the said partys to these presents shall or will at any time hereafter assign or Transfer his part or Share of or in the said work" and "that neither of the said partys shall or will during the time these articles shall continue in force either Directly or Indirectly Engage or concern himself in any Work or Undertaking of the like nature or kind or do or cause or wilfully permit or suffer to be done any act matter or thing whereby the Work or Undertaking may be prejudiced."

Allen and Gardner are to be allowed from time to time the "Customary price" for printing and publishing the work, but Smart and Rolt are on no account to have more than one quarter of the profits each. If either of them should be unable to write by reason of illness or other cause, he is to see that someone else does. The contract is to continue "in force during the Term of Ninety-Nine years, to commence from the publication of the first number." If, however, it should "happen that a loss shall at any time be sustained by the produce of the said work, not being sufficient to answer all charges relating for the space of Six Months together," it is lawful for any one or all of them, on giving the others notice, to be freed from the contract.

A minute book is to be provided in which, shall be entered "all such Orders, Agreements, and the Resolutions as shall be hereafter thought necessary by the said partys for the better carrying on the said work."

Lastly, each is bound to the other in the sum of two hundred pounds.

The agreement concludes as follows:—Sealed and delivered (being first duly stampt) in the presence of

	Christopher Smart
	Ri. Rolt
Thos. Rosoman	Edmd. Allen
Wm. Harborne	Thos. Gardner

(*Times Literary Supplement*, June 13, 1929, p. 474.)

quiry into the Learning of Shakespeare."[1] The contributions of Johnson, Smart, Percy, and Garrick are sufficient to distinguish any periodical of the eighteenth century; so the *Universal Visitor*, in spite of its short run, must claim its share of attention. In the history of periodical development, however, it was not important. It will probably be remembered chiefly for the unique contract under which Smart and Rolt conducted it—a document which illustrates clearly the low condition of authorship in the middle-eighteenth century.

In Edinburgh, Walter Ruddiman, Junior, established in July 1757, a miscellany to rival the successful *Scots Magazine*. The *Edinburgh Magazine*, as it was called, purposed to give notice to every meritorious essay and poem, and fittingly concluded its career in December 1762, with an announcement consisting of three columns of poetry, headed *Extremum hunc nobis Arethusa concede laborem*. When Walter Ruddiman put out his *Weekly Magazine* in 1768, he suggested that the new journal was the resurrection of the old, for its opening verses were entitled, *Resurgo*.[2]

[1] Other contributions of Smart are: "Further Remarks on Dr. Lowths Celebrated Prelections," "Thoughts on National Militia," "Faber Acicularius," "Anglice, a Pin-Maker" (a poem), "The Tea-pot and the Scrubbing Brush" (poem), "The Miser and the Mouse," "Care and Generosity, a poem," "Ad Cicadem," "To Health," and "The Furniture of a Beau's Mind."

David Garrick is credited with "A Dying Rake's Soliloquy," "To Mr. Hart," "An Epitaph," "A Recipe for a Modern Critick," "The Story of Amintor," and "A New Song." Besides many articles on politics, agriculture, and government, Rolt is assigned several poems—two of them being elegies on the death of his wife. Dr. Johnson's contributions, according to Anne Gardner, were "The Life and Writings of Chaucer," "Reflections on the State of Portugal," a humorous letter on the problem of how to dispose of surplus authors, a "Dissertation on the Epitaphs written by Pope," and "The Rise, Progress, and Perfection of Architecture among the Ancients." Finally, to Thomas Percy is given credit for a "Sonnet after the Manner of Spenser," and the "Sonnet on Leaving Bath (To Miss H——), June, 1755."

[2] Except for its department of poetry, the *Edinburgh Museum* (1763-4) was practically non-literary.

Walter Ruddiman's *Weekly Magazine of Edinburgh Amusement*, referred to as a sort of reincarnation of the *Edinburgh Magazine*, was the first weekly serial of the sort to appear in Scotland. That the poems of Robert Fergusson regularly appeared in it, from 1771, is sufficient to give it distinction. Grosart in his *Robert Fergusson* gives a list of the poet's contributions. He also says that the *Weekly* "leaped at a bound to unparalleled success" because of them.[1] There seems to be no doubt that Ruddiman and the poet were good friends, for the latter wrote

> To Walter Ruddiman, whose pen
> Still screened me from the Dunce's den. . . .

As for its success, it is recorded by Arnot, the historian of Edinburgh, that in 1776 the weekly circulation of Ruddiman's *Magazine* had reached three thousand copies.[2] With the title changed to *Edinburgh Magazine* (December 30, 1779–July 11, 1782), it was suspended for a year, to resume as the *Edinburgh Weekly Magazine* (Ruddiman had died June 18, 1781). It was finally concluded June 24, 1784. The *Weekly Magazine* was not filled entirely with original matter, by any means. For the most part, it appropriated its material, reprinting the "essence of all the magazines, reviews, newspapers, etc., published in Great Britain." It frankly advertised its predatory nature; and, no doubt, its success was very largely due to Ruddiman's judgment as a borrower.[3]

The *Royal Magazine* (1759-1771), as far as its contents are concerned, is merely another eighteenth-century magazine. It contained the usual components, and is in

---

[1] A. B. Grosart, *Robert Fergusson*, Edinburgh, 1898, pp. 90-98. See Ch. VIII for list of contributions.

[2] Hugo Arnot, *History of Edinburgh*, Edin., 1779.

[3] See G. H. Johnstone, *The Ruddimans in Scotland*, Edin., 1901.

no wise distinguished, except by Goldsmith's four essays.[1] But it illustrates well the persistence of the tradition which began with the *Journal des Sçavans* of 1665; and to be impressed by this fact one need only compare the excerpts from the preface of the *Journal* (see Chapter I) with the following from the first volume of the *Royal Magazine*:

> It has long been a complaint among the learned, that we are wholly ignorant of the labours of the ingenious in Italy, Spain, and many parts of Germany. It is also well known, and has been often lamented, that valuable observations are made, and forgotten; that they are beheld with pleasure and applause at their first appearance, but suffered to glide serenely down the current of time, till they are swallowed by the vortex of oblivion.
>
> We therefore propose to make a faithful collection of the valuable discoveries made by the literati of Europe, and publish them periodically for the benefit of our countrymen. Nor shall this be the boundary of our enquiries; we will endeavour to withdraw the veil of darkness which the ages of ignorance have extended over the discoveries of the ancients, and place them in a proper and conspicuous point of light. In short, we will assiduously labour to remove every difficulty that may oppose the progress of the arts and sciences, and smooth the rugged ascent to the temple of the muses.

As a matter of fact, the *Royal Magazine* contained little of literary interest besides the usual department of "Poetical Essays."

For a distinct advance over predecessors in quality of matter, we must look to the *British Magazine* of Tobias Smollett and Oliver Goldsmith (January 1760–December 1767). *The Life and Adventures of Sir Launcelot Greaves* ran serially through the earlier numbers, usually given the first place in its columns. Although the *British Magazine* was larger than the average miscellany, most of its matter was of an unliterary nature. Yet there were the score of articles from the pen of Goldsmith, notably

[1] See R. S. Crane, *New Essays by Goldsmith*, Chicago, 1927, pp. xxxiii and 12-47.

his "History of Mrs. Stanton," a series of articles on the
belles-lettres,[1] and his best known essay, "Reverie at the
Boar's Tavern in Eastcheap"—as well as serial novels,
oriental tales, biographies of men like Addison and Betterton, accounts of theatrical performances and actors,
reprinted essays from the *Idler*, and an essay attributed
to Johnson, on the bravery of English common soldiers,
which was added to the later editions of the *Idler* essays.
John Huddleston Wynne, later editor of the *Lady's
Magazine* was a member of the staff of the *British*, also.
The *British Magazine* was well illustrated, with more
pages and a larger amount of fiction than are to be found
in any other magazine before this date.

A department called "Modern Criticism" is to be
found in the *Imperial Magazine*, published "by His Majesty's authority" (1760-2). The modern criticism was a
kind of annotated book catalogue, although some general
critical articles are also to be found in this periodical,
as well as poetry, reviews of poems and plays, and an
essay on the use of learning. Set up the next year, the
Court Magazine is worthy of remark chiefly because of
its theatrical department called the "Green Room," although it also contained fiction. A life of Chaucer, illustrated, is also notable. Hugh Kelly was the conductor of
this serial, which ran into two volumes, as a fifty-page
monthly miscellany. Likewise, the *St. James's Magazine*
of Robert Lloyd had much literary material, especially
poetry. An essay on the advantage of measure in comedy, a translation of Klopstock's "Death of Adam," translations of the classics, and poems by Lloyd, Bonnell
Thornton, George Colman, Pope, Lord Lyttelton,
Christopher Smart, and many others, gave this serial an

---

[1] Attributed to Goldsmith; but see article by Dr. Caroline F. Tupper,
in *Pub. Mod. Lang. Ass.*, XXXIX (1924) 325-42; and comment thereon
by Ronald S. Crane in *New Essays of Goldsmith*, Intro. xiv, xix. It may
be that Smollett was the author.

exceptional claim to notice, although much of its content is obviously reprinted matter. Lloyd, the friend of Cowper and Churchill, was really a pioneer, in that he gave up the anonymity, the fictitious "Club," and the shopworn devices for attracting readers. With a title which did not suggest or promise anything, the *St. James's Magazine* was begun in September 1762, an eighty-page monthly, made up almost entirely of poetry and criticism. In March 1764, it became the *St. James's Magazine and Literary Chronicle*, with regular book reviews. Churchill's "Gotham" and "Candidate," and Shenstone's *Works* were subjects of interesting critiques. In fact, the *St. James's Magazine* is an extension of the poetry journal already remarked. The four volumes show it to have been quite the best thing of its kind up to this time.[1]

Collections of jests, bulls, stories, and sentimental fiction are found in the *Jester's Magazine* (October 1765-December 1766), a monthly of thirty-two pages; the *Court Miscellany; or, Lady's New Magazine* (later "Gentleman's and Lady's") of "Mathilda Wentworth of Piccadilly and Others" (1765-1771), contained sermons by the Rev. Laurence Sterne, reviews of the letters of Smollett, Swift, and others, much fiction, and criticism of Shakespeare and contemporaries, with biographies of Mrs. Cibber, Edward Young, Voltaire, Montesquieu, Prior, and Cervantes; while the *Oxford Magazine; or, University Museum*, "on a plan entirely new" (1768-76), reprinted *Poor Richard's Maxims* and published letters on English grammar, accounts of London dramatic performances, short fiction, and in later numbers an essay department called "The Scribbler, by Jonathan Eye-

---

[1] The *Universal Museum*, a sixty-page miscellany (1762-70), contained an interesting variation of the usual Parliamentary debates, known as "Debates in the Areopagus of Athens." Although this feature was accompanied by theatre notes, biographies, and some fiction, there is little in it to warrant a longer notice here.

bright, Esq." The last periodical contained crude copper-plate cartoons, to illustrate its letterpress.

The *Town and Country Magazine* (January 1769-December 1796), a very pretentious and successful serial, printed no less than forty contributions from the pen of Chatterton in 1769 and 1770, and then distinguished itself by refusing his *Balade of Charitie*, just before the author's death. It contained much to justify its subtitle, "a Universal Repository of Knowledge, Instruction and Entertainment." Besides articles on the British theatre and the department of poetry which attracted the youthful efforts of Chatterton, articles on Pope's pastorals, on Pope's "dispute" with Wycherley, on drama in England, on Rousseau, and on the works of Shakespeare, recommend it to the student of literature. Its conductor was Archibald Hamilton, son of the famous proprietor of the *Critical Review*. George Robinson, a bookseller, set it up.[1]

Scattering contributions of interest to students of literature are, from this point on, found in many periodicals of otherwise only ephemeral value. John Huddleston Wynne's *Lady's Magazine* of 1770-1832, had a "Sentimental Journey," obviously imitated from Sterne,[2] and a novel in installments; the *London Museum* of 1770 contained a letter from Mary Wortley Montagu "never before published," and among other articles on the stage one on the merits of Garrick as actor; the *Every Man's Magazine* of 1771 included two pages of poetry and an analysis of new publications; the weekly *Perth Magazine of Knowledge and Pleasure* (1772-3) had sentimental serial stories and much poetry of doubtful quality; and the *Monthly Ledger* (1773-5) relied chiefly on its occa-

[1] See Henry Curwen, *A History of Booksellers, Old and New*, London 1873, pp. 69 ff.
[2] Sentimental journeys were very popular in the columns of magazines during the next few years.

sional moral essays under the heads "Speculator" or "Censor."

The *Westminster Magazine* (1773-85) had an exceptionally literary character because of a department of reviews at the end of each number, another department on the theatre, and a regular periodical essay of a humorous kind under the head "Momus: or the Laughing Philosopher." Occasional features of interest were the attack on Pope's "puerilities" in his *Essay on Man*, biographical sketches of Garrick, Goldsmith, Churchill, and Robert Lloyd, and poetry by well known authors of the period. Isaac Reed is known to have been a contributor, and Goldsmith gave it four essays in 1773.

Emphasizing the "chastity" of its literary production, the *Sentimental Magazine* (1773-1777) began with an avowed purpose of amusing the mind, improving the understanding, and "amending" the heart. It contained a "sentimental" fable in French in each number, and a regular department of verse. Its chief value to-day lies in the information it contains regarding stage performances of the time—Murphy's *Alzuma*, Home's *Alonzo*, Goldsmith's *She Stoops to Conquer*, G. A. Stevens' *A Trip to Portsmouth*, and others—not because of the plays themselves, but because of the comment regarding how they were acted and received. Articles on sentimental comedy, the learning of Shakespeare, Glover's *Leonidas*, and similar subjects were interspersed with imaginary dialogues between historical characters—Cervantes and Herbert of Cherbury, Charles XII of Sweden and Cromwell, Eloisa and Mary Wortley Montagu. Sentimental biography was not omitted. The lives of Shakespeare, Pope, Sterne, Voltaire, and Wolsey are the most interesting to the student of today.[1]

[1] The *Scots Spy; or, Critical Observer* of 1776 was a well-intentioned literary periodical, but of little value and of questionable taste.

The *New Musical and Universal Magazine* (1774-5) was what its name implies, but contained a literary part of sixteen pages, devoted to parodies, verse, and "moral" tales. The *General Magazine* of 1776 began with an original feature—a "Modern Spectator," delineating the most striking characters in the reign of George III under fictitious names. But one of the most noteworthy variants of the magazine type was the *Novelist's Magazine* (1780-88), which apparently reprinted at length all the famous novels of the century, including *Joseph Andrews, Amelia, Pamela, Tom Jones, The Vicar of Wakefield, Roderick Random, Peregrine Pickle, Tristram Shandy, Robinson Crusoe*, and *Gulliver's Travels*.[1]

Meanwhile, in Ireland the *Hibernian Magazine; or, Compendium of Entertaining Knowledge* (1771-1810) carried on the good old tradition of the miscellany proper. Like most "magazines" of the forty years preceding, it carried in its columns everything from stocks to poetry, from news to sentimental fiction, dull biographies, and sheet music. Copper-plate engravings of actors or actresses of the day, in famous roles, as well as many pictures of fictitious characters or real figures, enlivened the pages of the *Hibernian*, or "Walter's," as it was later called. Like the *Gentleman's* and the *London*, it advertised on the title page its effort to meet all tastes—"a compendium of entertaining knowledge, containing the greatest variety of the most curious and useful subjects in every branch of polite literature."

An important enlargement of the miscellany form is found in the *European Magazine* (1782-1825). It began pretentiously, dedicated to the Prince of Wales, splendidly illustrated with copper engravings, and making an obvious appeal to wealth and fashion. The Philological Society of London set it up, with James Perry as the

[1] See also *New Novelist's Magazine*, 1786-7.

first editor. Isaac Reed, the Shakespeare scholar, was
one of the contributors and proprietors, and Stephen
Jones edited it from 1807. Its eighty pages contained regular departments of theatrical news, literary chronicles
and reviews, and verse. Early numbers contained Horace
Walpole's letter to "W. B." about Chatterton, and articles on the Rowley and Ossian controversies. Wordsworth's earliest printed poem appeared in its columns.
Thomas F. Dibdin sent it contributions. Of the oldest
devices to interest readers, the "Club" was still represented in the *European*. Headings that appeared regularly in early numbers were the "Man About Town," an
essay department, and the "London Review and Literary
Chronicle,"—a receptacle for miscellaneous contributions. A department of "Theatrical Intelligence" followed. As the Introduction to the first volume indicates,
the *European* was made to trim its sails between the serious and frothy, so as to please, if possible, all sorts of
readers. Its notable success is now well known. Eighty-
seven volumes had been published, in 1825, when it was
united with the *Monthly Magazine*.

The last days of the *European*, unlike those of most
magazines, were not days of dulness and decline. From
1820 its columns were almost wholly devoted to literature
and the fine arts, and its political complexion was exceedingly liberal. It attacked competing publications with
vigor, especially the new *Quarterly Review*, which it
scornfully declared was advocating "every antiquated
system of government." In its criticism it was no less tart.
A letter to Christopher North describes a common fault
of contemporary criticism—the critic is either silent in
the face of deserving work because he knows nothing
about it, or, because he knows a little about it, he tries
to raise his own reputation as a reviewer at its expense,
by tearing some details of it to bits, and creating the

impression that the critic is much wiser than the writer of the book (a method that seems to be still in vogue, in 1930).[1]

The *Bristol and Bath Magazine* and *North British Magazine* of 1782 have little to distinguish them, nor has the *British Magazine* of 1782-3. But another humorous periodical appeared in the *Wits' Magazine; or Library of Momus* (1784-85), with its "Story Teller" department (which was changed to the "Night-Walker," reminiscent of Dunton), its short dramas, its "characters" (including that of Samuel Butler, author of *Hudibras*), and its poetry department, which reprinted Cowper's "John Gilpin," delightfully illustrated. The *Newcastle Magazine* of 1785 is distinguished only by some observations on history and criticism, its "original" memoirs of Smollett, its poem by James Fordyce on the death of Dr. Johnson, and an article on the life and writings of George Colman. Among the short-lived periodicals of the next few years, the *Oxford Magazine* (1786) deserves mention—if we may believe the advertisement—as the first periodical to use copper plate illustrations pertinent to the matter of the columns. Many of the cuts are interesting as early cartoons. The literary contents were limited to anecdotes of James Woodhouse, the poetical cobbler, memoirs of William Wycherley, an essay on comedy, and accounts of plays.

To the *Edinburgh Magazine; or, Literary Miscellany* (begun, January 1785) belongs the credit for printing, in October 1786, the first review of Burns's *Poems*. It hailed the author "bursting through the obscurity of poverty and the obstructions of a laborious life," in a criticism

---

[1] *European Magazine* LXXXVII (May 1825), 435.

The *Edinburgh Eighth Day Magazine*, 1799, was of slight literary value, but interesting as the earliest example of the effort to dodge the newspaper tax by publishing every eighth day. Coleridge's *Watchman* of 1796 was an earlier example.

that brought the editor a letter of thanks from Burns. James Sibbald, the projector and first editor, began life as a farmer, but early removed to Edinburgh to engage in bookselling. Scott has left us a sketch of him—"a man of rough manners, but of some taste and judgment . . . and in his shop I had a distant view of some literary characters. . . . Here I saw Robert Burns."[1] Sibbald gathered around him an able staff of contributors. Lord Hailes was, perhaps, the most helpful in establishing the reputation of the *Magazine*. Sibbald withdrew from the editorship in June 1792. One of his successors was Dr. Robert Anderson, who is known to have greatly aided and encouraged literary talent in Edinburgh and to have been the first to appreciate warmly the work of Campbell. John Leyden (Scott's friend) published in the *Edinburgh Magazine* his translations from the Greek, Latin, and Scandinavian languages. Ritson and Scott were occasional contributors, and through them the *Magazine* furthered the revival of ballads and old romances. In 1802 David Brewster, a "natural philosopher," became editor; but the *Magazine*, after some changes in title, was soon merged with the *Scots Magazine*, the last number issued being that for December 1803.[2]

"Polite literature" was disseminated by the *Yorkshire Magazine* (1786), which contained the usual proportion of fiction and verse; the interest in stories was promoted for a short time by the *New Novelist's Magazine* of the same year, containing the *Unfortunate Lovers* of Smollett, the *Ethelgar* of Chatterton, and Johnson's *Vision of Theodore; The General Magazine and Impartial Review* (1787-91) for a time published a twenty-

---

[1] Lockhart's *Life of Sir Walter Scott*, Edin. 1837, i, 46.
[2] The *County Magazine* (1786-7) of Salisbury reprinted Joseph Warton's *Ode for the New Year*, Cowper's *Task*, and selections from *Ossian*, as well as the works of William Hayley, Congreve, and "Peter Pindar." It contained also anecdotes of Johnson, Swift, Pope, and Milton. It was continued as the *Western County Magazine*, 1790-92.

four page supplement containing Shakespeare's plays;
the *New Universal Magazine* of 1787-8 was distinguished
by a history of pre-Shakespearean drama, and by letters
and anecdotes of Johnson; the *Literary Magazine and
British Review* (really a miscellany, in spite of the title)
of the next year gave twelve of its eighty pages to reviews
of new publications, and was continued until 1794; *The
Aberdeen Magazine, Literary Chronicle and Review*
(1788-90), a fortnightly publication, was composed of
essays, fiction, and poetry, along with the usual non-literary matter; while the interest in biography, which had
begun in the miscellanies of Dunton and Motteux, now
produced several distinct serials—the *Biographical and
Imperial Magazine* of 1789-92, and the *Biographical
Magazine* of 1794.

The *Bee; or, Literary Weekly Intelligencer*, conducted
by James Anderson, is worth notice because of its "pre-
miums" offered for essays, stories, poems and translations,
as well as its criticism and biography of literary characters. It was published at Edinburgh from December 22,
1790 to January 21, 1794. Anderson interested Blacklock, the blind poet, in his venture, and tried to enlist the
services of Burns by sending him a rhyming epistle, in
which he described the then projected periodical as

> A work miscellaneous, extensive, and free
> Which will weekly appear by the name of *The Bee* . . .
> *The Bee* which sucks honey from every gay bloom.

In his letter of refusal, Burns called himself "A miserable, hurried devil, worn to the marrow in the function
of holding the noses of the poor publicans to the grind-
stone of the Excise."[1]

[1] For many non-literary or undistinguished Scotch periodicals, unnoticed in this study, the reader should consult the *Edinburgh Periodical
Press*, by W. J. Couper, Stirling, 1908.

The development of weekly miscellanies already noted was further
extended by the starting of the *Bystander* (August 1789-February 1790)

The *Monthly Mirror* "reflecting Men and Manners" published novels calculated to give "no shock to sensibility." It followed the path of the *Sentimental Magazine*, its sixty-four pages being largely taken up with literary features, a "Review of Literature" (some sixteen pages), a department called the "British Stage," wherein were discussed the uses and abuses of the drama, letters to the licenser, characters of authors and players living, a retrospect of first appearances, and a comparison of the theatres. Another department consisted of original poetry. Articles on Chatterton, Mary Wollstonecraft, Macklin, Middleton, and Mrs. Piozzi are worth remark, while reviews of Burke, Bürger's *Lenore*, Bowles' *Elegiac Stanzas*, Southey's *Joan of Arc*, Hayley's *Life of Milton*, the *Lyrical Ballads* (1800), and Malone's *Inquiry into the Authenticity of Ireland's Manuscript*, give the *Mirror* more than ordinary literary value. Moreover, it contained many signed articles, an unusual thing at this early date. It began in 1795 and was discontinued in 1810.

Samuel Taylor Coleridge's *Watchman* (March 1–May 13, 1796) although not of intrinsic literary value, deserves to be noticed as part of the life work of a great critic and poet. It was almost entirely unliterary in character, published "about once a week . . . That all may know the truth, and that the truth may make us free!" In form, the *Watchman* was a cross between the essay sheet and the miscellany, of thirty-two pages. Coleridge planned to avoid the stamp tax by publishing on every eighth day. Ten numbers were issued, filled with much pacifist propaganda and opposition to Pitt, a few reviews, and verse

published by a "Literary Association." Its single original feature was a history of literature, by Charles Dibdin, who was the editor.

The *Pocket Magazine* of 1794, a tiny periodical of seventy-two pages, had many articles signed by authors (from whose works they were borrowed), including one by Mary Wollstonecraft. The plan seems to have had some popularity, for a *Lady's New and Elegant Pocket Magazine* appeared in 1798, and several similar publications between 1800 and 1830.

contributions from the youthful Thomas Dermody and Thomas Lovell Beddoes, and prose from Thomas Poole and one Bringham. The *Watchman* cannot be regarded as of great importance in the development of literary serials, for its purpose was mainly political. It suffered extinction, as an organ of liberal propaganda, because of the great influence of the *Monthly Magazine*, which soon began to monopolize the talents of the young Radicals.

The *Cabinet Magazine; or, Literary Olio* (November 1796-July 1797) made a distinct advance in that it used signed articles almost exclusively. It contained a department called the "Projector," by "Plume Aircastle, Esq.," of prose contributions, and the "Cabinet of Apollo," a department of verse. The *English Magazine and Commercial Repository* (July 1796-97) was a meritorious performance, calculated to interest the business man especially. It included, however, a department called "Annals of Literature" and a section of poetry. The editor explained that he regarded the past as the age of solid learning, the present (with regret) as an age of light reading. On this theory he reviewed chiefly the more serious works.

The *Monthly Magazine, and British Register* (1796-1843) was set up by Richard Phillips, who had in 1792 founded the *Leicester Herald*, and was known among some of his contemporaries as a "dirty little Jacobin." Phillips rallied around him the young Radicals, and proceeded to give strong support to writers of liberal tendencies. John Aikin was his first editor. Godwin, "Peter Pindar" (Dr. Wolcot), and William Taylor of Norwich were contributors. Taylor's notable translation of Bürger's "Lenore" first appeared in the second number of this *Magazine*. Yet it had in it before 1800 little of literary importance, except a half-yearly "Retrospect of the State of domestic literature." In its earlier numbers, the *Monthly Magazine* was the usual mixture of miscellaneous elements—from literary essays to stock prices and items about provincial affairs. It contained, however, an excellent series of essays by William Enfield, called the "Inquirer," with the theme of each expressed in the form of a question at the head of the column. The first essay is thus introduced by the query, "Is verse essential to poetry?"[1] Later numbers contained lengthy reviews. Really distinguished contributions were Taylor's articles on German, Spanish and Italian literature. B. E. Hill and J. A. Heraud were later connected with the *Monthly*, and Thomas Lovell Beddoes and Douglas Jerrold were contributors. Its "Jacobinism" led to the founding of Colburn's *New Monthly Magazine* in 1814, and after that date the political warfare between these two periodicals was long and bitter. At the height of its career, the *Monthly Magazine* had a circulation of 5,000 copies.[2]

The *Monthly Magazine* and Coleridge's *Watchman* gave in 1796, a power to the Radical press, hitherto unknown. The ministerial party simply had to do something about it. It "inspired," therefore, a small but distinguished publication, the *Anti-Jacobin; or, Weekly Examiner* (November 20, 1797-July 9, 1798), which, although issued as a weekly, had the character of a miscellany, and, though wholly political in purpose, by the brilliance of its satire and parody won for itself a minor

[1] Arthur Beatty, in his *William Wordsworth*, (*University of Wisconsin Studies in Language and Literature*, Number 24, Madison, Wisc. 1927, 2nd ed., p. 55) has pointed out that Wordsworth was influenced by the debate between the "Inquirer" and Philo-rhythmus." *Monthly Magazine*, II, 453 ff. and 532 ff.

[2] C. H. Timperly (*Encyclopedia of Literary and Topographical Anecdote*, 2nd ed., London 1842, p. 795) gives the following figures for the numbers of copies of other literary periodicals sold at the end of the eighteenth century: *Gentleman's Magazine*, 4550; *British Critic*, 3500; *European Magazine*, 3250; *Universal Magazine of Knowledge and Pleasure*, 1750; *Analytical Review*, 1500; *New Annual Register*, 7000 to 8000 (annually). Timperly gives also a list of newspapers and periodicals published in the British Isles in 1838. See pp. 959-962.

place in literary history.[1] The "Friend of Humanity and
the Needy Knife Grinder," the "Loves of the Triangles,"
and the "New Morality" are now familiar to students of
the period. Southey, then in the days of his Radical youth,
was the chief victim of the parodists, although other
writers of liberal views came in for a share of ridicule.
Among the brilliant young men who contributed to the
Anti-Jacobin were George Canning, John Hookham
Frere, George Ellis—three who were to be later associated with the beginnings of the Tory *Quarterly Review*
—as well as Lord Morpeth, Henry Addington, George
Hammond, Edward Nares, John Macdonald, and William Gifford. The last was the *Anti-Jacobin's* editor; he
later became the first editor of the Tory *Quarterly Review*.

The *Ladies Monthly Museum* of 1798 was, on the
whole, the most substantial periodical for women thus
far issued. Its stock material of articles on fashion, cha-
rades, etc., was regularly varied with biographies of
women like Hannah More and Mrs. Barbauld, with a
monthly review of "female literature" such as Dr. Johnson's table talk, Walpole's writings, St. Pierre's *Paul et
Virginie*, and the works of Maria Edgeworth. Verse was
published under the head, "the Apollonian Wreath."[2]

The century may be fittingly concluded by reference to
two annual publications of note—Dodsley's *Annual Register* and the *Annual Anthology* of Bristol.

Dodsley's work was first issued in 1758, as a four hun-

[1] See Charles Edmonds, *The Poetry of the Anti-Jacobin*, 2nd ed. London, 1854, and *Poetry of the Anti-Jacobin,* ed. L. Rice-Oxley, Oxford, 1924.
[2] The short-lived *Historical Magazine* (1799-1800) "by Robert Bisset,
LL.D., with the assistance of Other Literary Gentlemen," surveyed poetry,
fiction, and drama.
    The *Arbroath Magazine*, a Scotch miscellany of 1799, was distinguished
during its brief career by the contributions of David Carey and Alexander
Balfour. (See *Bibliography of Arbroath Periodical Literature*, J. M.
M'Bain, Arbroath 1889.)

dred-page volume, and has been continued in an unbroken series to the present year. It is chiefly a compendium of general fact; but the last one hundred pages or so, devoted to general literature and poetry, are invaluable to the student who wishes representative selections from any year or period of years in the last century and a half. Edmund Burke was the first editor of the *Annual Register*.

The *Annual Anthology* first appeared in 1799, as a three hundred-page selection of poetry. It was intended as a periodical publication, but only two volumes were issued. Edited by Robert Southey, who contributed many poems, it was largely made up of the work of his friends —Charles Lloyd, Joseph Cottle (the publisher), Joseph Hucks, Charles Lamb, Robert Lovell, Samuel Taylor Coleridge, George Dyer, Humphrey Davy, Thomas Lovell Beddoes, "Perdita" Robinson, George Goodwin, Wm. Case, Jr., and others.[1]

Before 1800 the "magazine," or miscellaneous monthly periodical, had found a public and become a necessary part of the literature of the day. Readers sent letters, stories, poems, or essays to it; scholars inquired through its columns, or answered the queries of others. It supplemented the private library of the country squire or city merchant by furnishing copious extracts from most of the new books of importance, and the more important articles from the weekly and daily journals. It encouraged the young poet, and furnished him with models of the poetry of the masters. Although the major part of its contents were of a general and unliterary nature, this form of periodical had become by the end of the eighteenth century an indispensable vehicle of literature in all its forms.

There is no better way to summarize the development of the miscellany type of serial in the eighteenth century

[1] See note on Annuals, pp. 368-369 n.

than to compare the contents of the *Gentleman's Magazine* of 1731 with the *European Magazine* of 1800. From the *Gentleman's Journal* of Motteux, Cave inherited the idea of putting as many entertaining and instructive elements as possible between the covers of his serial. Possibly from hints in the *Grub Street Journal*, he got the idea of extracting the best of the weekly essays, and reprinting this mass of material—sifted of its chaff, as one might say—for busy readers. This borrowing idea gave him a new title. "Magazine," as Cave used the term, meant what the word suggests, a storehouse or repository of selected periodical literature. Thus the *Gentleman's* was, for many years, chiefly a compilation of the best things already published. A legion of imitators of the *Gentleman's*, continuing and extending this parasitical practice, show the miscellany to have been, before 1750, productive of little original literary matter. With the *Grand Magazine of Magazines* in 1758, the unscrupulous custom of preying upon other periodicals reached its logical extreme; it borrowed the best from the columns of other borrowers!

The reaction against this predatory method is early seen in the *British Magazine* of John Hill, in 1746, which goes as far as to parody the methods of Cave and his followers. From this point on, the miscellany (which is still called a "magazine") tends to become less and less a storehouse or selection of already published matter, but is gradually filled with original contributions. The variety of its appeals increases; it is adapted to the interests of science and agriculture and industry as well as literature and politics. Illustrations multiply, and the lighter features, such as stories and anecdotes, fill columns formerly devoted to political or religious controversy. "Novels" occupy many pages. The periodical essay, as has been noticed heretofore, is gradually absorbed into

AN ILLUSTRATION FOR THOMSON'S *Seasons*—
IN THE *Universal Magazine* OF 1747

the miscellany, as a feature. Biographical sketches, which since 1700 had always been found acceptable, are more frequent and more important. Criticism, although generally of a very conservative nature, in a few notable periodicals, such as the *Monthly Magazine* and the *Analytical Review* (see next chapter) encouraged, before the end of the century, the romantic reaction in English literature.

The increase in the circulation of newspapers, and perhaps a more rigorous enforcement of stamp duties, or the increase in these duties in 1797, discouraged the publishing of news summaries, one of the stock miscellany features. By degrees, the extracts from other periodicals were dropped entirely. The *Gentleman's Magazine* was one of the first to give them up. After 1770 the magazine was chiefly made up of original material. Thus the *European Magazine* of 1800 is more like Motteux's *Gentleman's Journal* of 1692 than is the *Gentleman's Magazine* of 1731. The vogue of the "magazine," in the strict sense, passed before the end of the century; and the monthly miscellany again became what it set out to be in the beginning—a miscellaneous periodical of instructive and entertaining original matter.

VII

EARLY CRITICAL REVIEWS—THE *MONTHLY REVIEW* AND ITS FOLLOWERS

In the history of English literary periodicals, the Review—the oldest and most noteworthy of types—has been also in evolution the most regular and dependable. Between the French abstract-serial of Sallo in 1665 and the English Reviews of 1790, a very gradual change transformed the abstract of a book into an abstract-with-comment, then into a review, of a sort, with copious excerpts from the work reviewed. Oldenburg, La Crose, and Dunton were the chief figures in the early development of the review from the abstract.[1]

Michael de la Roche, Huguenot friend of Bayle, who had served an apprenticeship in Holland, in 1710 continued this gradual development of the Review, in a serial publication which he called the *Memoirs of Literature*.[2] The *Memoirs* has been referred to as the "first English Review of original matter," but a glance at the contents, or even a reading of the conductor's preface, shows that characterization to be misleading. Its contents were not entirely original. La Roche admitted frankly that many of his abstracts were translated. His design was an old one—to give readers an account of learned books "beyond

---

[1] For convenience, it will be necessary hereafter to designate by the initial capital (Review) the periodical, in order to distinguish it from the contribution (a review).

[2] La Roche, unlike most Huguenot refugees, became a member of the Church of England. Before starting his first periodical enterprise, he served a kind of apprenticeship with London booksellers. As a journalist and critic, he was much influenced by his long friendship with Pierre Bayle. (See *Literary Journal*, iii, 1731, p. 116; and Agnew's *Protestant Exiles from France*, Edin. 1871, ii, 150 ff.)

the sea." He translated not only books but letters and dissertations, and said frankly that he found it necessary to publish some works of his own to fill up his columns.

In a sense, then, the *Memoirs of Literature* was a direct lineal descendant of the periodicals of La Crose, and more remotely of the *Journal des Sçavans*. But it was far more than that. La Roche made a distinct step forward, influenced much, we may believe, by the miscellanies of Motteux, Dunton, and others. He published in the *Memoirs of Literature* notes of addresses given before the Royal Academy, papers received, items about "professors" (chiefly continental) letters regarding manuscripts, news of academies, book notices, and reviews—some of the last two pages in length. The periodical was, in fact, largely made up of original matter. In the volumes for the three years during which it was issued as a monthly, are found many articles interesting to the student of literature in that period—a dissertation on pastoral poetry, one on the topic, "Whether those are not poets may judge poetry," letters on tragedy, an article on epic poetry, and a long article on the posthumous works of Thomas Browne, which is more like the later critiques in the *Monthly Review* than anything that had appeared up to this time. Of course, much attention was given to classical learning; the reviews of Bentley's works are of value today. Unlike La Crose's serials, the *Memoirs of Literature* contained articles on such subjects as the "benefits" of the tobacco habit. It is noticeable that La Roche was far less concerned than was his fellow Huguenot with purely moral and theological matters.

The *Memoirs of Literature* appeared originally as a monthly of sixty to eighty pages. The first series ended in 1714. It was resumed in January 1717, with the sub-title,

"English and Foreign Library." With the April number of the same year, it was finally discontinued.[1]

A few years later, Dr. Samuel Jebb, in his *Bibliotheca Literaria*, carried on for ten numbers (1722-4) the tradition of the "learned" type of serial. It was announced as a "Collection of Inscriptions, Medals, Dissertations, Etc." Selling for a shilling, it was issued as a forty-eight page bi-monthly. In the Introduction to No. 1, the projector stated his purpose:

> The undertaker of this work, having observed that many things which are useful and valuable are in a manner lost to the world by reason of their being too small to be separately published, has judged it will be acceptable to the Learned and Curious to have them collected into one body, and sent abroad as occasion shall require. The particulars which fall within the bounds of this design are,
>
> I. Inscriptions and medals, usually fugitive and lost.
> II. Small tracts of ancient and approved writers, which lie dispersed in libraries.
> III. Critical dissertations upon authors or things.
> IV. Whatever tends to the explaining any part of antiquity, notes upon the Fathers or Classics, emendations of corrupted passages, together with the readings of manuscripts not already collated.

Each number of the *Bibliotheca Literaria* concluded with two sections, one called "Labors of the Learned," containing the news of scholars, and the other devoted to announcements of books being prepared for the press.

La Roche, who concluded his *Memoirs of Literature* in 1717, went to Amsterdam to start a new undertaking— an English periodical in French, the *Bibliothèque Angloise ou Histoire Littéraire de la Grande Bretagne*, in collaboration with Armand de la Chapelle. The new serial seems to have been successful, for it was continued

[1] A forty-page monthly, called the *Delphick Oracle* (September 1719— March 1720) ought to be noticed in passing, as a late attempt to revive the question-and-answer periodical. Its matter of general information was "set forth through a correspondence held with the most learned scholars in the most famous universities of Europe . . . for the advancement of divine and human learning."

until 1727, with a total of fifteen volumes. As in the *Memoirs*, La Roche did more than abstract books. Comment (parenthetical, often) was added to the liberal excerpts which were quoted and translated for readers. Double titles were employed, in the original English and French, a device used thirty years before by La Crose in the *Universal Historical Bibliotheque*.[1]

In January 1725, La Roche evidently left the *Bibliothèque Angloise* in the hands of his collaborator, and returned to England; for we find him starting another monthly periodical, this time known as the *New Memoirs of Literature*. The reason for La Roche's return is explained in his preface. It was not from inclination, he says, but because of pressure from Innys, the publisher, that he took up the *New Memoirs*.

This periodical contained longer reviews than the former work, and was somewhat more varied in character. Each number consisted of about a dozen articles, up to twenty-five pages in length, with a total of seventy-six to eighty pages, usually. The last section contained notices of books newly printed or "to be printed." A representative article, that on Shelvocke's *Voyages* (January 1726), will give an idea how far La Roche had advanced toward the nineteenth-century review. He gave the full title of the book, name of the author, place of printing, price, and size of the book, in the modern manner. Then he quoted Capt. Shelvocke's preface, thus giving the reader an idea what to expect from the work, and made some comments thereupon. A concise summary of the story followed, with abundant quotations. As an example of the parts he selected and the manner of quotation—

The whales, grampusses and other fish of a monstrous bulk, are in such numbers on the coast of Patagonia, that they were very offensive. "For," says the author, "They would come sometimes so close to us, as

[1] La Roche seems to have had a hand in the *Memoires Littéraires*, also (La Hague, 1720-24).

"almost to stifle us with their stench when they blew, and would lie
"so near us, that I have frequently thought it impossible to escape
"striking upon them on every send of a sea. I am a stranger to the Green-
"land fishery (continues the author) and therefore cannot say why
"a trade might be carried on there. I may venture to affirm that it is a
"safer navigation; and I am apt to believe that here is a greater cer-
"tainty of succeeding."

In the last number of the *New Memoirs of Literature*
(December 1727), was the announcement of La Roche's
withdrawal from it. Another author was "taking up
the design" for the same publisher, under the title, the
Present State of the Republick of Letters.[1] Andrew Reid
was the one taking up the design, which became what
D'Israeli in his *Curiosities of Literature* calls, with La
Roche's periodicals, the best of the literary journals of
the time. Reid was interested in science, and was the
editor of an abridgment of the *Philosophical Transactions*, 1720-32. He began the *Present State of the Republick of Letters* with a good preface, setting forth the
advantages of England as a place for such a periodical.
No country in the world was more favorable to critical
undertakings, he said, where the greatest statesmen were
often highest in the world of letters, where there were
great universities and "liberty of the press."

Reid's periodical, although consciously modeled on the
learned serials of the past, by its monthly appearance
and its contents, shows how strong was the tendency toward the miscellany form. No. 1 consisted of five articles
and nine notices of books in eighty-eight pages, and that
distribution of matter was fairly well maintained. Scholars and translators like Richard Bentley and Mme. Dacier
were often mentioned and commented upon. Many

---

[1] For the source of the title, see the *Nouvelles de la République des
Lettres* of Pierre Bayle, and a book, *Republica Literaria*, translated in
1727, which was reviewed in the *New Memoirs* in July of that year.

articles were criticisms of classic authors. It was in the columns of this periodical that Warburton defended Pope, after the attack of Crousaz on the *Essay on Man*. There were some poems, usually complimentary verses—among them, Congreve's *Epistle to Lord Cobham*, here printed for the first time (March 1729). A long original dissertation on the use of morality in poetry reminds the reader of the *Monthly Miscellany or Memoirs for the Curious*. But at least one review is interesting to students of English poetry. Thomson's *Spring* was very appreciatively criticised in May 1728. The last section of the serial was devoted to the "State of Learning," with advices from Rome, Florence, Naples, Hamburg, London, etc. The *Present State of the Republick of Letters* was issued from January 1728 to December 1736, when it was united with the *Literary Magazine* to form the later *History of the Works of the Learned*.

Of less pretentious appearance was the *Mirrour*, started December 18, 1729, as a small octavo, and published irregularly, about one number a month. For the first few numbers, its criticism is notable. The contents are letters of many sorts—satirical, panegyrical, and humorous—for the purpose of showing the great improvement of wit, poetry, and learning. Moreover, we are informed by the author that the letters are introduced as "a mirrour for Mr. Alex. Pope and his creatures, the admirers of the famous *Dunciad*," with a . . . "legal conviction of Pope for dulness and scandal in the high court of Parnassus," because he had run counter to good manners and had "exerted his noble Billingsgate talents" in the most shameless abuse of his contemporaries. The author of this fairly well written work was probably Giles Jacob, known as one of Pope's victims. Yet the *Mirrour* justifies the attention of modern students by its attempt to show the lack in Pope of the *"mens divinior atque os . . . magna sonaturum . . .* which Spenser, Milton, Cowley, Dryden, Prior, and some others of our famous countrymen, have, in great measure come up to. Or is there anything"—asks the author—"in the poetry of Pope but trifling imitation of celebrated poets; or smooth-flowing words and jingling rhymes, adapted to the ear only . . . sinewless versification and sonorous nonsense?" This constituted a kind of review of Pope's third edition of the *Dunciad*. But this anticipation of an early nineteenth-century attitude toward Pope was by no means an indication that the *Mirrour* existed solely for the purpose of attacking this one poet. The five or six letters following contained criticisms of other authors and works, past or contemporary. Especially high praise was given Dennis. In later numbers, the author seems to have transferred his interest to other fields than literature. The bound copy of this publication is dated 1733, but indicates that the *Mirrour* ended with the issue of October 21, 1730.

The *New Memoirs of Literature* had been stopped at the end of 1727. In March 1730, La Roche came forward again with what, in a signed preface, he called a "continuation." It was a quarterly serial, the *Literary Journal*, designed to be published at Lady-Day, Midsummer, Michaelmas, and Christmas, and to be bound into volumes at the end of each half-year. As a matter of periodicity, this is of real importance; for later Reviews of the more serious type found the quarterly form to be the most satisfactory; and they generally adopted Roche's plan of binding up at the end of the half-year.

The *Literary Journal*, although it preserved its identity only a year and a half, was, while it lasted, a real Review in the modern sense, except that the extracts quoted to show the "quality" of an author were usually a little longer than was common later. Both in form and in its treatment of matter, it advanced a step toward the nineteenth-century Reviews. One ought to remark, in passing, however, that La Roche reviewed in a much livelier and more readable style than most of his predecessors in works of this sort. A characteristic review is that of Stevens's translation of Herrara's *General History of America*. The author begins, not unlike the critics of a century later, with two pages of comment and exposition, before he quotes from the book at all. Then he allows excerpts from the text to do much of the critical labor for him—a method yet to be improved upon. La Roche's ending of the article is worth quoting:

I suspect the Americans (Indians) have been represented by their cruel conquerors more vicious than they were; and if one had a mind to do them justice, Herrara's *History* would be sufficient for it. Regarding human sacrifices, he says "We have seen as great enormities among Christians. And indeed, what difference is there between sacrificing a prisoner of war, and burning a heretic alive; between a prisoner of war sacrificed by priests, and a heretic burnt alive at the desire of priests?"

It is true, of course, that the *Literary Journal* dealt not at all with English literature as we know it. Hardly a book was reviewed that is now remembered by title. La Roche's real contribution to the development we are tracing lay in his making the serious book-abstract publication of his predecessors into something very similar to the *Edinburgh Review* of the nineteenth century.

On the other hand, another periodical carried on in a most orthodox way the "learned" tradition of the past. Archibald Bower, while residing with Lord Aylmer and assisting him in reading the classics, conducted the *Historia Litteraria* "or an exact and early account of the most valuable books published in several parts of Europe" (1730-34). A markedly critical tendency characterized the contents of this eight-page monthly journal, although it dealt frequently with books of a theological or philological nature. Like many of its predecessors, it surveyed the "present state of learning," in a department near the end. A catalogue of books, usually with Latin titles, concluded the work.

A serial of the same learned type, although much more interesting here, was the *Miscellaneous Observations upon Authors Ancient and Modern*, by Dr. John Jortin, the ecclesiastical historian. It was published in yearly volumes (1731-32), to be sure, but deserves notice as a periodical work primarily literary. Although devoted to classical scholarship chiefly, it contained general criticism that has a wider appeal. The preface to volume one, for example, defends critical writing from those who ridiculed it. And a passage on incivility in criticism might have been read with profit by later reviewers. *Miscellaneous Observations* was translated into Latin and republished in Amsterdam by P. Burman and J. P. d'Orville, and by them continued after the original had been stopped.

Many a serial of this time employed—as we have seen —the time-honored device of a "Society of Gentlemen." The *Literary Magazine; or, The History of the Works of the Learned* (January 1735–December 1736), a successor of La Roche's publications, had its "society"— really Ephraim Chambers. It carried on the torch of erudition in the interval between the *Memoirs of Literature* and the later learned periodicals. The projector announced an intention of giving accounts of books, "with proper *observations upon each author*," and, in addition, of printing biographical memoirs, dissertations, and critical inquiries. Chamber's criticism is thus self-conscious. His conception of the critic's duty is illuminating:

We conceive it the duty of a journalist to give a faithful account of books which come into his hands. If he lies under a necessity of taking in the assistance of criticism, decency and good manners, probity and religion will prescribe him certain rules, from which he is never allowed to depart. When he affects the air and language of a censor or judge, he invades the undoubted right of the public, which is the only sovereign judge of the reputation of an author, and the merit of his compositions . . .

Bacon's *Letters and Remains*, Lobo's *Voyage to Abyssinia*, Pope's *Letters*, and Oldys' *Life of Raleigh* are among the interesting works reviewed. Regular departments consisted of extracts from the *Philosophical Transactions* and "Literary News."

Another *History of the Works of the Learned* (1737-1743) carried on rather ponderously the labors of La Crose and his kind. Without much advance in method over predecessors, this monthly compendium gave "accurate abstracts," "impartial" reviews of books, with critical reflections, a general view of the state of learning throughout Europe, and "memoirs of the most eminent writers." It was published by the proprietors of the *Present State of the Republick of Letters* and the *Literary Magazine*, as a substitute for both those serials, and consisted, therefore, of a rather remarkable mixture. The contents of one issue, for example, were:

    I. An abstract and epitome of the second volume of the *Life of David*.
    II. A critical review of a new edition of Fontenelle.
    III. An account of the origin and progress of surgery.
    IV. Microscopic observations on the louse, cheese, mites, etc.
    V. A catalogue of books lately published.

Had the *History* lived up to its pretensions, it might have made a permanent place for itself among periodicals. But, in truth, it was little more than a receptacle for dry treatises. Its literary value is therefore very slight.[1]

[1] The Preface of the *Literary Magazine* contains an interesting sketch of previous works of this kind, including references to Apollodorus of Athens and his *Library of the Origin of the Gods*, Diodorus of Sicily's *Historical Library*, and Photius' *Myrobiblia*. The author remarked that

William Oldys, librarian of the Earl of Oxford, issued a variant of the learned periodical, in the *British Librarian* (January-June 1737) a monthly of sixty-two pages.[1] Oldys, who had been engaged on the *Universal Spectator* and *Scarborough Miscellany*, designed in the new serial a "review and abstract of our most rare, useful, and valuable books . . . " As a result, the *British Librarian* contains matter valuable to students of literature. Articles ran to twelve pages, and were descriptive reviews in character. Gildas, William of Occam, William Prynne, John Wycliffe, are among the authors discussed; while especially interesting are criticisms of the *Historia Histrionica*, the *Dictes and Sayings of the Philosophers*, Froissart's *Chronicles*, Webbe's *Discourse of English Poetrie*, Hakluyt's *Voyages*, Dugdale's *Origines Juridiciales*, Glanville's *Plus Ultra*, Sir Thomas More's English works, Elyot's *Governor*, and Caxton's *Aeneid*. The scope of Oldys' critical interest may be measured by the following introduction to a review:

> The Boke of Eneydos, compyled by Vyrgyle; whiche hathe been translated oute of Latyne into Frenshe, and oute of Frenshe reduced into Englysshe, by me WILLIAM CAXTON, the 22 Daye of Juyn, the Yere of our Lorde 1490. Fol.
>
> This Work contains not an entire Version of two or three Books only of Virgil's *Aeneid*, as some might imagine from the slender bulk of the Book; nor is it here translated into Verse, as they might also expect, in imitation of the Original, and as nothing appears to the contrary in the Title above, printed at the End: but it is rather a Reduction of that Epic Poem to an historical Narrative in Prose; which, tho' a commendable Undertaking at that time, to familiarize the Contents; yet, as it is but a Translation of a Translation; as the Original itself is familiar enough now, and we have also many better Translations, even in Verse, directly from it; the very Table of Heads, no less than sixty-five, cannot be in this Place desirable. Therefore, we shall

---

at this date (1735) Holland produced more works of this sort than all the rest of the world.

[1] For authorship, see holograph letter in the British Museum copy.

only refer to a Note at Bottom, for a few Remarks upon the Work itself; and here recite the Translator's Preface; which contains such observable Proofs of the fleeting Fashions in our English Tongue, as may moderate the Conceits of those who depend upon a Style, or Manner of Expression, more than the Matter expressed, that will not, like most other things, become obsolete, but maintain its Perspicuity, and engage the Taste of all Ages. . . .

The most important predecessor of the *Monthly Review*, in form at least, was a quarterly, the *Literary Journal* of Dublin (December 1744-June 1749), better known as "Droz's *Literary Journal*." It was projected as another abstract periodical, giving the substance of German, Dutch, French, and Latin books in English, by adapting the "best abstracts to be found in foreign journals"—namely, second-hand abstracts. But in reality it was much more than this. Its two hundred pages contained many original articles; and a large part of its material, in later numbers, approached very closely the review form of the later *Monthly*, employing the method of analysis and quotation. The main purpose of the proprietor was to make foreign books accessible to Irish readers, and he was more concerned with controversial divinity than with literature. Thirty pages of the literary news of Europe concluded each number. Unquestionably, the *Literary Journal* was the first genuine Review published in Ireland.[1] Moreover, in the tradition of periodical literature, it may, for several reasons, be regarded as a bridge from the serious abstract serials of La Crose and La Roche to the *Monthly Review* of Griffiths, a few years later.

Discontinued in 1749, the *Literary Journal* was revived—after a fashion—in 1751, for a few numbers, as

[1] See R. R. Madden, *Limerick Reporter and Tipperary Vindicator*, May 1, 1894.
Droz reveals his identity in the Preface of Vol. I.

the *Compendious Library* "by V. Desvoeux." This one-hundred-page bi-monthly, issued in Dublin for the same publisher, was much more a literary periodical than its predecessor. Undoubtedly it borrowed the thunder of its London rival, the *Monthly Review*. Admirable critical restraint is expressed in Desvoeux's preface, when he says,

Though I shall sometimes intersperse a few observations of my own . . . yet I shall avoid positiveness, and it shall be my constant care never to give way to satyr, raillery, personal reflections, imputation of disowned consequence, or anything else that might give offense—my abstracts shall be short . . . my criticisms, if I ever venture upon any, such as I would thank any one for . . . on my own works.

Fielding's *Amelia* was favorably reviewed, in such manner as this:

Romances and novels, in general, have no great right to be in Literary Journals. Yet some exception may be made in favor of those not calculated for mere amusement; and we should be very sorry to look on any book as below our notice, that may tend to the Reformation of Manners and the Advancement of Virtue. This seems to be one, if not the chief, point from which Mr. Fielding's performance ought to be considered. . . . They who look for nothing else but entertainment will find here a plausible story, full of interesting incidents and moving situations, written in an elegant and lively style, and interspersed with many reflections that every man of taste must be pleased with.

The *Compendious Library* appeared from December 1751 to February 1752.[1]

Although the *Monthly Review* is looked upon as the first of the type of periodicals which was to become su-

[1] Following at once in the track of the *British Librarian* and the *Literary Journal*, the *Universal Librarian* (April-June 1751) gave accounts of new books, and included dissertations too small for separate publication. Like Droz's serial, it was a quarterly. It was issued by a "Fellow of the Royal Society."

Somewhat similar was the *Library* (April-December 1761), a monthly of fifty-six pages, set on foot by Dr. Andrew Kippis and some of his friends. Its subtitle was "moral and critical magazine," but it was more moral than critical. Essays on Shakespeare and Roger Bacon are almost its only "literary" contents.

preme in literary interest and influence, it did not emerge full-grown in 1749. In fact, Griffiths' publication was very far from the Review type, as represented by the *Edinburgh* and *Quarterly Reviews* of the nineteenth century. It began as a collection of digests or compends of books. The first number consisted of eighty pages, containing only five essay-abstracts. Evidently, Griffiths' early success must have been due to the appeal of the works selected for "review," rather than to any originality. His manner of condensing and commenting was exactly that of La Roche in several earlier serials. Moral philosophy, pindaric odes, the senses, patriotism, and a poem, the *Regicide*, "by the author of *Roderick Random*," were the subjects so dealt with in the first number.

In view of its size, general quality, and long career as a periodical, the justice of calling the *Monthly Review* the earliest Review of importance in English literature must be granted. But one has only to read the first few numbers to realize the continuity of periodical tradition. After three quarters of a century, the abstract idea was still predominant, as actually as in the days of La Crose and the *Weekly Memorials*. Readers in 1749 still looked to the periodical for a digest or epitome of books. That there had also developed a new idea—that of directing readers to the works of most merit, is of course true. Samuel Badcock, in a letter of May 9, 1783, advised Griffiths that the public demanded something more from the *Monthly Review* than mere abstracts. It is evident, therefore, that for more than thirty years of its career, the *Monthly* made little advance over its predecessors in the critical nature of its contents. After 1783, however, Badcock's advice seems to have been followed, for the *Monthly* rapidly improved its articles, until William Taylor of Norwich and other writers created what was to be for one hundred years the standard type of periodical criticism.[1]

The *Monthly Review* was set up by Ralph Griffiths, and was conducted by him and his son for over fifty-four years. Published originally at the "Sign of the Dunciad," in St. Paul's Churchyard, it was later moved to quarters in Paternoster Row, and then to the Strand. Dr. William Rose, master of an academy in Chiswick, prepared the first article, and continued for years to be one of the chief contributors. Owen Ruffhead, Andrew Kippis, James Grainger, John Langhorne, and James Mackintosh wrote for it. Hawkesworth was one of the most valued earlier assistants of the proprietor. In fact, Gilbert Stuart, another able contributor, feared in 1774 that the *Monthly* would not soon recover from the blow of Hawkesworth's death. It recovered, however; for the astute Griffiths saw that a periodical is known and lives by its contributors. He lost no time in adding new critics as old ones fell off. Among the successors of Hawkesworth were Samuel Badcock, whose informative letters to and from Griffiths are preserved at the Bodleian Library.[2] William Enfield of Norwich, who was one of the most prolific reviewers, William Taylor of Norwich (after September 1793), Alexander Hamilton of Edinburgh, who was always wanting advances, Richard Porson, who handled classical matters, Thomas Holcroft, whose reviews did much to give the *Monthly* a reputation for hostility to the State and Church, A. L. Geddes, John Wolcot, Richard Brinsley Sheridan, William Gilpin, Charles Burney, and Goldsmith labored to fill its columns, to say nothing of many others whose names are now forgotten. The air of liberal-

---

[1] William Taylor, in thirty-one years of periodical writing, is credited by his biographer with 550 articles in the *Monthly Review*, 764 in the *Monthly Magazine*, 361 in the *Annual Register*, 64 in the *Critical,* and fifteen in Aikin's *Athenæum* (see Robberds, *William Taylor of Norwich*, London, 1843, i, 126).

[2] Add. Mss. C 89, 90, and Add. Mss. VII, D. 11, 12.

ity which caused Johnson to tell the King that the
Monthly reviewers were Christians with as little Chris-
tianity as possible, inclined to pull down all establish-
ments, also impelled a clerical reviewer in 1793 to sever
his connection with Griffiths, protesting that he could no
longer stand the attitude of the *Review* towards principles he held sacred. In a reply to the latter, Griffiths
signed himself "an Old Whig and Consistent Protestant."[1]

The *Monthly*, by 1790, had become a substantial publication of 120 pages, divided into a dozen long articles
of ten pages each, followed by a section called the
Monthly Catalogue, which was composed of shorter treatments—from three to four pages each. An effort was made
to review in some manner *all* publications of the month;
and Enfield, who often advised Griffiths, wrote in 1793
that he believed this effort was "the one great point in the
Monthly's favor." The correspondence shows that a distinction in payment was made between the Catalogue
article and the review. Most of the writers (Holcroft,
for example) made a first appearance in the brief notices
of the Catalogue, and were later promoted to the rank
of regular reviewers.

Hazlitt affirmed that the style of philosophical criticism which later characterized the *Edinburgh Review*
was first introduced by William Taylor in the *Monthly*.[2]
Whether or not this is true, it is likely that Taylor, because of his interest in continental literature, brought to
English criticism (between 1793 and 1824) a broader
literary outlook, thus correcting to some extent the in-
sularity of British taste. For this corrective influence,
unquestionably a greater genius had prepared the way,
when Oliver Goldsmith between April 1757 and December 1758, contributed some twenty reviews to Griffiths'

[1] A *General Index of the Monthly Review* (Vols. 1-70) was published
in London, 1786, by Samuel Ayscough.
[2] *Spirit of the Age*, Lon. 1825, p. 308.

periodical. It is not the place here to examine the tradition which had given posterity the opinion that Goldsmith was infamously mistreated by Griffiths and his wife. It can only be noted—and with no intention of minimizing the importance of his connection with the *Monthly* —that Goldsmith, fresh from a post at Peckham School, was at the same time writing for the *Critical Review* and possibly for the *Literary Magazine*.[1] He was an obscure hack writer, like most of his fellow-reviewers. His literary energy was turned into other channels after 1758, and the prestige of the later *Monthly Review* owes little or nothing to him.

The *Monthly* was finally concluded in 1845 with the end of the fourth series. Many hasty and derogatory statements about it have been made by later writers who have had always in mind the comparison of this earlier work with the *Edinburgh* and *Quarterly* of the nineteenth century; but the *Monthly Review* will remain, like the *Gentleman's Magazine*, an important depository of information for students of the eighteenth century. Griffiths, in his effort for many years to notice every book published in London, made himself the creditor of all the generations of scholars and bibliographers who have followed him.[2]

The foremost rival of the *Monthly* was the *Critical Re-*

[1] But see R. W. Seitz, "Goldsmith and the *Literary Magazine*," *Review of English Studies*, V, 410-430.

[2] See George Paston, "The Monthly Review," in *Sidelights on the Georgian Period*, London 1902, pp. 147-166.

The *Edinburgh Review* of 1755, designed to be published every six months, attempted to include an account of all the books and pamphlets that had been published in Scotland during the half year, together with an appendix of books most worthy of notice in England and other countries. William Robertson, Adam Smith, Alexander Wedderburn, the Earl of Rosslyn, Hugh Blair, and others contributed to it. Mainly devoted to moral philosophy, it contains little that is interesting today except the review of Johnson's *Dictionary*, which, of course, caused it to be mentioned by Boswell. Its heavy learning and moral philosophy did not save it from an early demise. Two numbers only were published.

view, started February 1756, by Archibald Hamilton, a prosperous printer, who had been forced to leave Edinburgh by his share in the Porteous Riot. Tobias Smollett was virtually editor. The Reverend Joseph Robertson, a voluminous contributor, is credited with twenty-six hundred articles between 1764 and 1785.[1] Dr. Johnson wrote at least one review for it, that of Goldsmith's *Traveller*, while Goldsmith himself contributed sixteen articles between November 1757 and March 1760. The *Critical* was published ostensibly by a "Society of Gentlemen," really by a syndicate. The projectors took for themselves the admirable motto, "Nothing extenuate, nor set down in malice," which, unfortunately, they could not quite live up to. Their aim in criticism was—according to their preface—"To exhibit a succinct plan of every performance; to point out the most striking beauties and glaring defects; to illustrate remarks with proper quotations, and to convey those remarks in such a manner as might best conduce to the entertainment of the public." As a matter of fact, the *Critical* was established under Tory and Church patronage to maintain principles in opposition to those of the *Monthly*. Smollett wrote Dr. John Moore that the *Review* was conducted by four men of "proved abilities." These are conjectured to have been Dr. Thomas Francklin, David Mallet, Griffith Jones, and Joseph Robertson.[2]

Smollett's taste, wit, and miscellaneous learning qualified him highly for periodical writing and for editorial activities. On the other hand, he was often hasty and frequently a prejudiced judge. While himself applying the critical scourge without mercy, he resented any retorts from his victims. Thus he was easily led into petty squab-

---

[1] *Gentleman's Magazine*, LXXII (February 1802), 108; *European Magazine*, XIV (July 1788) 24; XXXI (April 1797), 260.
[2] See the anonymous satire *The Battle of the Reviews*, 1760; also *Letters of Tobias Smollett*, Ed. Noyes, Cambridge, Mass., 1926, pp. 148-150.

bles and clamorous contests of rejoinder, recrimination, and abuse. Among the controversies in which he became embroiled, the most unfortunate was that with Admiral Knowles, which led to imprisonment in 1759. A result of more literary interest was Churchhill's famous assault on Smollett's character and works. Other well known attacks on Smollett were those of Dr. James Grainger and John Shebbeare, the latter of whom was caricatured as Lawyer Ferret in *Sir Lancelot Greaves*. Although the controversies of Smollett were not all carried on in the columns of the *Critical*, the *Review* could hardly be unaffected by them.[1] Smollett came in time to resent greatly the obligations he had assumed as editor. He gave up all connection with the *Review* before he left England for France in June, 1763. Worry, ill health, overwork, and the attacks of his whiggish assailants, probably conspired to divorce him from this periodical enterprise.

In its rivalry with the *Monthly*, the *Critical* not only endeavored to cover most of the works published, but also prided itself on reviewing them immediately upon their appearance. It appeared at the same monthly intervals, as an octavo of 120 pages; it was made up likewise of long reviews, followed by a "monthly catalogue" of shorter reviews; and at the end of each number had a survey of public affairs—some twenty pages. Its position as a literary organ was soon established by capable criticism of Hume's *History*, Home's *Douglas*, Dyer's *Fleece*, Gray's *Odes*, Richardson's *Clarissa Harlowe*, Burke's *Essay on the Sublime and Beautiful*, and Butler's *Literary Remains*, the last by Goldsmith. The quality of the articles in the *Critical*, so Johnson maintained, was superior to that of the reviews in the *Monthly*. His comment on the methods of treating books by the writers in

[1] *Letters of Tobias Smollett*, Cambridge, Mass., 1926. See Letter No. 40, p. 57. Also pp. 70, 72, 96, 198.

these rival periodicals is well known.[1] Reviews of Grainger's *Sugar Cane* and Graham's *Telemachus* were among
Johnson's own contributions to the *Critical*. The *Critical
Review* continued to rival its more liberal contemporary
until 1790.

The importance of Johnson's prestige was discerned
by another publisher in 1756, and before the *Critical* was
well under way, the *Literary Magazine; or, Universal
Review* (May 1756-July 1758) had engaged his services.
He wrote the preliminary address, and some twenty-five
reviews, to say nothing of six original articles on matters
political. Boswell thought Johnson never gave greater
proofs of the force, acuteness, and vivacity of his mind
than in this periodical. But with the exception of a
critique on Warton's *Essay on the Genius and Writings
of Pope*, none of his contributions were of a critical nature. In fact, the *Literary Magazine* was chiefly non-
literary, in spite of the much that was written about Pope,
and Johnson's proposal for an edition of Shakespeare.
Even the twelve-page "Review of Books" was dropped
after the first volume. The major part of the *Magazine's*
contents range from a description of a sea-cow to historical memoirs. The *Literary Magazine* thus partook of the
nature of both miscellany and review—perhaps more of
the latter than of the former. Some verse is to be found
in later numbers. Johnson wrote for it until the fifteenth
number. Thereafter, the *Literary Magazine* gradually
declined, so Boswell affirms, and was discontinued in
1758, with the epithet "Anti-Gallican" applied to it.[2]

Like the foregoing periodical, the short-lived *Monthly
and Critical Review* of 1756 lays little claim to literary
values. Starting pretentiously like its model, the *Monthly*
of Griffiths, it abstracted and commented upon every-

[1] Boswell's *Life of Johnson*, ed. G. B. Hill, Oxford 1887, iii, 32.
[2] Boswell, *op. cit.*, i, 307, 320, 328, 505.

thing but literature. A review of Pope is the only essay that gives it critical interest. In a similar way, the *Monthly Record of Literature* (January-December 1767) apparently avoided literary matters, although Harrington's *Oceana* was reprinted serially and Farmer's *Essay on the Learning of Shakespeare* was reviewed. Its one hundred pages were chiefly occupied with essays in the interest of religion, virtue, and civil liberty. On the other hand, *Critical Memoirs of the Times*, which appeared monthly for nine numbers in 1769, contained a department of "modern literature," poetical originals (so-called), fugitive verses, a biography of Pope in a review of Ruffhead's *Life*, a long article on Voltaire's essay on Shakespeare, reviews of Pope's letters, and *Tom Jones, a Comic Opera*, as well as other features of interest. Joseph Warton's "Ode to Liberty" was printed among the "poetical originals." The *Universal Catalogue* (of contemporary literature) of 1772-74 was a direct descendant of the *Mercurius Librarius* of 1668. More than one hundred books were listed in the twenty-four pages of the first monthly number. The title of each book was given, with brief comment in italics; and books were numbered seriatim through the year. During the first year, 1511 books were thus treated. As comment became longer, in the second and third volumes, italics were used for the titles and ordinary type for the comment. The bibliographical value of this serial is obvious.

The *Edinburgh Magazine and Review* (October 1773-August 1776) was set on foot by Gilbert Stuart, who thought with rivalry to annihilate the *Scots Magazine*. The first numbers showed more talent than periodical publications usually exhibited. Dr. Thomas Blacklock, Professor William Richardson, Professor William Baron (possibly Adam Smith and David Hume), Reverend A. Gillies, William Smellie, whose *Memoirs* give us much of the available information regarding the project, and other names were implied by its "Society of Gentlemen" advertised on the title page. D'Israeli's *Calamities of Authors* describes its decline and fall. It was too full of abuse—so runs the condemnation.[1] Stuart's personal faults seem to have been largely responsible for its failure. Every clergyman in the Kingdom opposed it, and every magistrate threatened its destruction, we are told. Creech was the Edinburgh publisher, and John Murray sold it in London. When the untimely end came to the Scottish venture, Stuart went to London and persuaded Murray to set up the *English Review*, with what success will be seen later. While it lasted, the *Edinburgh Magazine and Review* was believed to exceed every other periodical of the day in "genius and originality."

Meanwhile in the English metropolis, the caustic William Kenrick was disturbing literary complacency and laying the foundations for the vituperative criticism of the nineteenth century. In January 1759, Kenrick was "appointed" to succeed Goldsmith on the staff of the *Monthly Review*. He wrote on foreign literature and also reviewed Goldsmith's *Inquiry* in November of that year, inserting at Griffiths' request so violent an attack on the author that even Griffiths was embarrassed. Kenrick was then obliged to explain away his insinuations in a favorable review of the *Citizen of the World* (June 1762). In 1766 Kenrick ceased writing for the *Monthly* and announced that he was about to undertake a new periodical. This was evidently the *London Review of English and Foreign Literature*, which did not appear, however, for nearly ten years. Beginning in 1775 as an eighty-page monthly, the new Review libeled the genius of the age, attacking Johnson, referring to Goldsmith's *Traveller* as

---

[1] For an extended account of the *Edinburgh Magazine and Review*, see Robert Kerr's *Memoirs of William Smellie*, Edinburgh 1811, i, 392-504.

a "flimsy" poem, finding the *Deserted Village* lacking in "dignity, genius, and fire," and generally running amuck among contemporary authors. It contains criticism of most of the literary works of this period, but makes little other than derogatory comment upon them. For that reason, the *Review* might with justification be ignored, were its criticisms not significant as forerunners of the infamous attacks published in the *Edinburgh Review* and *Quarterly Review*, a quarter of a century later. Kenrick was assisted in the editing by his son, William Shakespeare Kenrick, who after his father's death in 1779 continued the *London Review* for a year.

Henry Maty, son of Dr. Matthew Maty, who was Librarian of the British Museum, came forward in 1782 with the *New Review*, devoted to literary curiosities and intelligence.[1] Although it consisted chiefly of notices of foreign works, and is most valuable for its early recognition of the merits of German literature, the *New Review* is important also for its reviews of contemporary dramas on the English stage, its sketch of the Chatterton controversy, and articles on Pope, Warton, and Rousseau. As a monthly Review of sixty-four pages, it was continued for four years.

Although Gilbert Stuart's *Edinburgh Magazine* had been only slightly concerned with pure literature, the *English Review*, which he persuaded John Murray to start in London in 1783 was almost entirely of or about matters of literary interest. The "abstract" idea persisted in it, as is indicated by the sub-title, "An Abstract of English and Foreign Literature." The editor proposed to give an account of every book and pamphlet which should

[1] Matthew Maty, a physician from Leyden, settled in England in 1740. Ten years later he published at the Hague his bi-monthly *Journal Britannique*, which contained accounts in French of the principal books published in England. To this *Journal* and its reputation, he owed his appointment as under-librarian of the British Museum, at its first institution in 1753, and his appointment in 1772 as principal librarian.

appear in England, Scotland, Ireland, and America. This
Review may be distinguished as the first to include American books regularly. The eighty-eight pages of each number were occupied with fifty or more of reviews, ten or
twelve of monthly catalogue, ten of the theatre, and at
the end seven or eight of public affairs (a kind of continuation of Murray's annual *London Mercury* of 1780-
3). Moreover, there were valuable memoirs of famous
authors among the occasional features. Important contributors were Dr. John Whitaker, the historian of Manchester, Dr. John Moore, Sir John Leslie, William
Godwin, and William Roberts, who later published the
Looker-On. Again Stuart's personal antipathies operated
against the success of his project. He began a war with
his Scotch enemies, Blair, Robertson, and Gibbon. Moreover, he was not easy for the publisher to deal with; so
Murray himself soon relieved Stuart of the editorial
duties, and conducted the *Review* until his death in 1793.
It was carried on by his son, John Murray II, until 1796,
when it was incorporated with the *Analytical Review*,
which had been begun pretentiously in 1788.

Thomas Christie, a contributor to the *Gentleman's
Magazine* and a personal friend of John Nichols, became the first conductor of the *Analytical Review*. It was
a heavy quarterly of 128 pages, founded by Joseph Johnson, a Radical publisher, who issued the works of
Priestly, Tooke, Holcroft, and Mary Wollstonecraft.[1]
Not without reason did the *Anti-Jacobin Review* satirize
it in 1798, the year before its decease. Christie wrote the
preface and many of the articles. His interest in literature
and extensive reading of foreign journals, his classical,
theological, and philosophical leanings, all contributed
to his ability as an editor and author. Each number of the
Analytical consisted of from forty to seventy-five notices

[1] See Frank A. Mumby, *The Romance of Bookselling*, Boston 1911.

of books, varying in length from a long essay to a short paragraph, and followed by a few pages of "literary intelligence." An obvious attempt was made to comment in some way on every important book published, in imitation of the *Monthly Review*. The reviews followed what Christie called an "analytical plan." Lamb's *Rosamund Gray*, Disraeli's "romances," Bowles's poems, *Goetz von Berlichingen* in Scott's translation, Southey's *Joan of Arc*, Lewis's *Love of Gain*, Glover's *Athenaid*, and Campbell's *Pleasures of Hope*, were among the works upon which the "plan" was tried. It has been noticed that the *Analytical* reflected the romantic or sentimental drift of literature during the 1790's better than any other periodical; in particular, it may be remarked with some certainty that this *Review* did more than any of its contemporaries to sentimentalize the writing about external nature. Especially good examples of this progressive tendency may be seen in the long and appreciative articles on the "picturesque" studies of William Gilpin, and the discerning treatments of Wordsworth's *Evening Walk* and *Descriptive Sketches*.[1]

[1] Hundreds of references could be given, if space permitted, to show how the magazines and reviews of the second half of the eighteenth century reflected the public interest in Asiatic researches, British antiquities, Norse mythology, and other romantic concerns.

The following titles and quotations give a fair idea of the hundreds of Ossianic poems to be found in the periodical press: The *London Mag.*, IV (1785), 33, published "Selma, An Imitation of Ossian;" the *General Mag.*, II (June 1798), 32 had "Colna-Dona: a Poem;" the *County Mag.*, (September 1798) "Conlath and Cuthona;" the *Edinburgh Mag.*, VII (1788) 386 ff., "The Battle of Brabala;" the *General Mag.*, III (November 1789), 487 ff., "Cathlin of Clutha;" the *Town and Country Mag.*, XVIII (February 1796), 84-87, "Cathlava, an Erse Poem"; the *Lady's Magazine*, XXXVII (November 1796), 517 ff., a ballad from Ossian with twenty-nine stanzas, the first of which is, "Fair Moina sat on Tara's Height." See also *Gentleman's Mag.*, LV (March 1785), 198. The *Crit. Rev.*, 2nd Ser., XXXIV (February 1802), 164-170, quoted at length from Prof. Richardson's "Maid of Lochlin, a Lyrical Drama."

From 1784 the magazines and reviews were filled with *Werther* imitations, criticisms and translations. The following references, taken at random, indicate the periodical interest in "Wertherism"—*Gentleman's Magazine*, LV, 307, 385, 813; *Hibernian Magazine* 1785, 492; *Westminster*

The *Analytical Review*, because of its forward-looking tendency in politics and literature, is unquestionably one of the most important periodical sources for students of the late eighteenth century. Christie continued to edit the *Review* until his death in 1796. Arthur Aikin, afterwards the editor of the *Annual Review*, was one of the important later contributors. Among other things he wrote the article on Southey's *Joan of Arc*. The *Analytical* continued to be, in its last years, a faithful imitator of the *Monthly*, with its longer reviews followed by twenty or more short notices. It concluded as a 110-page monthly publication with little letterpress of literary importance.

Generously granting literature a place after politics and religion, the *British Critic*, begun in May 1793, was from the first an instrument of the Tory and High Church faction, and a real successor of the *Critical Review*. Although the founders of this periodical expressed a desire "to obtain criticisms from the most eminent persons in every field," the reviewer was in reality a counsel constantly retained by the Crown and the Establishment to defend these from the misrepresentation and calumny of writers who belonged to the Opposition—to call for "more common efforts in defense of British principles and British happiness." The Reverend William Beloe and Archdeacon Robert Nares were the joint-editors of the first series of forty-two volumes, which came to an end in 1813. T. F. Middleton, W. R. Lyall, and others conducted it until June 1825. At the end of the next year it was united with the *Quarterly Theological Review*, and published until 1843 as the *British Critic, Quarterly Theological Review and Ecclesiastical Record* under the

Magazine, XIII, 383; *European Magazine*, X, 214, 379; *English Review*, VII, 297; *Critical Review*, LXI, 357; *Edinburgh Mag.*, III, 370; *Monthly Review*, LXXX, 464; *Town and Country Mag.*, XXI, 186; *Bee*, I (April 13, 1791), 230.

direction of Edward Smedley, J. S. Brown, and John Henry Newman.

From the first, the *British Critic* consisted of about twenty-five rather short reviews occupying one hundred pages, a "British Catalogue" of five pages, and eight pages or less of brief notices. Numbers appeared monthly. Reviews of Steeven's *Shakespeare*, Burns's *Poems*, D'Israeli's *Curiosities of Literature*, and, in 1799, a favorable consideration of the *Lyrical Ballads*, are representative of its longer articles. To later numbers, Henry Nelson Coleridge contributed important critical appreciations of Crabbe and of his uncle, Samuel Taylor Coleridge. By the end of the century the "British Catalogue" had been increased to twenty-two pages, with only three pages of foreign books, while the main part of the *Review* consisted of twelve articles in seventy pages. The tendency to longer critical articles is significant, in view of later developments in periodical criticism. It cannot be said, however, that this defender of Church and Crown contains much valuable literary criticism. Time has proved that such predilections and reservations as the *British Critic* represented seldom result in enduring literary verdicts.

The *Monthly Epitome and Catalogue of New Publications* (1797-1802) was made up entirely of quotations from books. It is notable because no opinion was expressed. In fact, it was much like the earliest abstract-serials. Its aim was to present the reader with a sample of the author's work, and to allow him to judge its merit. "Our readers their own reviewers," expresses the idea of the projectors. Before the close of the century, the *Monthly Epitome* had thus presented to its public Tooke's *Diversions of Purley*, Moore's edition of Smollett's *Works*, Morritt's *Vindication of Homer*, Roger's "Epistle to a Friend," Southey's *Poems* of 1798, and, in two such "reviews," the poems of Wordsworth. In 1798, the *Lyrical Ballads* "with a few other poems" was noticed, with long quotations from the "Advertisement," "Lines Left upon a Seat in a Yew Tree," and "The Convict." In 1800, the *Lyrical Ballads, Vol. II* (really *Lyrical Ballads and Other Poems*) was represented by excerpts from "Lines Written in Germany," "The Reverie of Poor Susan," "Rural Architecture," and "The Old Cumberland Beggar." The *Monthly Epitome* was continued under a slightly different title, 1802-4, and then as the *Literary Magazine*, 1805-6.

The *Anti-Jacobin Review and Magazine, or Monthly Political and Literary Censor* (1798-1821), edited by John Richards Green, alias "John Gifford," was primarily a corrective organ, as its descriptive sub-title indicates; and therefore its service to literature was slight. Attacks on Holcroft, Godwin, and Mary Wollstonecraft implied its connection with the Tories and the Church. In fact, it continued in a less arresting way the opposition to liberal pens begun by the brilliant *Anti-Jacobin; or, Weekly Examiner* of 1797. In the first few years, Jonathan Boucher, divine and lexicographer, Samuel Henshall, an Oxford philologist, Robert Bisset, biographer and editor of the *Historical Magazine*, Richard Polwhele, a miscellaneous writer, William Heath, and Green himself, wrote nearly all the critical articles.[1] James Mill, the utilitarian, and John Horne Tooke handled works of a non-literary nature. The editor himself reviewed Bowles's poems, Charles Lloyd's work, German literature, and the poetry of many writers now well forgotten; Mary Wollstonecraft, Godwin, Holcroft, Charlotte Smith, and Arthur Murphy were consigned to the tender mercies of Bisset; Polwhele reviewed Scott's translation

[1] The names of contributors are indicated in the office set, now possessed by the British Museum.

of *Goetz von Berlichingen*, and the poems of Anna Seward, and viciously attacked Southey for his *Joan of Arc*; Boucher appreciated Hannah More; finally, William Lisle Bowles seems to have written one criticism—that of Polwhele's poems. Polwhele was the best of the critics, who, on the whole, were a poor lot. From the first, the *Anti-Jacobin Review* was the assailant of the "Lake School" (Coleridge, Southey, Lloyd, and Lamb, to whom it first gave this name), carrying on the campaign of detraction begun by the *Anti-Jacobin and Weekly Examiner*.[1]

If one wishes to learn at once the strength and weakness of the Reviews of the eighteenth century, he can do no better than to read the prospectus of the *New London Review; or Monthly Report of Authors and Books*, an ephemeral publication of 1799-1800. The first paragraph quoted below illustrates the critical spirit of the time at its best; the last paragraph reveals the characteristic weakness of periodical reviews of the eighteenth century.

It is not intended to make this Work a vehicle either of unqualified censure or applause . . . rather to point out what deserves praise, than industriously to search for what may incur blame. The Plan is suggested, and will be executed in the conviction, that few performances are wholly destitute of merit; that it is more useful to disclose latent excellence, than to exaggerate common faults; that the public taste suffers less from inaccurate writing, than from illiberal criticism; and that the vindication of literature is often but a pompous pretext for indulging invidious prejudice and petulant dogmatism.

The works to be noticed in *The New London Review* will receive that degree of consideration which they shall severally merit either by their magnitude or their utility. Attention will be given to each, in proportion to the labour it has occasioned, the excellence of the object at which it aims, and the likelihood of the means adopted for accomplishing it. Such, however, as have cost less pains, are on an inferior scale, more in a style of mediocrity, or betray a structure less lofty,

[1] Compare William Haller, *Early Life of Robert Southey*, N. Y. 1917, pp. 268-9.

ornamental, and finished, and occupy none of the higher walks of genius and taste, must be ranked with the common-place of the month, and be content, as in other Reviews, with such brief notice as the Catalogue admits.

Though no arrogance will be indulged in this Publication, whatever disturbs the public harmony, insults legal authority, outrages the best regards of the heart, invalidates the radical obligations of morality, attacks the vital springs and established functions of piety, or in any respect clashes with the sacred forms of decency, however witty, elegant, and well written, can be noticed only in terms of severe and unequivocal reprehension.

The beginning of the nineteenth century found the Review, i. e., a serial made up of articles purporting to be criticisms of books, existing as a distinct periodical type beside the more common Magazine. It had been developed from the abstract-serial of the seventeenth century, by a slow and regular evolution. The steps in this development are perceptible and easy to trace; and to show them clearly has been one of the main purposes of the author in the preceding pages. Denis de Sallo's personal habit of digest and epitome, which he gave readers of his *Journal des Sçavans* the benefit of, led to the epitomizing of books for busy readers—the abstract of the seventeenth century. The "author" of the *Universal Historical Bibliotheque* of 1687 decided to indicate "the quality of the author if known." The three fictitious critics of the *Mercurius Eruditorum* in 1691 selected for critical discussion only "what is most remarkable for beauty and defects in what comes out." Dunton's Athenian Society answered, in the *Mercury*, questions about the merits of authors, while La Crose marked out in his *History of Learning*, by use of italics, the "places best writ of every author." By 1693 the jog-trot summary of a book had evolved into an article of five or six pages—three pages of interpretative discussion followed by three more of abstract—as illustrated in Dunton's *Compleat Library*.

La Roche advanced the work of La Crose and Dunton by perceptible degrees, and his *Memoirs of Literature, New Memoirs of Literature*, and *Literary Journal*, between 1710 and 1730, contained long "reviews," much like those in the later *Monthly*. Finally, in the *Monthly* and *Critical*, in the *London Review* and *Analytical*, we may trace the beginnings of those characteristics which are now usually associated with the *Edinburgh Review* of 1802 and the *Quarterly* of 1809—the partisan bias, the vituperation, the dogmatism, the judicial tone, the air of omniscience and finality. Gradually, the abstract of a book in 1665 has become in 1800 a critical article about the author or the subject of the book.

Although much of criticism developed quite apart from periodical literature, and even though much critical writing has been since the seventeenth century an ingredient of other kinds of serials, yet the Review must be regarded by far the most important agent for the development of literary criticism in English before 1800. By that time it had little to do with creative literature, in one sense; but in another sense each of its articles was an original work, embodying of course more or less of compend or quotation from the book reviewed. It remained for the nineteenth century, with the critical writing of Jeffrey, Scott, Hazlitt, Macaulay, Carlyle, Lamb, and a hundred others, to elevate the substantial Review to a position of foremost literary importance and influence. That the two supreme examples of the type appeared within the first decade of the nineteenth century, indicated that the pioneer work had been well done. The reviewers of the *Edinburgh* and *Quarterly* have their fame or infamy; La Crose, Dunton, and La Roche, the pioneers, as well as most of the eighteenth-century reviewers, are now too generally forgotten.

VIII

THE *EDINBURGH, QUARTERLY,* AND *WESTMINSTER* REVIEWS[1]

In two ways the Review of the nineteenth century differed from earlier periodicals of the same type—it was comparatively free from the bookseller's influence, and it was affected as never before by political partisanship. John Dunton first made periodical criticism an adjunct of the book-selling and publishing business; he was the pioneer in comprehending and utilizing the advertising possibilities of early periodic publications to further the sale of books. Dunton frequently issued elaborate "reviews" before the books themselves were published. His *Compleat Library* of 1692 was an advertising medium for his own wares, just as his *Athenian Mercury* had been for some months before this.[2] It cannot be denied that in the century which followed, trade interests controlled to a large degree the reviewing of books in the columns of periodicals. The *Monthly* and the *Critical Reviews* lacked the independence of the later *Edinburgh* and *Quarterly.*

As for party politics in criticism, it does not appear that such an element was original with the nineteenth century. From early in the seventeenth century, politics and the press had enjoyed a sort of illicit connection. News writers in the reigns of Queen Elizabeth and James I were in

---

[1] The multitude of periodical enterprises in the nineteenth century makes it impossible, in a sketch of this sort, to attempt anything like a comprehensive treatment; and all that may be hoped for in the following pages is an outline of the main developments among reviews, magazines, and other literary periodicals during the last one hundred and thirty years.

[2] See R. P. McCutcheon, "John Dunton's Connection with Book Reviewing," *Studies in Philology,* XXV, 3 (July 1928), 346-361.

the employ of ministers of state; and political leaders
were quick to avail themselves of each new type of publication, that they might employ its influence on the
public mind. "Corantos" and "Occurrences" and "Intelli-
gencers" were, in the seventeenth century, the vehicles of
official journalism; and when the turn of the century
brought the newspaper into prominence, at the same time
revealing the division of political adherents into Whigs
and Tories, Tutchin's *Observator*, the *Flying Post*, the
British Gazetteer, and many another organ flourished in
support of the former party; while side by side with
them developed newspapers like the *Rehearsal*, the *Post
Boy*, the *Evening Post*, the *Weekly Packet*, and Mist's
Weekly Journal, issued in Tory interests.

No division of the press was entirely free from partisan influence. Even the essay sheet, the pervasive and
subtle leavener of public opinion, temperately aired Whig
or Tory views. Although the *Tatler* and *Spectator* and
Guardian had rather pale political complexions, the *Englishman* of Steele, the *Examiner* of Bolingbroke and
Swift, and the *Whig Examiner*, which absorbed Addison's energy during the period of its life, demonstrated
the partisan value of this form of periodical. In the two
hundred examples of the essay serial type which appeared
in the eighteenth century, the majority were probably
designed to exert some political influence. But at best the
essay sheet was an inconsequential force beside the daily
and weekly newspaper press, which developed enormous
power before 1800. The *Morning Post* of Daniel Stuart,
the *Morning Herald* of "Rolliad" fame, the *Morning
Chronicle* of James Perry, the *Sun*, the *Courier*, and the
Times of the Walters, father and son, and their noted
editor, Barnes, are perhaps the most important; while the
swarms of earlier, or less powerful and shorter-lived organs, aided here a demagogue, there a minister, to per-

petuate political prejudice or to convert apathy into heated partisanship.

After 1800, political influence in periodical literature became even more powerful. The Tories seem to have secured the preponderance of influence in the daily press; the other party had more than its share in the numbers and weight of the weekly newspapers, both in and out of London. In the "provincial" publications lay the real strength of the Whig and Radical press in the early nineteenth century. The tart *Anti-Jacobin*, the scurrilous *John Bull*, and *The Age*—except for these, the Tories had few champions in the weekly press. Opposed to them were not only the provincial press, but such London papers as the *Weekly Dispatch* of Harmer, Cobbett's *Weekly Register*, the *Atlas* of the Benthamites, the *Spectator* initiated by Joseph Hume and others, and most notable of all, the liberal *Examiner* of John and Leigh Hunt, rightly said to have opened a new epoch in journalism. Many of the weeklies belonged to that great army of journals known as the "unstamped press," which rebelled against the "taxes on knowledge" and did so much to free the newspaper from its shackles. Outside London, some six hundred "provincial" weeklies were published before 1850.[1] Pitt's manipulation of the early provincial press in the eighteenth century for his own ends is an interesting chapter in the history of journalism. Weeklies, like dailies, were not always consistent partisans. A change of editor or owner frequently brought a change of political face. But there is no disputing their influence on the English public in the days when reform bills, chartism, and agitation for repeal of the Corn Laws held general attention.

Politics were not confined to the newspaper press. The *Gentleman's Magazine* had published in the eighteenth

[1] H. R. Fox Bourne, *English Newspapers*, London 1887, ii, 133-135.

century the so-called "Debates in the Senate of Lilliput," reports of Parliamentary debates, in which the star "reporter," Samuel Johnson, took good care the Whigs should not have the best of it. In later years, the *Anti-Jacobin Review and Magazine* carried on monthly Tory defense in the spirit of its more brilliant weekly namesake. After its establishment, *Blackwood's*, by its force and startling individuality, easily took first place among Tory monthlies; the *London Magazine*, virtually the organ of the "Cockney School," *Fraser's*, a London "Maga," and the liberal Tait's *Edinburgh Magazine* were not far below *Blackwood's* in partisan effect. Yet the influence of the magazines, great indeed, was probably less than that of the Reviews. These were the crowning productions of a long century of development in the history of periodicals. Of the liberal *Monthly* or the conservative *Critical*, little further need be said; but the Whiggish *Edinburgh*, the Tory *Quarterly*, and the Radical *Westminster* were avowedly party organs, and their prodigious influence was due largely to the intelligent and rapidly increasing reading public to which they appealed. If, as has been wisely pointed out, these great Reviews molded the literary taste of England as the Academy directed that of France, their political influence was even more potent. Until 1855, stamp taxes limited the power of the newspaper press. But in the first half of the nineteenth century, the substantial quarterlies influenced the three factions which existed in English political thought with immediate and significant results.

In any study of politics and the English press, certain marked tendencies are observed. In the first place, those who wished to oppose the king or attack the government had a ready weapon. In spite of licensing acts and stamp taxes, they used it. And with all their severe repressions and punishments, kings and kings' ministers early learned

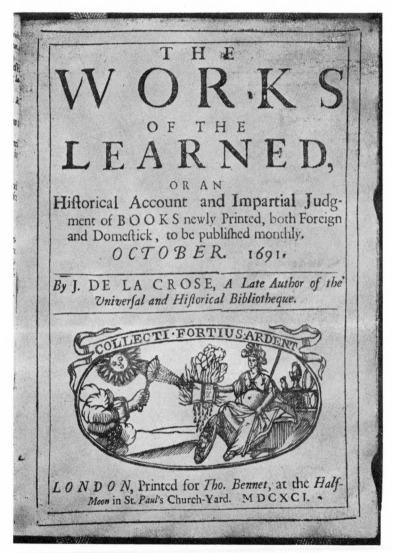

THE
WOR·KS
OF THE
LEARNED,
OR AN

Hiſtorical Account and Impartial Judgment of B O O K S newly Printed, both Foreign and Domeſtick, to be publiſhed monthly.
OCTOBER. 1691.

By J. DE LA CROSE, *A Late Author of the Univerſal and Hiſtorical Bibliotheque.*

COLLECTI·FORTIUS·ARDENT

LONDON, Printed for *Tho. Bennet*, at the *Half-Moon* in St. *Paul's* Church-Yard. MDCXCI.

AN IMPORTANT ANCESTOR OF THE MODERN REVIEW

that the only effective weapon for fighting the press was the press itself. So fire was fought with fire. So, also, for two centuries Tories and conservatives were, in a manner, on the defensive. L'Estrange's *Observator*, designed "to encounter faction and vindicate the government," the distinctly ministerial *Examiner* of Bolingbroke, the Whiggish *Test* of Murphy, offset by the *Con-Test* of Sir Philip Francis, the Tory *Critical Review* rivaling the Whiggish *Monthly*—these are a few notable examples of the deliberate use of English periodicals to oppose those of an attacking party. Thus, it was in a world long accustomed to political warfare, with attacks and counter-attacks carried on in every form of newspaper and periodical, that the two most pretentious organs of this kind, the *Edinburgh* and *Quarterly Reviews*, appeared in the first decade of the nineteenth century.

The *Edinburgh Review* (1802-1929) was not planned primarily as a party organ, although the politics of its youthful projectors were decidedly Whiggish. In the minds of its founders—Sydney Smith, Francis Jeffrey, and Francis Horner (and later, Henry Brougham), all of whom were between the ages of twenty-three and thirty-one—wit and fun were the first *desiderata*.[1] The idea was not to avoid politics altogether, but to allow them to be handled by the partisans of either camp, as long as they could provide amusement and information

[1] Lockhart, *Life of Scott*, i, 502.
Horner, in his journal for Sept. 30, 1802 (Horner, L., *Memoirs and Correspondence of Francis Horner*, Lon. 1843, i, 209) says, "This Review was concocted, about the end of last winter, between Jeffrey, Sydney Smith, and myself. The plan was immediately communicated to Murray, Allen, and Hamilton; Brown, Brougham, and the two Thomsons, have gradually been made parties." The generally accepted statement by Sydney Smith (*Memoir of the Reverend Sydney Smith*, N. Y. 1855, p. 31) was his recollection after half a century. See L. E. Gates, *Essays of Francis Jeffrey*, Bos., 1894, *Cambridge History of English Literature*, xii, 143; and J. L. Haney, *Early Reviews of English Poets*, Phil., 1904, xxiv, for accounts of the origin, based on Smith's untrustworthy memories.

for the reader.[1] But it was not long before the seductive tendency toward "witty whiggery" was leading them away from their original plan.

Sydney Smith supervised the publication of the first *Edinburgh*, with the assistance of Francis Horner. Afterwards, Jeffrey was formally appointed editor[2] and conducted the review until 1829. Sydney Smith spoke of the periodical to Constable as "independent," but Jeffrey seems to have tended more and more away from independent principles. On this point, the fall of the Whig government in 1807 caused a change in the views of his colleagues also. Horner, with his more serious turn of mind, saw the danger, and warned Jeffrey more than once against party politics in the articles he published.[3] But in spite of his warnings, the *Edinburgh*, which had commenced on principles of neutrality, became steadily more pronounced in its advocacy of party doctrines,[4] although wide variations of opinion were to be found in the Whig ranks on such questions as Spanish affairs, Catholic Emancipation, and Parliamentary and other reforms. In the early years, Scott and other Tories contributed articles on non-political themes. But the increasing boldness of other writers on national affairs offended this section of its readers and contributors. Flushed by success, the *Edinburgh* reviewers overstepped the bounds of moderation. Inevitable results were the estrangement of readers and that defensive activity of the Tories which led to the establishment of the *Quarterly Review*. When Horner wrote apprehensively to J. A. Murray, December 23,

[1] See Lockhart, *Life of Scott*, i, 383; ii, 157; Thomas Constable, *Archibald Constable and His Literary Correspondents*, Edinburgh 1873, i, 51; and *Quarterly Review*, XCI, 123-126.

[2] Possibly not until after the third number. (See Joline, *A Famous Reviewer*, N. Y. 1860, p. 108.)

[3] *Memoirs of Francis Horner*, London 1843, i, 514.

[4] C. C. Southey, *Life of Robert Southey*, London 1850, iii, 181. See also *Memoir of William Taylor*, London 1843, ii, 264; and Horner, *op. cit.* i, 523, 516, 493.

1809, that the *Edinburgh Review* had gone too far into merely personal and party considerations "in which the Review never engages without a loss of its proper character and usefulness,"[1] the mischief had been done. As a matter of fact, the idea of a rival periodical had been in the air for several years before the *Quarterly Review* appeared to dispute the political and critical influence of the *Edinburgh*.

Of Francis Jeffrey, the editor of the *Edinburgh Review* until 1829, much has been written and little may be added here. More than is usual with editors, he contributed essays to his *Review*, on subjects as various as Byron's poetry, jurisprudence, politics, and travels in Egypt. He wrote in October 1802 the first review in the first number, and contributed his last article in 1840.[2] For the most part, however, his interests were literary, and the burden of his essays are reviews of such writers as Swift, Goethe, Alfieri, Southey, Cowper, Campbell, Scott, Crabbe, Wordsworth, Miss Edgeworth, and Washington Irving. Jeffrey's attitude toward literature is now well understood—suggested in his early review of Southey's *Thalaba*: "Poetry has this much, at least, in common with religion, that its standards were fixed long ago, by certain inspired writers, whose authority it is no longer lawful to call in question."[3] With a dogmatism and an obstinacy worthy of a better cause, he valiantly defended his pseudo-classical citadel, long after the battalions of romantics had conquered the field. His was not the classicism of Dryden and Pope, but the degenerate classicism, which found in Campbell and Rogers and Crabbe virtues not recognized by most nineteenth-century critics. For him, there were "only two kinds of great

[1] Horner, *op. cit.*, ii, 14-15.
[2] See introduction to *Contributions to the Edinburgh Review*, by Francis Jeffrey, London 1844, pp. x-xi.
[3] *Edinburgh Review*, I (October 1802), p. 63.

poetry: the pathetic and the sublime." Later *Edinburgh* reviewers, and many of his contemporaries, did not sympathize with Jeffrey's critical position; but he unquestionably put his stamp upon the *Review* for a quarter of a century. The surprising result was that while less liberal in politics, the rival *Quarterly Review* appears today to have been, in its criticism of contemporary literary works, far more hospitable to novelty.

The *Edinburgh Review* from the start wisely abandoned the idea of noticing all the productions of the press. It was hoped it would be "distinguished, rather for the selection, than for the number, of its articles."[1] This, it must be pointed out with care, was a deliberate departure from the practice of the *Monthly* and *Critical Reviews*. The new plan seems to have been a fortunate one. In ten years the *Edinburgh's* circulation had grown to 10,000 copies; by 1818 it had reached its peak of 14,000. The first number consisted of twenty-nine articles in 252 pages. The system adopted in the enthusiasm of the beginning —"all gentlemen and no pay"—was abandoned, after the first two numbers, for the wiser one of generous stipends to editor and contributors. Rapidly, the *Edinburgh* assumed a foremost place among the organs of literary criticism. For although the judgments of Jeffrey and other reviewers, who arrogated to themselves "an authority hardly less than pontifical," have not always been confirmed by the judgments of posterity, on the other hand, they have in many cases been fully vindicated. During the first quarter-century, however, in spite of general impressions, it must be admitted that the rival *Quarterly* contained far more individual criticisms that have stood the test of time.

As the first editor, Jeffrey gathered about him an excellent group of contributors. Walter Scott was an im-

[1] See Advertisement to the first number, October 1802.

portant reviewer, until, in 1808, he became interested in the plans for a rival organ. Between 1802 and 1829, reviews were secured from the pens of Thomas Brown, James Mackintosh, Peter Elmsley, Thomas Campbell, William Hazlitt, John Playfair, George Ellis, T. R. Malthus, Henry Hallam, Thomas Jefferson Hogg, Payne Knight, Francis Palgrave, Thomas Arnold, T. B. Macaulay, and Thomas Carlyle.[1] Macvey Napier (originally Napier Macvey), who had been a contributor to the *Edinburgh* since 1805, in 1829 took the editorial chair, when Jeffrey retired to become Dean of the Faculty of Advocates. Napier brought to his new task the experience acquired as general editor of a supplement of the sixth edition of the *Encyclopedia Britannica*, and carried on the work of Jeffrey with less dogmatism and quite as much energy. In 1847 William Empson succeeded him, to be followed by George Cornewall Lewis, in 1852. Lewis conducted the *Review* for three years, during which he contributed eighteen articles, then quitted the editorial chair when he succeeded to the baronetcy of his father, Sir Thomas Frankland Lewis. For the next forty years Henry Reeve took charge of the *Review*, after fifteen spent in guiding the foreign policy of the *Times*. In 1865 he edited the *Greville Memoirs*, for which he is more likely to be remembered today. It is probable that his long connection with the *Review* changed the character of the periodical somewhat, and made it less important as a medium of literary criticism. When, in 1895, Arthur R. D. Elliot took it over, it had a lower standing as a critical periodical, whatever its political merits.[2]

In July 1912, Harold Cox took the helm of the *Edin-*

[1] W. A. Copinger, *The Authorship of the First Hundred Numbers of the Edinburgh Review*, Manchester 1895. See also P. L. Carver, "Hazlitt's Contributions to the *Edinburgh Review*," *Review of English Studies*, IV, 375-393.

[2] Elliot was the author of the excellent chapter on magazines and reviews in the *Cambridge History of English Literature*, xii, 140-163.

burgh and guided its policy until its demise in October 1929. Anonymity, that time-honored cloak of critical authorship, was cast aside at the beginning of his editorship. The names of writers enticed readers, who had been obliged, before 1912, to be content with the frequently lesser attraction of the subject. Edmund Gosse, Walter de la Mare, E. S. Roscoe, Orlo Williams, Lytton Strachey, Gilbert Murray, A. Quiller-Couch, W. P. James, John Drinkwater, Lord Ernle, J. St. Loe Strachey, and Michael Sadleir, are some of the familiar and alluring names that have caused readers to pick up the blue-covered quarterly with eagerness and read it with pleasure. After 1924, William Rountree conducted a department of short criticisms at the end of the *Review*, called "Recently Published Books."

It is worth observing once more that the *Edinburgh Review* gave a new turn to the periodicals of this type, in that, unlike its predecessors, the *Monthly* and *Critical*, it made no pretense of reviewing all the books published. On the contrary, it discussed only those which could be made the texts of articles on subjects of current interest. Rigidly selective in its method, therefore, the *Edinburgh* was the first to acquire certain characteristics which are noticed in all the later reviews of the nineteenth century. Macaulay writing on Milton, or Jeffrey reviewing "Alison on Taste," seized the opportunity to present their own views of the general subject rather than their reactions on the methods or materials of the author. Pursuing this method, inaugurated more than a century and a quarter ago, the *Edinburgh Review* was never seriously rivaled, except by the conservative *Quarterly Review*. It is remarkable that during its entire career the *Edinburgh* was associated with the house of Longman,[1] just as the

---

[1] Published in 1809 by Archibald Constable and Co. of Edinburgh, it was sold from the first by the Longmans in London. After the financial disaster of Constable in 1826, the Longmans took over the *Review*.

Quarterly has always been a property of the house of Murray. It is noticeable that in its later years the *Edinburgh*, however, was less of a literary organ than its great rival.

The success of the *Edinburgh Review* spelled the failure of other publishing enterprises. Among these was the *Annual Review* of Arthur Aikin, a chemist and writer on scientific subjects, whose interests naturally were reflected in this periodical. The *Annual* (1803-1808) was very much of a family affair, for it was contributed to by Aikin's father, the Reverend John Aikin, his aunt, Mrs. Barbauld, and his sister Lucy, the biographer of Addison and of her father. Mrs. Barbauld, with Robert Southey and William Taylor of Norwich, gave the *Review* whatever scanty literary values it has today. The *Annual Review*, the *Eclectic Review* (1805-1868), a sectarian religious organ of the Dissenters, and several other periodicals of the type were close imitators of the *Edinburgh*.

The prestige of the *Edinburgh Review* and the influence of its "invisible infallibles" were ineffectively challenged in 1809 by the seventy-seven-year-old Richard Cumberland and his *London Review*, a periodical erected by Tipper, the bookseller—a premature protest against the critical cowardice of anonymity. Hewson Clarke was a partner, and Henry Crabb Robinson had a hand in "getting up" this original enterprise, as he relates in his *Diary*.[1] The *London Review* is distinguished by the fact that each contributor put his name to his review. It was a courageous design, in an age of irresponsible criticism, and one worthy of a better fate than that which overtook it. Except for La Crose's voluntary assumption of responsibility at the beginning of the eighteenth century, there is no other example of such critical frankness in periodicals before the middle of the nineteenth century.

[1] *Diary, Reminiscences, and Correspondence of Henry Crabb Robinson,* ed. Thomas Sadler, London 1869, i, 295.

Cumberland expresses his convictions rather testily in his Introductory Address:

The Man, who in the genuine spirit of criticism impartially distributes praise or blame to the work he reviews, has no more need to hide his name than the tradesman has, who records himself over his shop-door; for whom has he to fear, or of what to be ashamed? Learning has no truer friend; genius no better counsellor, no safer guide.

Every one must confess, that there is a dangerous temptation, an unmanly security, an unfair advantage in concealment: why then should any man, who seeks not to injure but to benefit his contemporaries, resort to it? . . . a piece of crape may be a convenient mask for a highwayman; but a man, that goes upon an honest errand, does not want it and will disdain to wear it.

It sounds very reasonable, as we read it today, but it did not spell success in 1809. Crabb Robinson wrote one review—that of Wordsworth's Cintra pamphlet. James and Horace Smith, Horace Twiss, G. W. Crowe, and Poet-Laureate Henry Pye, other contributors to this original undertaking, did not give it the brilliance to compete with the *Edinburgh* and *Quarterly*, whose writers "carried on their operations under casemates or by ambuscade." In truth, the *London* was cursed with "original dulness."[1]

If Cumberland and his *London Review* were anticipating what became the almost universal practice of reviewers in the twentieth century, it can have given him little satisfaction. Apparently readers did not yet wish to have the veil of anonymity drawn aside. The bold undertaking languished, and was finally given up, after four half-crown, quarterly numbers had been published. Copies of the Review are now rare curiosities—reminders of a day when men had more faith in the mysterious oracle than in the known critic.[2]

[1] Introductory address of *London Review*. See also Moore, *Works of Lord Byron*, Murray Ed., ix, 62 n.

[2] In 1806, William Nicholson, who was also (1791-1815) the editor of the *Journal of Natural Philosophy*, advertised the *General Review of*

For the origin of the *Quarterly Review* (1809 ff.) three factors may be regarded as responsible—the Administration, represented by George and Stratford Canning; the enterprising and far-sighted young publisher, John Murray (second of the name) ; the reaction of men like Scott and Southey from the politics of the *Edinburgh*, and the harsh criticisms of their own works in the columns of this Scottish *Review*. The complicated plans and activities of the group of Tories who founded the *Quarterly* have more to do with politics than literature. Yet, since they involve one of the greatest literary figures of his generation, they are not out of place in a story of this, the oldest existing and most important Review in the history of English periodicals.[1]

It is hard to determine what individual first conceived the plan of a Review to rival the *Edinburgh*. Only two direct claims were made, one by Southey, which may be dismissed, the other by Stratford Canning, the diplomatist, a cousin of George Canning. While walking along Pall Mall one day, early in 1808, Stratford Canning made a plan for a Tory organ, conducted along the lines of the *Edinburgh*.[2] He proposed the idea to George Canning, who referred him, with evident satisfaction, to William Gifford. Stratford Canning declared that the name as well as the idea originated with him and his friends, and that he drew up the sketch of a prospectus. Later he introduced John Murray to William Gifford. This may have been the initial step toward the establishment of the *Quarterly*. Stratford Canning's part in originating this *Review* was at least an important one, for John Murray

---

British and Foreign Literature, as "conducted" by him. The venture was an eighty-six-page monthly periodical of general articles and reviews, with an added "monthly catalogue" of ten pages. A review of the Ossian Committee report, and critical articles on Southey's *Madoc* and James Montgomery's poems, are interesting contributions.

[1] See my *Tory Criticism in the Quarterly Review*, 1809-1853, N. Y. 1918.
[2] S. Lane-Poole, *Life of Stratford Canning*, London 1888, i, 192 ff.

sent him a complimentary copy of the first number on March 12, 1809, and referred to it as "a work which owes its birth to your obliging countenance and introduction of me to Mr. Gifford."[1]

It is possible, however, that Stratford Canning's suggestion was anticipated by a letter which Murray wrote to George Canning as early as September 25, 1807, advising that some means equally popular ought to be adopted to counteract the dangerous tendency of the *Edinburgh*. Murray offered to engage his "arduous exertions to promote its success."[2] As far as we know, Canning did not answer Murray's letter in writing, and it is probable— although it cannot be proved—that in the delay before negotiations were taken up, the plans and suggestions which Stratford Canning and his friends had made were communicated to the minister and to William Gifford. At any rate, it was through Stratford Canning that negotiations were finally opened with Murray. The meeting of Murray and Gifford was in January. It was not until the first of September, evidently, that Canning asked Gifford to take the editorship.[3]

But, during the months before practical steps could be taken, Walter Scott was enlisted in support of the plan. Formerly a prominent contributor to the *Edinburgh*, he had become alienated from the Scottish publication by a severe review of *Marmion* in April 1808, by the general tone of the political articles, by the injudicious remarks of Constable's partner, Hunter, regarding the contract made with Scott for an edition of Swift, and by Constable's treatment of Weber, Scott's amanuensis. Murray

---

[1] Samuel Smiles, *A Publisher and His Friends*, London 1891, i, 152.

[2] Smiles, *op. cit.*, i, 93.

[3] See Gifford's letter to Canning, Smiles, *op. cit.*, ii, 163. For evidence that Murray did not make the first proposal to Gifford—Smiles, *op. cit.*, i, 99. I have not been able to find proof to support the assertion that Scott successfully pressed the editorship upon Gifford (Elliot, A. R. D., *Cambridge History of English Literature*, xii, 150).

had the astuteness to see that Scott's feelings were hurt, and easily secured him for the Tory *Review*. Thus drawn into the *Quarterly* group, Scott soon became the chief figure. He was not the original suggestor of the *Review* "to some of the men in power," as Southey declared.[1] He was more than that. His letters to Gifford, Murray, Ellis, and his brother, Thomas Scott, indicate that his was the guiding hand during the critical period of its infancy. Southey was nearer the truth when he called Scott the "proprietor."[2] The latter's letters of direction, encouragement, and warning to the men most interested, tell the story. Scott was almost the *creator* of the Tory organ. Many years later he referred with satisfaction to the time when he had "the principal share in erecting this *Review* which has been since so prosperous."[3] How important he was to its success is shown clearly by Gifford's letters to him at this time.[4]

It is clear, then, that the outstanding figure in the group of Tory conspirators, in the later months of 1808, was Scott. Once the *Quarterly* was in progress, and the difficulties and dangers of its birth and infancy largely over, he threw the greater part of his valuable energy into other literary channels, believing it would be comparatively easy to keep the *Review* going. Yet until he was sure of its success, he was the leading spirit in editorial councils, the driving personal force behind the project. Although there was plenty of talent among the others engaged in the venture, he alone had the tact and adroitness to carry through an enterprise which required so much delicacy. Murray felt that the defensive power of the Tories in this conflict "with other principles and doc-

---

[1] Warter, John Wood, *Selections from the Letters of Robert Southey,* London 1856, ii, 107.

[2] *Ibid.,* ii, 194.

[3] *Journal of Walter Scott,* Edinburgh 1891, p. 22.

[4] *Familiar Letters of Sir Walter Scott,* Edinburgh 1894, App. I, ii, 399-401.

trines" was undoubted, but without the generalship of
Scott it would have been difficult to have drawn them
into action at this time.[1]

The two great reviews, the *Edinburgh* and the *Quarterly*, had much in common politically in the interests of
the landed aristocracy; they likewise agreed fundamen-
tally on matters of literary criticism. Both depended
largely upon established standards, and uttered their verdicts with the same legalistic and all-knowing finality.
Both agreed that critics were persons eminently fitted by
a natural sensibility, as well as reflection and long experience, to perceive all the beauties that exist and to settle
the relative value of works of literature. "Taste" was
thus regarded as in a measure inherent and to some extent acquired. Both Reviews were generally loyal to Pope,
and in them reviewers occasionally defended classical
principles. Yet they were cautious in literary verdicts as
in political. Neither Review desired any great change
from the established order of things, yet neither came out
with any great partiality to the dying classicism of the
late eighteenth and early nineteenth centuries. And both
were capable of anarchic individualism upon occasion.

But the *Quarterly* was established to oppose the utterances of the northern Whigs. So, on questions of literary merit, appreciably diverse positions were found on
grounds where they were in fundamental agreement. One
reason for the founding of the *Quarterly* was the fact
that Scott, Southey, and other Tories were smarting under
the lash of carping Whiggish criticism. This led inevitably to the expression of critical opinion, the value of
which was modified by political prejudice and favoritism.
One of the most remarkable results of this divergence
from the sacred criteria of the past in search of issues
upon which to defend patrons of Tory favor is mani-

[1] Smiles, *op. cit.*, i, 110.

fested in the more liberal attitude of the *Quarterly* toward novelty, whether it appeared in the method or the material of literary work. A virtual championship of the "Lake School" was the result, although the *Quarterly* always refused to recognize that this term had any value as a name. In defence of Scott and Southey, this countenance of novelty was most often expressed; and often these two were the defenders.

It must be noted that the *Quarterly* was, above all else, the champion of the Established Church, the palladium of privileged aristocracy. The *Edinburgh's* critical articles often contained political aspersions, and Jeffrey frequently formed his judgments on other than literary grounds. But it is true and natural that *Quarterly* reviewers showed a much greater inclination to partiality on matters affecting Church and Crown. Whatever tended to decrease general respect for the established order, the Church, the monarchical form of government, the laws, the King, and the landed aristocracy, was evil. Modified and varied by its applications, this was always the major consideration.

For this reason, the *Quarterly Review*, during the first half of the nineteenth century, earned a reputation for unfairness and vituperation. The abusive and usually unwarranted castigations of Keats, Leigh Hunt, Hazlitt, Lamb, Shelley, Tennyson, Macaulay, Carlyle, Dickens, and Charlotte Brontë owed their virulence to party or religious prejudice. John Wilson Croker, Lockhart, John Taylor Coleridge, H. H. Milman, W. S. Walker, James Russell, William Gifford, and Miss Rigby (afterwards Lady Eastlake) are now known to have been the most relentless of these champions of Church and State. Only Lockhart and Gifford were even remotely qualified to be critics, and they were too frequently blinded by party or personal rancor.

But time has paid well the unjust judges. Croker and Gifford and Lockhart, like Jeffrey, are now remembered, not for their best criticism, but for their worst. As a matter of cold fact, all wrote well on occasion. And the *Quarterly* had other better critics, such as Henry Nelson Coleridge, Henry Taylor, Charles Lamb, Walter Scott, John Sterling, Whitwell Elwin, Francis T. Palgrave, Isaac D'Israeli, George Ellis, Washington Irving, Abraham Hayward, and Robert Southey. Some of them, like Southey, may have erred on the side of mercy, but the major part of their critical writing showed both justice and discernment.[1] The faults of the *Quarterly* reviewers are too much dwelt upon. It should not be forgotten that many of what are now regarded as the commonplaces of modern criticism first appeared in print in the *Quarterly Review* or the *Edinburgh*, in appreciations of Wordsworth, Coleridge, Scott, Byron, Maria Edgeworth, Jane Austen, Crabbe, Lamb, Thomas Moore, Tennyson, Dickens, Thackeray, and Washington Irving. A few wrong sentences hastily given, in the courts of literary criticism, should not be allowed to outweigh many just verdicts.

The story of the first century of prosperity which the *Quarterly Review* enjoyed has been well told in the Centenary articles, and need not be repeated.[2] "Juvenal" Gifford, who had formerly made himself useful to the Tories as editor of the *Anti-Jacobin and Weekly Examiner*, occupied the editorial chair until 1825; John Taylor Coleridge, a nephew of the poet, acted as editor for one full year; Lockhart served in that capacity from 1826 to 1853; Whitwell Elwin then took up the task, resigning it in 1860 to continue the great edition of Pope which

---

[1] Lockhart declared that the *Quarterly* owed its success to Southey, more than to any other single writer. But Southey seldom reviewed works of literature. (*Life of Scott*, ii, 224.)

[2] *Quarterly Review*, April and July, 1909, Nos. 419 and 420.

Croker, who died in 1857, had begun; William Macpherson succeeded him for a period of seven years; William Smith followed between 1867 and 1892; Rowland E. Prothero (now Lord Ernle) conducted the *Review* until 1899, when Sir George Prothero took charge. Upon his death in July 1922, Sir John Murray, head of the famous publishing house, conducted the *Quarterly*, in joint-editorship with C. E. Lawrence. The latter has remained, since Sir John Murray's decease in 1928, joint-editor with Sir John's son, Lt. Col. John Murray.

The second half of the nineteenth century brought to the *Review* not only new editors but many new critics. Some were mere dabblers in literature, like Gladstone and Lady Eastlake. But throughout its long life the *Quarterly* has at no time been without respected names among its contributors of critical reviews. Elwin added to its staff Mark Pattison, Bulwer-Lytton, John Forster, Thackeray, and Harriet Martineau; Macpherson enlisted George Borrow; Smith secured contributions from such new critics as J. Addington Symonds, Matthew Arnold, J. Churton Collins, and Swinburne. At the end of its first century, the *Quarterly* contained literary reviews by Austin Dobson, Bertram Dobell, F. Y. Eccles, Emil Faguet, Alfred Austin, and Sir Sidney Lee. Recent contributors —Lord Ernle, Laurence Binyon, Evelyn Underhill, A. C. Bradley, Abbé Dimnet, S. L. Bensusan, G. M. Fraser, Walter Jerrold, Ernest Weekley, and Horace G. Hutchinson—have assured the continuance of its high standard.

Much space has been given in this sketch of literary periodicals to the two great Reviews, whose unparalleled success and astonishing prestige, even up to our own day, have caused them to overshadow all similar enterprises. They dominated the nineteenth century. Their religious, political, and critical opinions found assent in the minds of thousands of readers; their magisterial finality quieted the doubts of generations. With honest conviction, the English squire told Tennyson's father that the *Quarterly* was "the next book to God's *Bible*." The critical importance of these Reviews waned as scores of more specialized magazines and literary journals entered the field. Their literary values have always been subordinated to those of politics. Yet their influence upon literature has been profound, if not always salutary. Their development of such writers as Scott, Macaulay, and Hazlitt is significant. They have done much to stabilize criticism during the last century. And, almost without exception, it may be said that the scores of English and American Reviews which have appeared since 1802 have been frank imitators of the *Edinburgh* and the *Quarterly*.[1]

In the meantime, antiquarian interest and love of older literature had brought about the establishment in 1820 of the *Retrospective Review*. It was founded by Henry Southern and edited by him alone in the first series, 1820-1826, after which he was assisted, between 1826 and 1828, by Sir Nicholas Harris Nicholas, a barrister and famous antiquary. Charles Wentworth Dilke was for several years one of the *Retrospective's* chief supporters. It was issued as a large periodical of the Review type (176 pages), unique in its make-up. The periodical consisted of critiques written in the same manner as those of the

[1] An evangelical periodical, the *British Review and London Critical Journal*, would scarcely be remembered now, but for the editor's quarrel with Byron. Hostile criticism of the poet's work led to the latter's sardonic retort,

> ....My epical pretensions to the laurel:
> For fear some prudish readers should grow skittish,
> I've bribed my Grandmother's Review—the British.
> 　　　　　　(*Don Juan*, I, ccix)

William Roberts, the editor, seems to have assumed that the charge of bribery was to be taken seriously, for he denounced *Don Juan*, Cantos I and II, in the *Review* in 1819 (No. xxvii), and answered the apparent accusation. Byron replied in his "Letter to My Grandmother's Review," in the *Liberal* 1822. Beyond this well known duel with Byron, there is little of literary interest to recommend the *British Review* to our notice. It was issued 1811-1825.

Quarterly or *Edinburgh*, except that the titles which gave
the pretexts to the various articles were not titles of newly-
published works but rather those of works of merit published in the past. The dates of the volumes reviewed
ranged from 1500 to the eighteenth century, although
they were criticised in the modern manner. The dramas
of Thomas Nash and Shadwell, the works of Thomas
Browne, Heinsius, Du Marsais, or Ben Jonson, or the
"Letter of John Ashwell, 1527," were thus presented to
the public, as if fresh from the press. Southern's preface
to the first volume indicates his original purpose:

> The design of this review of past literature had its origin in the
> decisively modern direction of the reading of the present day—, it is
> an attempt to recall the public from an exclusive attention to new
> books, by making the merit of old ones the subject of critical discussion.
> The interesting form and manner of the present Reviews it is intended
> to preserve; though, from the nature of the work, and from our un-
> feigned horror of either political or personal invective, we shall neither
> pamper the depraved appetites of listless readers, by piquant abuse—
> nor amuse one part of the public, by holding up another to scorn and
> mockery;—at any rate, we shall not be driven to a resource of this
> description through a paucity of interesting matter which we may
> legitimately present to our readers. While the present Reviews are con-
> fined to the books of the day, we have the liberty of ranging over the
> whole extent of modern literature. Criticism, which, when able and
> just, is always pleasing, we shall combine with copious and characteristic
> extracts, analyses, and biographical accounts, so as in some measure to
> supply the dearth of works on the history of literature in our own lan-
> guage; for it is to be lamented, that except the unfinished work of
> Warton, and a few detached Essays, we have no regular history of
> English poetry—and that of the prose writers, their language, style,
> spirit, and character, there exists no account at all.[1]

Comparison of the older writers with the "moderns"
was a common method of Southern and his staff. An ex-

---

[1] Southern has the following note:
"We must not, however, omit to mention, that this department is emi-
nently indebted to the elegant productions of Dr. Drake, his Essays on
Periodical Literature, and other works."

cellent example of their criticism, the following excerpt from a critique on the works of John Dennis contains interesting comment upon critical methods:

The critics of the age of Dennis held, in their claims, a middle course between their predecessors of old time, and their living successors. The men who first exercised the art of criticism, imbued with a deep veneration for the loftiest works of genius, sought to deduce rules from them, which future poets should observe. They did not assume the right of passing individual judgments on their contemporaries—nor did they aim at deciding even abstract questions of taste on their own personal authority—but attempted, by fixing the laws of composition, to mark out the legitimate channels in which the streams of thought, passion, and sentiment, should be bounded through all ages. Their dogmas, therefore, whether they contained more or less of truth, carried with them no extensive weight, were influenced by no personal feelings, excited no personal animosities, but simply appealed, like poetry itself, to those minds which alone could give them sanction. In the first critical days of England—those of the Rymers and the Dennises—the professors of the art began to regard themselves as judges, not merely of the principles of poetry, but of their application to living authors. Then commenced the arrogance on the side of the supervisors, and the impatience and resentment on that of their subjects, which contemporary criticism necessarily inspires. The worst passions of man were brought into exercise in reference to those pure and ennobling themes, which should be sacred from all low contentions of "the ignorant present time." But the battle was, at least, fair and open. The critic still appealed to principles, however fallacious or imperfect, which all the world might examine. His decrees had no weight, independent of his reasons, nor was his name, or his want of one, esteemed of magical virtue. He attacked the poets on equal terms—sometimes, indeed, with the poisoned weapons of derision and personal slander—but always as a foe to subdue, not as a judge to pass sentence on them. Criticism, in our own times, has first assumed the air of "sovereign sway and masterdom" over the regions of fantasy. Its professors enforce not established laws, contend no longer for principles, attack poets no more with chivalrous zeal, as violating the cause of poetic morals, or sinning against the regularities of their art. They pronounce the works, of which they take cognizance, to be good or bad —often without professing to give any reason for their decision—or referring to any standard, more fixed or definite than their own taste, partiality, or prejudice. And the public, without any knowledge of their fitness for their office—without even knowing their names—receive them as the censors of literature, the privileged inspectors of genius! This strange supremacy of criticism, in our own age, gives interest to the investigation of the claims, which the art itself possesses to the respect and gratitude of the people. It is on the whole beneficial to the world, it must either be essential to the awakening of genius—or necessary to direct its exertions—or conductive to the keeping alive and fitly guiding of public admiration and sympathy with the poet's noblest and holiest creations. . . .

One hundred pages of such "retrospective" reviews were followed by another section, "the Historical and Antiquarian Magazine," made up of articles on subjects of historical or antiquarian interest. Another section at the end of the *Review* contained critical notices of contemporary works. The *Retrospective* was advertised as a Review containing "criticisms upon, analyses of, and extracts from curious, valuable, and scarce old books." It was discontinued after 1828, but revived in 1853-54, as a one-hundred-page publication containing some seven or eight "reviews," followed by a section of "Anecdota Literaria." Altogether the *Retrospective* was an original and interesting performance, and deserving of a longer life.

The most important imitator of the *Edinburgh* and *Quarterly* was the *Westminster Review*, whose rise roughly corresponds with the rise of a third party in English politics. It was set up in the spring of 1824 by James Mill, utilitarian philosopher and disciple of Jeremy Bentham, who at the start provided the funds for it. In its earlier years, therefore, the *Westminster* was truly a Benthamite organ. James Mill, who had contributed to the *Edinburgh Review* between 1808 and 1813, helped the *Westminster* to begin its career effectively by writing for the second number an attack on the *Edinburgh* reviewers, whom he characterized as political trimmers. In the fourth number, he attacked the *Quar-*

terly Review for its obstinate conservatism. Having made
plain the political views of the "philosophical radicals,"
its supporters, the *Westminster*, edited by John Bowring
and Henry Southern, continued to serve the purposes of
Bentham and the Mills, James and his son, John Stuart
Mill; and, inspired by the methods of the *Quarterly* and
Edinburgh, its two great precursors, attempted to employ
literary criticism in the service of utilitarian doctrine.

Financial success did not crown the efforts of the earlier
proprietors of the *Westminster Review*, however. In
1828, they were obliged to call on Col. Perronet Thompson for assistance, and to place the *Review* in his hands.
In 1836 it was amalgamated with a new *London Review*,
which had been started the preceding year by Sir William
Molesworth; and it continued its career, without any
great change of political face, as the *London and Westminster Review*. Molesworth, in 1837, transferred the
proprietorship to John Stuart Mill, who, though his official position with the East India Company prevented
his being known as the actual editor, superintended the
work, with assistance from Thomas Falconer and the
Aberdonian, John Robertson.[1] In 1840 Mill transferred
the *Review* to William E. Hickson, who edited it until
1847, but was finally glad to dispose of it for £350 to
John Chapman.

As the *Westminster and Foreign Quarterly Review*, it
became in October 1851 a rejuvenated publication, with
Chapman as editor and proprietor. Chapman gathered
around him able contributors—such men as Froude,
Mark Pattison, and later, Frederic Harrison and Walter
Pater—and brought Mary Ann Evans ("George Eliot")

[1] See Alexander Bain, *Life of James Mill*, London 1882, p. 46 ff.; C. M.
D. Towers, "John Stuart Mill and the London and Westminster Review,"
Atlantic Monthly LXXIX, (January 1892), pp. 57-74; *Autobiography,
of John Stuart Mill*, ed. J. J. Coss, N. Y. 1924, p. 145; *The Philosophical
Radicals of 1832, Comprising the Life of Sir William Molesworth*, Lon-
don 1866.

into notice as his assistant-editor. For two years Miss Evans bore the brunt of the editorial labor, helping to write the prospectus, and herself contributing reviews of Carlyle's *Life of John Sterling* and many other works. The *Review* had by this time become the organ of advanced theological thought, advocating reforms within the Church as well as in Society and the State.[1]

The earlier critical attitude of the *Westminster Review* was unique, although suggested, of course, by the political bias of the *Edinburgh* and *Quarterly* reviewers. Ordinarily, a single number contained ten long reviews, and from six to ten shorter critical notices. When these concerned works of pure literature, such as Scott's *Redgauntlet*, some good critical evaluations appeared, almost invariably biased by political prejudice, and vitiated by the obvious efforts of the reviewers to stimulate the flagging energies of the philosophical radicals. John Stuart Mill's review of the *Poetical Works of S. T. Coleridge*, (1829)[2] presents a good example of their critical weakness. It is one of the few favorable contemporary interpretations of Coleridge's work, and, in the light of nearly a century, one of the most praiseworthy attempts to advance the reputation of the poet. Yet Mill felt that Coleridge's general qualities as poet were exemplified in his desire to promote the happiness in the world, in the logic of his conclusions, and in his psychological treatment of character. Certainly, only a Benthamite critic would have regarded these as evidences of poetic genius, and only a Radical would have given such disproportionate attention and praise to Coleridge's revolutionary poems. Tennyson, who had been overwhelmed by Croker's de-

[1] The *Foreign Quarterly Review* (1827-35) was edited by J. G. Cochrane, who is now remembered as an editor of the *Caledonian Mercury*, and the cataloguer, in 1838, of Walter Scott's Abbotsford library. After the thirty-seventh volume, the *Foreign Quarterly* was incorporated with the *Westminster Review*.

[2] *Westminster Review*, XII (January 1830), 1-31.

risive review in the *Quarterly* of 1833, was, in July, 1835, warmly defended by Mill in the *Westminster* in one of the most favorable criticisms the young poet had yet received.[1] In July 1837, Carlyle's *French Revolution* was welcomed by the same reviewer. Scott was usually badly handled by the *Westminster* because of his well-known Toryism, while Byron, because of his last journey to Greece in the interest of freedom, was tenderly dealt with.

In the first half-century, at least, we find in the *Westminster*, quite as much as in the *Edinburgh* and *Quarterly*, criticism of literary works qualified by political axe-grinding. Reviewers attempted to put the *belles-lettres* into Utilitarian envelopes. It cannot be held, however, that in this Radical organ the reviewers often rose above the ulterior purpose and produced lasting critical opinions and interpretations, as was the case in the *Edinburgh* and *Quarterly*. Whatever John Stuart Mill's standing as a political philosopher, he cannot be regarded as a great judge of literature. Nor can we find among the names of notable earlier contributors—Carlyle, Sterling, Bulwer, Charles Buller, Roebuck, Harriet and James Martineau, Mazzini, W. J. Fox, Henry Coke, James Mill, and William Hickson—any, with the exception of Carlyle and John Sterling and Fox, perhaps, who had the qualifications of true literary critics.

The later years of the *London and Westminster Review* warrant little comment here. In 1887 the quarterly form was abandoned for the monthly. As a monthly review it appeared until 1913, when, with many of its brethren of the press, it disappeared on the eve of the Great War. In the new form, the *Review* made no pretence of reviewing, but published articles on various subjects of national interest, a very small percentage of which had

[1] The works reviewed were: *Poems, chiefly Lyrical* (1830) and *Poems* (1833).

any connection with pure literature. At the end of the *Review* was a department entitled "Contemporary Literature," divided under the minor headings of Science, Politics, Sociology, Voyages, Travels, History and Biography, and *Belles-Lettres.*

IX

THE LATER REVIEWS AND THE *FORTNIGHTLY*

Several excellent periodical publications are worth notice as obvious efforts to exploit the success of the *Edinburgh, Quarterly* and *Westminster.* The *Investigator,* was a 240-page quarterly review, edited 1820-24 by W. B. Collyer, T. Raffles, and J. B. Brown. Its only claim to interest here lies in its occasional criticisms of contemporary authors. The *British Critic, Quarterly Theological Review and Ecclesiastical Record* (1827-1843), as its title implies, devoted itself mainly to religious matters. Under the successive editors, Edward Smedley, J. S. Boone, John Henry Newman, and others, it published, in spite of its theological bias, some criticism of value. The *Dublin Review* of London, which was begun in 1836 and is now approaching its centenary as a prosperous enterprise, is a better example of a real imitator. Up to 1890 it contained occasional critical reviews of significance, but in recent years has been almost completely non-literary. India in English literature was extensively treated through the excellent 250-page quarterly, the *Calcutta-Review* (1844-1869), a popular and interesting imitator of the great London and Edinburgh Reviews. The *North British Review* of Edinburgh, a heavy quarterly publication of 284 pages, edited by Dr. David Welsh and contributed to by David Brewster, contained much good material in occasional literary articles, and was a conscientious imitator of its great rival, the *Edinburgh Review.* It appeared from 1844 to 1877. The *Irish Quarterly Review* of 1851 (Dublin) was another slavish follower of the *Edinburgh* tradition, but the *New Quar-*

terly Review of London (1852-1862) shows an ambitious effort to revive the eighteenth-century methods exemplified in the *Critical* and *Monthly*. This periodical, a production of Hookham and Sons, really attempted to notice everything of importance in the world of books. Melville's "The Whale" (*Moby Dick*) received a whole page of appreciation; another novel, two inches. The reviews averaged something less than a page to a book. The scope of the periodical is revealed in the sub-title, "And Digest of Current Literature, British, American, French, and German." Each number concluded with a "Quarterly List of New Publications."

Finally, the *London Quarterly Review*, which was established in 1853 as an organ of the Methodists, contained some short reviews, but was otherwise only a medium of religious propaganda. It illustrates well the characteristics of the Review turned to a strictly sectarian purpose. Probably it has derived vitality from this definite aim, for it is still in progress. A similar sectarian purpose and a high standard of excellence was attempted by Richard Holt Hutton, in his Unitarian *National Review* of 1855-1864. Walter Bagehot was co-editor with Hutton. The latter's experience as editor of the *Inquirer* (1851-3) gave him a knowledge of contributors who could carry out a Unitarian program in the new Review. Among the former pens of the *Inquirer* whom he again enlisted, was James Martineau, a Unitarian divine, the brother of Harriet Martineau, who was likewise pressed into service. W. C. Roscoe, a brother-in-law of Hutton, was also added to the staff.[1] But the *National* of 1855, in spite of its reviews, is less significant, as a literary periodical, than its successor which began in 1883.

Quite the most important literary periodical of the lat-

[1] See Hutton's *Poems and Essays of W. C. Roscoe, Edited, with a prefatory Memoir*, Lon. 1860.

ter half of the nineteenth century was the *Fortnightly Review*, set up on May Day 1865. Much of its early success was due to the editorial policies of George Henry Lewes, who, after a varied career as actor, critic, novelist, biographer, and writer on scientific subjects, and some editorial experience with the *Leader* in 1850, undertook to guide the destinies of this new periodical. The *Fortnightly* was not an ordinary English Review. It was modelled, in fact, on the *Revue des deux Mondes*, that extraordinarily successful Paris periodical. This is an important fact. It shows English periodicals, nearly two centuries after the founding of the *Journal des Sçavans*, still influenced by French journalistic invention.[1] Following the example of the *Revue*, the editor of the *Fortnightly* included in his pages a variety of miscellaneous contents, like most of the magazines. In fact, the *Fortnightly* combined in itself the merits of both "magazine" and Review, as its French model had done from the beginning. Likewise, it abandoned the traditional secrecy regarding the identity of contributors. John Morley, writing in 1889,[2] on the effect of the "signed article" on literature, referred to it as "an experiment which Henry Lewes, the founder of that review was the first to make." Of course this leaves out of account the brave attempt of

[1] The *Revue des deux Mondes* was established in December 1829, in Paris, under the editorial direction of François Buloz. It was a fortnightly publication, containing not only critical contributions but fiction (sometimes in serial form), plays, and other features of the miscellany. From the first, nearly all contributions were signed with the names of the authors; Dumas, Balzac, Sainte-Beuve, and Montalembert were among the early names. Although the *Fortnightly Review*, in England, failed to carry out the plan of publication suggested by the title, and soon became a monthly, the *Revue des deux Mondes* continues to appear bi-weekly. It is now a 240-page periodical, selling for six francs; and its contents are still as miscellaneous as those of the magazines. "It has never had an effective rival." The successors of Buloz—Brunetière, Francis Charmer, and René Doumic—have continued his literary policy, to make the *Revue* unrivalled as a medium for the foremost men of letters. ("The 'Revue des deux Mondes'," *Times Literary Supplement*, Dec. 5, 1929, pp. 1009-1010.)

[2] *New Review*, i, 514.

Richard Cumberland in the *London Review*, an attempt which Morley was probably unaware of; and gives no credit to the *Fortnightly's* real prototype, the *Revue des deux Mondes*. It reveals, however, that a change had come over the English reading public in fifty years. The time had passed for universal anonymity. Perhaps the rapid growth of a fiction-reading public had done more to effect this change than any other one thing. Henceforth, the names of authors worked their magic to claim public attention, which in an earlier day, had been seduced by mysterious societies of gentlemen and "invisible infallibles."[1] Thus the *Fortnightly* appeared originally as a frank and self-confessed rebel in the world of periodicals, striking at one of the most cherished tenets of English journalism—that opinion or judgment lost weight if it was known to be "the expression of a single individual instead of a group of pundits."[2]

[1] J. Boyd Kinnear wrote in the *Contemporary Review* in 1867 (V., 338, in an article on "Anonymous Journalism") "It seems evident, at all events, that the idea (of signed articles) is gaining ground. The increasing influence of journalism is attended with a rise in the position of journalists, and with, at the same time, an inclination in the public to discover the individual writers and a desire in the writers to be personally recognized. Novelists, travellers, philosophers, statesmen, are all known to be among the contributors to the columns of leading journals, and even ministers of the Crown add to their weight by being understood to write in daily papers. There is no reason that they should not. The function thus exercised is, next to that of addressing the House of Commons, the most powerful means of swaying political opinion. In some respects it even surpasses in influence that more distinguished organ. But the very magnitude of its influence increases the necessity for its being exercised under the chastening influence of direct responsibility. Aspiring to form and to lead public opinion, and in great measure attaining its pretension, there is the more urgent necessity for its reciprocal subjugation to the salutary constraints which public opinion imposes upon the individual depositories of power. And when the best men are ready to accept these conditions, and recognize that by adoption of them their power for good will be enhanced, . . . the establishment of the principle cannot long be deferred. . . . Where power is assumed, responsibility must be affixed.

[2] Arthur Waugh, "The Biography of a Periodical," *Fortnightly Review*, October 1929, pp. 512-524. Compare the Preface to Number 1: "We shall endeavor to further the cause of progress by illumination from many minds . . . every contributor to speak on his own responsibility. . . . In all matters of conduct and discussion *The Fortnightly Review* is to be impartial and absolutely honest, thoroughly eclectic, opening its columns

Frederic Chapman and George Henry Lewes were among the "little group" of men who put together a few thousand pounds and founded the *Fortnightly* in 1865. The early numbers were brilliant but not financially successful; so the group made over their copyright to the publishing firm of Chapman and Hall, and the *Fortnightly* became a monthly Review at the end of eighteen months, although to this day it has retained its original title. It was, and continues to be, a miscellaneous publication, practically every number made up of an installment of a serial novel, articles of a general or critical nature, a "Department of Public Affairs," and another called "Notices of New Books." The *Review* was really a mixture, unprecedented in England, of reviews, stories, serious articles, and poems. The first chapters of Anthony Trollope's novel, "The Belton Estate," appeared in the first number—"to relieve and sweeten the imagination." Other contributions were from the pens of George Eliot, Robert Buchanan, Thomas Henry Huxley, and Lewes himself—not forgetting the article which opened the first number, the first installment of Walter Bagehot's *The English Constitution.*

Lewes, being obliged by ill health to give up the editorial reins of the *Fortnightly* in 1866, resigned in favor of John Morley, who guided the policies of the review for fifteen years—quite the most brilliant years in its history. He raised the already admirable periodical to an "impregnable position among the honorable organs of human thought and progress." As leader of the Comtist party in England, Morley made the *Fortnightly* the mouthpiece of the positivists—the standard bearer in the battle of rationalism against orthodoxy. During Morley's absence in America, George Meredith acted as pilot of

---

to all opinions, without any pretensions to editorial consistency or harmony."

the *Review*. Morley's editorship was followed in 1883 by that of T. H. S. Escott, which lasted a few years, to give way to the eight-year term of Frank Harris.[1] Both were able editors, but W. L. Courtney, who followed them in 1894, had qualities and opportunities not usually possessed even by literary journalists. For thirty-four years, until his death in December 1928, Courtney maintained the high standard of this remarkable periodical, securing contributors from the ablest of his contemporaries, not only on subjects of literary interest but in many other fields. As has been said, his opportunities were exceptional. He was for many years a director, and at one time chairman, of the publishing house of Chapman and Hall; and for a period almost coincident with his long editorship, he was a leader writer on the staff of the *Daily Telegraph*. During the Great War, especially, he was able to secure many articles about the conflict which gave the *Fortnightly* an enviable prestige and authority in the periodical world. Incidentally, during the trying days of the War, the *Fortnightly*, like many other Reviews, found it expedient to resort once more, for obvious reasons, to the old device of anonymity.

The roster of the *Fortnightly's* contributors during the last fifty years reads like an index to the Hall of Fame. A large proportion of these names have no interest to students of pure literature or literary periodicals. But toward the end of the nineteenth century, the *Fortnightly* included in its columns the work of George Meredith, Walter Bagehot, Matthew Arnold, G. J. Whyte Melville, John Dennis, Moncure D. Conway, J. Addington Symonds, Grant Allen, Sidney Colvin, Alfred Austin, Edward Dowden, William Morris, Walter Pater, W. M. Rossetti, Leslie Stephen, and George Saintsbury.

[1] T. S. H. Escott, *Masters of English Journalism*, London 1911.
Oswald Crawford was connected with the staff of the *Fortnightly* in the 'nineties.

Since 1900, the importance of the *Fortnightly* has been no less evident. In fact, it remains after half a century much the same periodical as it began—more miscellany than review, more review than magazine. It began as a fortnightly periodical of about 130 pages; it is now a monthly averaging 140 pages. Maurice Hewlett, George Gissing, Stephen Gwynn, Andrew Lang, William Sharp, Arthur Symons, James Joyce, Alice Law, Maurice Maeterlinck, Ernest Rhys, Harold Spender, St. John Hankin, Francis Gribble, William Archer, Henry James, Sir Henry Newbolt, "Lewis Melville," Henry Arthur Jones, Professor William Knight, Vernon Lee, John Galsworthy, Ezra Pound, David Alec Wilson, Walter Sichel, Stewart M. Ellis, Arthur Waugh, Richard Curle, and Sir Arthur Quiller-Couch, have by their critical and creative talents enhanced the value of this publication. Fiction has continued to be one of its attractions—the stories of Trollope, Meredith, Swinnerton, "Fiona Macleod," Eden Philpotts, Kipling, H. G. Wells, and F. Tennyson Jesse, securing a popular but discriminating reading public. Poetry has remained one of its staples, including the verse of Thomas Hardy, Emile Verhaeren, Alfred Noyes, Herbert Trench, Alice Meynell, W. W. Gibson, John Drinkwater, and John Masefield. Barrie's first serious play, the *Wedding Guest*, was published as a supplement to the *Review*.

The influence of the *Fortnightly* was seen in 1866 in the *Contemporary Review*, a religious periodical, primarily, set up by Alexander Strahan. It was not in any real sense a literary journal; although the publication in its pages of Tennyson's "The Last Tournament" in 1871, and a few less important contributions, makes it impossible for one to ignore it entirely. The articles of literary nature were very occasional, however, although bearing the names of Walter Besant, Augustine Birrell, Norman

Hapgood, and Edmund Gosse. It was edited, 1882-1911, by Sir Percy William Bunting, who made it an organ of social reform. On the whole, its chief importance in this survey of literary periodicals is due to the department called "Some Recent Books," which began in 1901, and in 1908 became the "Literary Supplement," as it remains to this day.

The *Nineteenth Century*, which was begun in March 1877, also derived something from the example of the *Fortnightly*. Issued monthly, it was from the first a mixture of general articles and poetry. Usually each number was opened with a poem, and consisted of ten articles of 176 pages. James Knowles was the first editor. The first number of the *Review* contained a "Prefatory Sonnet" by Alfred Tennyson, Poet Laureate, followed by Matthew Arnold's essay, "Falk-land," Frederick W. H. Myers' critical article on George Sand, Henry Irving's "An Actor's Notes on Shakespeare," and other equally interesting contributions. Several other poems were contributed by Tennyson to later numbers, including the sonnets, "Montenegro" and "To Victor Hugo," "Achilles Over the Trench," "The Revenge; A Ballad of the Fleet," "The Defence of Lucknow," "De Profundis," and "To Virgil," while other poetic contributions were from the pens of Matthew Arnold, Swinburne, Aubrey de Vere, and Walter H. Pollock. General articles appeared over the well-known names of J. A. Froude, Frederic Harrison, James Spedding, W. E. Gladstone, John Ruskin, James Payn, H. D. Traill, Justin McCarthy, J. H. Shorthouse, Edmund L. Godkin, W. J. Courthope, and Henry Morley. The most notable of these, if literature be considered, are the many essays by Matthew Arnold and the "Department of Recent Literature" (of some twenty pages) contributed to each volume, for several years, by Henry Morley. The last contained some of the most scholarly and sagacious critical reviews of the period, and was followed by a list of books recommended to readers. The *Nineteenth Century* is now edited by Carrol Romer.

The greater *National Review* was set up in 1883, with Alfred Austin as its editor. It was a conservative organ in politics. At the beginning, it appeared as a monthly of 150 pages; by 1904 its size had been increased to 300 pages the month. It is still in progress—a monthly review of 150-180 pages. W. J. Courthope, who was Austin's assistant editor from 1883 to 1887, gave it most of its literary values by publishing in its pages his own critical labors and by attracting to it some of the foremost writers of the day—Leslie Stephen, William Watson, H. D. Traill, and William Archer. Directed for some years by W. Earl Hodgson, *The National* has been since 1894 edited by L. J. Maxse, and has become almost non-literary. In contrast with the *Fortnightly* and the *Contemporary*, the two *National Reviews* represent the old tradition established by the *Quarterly* and *Edinburgh*, a line of development in periodical journalism which seems to have begun to pass away, as recently illustrated by the regretted decease of the *Edinburgh Review* after more than a century and a quarter of prosperity.

The most pretentious literary periodical of the nineteenth century, in appearance, at least, was the *Universal Review* (May-August 1888–September-December 1890). Its title was inherited from earlier periodicals of 1824 and 1856—the latter chiefly a magazine of art—and the periodical of 1888 was more important for its art than its literature. With a page eleven by seven inches in size, the *Universal Review* averaged 648 pages to a number. It was quite the largest Review that had appeared. Its profuse illustrations gave it standing with the best art journals of the century. Its pages included reproductions of the works of George F. Watts, Holman Hunt, Sir

Frederick Leighton, Hubert Herkomer, Edward Poynter, Walter Crane, J. W. Waterhouse, Alfred Hunt, Sir John Millais, and others. Perhaps it should be regarded as a late Pre-Raphaelite organ, for the "Brotherhood" supplied the most striking of its profuse illustrations.

The *Universal Review* contained only an occasional article on literature, but usually this was a good one. Grant Allen, William Archer, Sir Edwin Arnold, Samuel Butler, Wilkie Collins, Alphonse Daudet, Sir Charles W. Dilke, W. E. Henley, Henry James, Richard Garnett, A. W. Pollard, and Laurence Housman were among its galaxy of famous contributors. It was ably edited by Harry Quilter, art critic and journalist, who had made himself well known previously by work on the staff of the *Times* and the *Spectator*.

Another monthly publication of the same period was Longman's *New Review*, 1889-1897, edited at first by Archibald Grove, and then (between 1894 and 1897) by William Ernest Henley. Although much less pretentious in form than the *Universal*, it lacked nothing in talent, for its letterpress contained notable contributions from Lord Coleridge, Henry James, Augustine Birrell, Andrew Lang, Bret Harte, William Archer, Grant Allen, Thomas Hardy, A. C. Swinburne, Frederic Harrison, Rider Haggard, George Moore, and others now known to fame.

Henry James and George Moore were assistants in another and more startling periodical enterprise, the *Yellow Book* (April 1894-April 1897), "an illustrated quarterly—one that was both review and magazine. It was called the "Oscar Wilde of periodicals." "Clever enough to catch the public by serious endeavor, its contributors prefer to use mountebank methods!" said the contemporary American *Critic*.[1] Others damned it as impertinent and vulgar. In truth, the *Yellow Book* contained some of

[1] *Critic*, XXII, 360.

the most brilliant writing of the 'nineties in its 280-page numbers. It was humorous and cerebral. Its writers revealed a tendency to conceal the meaning of their stories by studious avoidance of the obvious. The "frosty genius" of James, the humor of Aubrey Beardsley—at its best here, perhaps—the work of George Gissing, Lionel Johnson, Ernest Dowson, Max Beerbohm, Charlotte Mew, William Watson, A. C. Benson, H. G. Wells, and Kenneth Grahame, raise it well above the "conscientiously original mediocrity" with which it was charged. Its editors, Beardsley and Henry Harland, sought and included within its pages the work of more orthodox pens—Saintsbury, Symons, Gosse, Arthur Waugh, John Davidson, Garnett, John Buchan, and Walter Raleigh. Beautifully printed and illustrated with individual taste, the *Yellow Book* was a sensation in its day. In style it followed the *Fortnightly*, mingling its reviews, fiction, and poetry indiscriminately, to produce a periodical of pure literature quite without precedent.

The dawn of the twentieth century brought to complete accomplishment a tendency which had been obvious since the establishment of the *Fortnightly Review* in 1865.[1] After that date, the quarterly periodical began to assume the appearance of a monthly miscellany; the miscellany—no longer necessarily a monthly—began to acquire the functions and qualities of the Review. Poetry and fiction appeared in the Reviews; reviews became a more common ingredient in the magazines. This confusion of the long-respected types is well illustrated by five excellent literary periodicals which were founded within the first thirty years of our century.

Murray's *Monthly Review*, founded in 1900, with Henry Newbolt as editor, was a more attractive and

[1] It is true, of course, that rare examples of this mixed character may be found as early as 1756 in the *Literary Magazine or Universal Review*. See also the *Critical Memoirs of the Times*, 1769.

expensive publication than any which had yet appeared, with the possible exception of the *Universal*. Anthony Hope's "Tristram of Blent" represented the quality of its serial fiction. Other stories appeared from the pens of Hope, Alfred Ollivant, Quiller-Couch and Kipling. Poetry was supplied by W. B. Yeats, Newbolt, Alice Meynell and Laurence Binyon. Arthur Symons, Andrew Lang, Francis Thompson, Leslie Stephen, Edith Sichel, William Archer, George Meredith, Edward Garnett, T. Sturge Moore, and Quiller-Couch contributed articles and critiques to give the *Monthly* the highest literary quality of the time. With some political editorials and articles, much about art, its 196 pages printed on antique finish paper, and with numerous splendid illustrations (chiefly of works of art) this periodical made the bravest appearance of any of its contemporaries, until its end in 1907.

Within a year it had a worthy successor, the *English Review*, which also began pretentiously, in December 1908, a 200-page miscellany, with Ford Maddox Hueffer as editor. The initial poem by Thomas Hardy was followed by "The Jolly Corner" of Henry James, "Some Reminiscences" by Joseph Conrad, a story called "The Fisher of Men" by John Galsworthy, an article, "Stonehenge," by W. H. Hudson, "The Raid," a story by Leo Tolstoi, and the first chapters of "Tono-Bungay" by H. G. Wells. This feast of good things was supplemented by "The Month," a department containing editorial, political and social paragraphs, and the whole garnished with reviews, one by Conrad. Obviously, the *English Review* began with all the well known features of a monthly miscellany and a quarterly review.[1]

[1] Hugh Walpole, in *Books* (New York, June 22, 1930, p. 9), recently wrote "May England never forget that the first two years of that paper (the *English Review*) under Hueffer's editorship was a magnificent re-

Vigorously edited and managed, it attracted to itself a large share of the available talent of the time. In March 1910, Austin Harrison took over the editing of the *Review*, and recently—in June 1925—Ernest Remnant, the present editor, entered upon his duties. Mr. Vernon Rendall is now the literary editor. Among early contributors were George Saintsbury, G. K. Chesterton, Norman Douglas, Hillaire Belloc, W. B. Yeats, Walter de la Mare, Granville Barker, A. C. Swinburne (the last year of his life), Arnold Bennett, T. Sturge Moore, Richard Garnett, Edward Hutton, W. H. Davies, Thomas Burke, Laurence Binyon, Alfred Noyes, Edward Thomas, and Gerhart Hauptmann. These were later reinforced by Lord Dunsany, John Masefield, Richard Middleton, James Elroy Flecker, Henry Newbolt, A. C. Benson, Ernest Rhys, Austin Harrison, George Moore, Clemence Dane, D. H. Lawrence, and John Drinkwater. As this list of contributors suggests, the *English Review* was exceptionally hospitable to poets and poetry, for some time paying special attention to the "Parnassians." In spite of the undeniable quality of its content, however, the *Review* did not materially prosper. Its size was gradually reduced to 120 pages; and it continues today, a hybrid periodical of modest appearance, selling for a shilling a copy. It remains a not popular but exceedingly distinguished publication. Its columns receive some of the best written prose and poetry of our day.

Somewhat more widely read, perhaps, is the *London Mercury*, a three-shilling, monthly miscellany set up in November 1919 with J. C. Squire as editor. Like the *English Review*, it is of uncertain parentage—its pages containing a mixture of elements, fiction, poetry, articles, and reviews. It makes a showy appearance, as every suc-

---

nascence of wonder! There never was anything else in English periodicals so good."

cessful serial must in these days of novelties, with its yellow covers, and distinguished format and printing. But the editor knows the secret of all successful editing, and sees that its columns are filled regularly with a variety of the best. "No other literary review in the World commands such talent"—reads the blurb, in a claim hard to deny. The brilliance of its staff of contributors is generally recognized—its criticism is known to be hospitable towards every kind of sane experiment, but "chilly towards anarchical cleverness." Edward Shanks, the late John Freeman and C. E. Montague, Edmund Blunden, Walter de la Mare, Aldous Huxley, James B. Orrick, Michael Sadleir, G. K. Chesterton, J. B. Priestly, Maurice Baring, Hillaire Belloc, Max Beerbohm, Arnold Bennett, Robert Bridges, Joseph Conrad, W. H. Davies, D. H. Lawrence, Shane Leslie, Maurice Hewlett, Alfred Noyes, Lord Alfred Douglas, Robert Nichols, Siegfried Sassoon, Bernard Shaw, W. B. Yeats, Rose Macaulay, Robert Lynd, V. Sackville-West, and Sturge Moore are some of the authors whose names have ornamented its pages. Like the *English Review*, it is a specialized result of two centuries of critical evolution; it is concerned with books and authors primarily.

The *Criterion*, a 200-page quarterly, which sells for seven-and-six the copy, further illustrates the current tendency. Founded in 1923, and edited since its beginning by T. S. Eliot, it embodies a mixture of miscellaneous components similar to those of the *English Review* and the *Bookman*—articles, reviews, and occasional poetry. It is the medium of most advanced thought, a forum for the intellectual debates of the day. Reviews by Charles Whibley, John Gould Fletcher, Arlo Williams, Bonamy Dobrée, F. S. Flint, Edith Sitwell, Richard Church, W. H. Thorpe, and John Haywood, and articles by Allen Tate, W. J. Lawrence, Harold Munro, H. J. C. Grierson,

D. H. Lawrence, and G. K. Chesterton, make the *Cri-terion* a critical organ to be reckoned with in present-day literature.

Finally, the *New Adelphi*, a half-crown quarterly of 200 pages, edited by John Middleton Murray, although of too recent a beginning to come properly within the limits of this survey, is a valuable exemplification of the drift of tendency in literary periodicals. According to the standards of the eighteenth or nineteenth centuries, it is an anomalous periodical—made up of fiction, articles, poems, and reviews. Really, it is the logical result of the movement initiated by the *Fortnightly Review* more than half a century ago. The old and famous *Edinburgh Review* ceased publication in 1929, with a comment by the editor on the "different conditions" and increased competition from daily press, monthly magazines, etc. Although the *Quarterly Review* and a few other similar serial publications survive, faithful to the older tradition, it seems likely that the age is not kind to Reviews of the old, narrow type. The *Fortnightly* and its imitators have responded more sensitively to the taste of the time. The day of the *Monthly, Critical, Analytical* and *Edinburgh* has gone. The present-day reader sees nothing incongruous in a mingling of fiction, poetry, general articles, and reviews within the covers of his quarterly or monthly literary periodical.

X

LITERARY MAGAZINES SINCE 1800

There is a very good reason for distinguishing between the magazines before 1800 and those which were begun later. The *Gentleman's Magazine*, the *London*, the *Universal Magazine of Knowledge and Pleasure*, the *Scots*, and others which followed the general plan of Cave's periodical, were for the most part what the term "magazine" implies—storehouses of miscellaneous information, repositories of all sorts of facts and fancies. Much of the entertainment they provided was far from "literary;" their editors sought to amuse readers with mathematical problems, conundrums, rebuses, dances and songs (with musical scores) ; with lists of births, deaths, marriages, preferments, promotions, bankrupts, and sailings of vessels. Some original matter appeared in their columns before 1750, but the magazine as a periodical made up primarily of original literary material was slow in taking shape. Poems, essays, fiction, and drama, had, since 1692, been used to some extent; yet the modern magazine— that is, a miscellany of original works of the imagination, like the *New Monthly Magazine* of the 1840's and the *Cornhill Magazine* of 1860—was not conceived before the beginning of the nineteenth century.

Strange as it may appear, the *Gentleman's Journal* of 1692 and the *Muses Mercury* of 1707-8 were more "modern" in character than many of the periodicals which followed them. They were mainly composed of fiction, verses, and essays, and while they attempted to provide that exhaustive variety of appeals which characterized the magazine during the next fifty years, they actually gave a larger proportion of space than did the eighteenth century magazine to the same kinds of "original" material that we now find in our popular monthly miscellanies.

The type of miscellaneous publication created by Edmund Cave and his imitators was represented in the early nineteenth century by John Aikin's *Athenaeum*, 1807-9. Aikin was a physician who, forced in 1798 to give up his practice because of physical infirmities, was able to devote the last twenty-four years of his life to his favorite studies and literary interests. He had assisted his nephew, Arthur Aikin, with his *Annual Review*; and was the friend of Southey, Erasmus Darwin, Priestly, James Montgomery, and William Enfield. Aikin's *Athenaeum*, although giving the name later to a weekly literary journal, was itself a 100-page monthly magazine, little different, in form or contents, from the *Gentleman's Magazine*. It is only interesting here because it shows how the force of tradition made editors include in their columns not only poetry and essays, but meteorological reports, discoveries and improvements in the arts and manufactures, obituaries, domestic and foreign occurrences, bankrupts, a retrospect of public affairs, commercial reports, prices of stocks and agricultural notes. From a survey of the contents of such a magazine, one may conclude that important movements took place in the nineteenth century, toward selection and specialization, in the materials to be used in miscellaneous periodicals. We shall see that this tendency to specialization affected all branches of periodical literature, and at length developed the various literary serials that we read today.

No great change is seen in the *Monthly Repository of Theology and General Literature*, 1806-1837. It was for a time the mouth-piece of the Unitarians, beginning its run with Robert Aspland and William Johnson

Fox, preacher, politician and author, as its editors. The latter, in 1831, purchased the periodical and changed its character, making it a noteworthy medium of criticism and a very interesting magazine of literature. He secured as contributors John Stuart Mill, Harriet Martineau, Henry Crabb Robinson, Robert Browning, and Ebenezer Elliott; and in the next few years published good reviews of Wordsworth, Tennyson, Hazlitt, Browning, a defence of the "Cockney School," and articles on Lamb and Coleridge. In form, the *Monthly Repository* was of transitional significance. It combined, within its covers, the old news-with-comment feature of the eighteenth century and early examples of the serial narrative which later became so great an attraction of the *Cornhill*.[1] A few of its articles bore the names of authors—a significant fact, at this time. Later numbers contained much of the work of Leigh Hunt and Richard Hengist Horne, including the latter's play, "The Death of Marlowe" and the former's "Blue-Stocking Revels." When Fox relinquished the editorship in June 1836, Horne and Hunt successively carried on the task until the end of the *Repository's* career in 1837.[2]

Several magazines that are worth at least a passing notice came into prominence early in the century. The *Dublin and London Magazine* of 1825-26 was an illustrated miscellany of forty-eight pages, which contained much about Thomas Moore and about Michael James Whitty, author of the "Tales of Irish Life," who was a contributor, and perhaps, editor, as well as a feature called "Sittings of the Eldon Club," an imitation of the "Noctes Ambrosianae" of *Blackwood's*. The *Cambrian Quarterly Magazine* of 1829 to 1833 was a 150-page mis-

[1] It should be noted, however, that rare examples of the serial story were published as early as 1710 in *Records of Love; or Weekly Amusements for the Fair Sex*.

[2] The *Literary Panorama* (1806-19) was, in spite of its title, almost completely non-literary.

cellany which evidently found its chief inspiration in the statement of *Fraser's*, "the Welsh are not a literary people." It contained a great deal about the *Mabinogion* and the ancient Welsh legends, mingled with fiction, essays, and poetry. Throughout its career of nearly half a century, it published many poems, articles on Irish life, and intelligence of the learned societies of Dublin, Belfast, and other Irish centers of culture. It concluded with six or eight pages of critical notices. But fiction was always its most important element. Charles James Lever was its editor, 1842-5, and Sheridan Le Fanu, between 1869 and 1872. The *Dublin University Magazine* of 1833-1880 was a meritorious monthly of 110 pages, containing many signed contributions, most important of which were the stories of Samuel Lover, who helped to found this periodical, William Carleton, G. P. R. James, Lever, and Le Fanu. The *Cambridge University Magazine* of 1839-43, an eighty-page monthly, by a series of articles on "Poets of England who have died young," assiduously promoted the posthumous fame of Shelley and Keats. It contained many other notable articles—on Wordsworth, Byron, on Mrs. Shelley's edition of her husband's works, on "Prometheus Unbound," on Ebenezer Elliot, a series of long articles on living dramatists of England, and several essays on poetry, its nature and effects. This is not to be confused with another and much less important *Cambridge University Magazine* of 1835.

Before the founding of *Blackwood's Magazine* in 1817, periodical literature in Edinburgh had been almost a Whig monopoly. There was no literary organ, in other words, to offset, by the artful mingling of politics with literature, the partisan influence of the *Edinburgh Review*. Tory opposition began in William Blackwood's *Edinburgh Monthly Magazine*, under the incompetent joint-editorship of James Cleghorn (editor of Constable's *Farmer's Magazine*, 1800-1825) and Thomas Pringle, a rustic "genius." The *Magazine* was uninspired and undistinguished, and was made up of the orthodox materials such as articles on the symbolical uses of salt, on the sculpture of the Greeks, on combustion, and on the pastoral life, and a "chronicle" section consisting of births, deaths, marriages, promotions, bankrupts, etc. In short, it followed slavishly the older magazine tradition. After the sixth number, Blackwood dispensed with the services of these weak editors and turned the *Magazine* over to three young assistants, John Wilson ("Christopher North"), James Hogg, and John Gibson Lockhart.[1] He changed its name to *Blackwood's Edinburgh Magazine*, and proceeded to sting his contemporaries into attention with the extraordinary "Chaldee Manuscript," attacks on the "Cockney School" of poetry, and unwarrantedly savage criticism of S. T. Coleridge and others. The effect produced by the "Chaldee Manuscript," a local satire done in somewhat blasphemous scriptural language, is hard to believe, although testified by a cloud of witnesses. It is only by comprehending, to some degree, the circumstances of this extraordinary *jeu d'esprit*, that its astonishing effect on its readers can be understood. One reason for the excitement it created is clear—it was loaded with the most venomous, if innocent-looking, personal allusions, many of which carried their virulence to the last extreme of slandering character and ridiculing physical infirmities.[2] Thus *Blackwood's* gathered a harvest of well-deserved obloquy at the very outset of its career, and

---

[1] R. P. Gillies may have suggested the founding of *Blackwood's* to Hogg (see *Memoirs of a Literary Veteran*, London 1851, ii, 230; also the review of Mrs. Gordon's *Christopher North* in *Quarterly Review*, CXIII, 208-240).

[2] For a full but unfortunately partisan account of the establishment of *Blackwood's*, see Mrs. Oliphant's *William Blackwood and His Sons*, Edin. 1897, i, 93 ff.

took its place among the infamous few periodicals which, through political bias and the besmirching of literary reputations, wrote a regrettable chapter in the history of criticism. This vilification had a definite motive behind it, for the most part, as in the case of the notorious reviews in the *Quarterly* and *Edinburgh*. *Blackwood's* was set up as a more pert and nimble *Quarterly*, as a Tory organ, designed to give smart opposition to the *Edinburgh Review*. Lockhart, although himself a Tory, expressed the views of its founders and sympathizers when he wrote in 1818 that he loathed the "blundering and bigoted pedantry of the *Quarterly Review*, especially of Croker and Southey." Something better was needed, the Tories felt, if they were to meet the Whigs on even terms.

The success of Blackwood's venture was secure after his startling October number had appeared. A libel suit did not stop it, nor did adverse criticism, and the counterassaults of its victims. Its attacks on Coleridge, Hunt, and Hazlitt were in a measure offset by discerning criticisms of Shelley, Wordsworth, and other authors. *Blackwood's* introduced original criticism into the magazine, as a more important element than it had ever been before—a fact of great interest to the historian of periodical literature. Men of letters rallied to it. Walter Scott, one of the earliest contributors, gave *Blackwood's* his invaluable support and countenance, when they were most needed. Henry Mackenzie, author of the *Man of Feeling*, likewise brought it prestige, although he was forced to remonstrate over its politics. Samuel Taylor Coleridge became a somewhat reluctant contributor in 1819, and in October 1821, a selection from his correspondence was published in it.[1] John Galt's first literary success, *The Ayrshire*

[1] See J. D. Campbell, *Samuel Taylor Coleridge*, London 1896, pp. 241, 249.

THOMAS CAMPBELL, Esqʳ

AUTHOR OF THE PLEASURES OF HOPE, &c, &c.

Published by T. Richardson 96 High Holborn.

A FAMOUS MAGAZINE EDITOR

AN ILLUSTRATION FROM THE *Literary Speculum* OF 1822

Legatees (1820) appeared in "Maga." In later years, when a novel of Bulwer-Lytton was running in fifteen installments and George Eliot was making her début in its columns with "Amos Barton," *Blackwood's* was famous for its "trumpet-tone."

After a few years of lusty youth, *Blackwood's* became less extravagant in its critical attacks. The "Noctes Ambrosianae"—results of evenings at Ambrose's—began to appear in 1822 and were continued until 1835. William Maginn, the witty Irishman who was later to be one of the founders of *Fraser's Magazine*, had by this time become a contributor to "Maga," as *Blackwood's* was nicknamed. He assisted Lockhart, Hogg, R. P. Gillies, and Wilson in writing the earlier installments of the "Noctes"; but it was Wilson who alone carried them along in the later years. Wilson wrote at least forty-one of the seventy-one papers, and did more than any other to make them perhaps the liveliest and most popular series of periodical literary sketches ever given to the world. They acted as a safety-valve for the ebullient spirits of the gifted young men who made up the anonymous staff of "Maga."

It is manifest, however, that even the *Blackwood's* of 1825 was not comparable to the modern magazine of original literary matter. "Maga" carried dutifully its pages of "Chronicle" for several years longer—deaths, births, marriages, stock prices, etc. Gradually, under the influence, perhaps, of the *New Monthly Magazine*, these pages became fewer; by 1827 the "Chronicle" head was dropped, and the few pages of this material (in fine print) appeared irregularly. In 1831 such matter disappeared entirely. The modern literary magazine had appeared at last, made up entirely of original articles, fiction, and poetry. Its evolution was probably hastened by the beginning of weekly journals like the *Edinburgh*

Literary Journal and the London *Athenaeum*, both of which were set up in 1828.

At the end of the nineteenth century, *Blackwood's* was a prosperous monthly miscellany of 160 pages, chiefly made up of fiction and criticism. It was still liberal in literature and conservative in politics. The quality of its later narrative contents is illustrated by Conrad's *Lord Jim*, which appeared serially throughout the year 1900. Professor C. Gregory Smith's review of M. Jusserand's *Literary History of the English People* represents its criticism. The poetry of Alfred Noyes had given it distinction for many years. Such names as those of May Sinclair, Andrew Lang, Quiller-Couch, Percival Gibbon, Stewart Edward White, Locker-Lampson, Neil Munro, and Charles Whibley, in its tables of contents, have, since 1900, revealed the fact that "Maga"—the oldest of the now existing magazines in English—has maintained its position over more than a century. It has been the medium through which many great modern reputations have been made. The dean of our contemporary magazines, it is still a literary periodical of first importance.

Blackwood's was started ostensibly because of the need of a "nimbler and more familiar" kind of criticism in Edinburgh. Three years later the need was evidently felt in London, for the *London Magazine* (1820-9) appeared to give the warmest sort of rivalry to its northern prototype. Printed for Baldwin, Cradock and Joy, it was edited, until his untimely death, by John Scott, who had written some discerning criticisms of Wordsworth and Keats in the *Champion*, between 1814 and 1817. Scott had proved himself an able editor of the weekly journal, and came to the editorial chair of the *London Magazine* prepared to give the metropolis a monthly periodical of "sound principles in questions of taste, morals, and politics." The *Prospectus* of the *Magazine* is worth quoting:

> We have been induced to revive the Title of a once well-known but discontinued Magazine, and to appropriate it to our new undertaking, in consequence of its occurring to us as singular, that while secondary towns of the Kingdom give name and distinction to popular Journals, the METROPO-LIS should remain *unrepresented* in the now strenuous competition of Periodical Literature. This circumstance has induced us to enter the lists under the auspices of LONDON; and one of the principal objects of the LONDON MAGA-ZINE will be to convey the very "image, form, and pressure" of that *"mighty heart"* whose vast pulsations circulate life, strength, and spirits, throughout this great Empire.

There is little suggestion of literary values in this. But the *London Magazine* was destined, under the editorial influence of Scott, to shine brilliantly in the literary firmament.

The *London* began its career as a 118-page miscellany, with considerably more of its contents devoted to writers and books than is to be found in any preceding periodical of the kind. De Quincey's "Confessions of an Opium Eater," the "Essays of Elia," and the "Table Talk" of Hazlitt indicated the taste of the editor and the ability of the contributors. John Scott was, without question, one of the most discriminating judges of literature in his generation. His appraisals of Walter Scott, Shelley, Keats, Wordsworth, and Byron, put to shame the blundering ineptitudes of most of his contemporaries—Lockhart and Jeffrey, in particular. The *London Magazine*, during Scott's life, was therefore, a remarkable journal of criticism.

Scott, without doubt, wrote the several critical attacks on *Blackwood's Magazine*: "Lord Byron; his French Critics, the Newspapers, the Magazines," May 1820; "Blackwood's Magazine," November 1820; "The Mohock Magazine," December 1820; and "Town Conversation," January 1821. The first must today be looked upon as a rather fair description of the strength and weakness of *Blackwood's*. Six months later, however, Scott launched an attack "in a style of uncompromising denunciation." Scott believed that the good name of literature was concerned—that much is clear to-day. Himself a better critic than his antagonists, he flung them a challenge—denounced their "duplicity and treachery, as mean and grovelling as their scurrility has been foul and venomous." He pointed directly at Lockhart.

Complicated negotiations followed, too involved to be narrated here.[1] The result, was, briefly, a stupid misunderstanding, a blundering duel at Chalk Farm between Scott and J. H. Christie, Lockhart's second, and the death of Scott. The irresponsible and anonymous criticism of those blackguarding days had at last brought its tragedy. John Scott died, on February 27, 1821, at the peak of his career as editor and critic.

Without Scott, the proprietors of the *London Magazine* were in a quandary. They attempted to enlist Hazlitt, but he, although willing to substitute for a month or two, hesitated to assume the responsibility. In the meantime, Taylor and Hessey purchased the *Magazine,* and the ambitious Taylor determined to act as editor himself, with Thomas Hood as a kind of sub-editor. It was a disastrous decision. One result, however, was the inauguration of the famous "Magazine dinners," which were attended by Henry Francis Cary, Lamb, T. G. Wainewright, the art critic, Thomas Noon Talfourd, Allan Cunningham, B. W. Procter ("Barry Cornwall"), C. W. Dilke, J. H. Reynolds, James Kenney, the farce-writer,

---

[1] See obviously partial stories of the quarrel in Andrew Lang's *Life and Letters of Lockhart,* Lon. 1898, i, 250-282; Mrs. Oliphant's *William Blackwood and His Sons,* Edin. 1897, i, 229, 232, 379; and probably the fairest account in Jacob Zeitlin's "The Editor of the *London Magazine,*" *Journal of English and Germanic Philology,* XX, 328-354. A recent survey of Scott's Career, by T. R. Hughes is "John Scott: Editor, Author and Critic," *London Mercury,* XXI (April 1930), 518-528.

an old friend of Lamb's, Hazlitt, and De Quincey, as well as other lesser lights, like George Darley, John Clare, and William Crowe. Another result of Taylor's unfortunate decision was the steady decline, after a brilliant year or two, of the *Magazine*, as its writers became more and more dissatisfied. Taylor, with the ablest group of contributors available, would not give them what every author desires—a free hand. Hazlitt ceased to write for him. Lamb complained in 1823, "The *London*, I fear, falls off." Procter's and Reynolds' papers were rejected. In April, 1824, Beddoes, Procter's friend, wrote "Exit *London*." By the autumn of 1824, the *New Monthly* was gaining ground and the *London* was in desperate straits. Lamb sent his first contribution to the rival magazine in January 1825, and his last article in the *London* appeared in the August number. In September, the *London Magazine* passed into the hands of Henry Southern and sank into insignificance. Its end came in 1829. The story of the later days of the *London* is well told in King's biography of Henry Francis Cary.[1]

It cannot be denied that during the first few years of its brief career the *London Magazine* surpassed all its contemporaries as a literary periodical. Lamb contributed for a period of five of his most productive years. Hazlitt gave it some of his most discerning critical essays. Carlyle's "Schiller" first appeared in its columns, in installments running from October 1823 to September 1824. Henry Francis Cary, the translator of Dante, was a constant contributor after 1821; and the several others who have been mentioned as participants in the "Magazine dinners" coöperated to give it significance as a medium of critical and creative effort. Moreover, the fact should not be overlooked that the *London* was a more

---

[1] R. W. King, *The Translator of Dante*, London 1925, pp. 124-177. See also Walter Jerrold, *Thomas Hood*, London 1907, pp. 92-122.

critical monthly magazine than any which preceded. It promoted the tendency already remarked in *Blackwood's*, to make the miscellaneous periodical a medium of critical writing.[1]

Meanwhile, the year 1814 had seen the beginning of the *New Monthly Magazine and Universal Register*. Henry Colburn, the publisher, evidently believed his motto (quoted from Dr. Johnson)—"Every art is improved by the emulation of competitors." On the title page for several years was printed the following:

> *Monthly Magazines* have opened a way for every kind of inquiry and information. The intelligence and discussion contained in them are very extensive and various; and they have been the means of diffusing a general habit of reading through the nation, which in a certain degree hath enlarged the public understanding. HERE, too, are preserved a multitude of useful hints, observations, and facts, which otherwise might have never appeared.—Dr. Kippis.

The *New Monthly* began its career as a definitely political organ, like most of the magazines and reviews of this age. The "address to the public" (1814) contains the following explanation of its rise:

> We need but to cite the *Monthly Magazine*, whose Editor, nursed in the school of Jacobinism, commenced his career as a promulgator of Paine's *Rights of Man*, and who, with all the consistency of our pseudo-patriots, has of late years been one of the most zealous worshippers of that Moloch, Buonaparte. The political poison so artfully introduced into every department of that work, and mixed up with a due proportion of

---

[1] *Ollier's Literary Miscellany*, 1820, "in prose and verse," set out to be the best critical and literary miscellany of the times. Only one number appeared, but this consisted of two hundred pages. The *Miscellany* is remembered for the fact that it contained Peacock's "The Four Ages of Poetry" which evoked Shelley's *Defence*. It should be noted also that it contained sixty pages of German criticism, that of A. W. Schlegel, in particular. Moreover, in its columns are found the publishers' advertisements of Shelley's poems, Lamb's works, Hunt's books, and the *History of a Six Weeks Tour*. Virtually all the then published volumes of Shelley's poetry were advertised in this *Miscellany*.

ribaldry and irreligion, was calculated to produce a mischievous impression upon the minds of the unthinking and inexperienced at home, and to misrepresent and degrade the character of the country abroad. These considerations could not but excite in every honest mind a thorough abhorrence of its principles and a strong desire to counteract its tendency. To such feelings the *New Monthly Magazine* owes its existence.

The *New Monthly* possessed all the regular ingredients of the *Gentleman's Magazine*, and, indeed, appeared much like it in form. Each number consisted of one hundred and twenty pages, which included everything entertaining and informative, many "memoirs," and columns of "Dramatic Register" and "Provincial Occurrences." Articles were usually signed by initials or pseudonyms. It was not until 1820 that the *New Monthly* became an important literary organ. With Thomas Campbell's acceptance of the editorship, the periodical assumed the title, *New Monthly Magazine and Literary Journal*. As this change of title implies, Campbell, who had had experience as a journalist on the *Morning Chronicle, Star,* and *Courier,* determined to make the magazine less of a political and more of a literary periodical than it had been before. His contract with Colburn called for twelve articles, six in prose and six in verse, for a salary of five hundred pounds a year.[1] The character of the *Magazine* changed still further in 1824, when it was made up of reviews, original articles and poetry—some articles signed by the writers—and the "Historical Register" section was issued separately, in the bound editions. Excellent critical appreciations of Wordsworth and of Lamb appeared, from the pen of Thomas Noon Talfourd, and a very notable contribution in 1820 was an anonymous review of Keats' *Lamia* volume, a highly favorable appraisal of the work of the young poet. Many poetic contributions

[1] William Beattie, *Life and Letters of Thomas Campbell,* London 1850, ii, 357.

in the columns of the *New Monthly* were signed with the
initials of Talfourd, Douglas Jerrold, James Montgomery, and Bernard Barton, the Quaker poet; and the
collaborated verses of Keats and Charles Armitage
Brown on the skulls of Beanly Abbey first appeared in it.

Campbell's own lectures on poetry and several of his
most popular poems, such as "The Last Man," helped to
improve the quality of the *Magazine*. Campbell gathered
about him a group of well-known writers, but his editorship, which lasted for nine years, does not seem to have
been signally successful. Edward Bulwer-Lytton, first
Baron Lytton, succeeded him from 1831-2;[1] Theodore
Edward Hook, another novelist, was editor from 1836-
41; Peter George Patmore occupied the chair from
1841-52, assisted by Thomas Hood for a time; William
Harrison Ainsworth acquired the *Magazine* in 1853, and
it was edited by his son, William Francis Ainsworth,
from 1871 to the end in 1884. Its succession of famous
editors, and the large number of critical articles it contained, give the *New Monthly* a high place among the
magazines of the century. Moreover, it contained many
early examples of signed contributions; and in the original nature of its letterpress it was, from 1820 on, one
of the most progressive of periodicals.

The periodical of highest literary quality in the first
quarter of the nineteenth century was unquestionably
Leigh Hunt's and Byron's *The Liberal*, described as
"Verse and Prose from the South." In fact, it can be
declared that the high level of its contributions has been
but seldom attained since it appeared in 1822. Suggested
by Shelley to Thomas Love Peacock as early as February
1818, the plan for the magazine was finally realized when
Byron and Leigh Hunt—after Shelley's tragic death on

[1] Bulwer-Lytton contributed regularly to the *New Monthly*, as well as
to the *Edinburgh Review, Westminster Review, Monthly Chronicle, Examiner, Literary Chronicle*, and other periodicals.

the eve of the launching of this enterprise—carried on the periodical labor in which Shelley's was to have been the enthusiastic and guiding spirit. Hunt, to whom Byron was indebted for defence of him at the time of his separation from Lady Byron, had journeyed to Italy with his family, at Byron's expense, for the sole purpose of editing the periodical; so, in spite of Shelley's death, there was nothing for them to do but go on with the undertaking. Byron financed Hunt for a while, and half-heartedly supported the *Liberal*. But he and Hunt for various reasons did not get on well. So the *Liberal* was destined to have a brief existence.

While it lasted, the *Liberal* was—as has been remarked—an extraordinary literary periodical, and, within a limited circle of readers, the sensation of its day. Only four numbers appeared, issued "occasionally" and "Printed by and for John Hunt," in London. The Preface to the first volume and Advertisement to the second were written in Leigh Hunt's most cocky and offensive vein. But the "Vision of Judgment," which opened the first number, is the greatest satire that ever filled the pages of an English periodical. Other contributions from Byron were the "Letter to the Editor of My Grandmother's Review," the "Epigrams" on Castlereagh, and the translation of the first canto of the *Morgante Maggiore* of Pulci, the "Blues," and "Heaven and Earth." Hazlitt contributed several of his best essays, including "My First Acquaintance with Poets," and "Shakespear's Fools"; while from Shelley's unpublished remains were printed the exquisite "Song for an Indian Air," his "Lines to a Critic," and the "May-Day Night" fragment of his translation of *Faust*. Hunt wrote half the letterpress, including in it his "Book of Beginnings" and his "Letters from Abroad." Yet with all its quality of contents, the *Liberal* was from the beginning doomed to a short career. Had Shelley lived, its story might have been a different one.

Knight's Quarterly Magazine, 1823-4, was set up by Charles Knight, author and publisher, whose experience with periodical enterprises had already included labor on the staffs of the *Globe*, the *British Press*, the *Windsor and Eton Express*, the *Plain Englishman*, and the *Guardian* of 1820-2. Although rather original in its design and of pretentious purpose, the *Quarterly Magazine* was not greatly inspired. Some interesting parodies of Byron and Wordsworth and a few reviews give it a mild interest to students of the period. It had a kind of successor in the *Literary Magnet of Belles-Lettres, Science, and the Fine Arts*, "by Tobias Merton, Gent." (1824-6), printed monthly for Charles Knight, and, like the *Quarterly Magazine*, ambitious in design. The contents of each 56-page number consisted of (1) "Original essays on subjects of permanent interest," (2) sketches of society, (3) tales and romances, (4) notices of new publications, (5) poetry, and (6) early intelligence of all matters connected with literature and the fine arts. Four of the six departments were "literary"; the *Literary Magnet* set out to be an organ of importance in the world of letters. Perhaps the most interesting thing in it today is its series of articles on the "living poets of England"—Wordsworth, Mrs. Hemans, etc. In the poetry department, much of the work of M. G. Lewis, Mrs. Hemans, Wm. Lisle Bowles, Akenside, and others, was reprinted. It is now well known that Macaulay began his real literary career in *Knight's*.

(John) *Sharpe's London Magazine* of 1829, a 128-page monthly, was a genuine literary periodical. The initial number was divided into three parts—the first devoted to "poetry and romance," by such authors as Theodore Hook, Robert Southey, Allan Cunningham, and

George Darley; the second, to essays, criticisms, and characters; the third, to society and manners. The second number was somewhat different. The table of contents listed contributions and authors without classification (unusual at this time) and gave the names of contributors —George Darley, Miss Mitford, Mrs. Hemans, Francis E. Smedley (who was editor, 1847-52) James Hogg, W. Kennedy, T. H. Bayley, and John Cumming. A sonnet of S. T. Coleridge's—"Oh, it is pleasant"—is included as published "for the first time."[1] Discontinued after three numbers had appeared, *Sharpe's* was revived in 1846-49, and published, 1849-52, as *Sharpe's London Journal*. Then, with the old title of *Sharpe's London Magazine*, it was continued until 1870, under the editorship of Mrs. S. C. Hall, who had succeeded Smedley as editor for a year in 1852-3.[2]

Among the not greatly distinguished but still important magazines of the 'twenties and 'thirties must be named the *Literary Speculum* (November 1821-May 1822). Of the two volumes, the second gives today no indication that it was anything more than an annual. The first volume, however, shows that the *Speculum* was originally published as a 72-page monthly miscellany, entirely devoted to literature. A *National Magazine*, of 1826, consisted of sixty-six pages of poetry (mostly reprinted) and general articles. A series of articles on old English drama, and another on the literature of England, are notable contents. A popular magazine from 1831 to 1857 was the *Metropolitan*, a monthly miscellany of 128 pages devoted to light fiction, with from sixteen to thirty-two pages of book notices at the end of each number. Its chief interest here lies in the fact that Captain Frederick Marryat, author of *Peter Simple*, and of many

[1] Actually, it had first appeared in *Blackwood's* in November 1819.
[2] Smedley acted as editor of *George Cruikshank's Magazine*, during its brief career of two numbers in 1854.

other stories which appeared in its columns (at the rate of sixteen pounds a sheet), edited it from 1832-35, with Edward Howard, author of *Rattlin' the Reefer*, as his sub-editor.[1]

Fraser's Magazine for Town and Country, 1830-82, a 128-page periodical, was published by a Scotch printer, James Fraser, although not given his name, as might be supposed. The starting of this serial, which was for a short time one of the leading literary organs, was brought about by two rollicking bohemians of the day, William Maginn, late of Paris, and his friend, Hugh Fraser (for whom the *Magazine* was named) who became its joint-proprietors, with editorial assistance perhaps from F. S. Mahoney.[2] Maginn had ceased writing for *Blackwood's*, and in 1830 was free to devote his not inconsiderable talents to the new undertaking. "Regina," as the new magazine was familiarly called, was an avowed imitation of "Maga." Containing much excellent criticism and other literary material, it was, for a time, a keen competitor. The contributions of Ruskin and Thackeray combined to make it for several years the best of the English literary monthlies. Ruskin's "Munera Pulveris" and Thackeray's "History of Samuel Titmarsh," 1837-8, the "Yellow-plush Correspondence," 1838, "Catherine," 1839-40, and in 1844, "The Luck of Barry Lyndon," were accompanied by lesser literary works of "Father Prout" (F. S. Mahoney), Thomas Love Peacock, James Anthony Froude, and William Allingham, the last of whom edited *Fraser's* from 1874 to 1879. Maginn's contributions were no small factor in its popularity. The famous "Gallery of Illustrious Literary Portraits" (with

---

[1] *The Critic*, a monthly magazine, appeared in 1832 for only two numbers. It was an admirable 100-page miscellany, consisting of critical articles—including reviews of Moore's *Byron*, Fanny Kemble's dramatic writings, and Mrs. Trollope's *Domestic Manners of the Americans*—as well as several original papers on drama and considerable fiction.

[2] See Mrs. Gordon's *Christopher North*, Edin. 1862, ii, 99.

the drawings by Daniel Maclise and the letterpress by Maginn) appeared between 1830 and 1838 and was unquestionably one of the most attractive features of the magazine. Carlyle gave *Fraser's* more than twenty contributions, including his "Sartor Resartus" (in installments, 1833-34).

After James Fraser's death in 1841, "Regina" declined in quality and prestige. G. W. Nickisson published it until 1847, when it was transferred to John W. Parker; he and his successor continued it until 1882. It was then superseded by *Longman's Magazine*, the Longmans having owned it since 1863.

Tait's Edinburgh Magazine, a monthly of 138 pages (1832-64) issued by William Tait, was one of the first of the cheaper shilling magazines (a half-crown had been heretofore the usual price); and it carried on, in the Northern capital, the political work of the *Westminster Review* in London. In other words, it was an organ of Radical politics, contributed to by John Stuart Mill, Richard Cobden, and John Bright. Each number of the *Magazine* began with a political essay. The literary influence of *Tait's* was slight. It contained little fiction and poetry, and no very important criticism; although a regular department of ten pages was called the "Monthly Register of New Publications."

Among the periodicals of lesser importance, *Cobbetts' Magazine,* "By Messrs. John and James Cobbett" (1833-4), distinguished itself by an attack on Wordsworth and the other "Lake Poets." It began as a one hundred-page monthly which lasted for little more than a year, and then was continued as the *Shilling Magazine.* Douglas Jerrold's *Shilling Magazine*, of 1845-48, contained several installments of P. G. Patmore's "Recollections of Hazlitt," fiction by Jerrold himself, and the letters of "Juniper Hedghog." This periodical was pub-

lished "for the good of the people." The editor announced, "It will be an earnest desire to avail ourselves
of all and every variety of literature, if illustrating and
working out some wholesome principle." *Sherwood's
Monthly Miscellany* (later *London Monthly Miscellany*) of 1838-39, was notable for one thing only—all its
stories were signed. This was a new departure in magazines containing much fiction. Thus we learn from the
table of contents that C. W. M. Reynolds, Calder Campbell, Thomas Egerton Wilks, Hal Willis, H. J. Miller,
W. H. Harrison, and Cornelius Webbe, were the authors
of the sentimental poetry and romantic fiction in its
pages. Although its literary value is slight, *Sherwood's*
is of interest as the first magazine to adopt regularly and
completely the now almost universal practice of signing
contributions.

Edward Moxon's *Englishman's Magazine* (1831) was
a really ambitious undertaking, a monthly of 120 pages,
selling for a half-crown. By reason of its contributors
it has clear title to a place among the better literary
magazines of the century, in spite of its short career of
little more than a year. Tennyson, at that time almost
unknown, Thomas Hood, Charles Lamb (signing himself "Elia"), Leigh Hunt, John Sheridan Knowles,
Thomas Pringle, Mrs. Norton, William Motherwell,
John Clare, and the precocious Arthur Henry Hallam
were represented in its columns. Although its poems were
numerous, it is better remembered today for its criticism
and its essays. In some ways the most interesting contribution (excepting, of course, Lamb's Essays) was Hallam's
review of Tennyson.[1] Hallam began his critique with a
boyishly ardent attack on James Montgomery, the *Edinburgh Review*, the *Gentleman's Magazine*, and the older

[1] Number 5, pp. 616-627.

critical journals in general, and proceeded to praise of Wordsworth, a defence of the "Cockney School, and deification of Shelley and Keats (with a good word thrown in for Leigh Hunt). He then connected his young contemporary, Tennyson ("this faithful Islam poet") with those whom he called the poets of sensation. His praise for Tennyson knew no bounds. He quoted most fully and with the most fervid admiration "Recollections of the Arabian Nights," "Oriana," and "Adeline." This article, which had the title, "On some Characteristics of Modern Poetry, and on the Lyrical Poems of Alfred Tennyson," unquestionably had much to do with causing Tennyson's next volume to be the object of almost universal critical derision. The *Englishman's Magazine* bore a name reminiscent of Defoe, whose portrait graced its cover. Like many of its contemporaries, it gave its later columns to short sections of musical notes, and reviews of art works, drama, etc. More than half its contributions were followed by the author's names.

The significance of the miscellany or "magazine" in the literary life of the nineteenth century is nowhere better illustrated than in its relation to the closely associated figures, William Henry Wills, Richard Bentley, and Charles Dickens. Bentley (1794-1871) learned the printing business in the office of his uncle, John Nichols, who, with the senior Bentley, was among the later publishers of the *General Evening Post*. In 1819 Richard Bentley joined his brother Samuel in undertaking a printing and publishing business; ten years later he became the partner of Henry Colburn for a time. By 1836 Bentley had become well established as a publisher; and in this year he projected a monthly magazine, to be started the following January. On the 22nd of August he secured, by signed agreement, the services of Dickens as his first editor. "Boz" was already rising toward the crest of his fame. At the age of nineteen he had made his first appearance in the "Gallery" as a parliamentary reporter of the *True Sun*, a morning newspaper; afterwards, for two sessions he had written for the *Mirror of Parliament*, originated and conducted by one of his uncles; and, in his twenty-third year, he had become a reporter for the *Morning Chronicle*. Some little sketches were contributed to Holland's *Monthly Magazine*, the tenth and last in February 1835. One which appeared the preceding August first bore the signature of "Boz." The sketches were continued in the *Evening Chronicle* in 1835, at the instance of George Hogarth, who became in April 1836, his father-in-law. In the following year appeared in book form the *Posthumous Papers of the Pickwick Club, edited by Boz.*

As the first editor of *Bentley's Miscellany*, Dickens contributed more than any other writer of his staff. "Oliver Twist" appeared serially throughout the years 1837 and 1838. The author's fame and the popularity of *Bentley's Miscellany* grew apace. Dickens became embarrassed by his agreement with Bentley, which called for other literary efforts on the same terms—impossible in view of the fact that the publisher was becoming enriched while the author was receiving a "paltry, wretched, miserable sum."[1] As a result, with the conclusion of "Oliver Twist" in 1839, Dickens was relieved of his obligations to the publisher; and William Harrison Ainsworth succeeded him in the editorial chair, 1840-42.

Bentley's Miscellany was begun in January 1837, as a periodical of one hundred pages. The initial number contained a prologue by Maginn, following "Our Song of the Month," and succeeded by "Our Opening Chaunt"—

[1] See letter, Dickens to Bentley, dated 21st of January, 1839, quoted in John Forster's *Life of Charles Dickens*, Lon. 1904, i, 106-107.

Come around and hear, my public dear,
Come hear, and judge it gently,—
The prose so terse, and flowing verse,
Of us, the wits of Bentley.

Those who admire a merry lyre
Those who would hear attent'ly
A tale of wit, or flashing hit,—
Are asked to come to Bentley—

A bantering, humorous introduction to the public disclaimed any deep interest in romance or science or politics. The contents of the magazine consisted of poems, essays and stories—more pages devoted to fiction than to any other *genre*.

During the first year Theodore Hook, Samuel Lover, Thackeray, "Father Prout," John Hamilton Reynolds, Charles Whitehead, William Jerdan, "Thomas Ingoldsby" (R. H. Barham), George Hogarth, J. Sheridan Knowles, J. A. Wade, and C. J. Davis were some of the contributors. Ainsworth's novels, "Guy Fawkes," "Jack Sheppard," etc., appeared for years in the columns of *Bentley's*. Notable among the contents of the *Miscellany* were the poems of Henry Wadsworth Longfellow, then exceedingly popular in Great Britain. It contained also biographical and critical articles on nearly all the important writers of the early nineteenth century. Illustrations by George Cruikshank and John Leech enhanced the attractiveness of this magazine. It was continued until 1869.

William Henry Wills, who had begun his career by contributing to the *Penny* and *Saturday Magazines*, sent in 1837 two pieces to Dickens, then editor of *Bentley's Miscellany*. One of these was accepted, and further contributions were invited. In 1841 he had got himself sufficient reputation to be asked to aid Ebenezer Landells, Henry Mayhew and Mark Lemon, in founding *Punch*. He acted at one time as its dramatic editor, and supplied prose and verse until 1848. In the meantime, he had (in 1842) been for a short time assistant editor of *Chambers' Journal* in Edinburgh. The year 1845 saw him engaged in another journalistic adventure in London—as chief of the sub-editorial staff of the *Daily News*, established under the editorship of Dickens, to whom Wills also became a kind of secretary. When, in 1850, *Household Words* was started by Dickens, with the joint-proprietors, William Bradbury, Frederick Mullett Evans, John Forster, and Wills, the last became again Dickens' assistant.[1] From 1859 to 1869, he likewise was Dickens' sub-editor on a new publication, *All the Year Around*, which, owing to differences with Messrs. Bradbury and Evans, Dickens and Wills set up as a successor, Dickens, in the meantime, having purchased *Household Words*. Wills' place, on his retirement in 1869, was taken by Charles Dickens, Jr.[2]

Household Words and *All the Year Around* represent, in scope and aim, a popularizing of periodical literature which had been going on for half a century, in response

[1] *Household Words* was the first important example of a popularizing tendency which had been apparent since 1815, when several low-priced and low-quality periodicals began to appear on the market. The political agitation of 1831-2 led to greater popular demand, and a supply of cheap and wholesome serials commenced with *Chambers' Journal* (1832 ff.), the *Penny Magazine* (1832-45) of Charles Knight, and the *Saturday Magazine* (1832-1844). In this one year (1832) were started also the *Half-penny Magazine*, the *Christian's Penny Magazine*, the *Ladies' Penny Gazette*, the *London Penny Journal*, the *Girl's and Boy's Penny Magazine*, the *Boy's and Girl's Penny Magazine*, the *True Half-Penny Magazine*, *Dibdin's Penny Trumpet*, and the *Penny Comic Magazine*. These sold for a penny or a penny and a half. Only the *Penny Magazine* deserves notice as a periodical of literary merit. This was contributed to by the best writers of the day, and soon reached a circulation of 200,000, in weekly numbers and monthly parts. Cheap periodicals of lower tone followed—the *Family Herald* (1843) the *London Journal* (1845) and Lloyd's *Weekly Miscellany* (1850-51). It remained for Dickens and his colleagues to improve once more the quality of the weekly magazines, and to bring to the household and fireside reading matter both excellent in quality and low in price.

[2] See R. C. Lehmann, *Charles Dickens as Editor*, London 1912, p. 390.

to the gradual spread of education. The various penny and half-penny magazines which appeared between 1800 and 1850 show that extension of the reading public among the lower classes which was one of the most remarkable signs of the times. Dickens described *Household Words* to Mrs. Gaskell as a "new cheap weekly journal of general literature. . . . No writer's name will be used, . . . every paper will be published without any signature, and all will seem to express the general mind and purpose of the journal, which is the raising up of those that are down, and the general improvement of our social condition."[1]

Household Words, "conducted by Charles Dickens," originally appeared on Saturday, March 30, 1850, as a twenty-four-page miscellany. Poetry, anecdotes, stories, biographical incidents, and letters, made up the customary contents of a number. Little of its matter can be regarded as "literary" in any but a qualified sense. It was written for the people, whom Dickens loved. Yet a roster of the contributors to *Household Words* is a cross-section of the secondary literary talent of the day, with not a few of the best authors included. Among these whose names are to be found in the "office book" are Richard H. Horne, Henry Morley, Mrs. Catherine Crewe, Mrs. Gaskell, Mrs. Chisholm, Harriet Martineau, John Forster, F. K. Knight, Alexander Mackay, Coventry Patmore, Charles Knight, E. C. Grenville Murray, George Augustus Sala, Henry Austin (Dickens' brother-in-law), James Hannay, Hon. Mary Boyle, Leigh Hunt, W. H. Dixon, William Howitt, John Poole, Geraldine Jewsbury (the friend of Mrs. Carlyle), William Moy Thomas, Georgiana M. Craik, William Allingham, Wilkie Collins, and his brother, Charles A. Collins,

[1] Letter dated January 31, 1850. *Letters of Charles Dickens*, N. Y. 1879), i, 250.

Adelaide Procter, C. H. Townshend, James Payn, Edmund Yates, John Oxenford, and George Meredith.

The last number of *Household Words* was published on Saturday, May 28, 1859; the first number of *All the Year Around* appeared on Saturday, April 30th, the two periodicals thus overlapping by five numbers. The second was sold at the same price as the first—twopence. Dickens purchased the former journal at auction on May 16. After the fifth number of *All the Year Around*, he added to the title of the new periodical the words—"with which is incorporated *Household Words.*" By a formal agreement Dickens became proprietor of three fourths of the new property; Wills, one fourth. One can be certain of only Dickens' contributions to *All the Year Around*, for there exists no such Office Book as that which reveals the identity of the contributors to *Household Words.*[1] Probably many of the old *Household Words'* staff contributed to the new enterprise. Dickens' letters reveal the fact that among them were Wilkie Collins, Edmund Yates, George Walter Thornsbury, Charles Collins, Bulwer-Lytton, Henry Morley, Charles Reade, Miss Harriett Parr, Mrs. Gaskell, Percy Fitzgerald, J. C. Parkinson, and Charles Lever. Sheridan Le Fanu is known to have contributed short stories.

All the Year Around began brilliantly on Saturday, April 30, 1859, with the first installment of "A Tale of Two Cities." Identical in size and format with *Household Words*, it continued until 1895, when it was incorporated with a new *Household Words*, a re-incarnation of the periodical it had once absorbed. Charles Dickens, Junior, carried on the publication of *All the Year Around*, after his father's death in June 1870, until its

[1] See R. C. Lehmann, *Charles Dickens as Editor*, New York 1912, p. 262; *Works* of Dickens (Chapman and Hall) 1908, vols. xxxv and xxxvi.

close, and issued from 1881 the new *Household Words* which absorbed it.

Other monthly miscellanies, in the middle years of the century, were demonstrating the popularity of this form. *Ainsworth's Magazine*, illustrated by Cruikshank, and beginning in 1842 with some critical pretensions, became more completely than any that had preceded it, a miscellany of fiction. It was a monthly of sixty-four pages. Its neglected files contain the poems of Tupper, travel sketches by Francis Ainsworth, Thomas Medwin, and Charles Hervey, serious articles by Samuel Laman Blanchard, and John A. Heraud, translations by Edward Vaughan Kenealy, and fiction by John Oxenford, Charles Ollier, G. P. R. James, Miss Pardoe, Charles Kirkpatrick Sharpe, Mrs. Humphrey Ward, and Charles Lever. William Harrison Ainsworth's novels, "The Miser's Daughter," "Windsor Castle," "Modern Chivalry," etc., with reprints of others, here appear, with "Ehrenstein" by G. P. R. James, Leigh Hunt's "A Jar of Honey from Mount Hybla," and a translation of Dumas's "Count of Monte Cristo"—all in installments. Many illustrations brightened the pages of this once popular magazine.

A very high quality of literature was represented in the contents of *The Germ*, the famous little organ of the Pre-Raphaelites, which appeared in January 1850. Its explanatory sub-title was "Thoughts toward nature in Poetry, Literature, and Art." After the second number, the title, which had dissatisfied many of the Brotherhood, was changed to *Art and Poetry*. The fourth number was the last. This small monthly miscellany of forty-eight pages, selling for one shilling, was chiefly the work of Dante Gabriel Rossetti, who was the leading spirit of the Pre-Raphaelite Brotherhood. It was, while it lasted, a

good example of the magazine with a special purpose—
with artistic propaganda to disseminate.

Among the contributors were Coventry Patmore, who
wrote the article on *Macbeth*, Christina Rossetti ("Ellen
Alleyn") who contributed her poem "Repining," and
J. L. Tupper, who supplied the "Papers of the 'MS Society' " and several poems, while from F. G. Stephens came
an article on "Modern Giants," from William Michael
Rossetti his "Evil under the Sun," and from the editor
his "My Sister's Sleep," "Hand and Soul," "The Blessed
Damozel," "The Carillon, Antwerp and Bruges," "From
the Cliffs, Noon," "Pax Vobis," and "Sonnets for
Pictures."[1]

After the failure of *The Germ*, much of the effort of
the Pre-Raphaelites was turned into the *Oxford and
Cambridge Magazine* (London) of 1856, a pretentious
monthly of 128 pages. This miscellany, which lasted only
a year, is now of great value to students of the Victorian
period, for it contained criticism of Thackeray, Macaulay, Carlyle, Charlotte Brontë, Ruskin, Longfellow,
Browning, Kingsley, and other eminent writers of the
middle nineteenth century. The periodical was divided
into four parts—essays, tales, poetry, and notices of books.
A series of three long articles on Tennyson and his work
by the editor, W. Fulford, illustrates its value as an organ
of contemporary criticism. A list of its contributors, supplied by Vernon Lushington and W. Bell Scott, in a copy
which recently came on the market, shows that several
of the foremost of the Pre-Raphaelites were among its
quite extraordinary array of talent. It reveals the full list
of the contributors as follows: Wilfred Heeley, Edward
Burne-Jones, William Morris, Dante Gabriel Rossetti,
Vernon and Godfrey Lushington, Lewis Campbell,

---

[1] For a full account of the contributors see W. M. Rossetti's introduction to *The Germ . . . being a Facsimile Reprint . . .* London 1901.

B. Cracroft, Miss Macdonald, and W. Fulford. It reveals also that Burne-Jones's contributions were "The Newcomes," "The Cousin," "Druid and Maiden," and a review of "Ruskin's New Volume"; that Morris wrote "Ruskin and the Quarterly," "Churches of Northern France," "The Death of the Avenger," "A Dream," "Frank's Sealed Letter," "Golden Wings," "Winter Weather," "Hands," "Chapel in Lyonesse," and "Pray but One Prayer"; that Rossetti contributed his "Nineveh," and reprinted in it his "Staff and Scrip," and "Blessed Damozel." It shows also that most of the criticism of contemporary writers was written by W. Fulford, Vernon Lushington, B. Cracroft, and Miss Macdonald—critics who are forgotten today, but whose work is of such quality as to make them appear deserving of a better fate.[1]

A prosperous periodical which attracted a galaxy of unusual talent, during the second half of the nineteenth century, was *Macmillan's Magazine*, an enterprise of the publishing firm of Macmillan. It was established in November 1859—a year in which no less than one hundred and fifteen periodical undertakings were started in London alone—and continued until 1907. At first, it consisted of eighty pages of articles, stories, and poems, with the names of the authors plainly indicated beneath the titles—Thomas Hughes, Herbert Coleridge (the grand-nephew of S. T. Coleridge, and first collector of materials for what is now the great *New English Dictionary*) W. E. Forster, Franklin and Henry Lushington, David Masson, the editor of Milton, F. D. Maurice, Richard Monckton Milnes, Alexander Smith, Francis T. Palgrave, and Alfred Tennyson. The first six numbers of the *Magazine* contained *Tom Brown at Oxford* in install-

---

[1] I must acknowledge the kindness of Messrs. W. Heffer and Sons, of Cambridge, for the list of contributors.

ments, and subsequent numbers printed serially many stories well known today. Of Tennyson's poems, "Sea-Dreams," 1859, "Wages," and "Lucretius," 1868, "The Charge of the Heavy Brigade," 1882, "Vastness," 1885, and "Carmen Sæculare," 1887, first appeared in *Macmillan's Magazine*. Thirty years after its beginning, the novels of Marion Crawford were appearing in installments, as well as the works of J. C. Bailey, Bret Harte, Ernest Rhys, and Gilbert Parker. *Macmillan's* was edited successively by David Masson, 1859-68; George Grove, 1868-83; John Morley, 1883-85; and Mowbray Morris, 1885-1907. Not primarily a literary periodical —it included many articles on travel, history, politics, manners, and things in general—and is noteworthy as one of the first magazines to use signed articles only. The display of talent among its contributors is very significant, illustrating the importance of the magazine as a literary medium in the second half of the century.

After *Blackwood's*, the *Cornhill Magazine* is the oldest English miscellany now published. George Smith, of the publishing firm, Smith, Elder, and Co., was the originator of this enterprise. Existing magazines were few, and when not high-priced, were narrow in literary range. It occurred to him that a shilling magazine which contained, in addition to other first-class literary matter, a serial by Thackeray, must command a large sale. His plan succeeded. After the first month, one hundred thousand copies were printed. Number one contained a section of Anthony Trollope's "Framley Parsonage" for an opening contribution, and concluded with a "Roundabout" paper ("On a Lazy Boy") by Thackeray. A horn-of-plenty cover which was to become famous was designed by Godfrey Sykes—of which "Father Prout" wrote

With Fudge, or Blarney, or the Thames on fire
Treat not thy buyer;
But proffer good material—
A genuine cereal,
Value for twelve pence, and not dear at twenty;
Such wit replenishes thy Horn of Plenty.

Smith's idea was to combine the critical review and the
serial novel (then published in monthly installments)
and give the result to the public at the price of the cheap-
est magazine. Macmillan had entered the field with a
shilling magazine two months before; but *Macmillan's*
made no great specialty of fiction. The *Cornhill*, with its
successive narratives from such story tellers as Thackeray, Trollope, Charles Lever, George Eliot, Mrs.
Gaskell, Wilkie Collins, Charles Reade, William Black,
James Payn, Henry Seton Merriman, Thomas Hardy,
Mrs. Humphrey Ward, and E. F. Benson, has presented,
since 1860, an outline of British fiction. Moreover, its
success definitely put the serial novel into periodical
literature, as an attractive feature that has never lost its
popularity.

It was a happy thought of the founder which made
Thackeray his first editor, even though the novelist
proved but an indifferent executive. His reputation made
him invaluable in the early days of the *Magazine*. Its
immediate and brilliant success during the two and one-
half years that Thackeray sat in the editorial chair,
indicate that he could not have been the worst of pilots,
Anthony Trollope to the contrary notwithstanding.

Thackeray's later novels, the efforts of Charlotte and
Emily Brontë, the first appearances of many a poem of
Tennyson (see "Tithonus"), Robert Browning, Mrs.
Browning, Meredith, Swinburne, and articles by Mat-
thew Arnold, John Addington Symonds, Leslie Stephen,

and Robert Louis Stevenson, are to be found in the files of the *Cornhill*. Thomas Hood, Washington Irving, G. H. Lewes, Bulwer-Lytton, George Macdonald, Richard Monckton Milnes, Laurence Oliphant, Adelaide Proctor, "Father Prout," and Ruskin, were other contributors of poetry and prose who united to give the *Cornhill* a higher literary quality than any other magazine of the century. Indeed, the passing years have seen its lustre dimmed but little. With the names of Margaret L. Woods, W. H. Hudson, A. E. W. Mason, Violet Jacob, the late Stanley J. Weyman, Arthur C. Benson, J. C. Snaith, Henry James, Percival Gibbon, Edmund Gosse, Sidney Colvin, Churton Collins, Birkbeck Hill, Grant Allen, W. M. Letts, William Watson, Quiller-Couch, A. A. Milne, Thomas Seccombe, Maurice Hewlett, and Laurence Housman, the *Cornhill* has held its own against a steadily increasing number of competitors—and now, after seventy years, is a necessity for every well-furnished library or reading room table.

Thackeray and the *Cornhill* introduced something new and better into the world of literary periodicals; and, after the first editor had withdrawn, the Thackeray tradition survived. For many years there was "somewhat of the Thackeray touch" in the *Cornhill*.[1] The novelist continued to contribute to it after his resignation. He was succeeded by a sort of commission-editorship, shared by Dutton Cook, Frederick Greenwood, and George Smith, himself. In 1871 Leslie Stephen was appointed to the chair, a worthy successor to his father-in-law. Dr. A. W. Ward of Peterhouse pointed out that no other English magazine had been "so liberally interfused with literary criticism of a high class," and at the same time had remained such pleasant reading, as the *Cornhill* under

[1] See "The Jubilee of the Cornhill," *Cornhill Magazine*, 101 (January 1910), 1-27.

Stephen's management.[1] Stephen resigned in 1882, and
a new era began under his friend and successor, James
Payn, a veteran of other editorial wars, whose regime
lasted fourteen years. Then J. St. Loe Strachey took command for one year (1896-97), to be followed by Reginald
John Smith, of the firm (1897-1916). Under the able
leadership of Leonard Huxley, the *Cornhill* has taken
since 1916 a new lease of life. As in the beginning, it has
still its serial narratives, intermingled with poetry and
articles of general and critical nature. It has changed its
publisher but not its character. The second oldest of the
existing magazines, it is yet one of the best.

Emerging from the multitude of mediocre miscellaneous periodicals of the second half of the century, the
Temple Bar Magazine (1860-1906) deserves mention.
It carried from the first nearly one hundred and fifty
pages of stories and articles, and some, but not a great
deal of, poetry. The first editor was George Augustus
Sala, who had begun a career of multifarious literary
activity by contributing to *Chat, Household Words, All
the Year Around*, the *Train*, and the *Illustrated Times*;
had edited the *Welcome Guest* (1858-61); long contributed the "Echoes of the Week" column to the *Illustrated London News*; and had—after some contributions
to the *Cornhill Magazine*—established as a rival the
Temple Bar. Edmund Yates, the dramatic critic, was his
sub-editor. Sala remained editor of the *Temple Bar* until
1866, when Bentley purchased the magazine.

A superior work of a somewhat popular nature was
Longman's Magazine (November 1882–April 1891), a
monthly miscellany chiefly made up of fiction. Each
copy, consisting of 124 pages, contained installments of
two serial novels, besides poems and some critical ar-

[1] Article in *Manchester Guardian*, Feb. 23, 1904. See F. W. Maitland's
Life and Letters of Leslie Stephen, N. Y. and Lon. 1906, pp. 257 ff.

ticles. Before the end of the century, with contributions from Grant Allen, F. Anstey, Austin Dobson, J. A. Froude, Thomas Hardy, William Dean Howells, Jean Ingelow, Richard Jeffries, William Archer, Walter Besant, John Burroughs, George W. E. Russell, R. E. Prothero, Eden Philpotts, Rider Haggard, Andrew Lang, Mrs. Oliphant, James Payn, Samuel Smiles, Justin McCarthy, Bret Harte, and Kipling, *Longman's Magazine* was second to none, although its really distinguishing feature lay in the number and quality of its serial stories. Only after 1900 was the identity of authors freely revealed. The names of John Oxenham, Charlotte Mew, W. L. Courtney, Michael Macdonaugh, Lewis Melville, C. E. and E. F. Benson, Beatrice Grimshaw, Laurence Housman, Walter de la Mare, Mrs. Edmund Gosse, Edward Thomas, John Masefield, Laurence Binyon, and Winifred M. Letts, then greeted readers, and gave a quality to its contents that should have ensured a longer life.[1]

Under the inspiration of the weekly journals, the *Athenaeum* and *Academy*, etc., the *Bookman*, a monthly magazine of *belles-lettres*, began in 1891 its colorful career. To-day it is in some ways the crowning achievement of that highly specialized interest in books and writers which a century of development in periodical criticism has produced. Of large size, as attractive as format and illustration can make it, the *Bookman* presents an appearance in extreme contrast to the literary journal of the past. It completely comprehends the field of its special interest. Every writer of note, every book of consequence to a literary public, finds consideration in its columns. Edited with distinction since 1923 by the late Arthur St. John Adcock, himself the author of no

[1] The *Strand Magazine* (1891 ff.) is even more popular in its appeal. Among its early contributors were Conan Doyle, E. W. Hornung, P. G. Wodehouse, Jacobs, Vachell, and H. G. Wells.

less than thirty books, its pages have been enriched by contributions from a large proportion of the living English critics.[1] It now appears as a folio of 100 to 170 pages; and its contents from year to year include invaluable biographical and critical articles concerning every author of importance. An enumeration of the department headings reveals the thorough manner in which it covers the subject of contemporary letters. These are "Books and Their Writers," the "Bookman's Diary," the "Bookshelf," "Novel Notes," the "Bookman's Table," the "Bookman Gallery," "Books of the Month," and the "Short Story Competition"—a department of fiction. The potent influence of the *Fortnightly Review* is here apparent, in the mingling of such elements as reviews with occasional poetry and fiction and biography. The *Bookman* again illustrates that interesting phenomenon, the breaking down of the traditional classifications, which marks the most characteristic change in the nature of English literary periodicals at the beginning of the twentieth century. It is illustrated as attractively as a popular magazine, and combines the most useful and alluring features of quarterly review, weekly journal, and monthly miscellany.

Two highly specialized periodicals deserve especial comment. The *Sir Walter Scott Quarterly*, issued from April 1927 to January 1928, was an admirable, if short-lived, miscellany. Its contents were entirely made up of anecdotal, critical, or descriptive articles about Scott. Edited by W. Forbes Gray, it consisted of fifty-six pages of articles from the pens of John Geddie, Sir George Douglas, Professor Rait, Historiographer Royal of Scotland, Alasdair Alpin MacGregor, Winifred Duke, Hugh Littlejohn, John Hogben, Davidson Crook, Robert Cochrane, A. M. Williams, D. S. M. Meldrum, James

[1] Mr. Adcock's death occurred on June 9, 1930.

W. Herries, Stewart A. Robertson, Vernon Rendall, J. A. Lovat-Fraser, H. G. L. King, and others. Probably the most valuable contribution was a heretofore unpublished series of Scott's letters to Lockhart, which runs through two numbers. These were supplied by Davidson Crook. The *Dickensian*, first published in January 1905 and still in progress, appeared as a monthly magazine under the editorial direction of B. W. Matz, and was continued after his death in July 1925 by the present editor, Mr. Walter Dexter. It is published by the Dickens Fellowship at the Dickens House, and is filled with articles written by lovers of "Boz"—a tribute to the perennial charm of the great English story teller. Since 1921 it has been issued quarterly. It consists of about eighty pages, with many illustrations; and each number is usually concluded by a bibliography of newspaper and magazine articles called "Dickensiana of the Quarter." The contributors to the *Dickensian* have been Percy Fitzgerald, Edwin Pugh, G. K. Chesterton, Peggy Webling, H. Pearl Adam, J. W. T. Ley, Arthur Waugh, Edward Wagenknecht, W. C. Day, T. Sturge Cotterell, Sir Alfred Robbins, J. K. Thompson, the Hon. Charles Jameson, H. Brookes Cross, F. R. Dean, and, in fact, every Dickens authority of note, in England or America. The *Dickensian* now enjoys the distinction of being the only periodical of its kind. Devoted to one great figure in English letters, it has existed for twenty-six years. Both in its character and in its astonishing career, the *Dickensian* is unique.

Another exceedingly important periodical, characteristic of the time, is *The Bookman's Journal and Print Collector*, which began publication October 31, 1919, as a 24-page weekly journal selling for threepence—"a paper for all literary men and collectors." In October 1921, it entered a new series, in the form of a monthly miscellany of thirty-six pages, with better typography and many splendid illustrations. Edited throughout its career by Wilfred G. Partington, the *Bookman's Journal* is a very important literary periodical, whether in weekly or monthly form, because of the amount of information it publishes regarding contemporary authors. In especial, Henry Danielson's bibliographies of modern authors— Flecker, Masefield, Brooke, Beerbohm, Middleton, Leonard Merrick, Francis Ledwidge, Hugh Walpole, Drinkwater, Lionel Johnson, Gissing, Hardy, etc.—make it invaluable to the student of contemporary letters. Through several years, the poems of Walter de la Mare gave its columns distinction with welcome regularity. In addition to a quantity of ordinary reviewing in each number, this journal has been almost never without a significant article on literary men or concerns, from the pens of Henry Savage, Morley Roberts, Clement K. Shorter, John Drinkwater, Horace Wyndham, George Saintsbury, Michael Sadleir, William Jaggard, Louis Golding, or the editor himself. A department entitled "Forgotten Books" is one of the most attractive features of the earlier *Bookman's Journal*. In its later numbers, the "Print Collector" side of the publication appeared to outweigh more and more the book lover's sections. Nevertheless, from first to last, the *Journal* was an admirably conceived and edited performance, and its files are now rich sources of material for the student of literature.[1]

A backward glance, as we reach the milestone "1930" reveals vital changes in the character of English literary

[1] The most recent and specialized of our literary magazines, although also of exceedingly narrow appeal to the reading public, is *Life and Letters*. It is edited by Mr. Desmond MacCarthy and obviously addressed to a limited body of readers. A typical number contains four or five contributions in seventy pages, and concludes with twenty pages of "Readers Reports." Recent contributors include Aldous Huxley, Dilys Powell, Logan Pearsall Smith, W. J. Lawrence, Robert Trevelyan, and Augustine Birrell, as well as the editor. *Life and Letters* is issued as a shilling quarterly, and is now in its fourth volume.

magazines since the beginning of the nineteenth century. The *Monthly*, the *Scots*, the *European*, and other eighteenth-century magazines which continued after 1800, carried faithfully the old news summaries, lists of stocks, births, deaths, marriages, etc. They were still, in some cases, predatory rather than original. They were unattractive in appearance; they preserved an obstinate and consistent anonymity; and it was still true that to furnish information rather than to entertain was their chief purpose. What is more important—the eighteenth century held out meagre compensations for authorship. The profession of letters was not yet a substantial or attractive one.

It remained for the magazines of the nineteenth century to increase the rewards of literary craftsmanship, and thus improve the quality of contributions by attracting a host of ambitious young writers. The *New Monthly*, *Blackwood's* and *London*, eliminated the obsolete "chronicle" matter from their columns. They improved the quality of their criticism, and made this ingredient important and stimulating. The *Monthly Repository*, and later *Bentley's* popularized the "continued" novel, which later magazines—the *Cornhill, Ainsworth's, Macmillan's* and *Longman's*—carried to a high place in the favor of readers. Magazines appeared in attractive covers and with illustrated letterpress—the work of the best artists. They secured contributions from the greatest poets of the century. Finally, under the influence of *Sherwood's Monthly* and *Bentley's Miscellany*, perhaps, they abandoned the old veil of anonymity. The modern literary magazine, a miscellaneous periodical consisting of original fiction, criticism, poetry, and general articles, is really a product of the nineteenth century. It is best illustrated today in *Blackwood's* and the *Cornhill Magazine*, or the more specialized *Scots* and *Bookman*.

XI

THE WEEKLY JOURNAL OF *BELLES-LETTRES*

For the beginning of the weekly journal devoted to *belles-lettres*, we are accustomed to look to the *Examiner* of Leigh Hunt, which began in 1808 and was conducted with independence and brilliance, by various editors, until 1881. The *Examiner* is a work of vital interest in any literary history of England, because of its criticisms, although its literary significance was less deliberate than accidental—chiefly the result of Hunt's championship of his friends. When the occasion for this championship had passed, the literary influence of the *Examiner* to a large degree vanished. It was only during the first twenty years, therefore, that the *Examiner* was a critical periodical of great value. Yet the success of this weekly paper unquestionably caused it to affect the form and the quality of later literary journals.

The *Examiner* was anticipated by at least two periodicals whose influence on later publications may be discerned. One was the *Literary Journal*; "a review of literature, science, manners, and politics," of 1803, a Thursday publication of thirty pages, selling for one shilling. At first its "literary" values were limited to one small department of poetry, although the letterpress of belletristic nature steadily increased in volume and importance. The *Journal* was projected and edited by James Mill and, until its conclusion in 1806, was his chief interest. It was the earliest true precursor of the *Literary Gazette* and *Athenaeum*.[1]

[1] See Alexander Bain, *Life of James Mill*, Lon. 1882, pp. 41-47. James Anderson's *Bee, or Literary Intelligencer* (Dec. 22, 1790–Jan.

Mill's serial was followed in 1808 by another weekly literary journal called the *Director*, edited by Thomas Frognall Dibdin. This ran to a modest total of twenty-four numbers. Its failure was not due to lack of pretentious plan. Sir Thomas Bernard founded the *Director*, and Dibdin wrote two-thirds of the contents. It was a 32-page, one-shilling octavo serial which included in its columns essays in literature, art and manners, "bibliographiana," analyses of the lectures at the Royal Institution, and descriptions of the pictures for sale at the British galleries. The most valuable parts of Dibdin's work are, undoubtedly, the comment upon and facts about Gough's, Harley's, and Rawlinson's libraries, and the Landsdowne manuscripts. But the *Director* is also worthy of remark for its extraordinary condemnation of the *Beggar's Opera*, its essays on the structure of contemporary theaters, on Shakespeare's plays, and on neglected literature. Moreover, Dibdin here exploits his own history of English literature, and furnishes valuable biographical data regarding many half-forgotten persons, like John Henley and Osborne, the bookseller. Other contributors were Bernard himself, Sir Humphrey Davy, Sir George Beaumont, Prince Hoare, William Crowe, and Mrs. Edward Forster.[1]

Neither of these earlier weekly journals may be said to have established the form which was to be standard for the next half-century, even—with some modifications— to our own day. For the form, at least, we must look to the *Examiner*, although, as is seen, it hardly deserves the

21, 1794) of Edinburgh should be noted, on account of its weekly periodicity. Its contents, however, were derivative and of inferior quality. It does not anticipate, in any true sense, the later weekly critical journal. Ruddiman's *Weekly Magazine* is likewise not a true precursor of the journal of *belles-lettres*, in spite of its literary content. The same may be said of the *Grub Street Journal*.

[1] See T. F. Dibdin, *Reminiscences of a Literary Life*, Lon. 1836, i, 249-252.

title sometimes given it of "the first weekly literary journal." Except for a department called the "Theatrical Examiner," which mainly concerned itself with the contemporary stage, literature was virtually ignored by the editors, until Shelley and Keats began to need critical support from Leigh Hunt. Aroused by the campaign of detraction and vilification waged by Croker, John Taylor Coleridge, and others of the *Quarterly* group, Leigh Hunt—before his removal to Pisa to edit the *Liberal*—took up his pen again and again in defence of his friends. The immediate value of his critical efforts is difficult to determine, for often his valiant championship only brought the defended greater measures of wrath and contumely. Hunt was a marked man in those days, and what the Tories found it hardest to forgive Shelley and Keats was their association with him. But other generations, without the prejudice of the Eldon Tories, now appreciate the service of Hunt—his heroic critical defence of friends whom he rightly believed to be great poets. In the *Examiner*, between 1816 and 1822 were criticised, or quoted approvingly, or published for the first time, eleven of Shelley's more important poems. They were "Alastor," "The Hymn to Intellectual Beauty," "The Revolt of Islam," "Ozymandias," "Rosalind and Helen," "The Cenci," "Prometheus Unbound," "The Ode Written October 1819," "To a Skylark," "Lines Written Among the Euganean Hills," and "Adonais." During Shelley's lifetime, no other periodical contained so many articles about his work as the *Examiner*; and no contemporary writer approached Leigh Hunt as sympathetic and discerning critic of his poetry.[1] Of Keats and Byron, also, Hunt wrote many defences and

[1] See my "Shelley's Debt to Leigh Hunt and the *Examiner*," *Pub. Mod. Lang. Assoc.*, XL, 185-192, March 1925.

critical appreciations, presenting the beauties of their works in long and judiciously selected quotations. Thus, for a short time, at least, he made the *Examiner* the most valorous critical champion of the young Romantic poets.

The *Examiner* appeared on Saturdays as a sixteen-page weekly journal. Its department called the "Political Examiner" was the first and principal part of it, and contained the most fearless political writing of the day. The "Theatrical Examiner" followed, famous for Leigh Hunt's impartial and outspoken criticism of contemporary dramatic productions. In the 1820's the form of the paper was changed and a good deal of poetry was included, as well as criticism, and a department of short reviews called the "Literary Examiner." After 1830, however, the *Examiner* contained almost no literary interest whatsoever, except the reviews of the "Literary Examiner" department, which seldom were criticisms of value, and the now occasional "Theatrical" section.

Hazlitt could write contemptuously in 1822, "The Weekly Literary Journals, Gazettes, etc., they are a truly insignificant race—a sort of flimsy announcements of favored publications—insects in letters, that are swallowed up in the larger blaze of full-orbed criticism." He admitted, however, that the *Examiner* led all the other weekly Journals in "steadiness and principle," and was the ablest and most respectable of them. By 1845 the *Examiner*—then the property of Albany Fonblanque—had a circulation of 6,000 a week; and its readers were "the intelligent and educated classes."[1] John Forster was associated with Fonblanque for a time, and occasional reviews of great vigor and discernment reveal his influence on the literary function of the periodical. The *Examiner* was

[1] See the *London Journal* of 1845, an unimportant sixteen-page weekly journal. The first volume has a valuable series of sketches of the London Press.

continued as a weekly journal until February 26, 1881, after which it became an annual publication.[1]

Under the leadership of the *Examiner*, the form of the weekly journal of *belles-lettres* became standardized. This type of periodical was, with few exceptions, a sixteen-page folio, issued on Saturdays, and containing reviews of various lengths, poetry, letters of contributors, and gossip of books and authors.[2] It is exemplified in the *Literary Gazette* of 1817-1862, which was founded by William Jerdan and edited successively by him (1817-50), by Samuel Phillips, L. Reeve, J. M. Jephson, Shirley Brooks, Henry Christmas, W. R. Workman, F. Arnold, John Morley, and C. W. Goodwin. Its title-page promised "original essays on polite literature, the arts and sciences, a review of new publications, poetry; criticisms of fine arts, the drama, etc.; biography, correspondence of distinguished persons, anecdotes, *jeu d'esprit*, proceedings of literary societies, and literary intelligence." In 1862, it was incorporated with the *Parthenon*, a weekly journal edited by W. C. Goodwin.

The greater importance of the *Literary Gazette*, however, lay in its "novel" plan and "experimental" nature. At the end of the second year of unqualified success, the *Gazette* contained a self-congratulatory article—apparently by the editor, Jerdan—in which it was declared that over four hundred new works had been reviewed, "with extracts"; that some fifty biographical memoirs had been published; and that the *Gazette* had omitted "no notice of consequence to the fine arts or science."[3]

[1] A qualified success in this form of periodical was the *London Review and Weekly Journal* of 1860-69. Started by Charles Mackay, it was contributed to by Laurence Oliphant and William Black, the novelists. It was finally incorporated with the *Examiner*.

[2] It is impossible to ignore the *Champion* of John Scott, later the unfortunate editor of the *London Magazine*. Formerly *Drakard's Paper*, the *Champion* appeared (1814-1822) as an eight-page Sunday newspaper, containing some theatrical notices, and much miscellaneous literary matter.

[3] See *Literary Gazette*, Jan. 2, 1819, and William Jerdan, *Autobiography*. London 1852-3.

Actually, scientific matters were very minor elements in
the content of the journal. Its columns were almost entirely filled with letterpress that concerned books and
authors. Each number contained, on the average, two
long reviews that included copious extracts from the
works criticised. Indeed, the *Literary Gazette* was aston-
ishingly similar to the highly specialized weekly literary
journals of the present time. The high aim of the founder
and first editor was thus set forth in 1819:

> To the lovers of literature, these volumes, when they have outlived
> their year, may not be so unimportant, but rather constitute a great
> portion of literary history, and be indeed the annals of the republic
> (of letters).

The yellowing volumes of the *Literary Gazette* comprehend, in truth, "a great portion of literary history." The
form of this journal and the character of its contents
never changed during its career of nearly half a century.
The work of George Crabbe, Mary Russell Mitford and
Barry Cornwall gave early distinction to its columns.
Indeed, in its pages, the student may find a cross-section
of the literary activity of three decades—the "annals of
the republic" of letters.

The purest early example of this type of literary periodical is seen in the *Literary Journal, and General Miscellany of Science, Arts, History, Politics*, etc., of
1818-19. This was a sixteen-page weekly paper, selling
for sixpence—what was hereafter for a time the standard
price—very similar to our modern weekly journal of
books. In other words, it was almost entirely made up of
book reviews or matter concerned with books and authors. While it lasted, it was unquestionably the best of
the weekly critical publications. In the very rare copies
that survive, we find long critical articles on such writers
as Wordsworth, Lamb, Hogg, Scott, Cobbett, and Byron.
In fact, it contains contemporary opinions on all the im-

portant authors and the most valuable books of the two years it covered.

Almost equally good is the *Literary Chronicle and Weekly Review* (became—Nos. 59-260—*Country Literary Chronicle*) which began, 1819, in the standard form of a six-penny Saturday paper. It included well-written reviews of Byron, Lockhart, Crabbe, and other contemporary authors, with somewhat wrong-headed, perhaps, but vigorous and arresting criticism. In 1828 it was incorporated with the *Athenaeum*, which had been founded on January 2. Another Saturday journal, the *Verulam*, of sixteen pages, was begun on March 1, dealing with almost anything except literary matters. On May 17 (with No. 12) the *Verulam* was likewise merged in the prosperous new publication, which James Silk Buckingham, the founder and proprietor, wanted to make a reincarnation of the Athenaeum of antiquity—the "resort of the most distinguished philosophers, historians, orators and poets of our day." Buckingham, who had been expelled from India in 1823 for the boldness with which he attacked in his *Calcutta Journal* the Government abuses, opened the career of the *Athenaeum* with an assault upon the conservative *Quarterly Review* and its method of mingling political bias and critical judgments. Among the chief contributors to the *Athenaeum* during the first two years were Frederick Denison Maurice and John Sterling, former Cambridge "Apostles," who represented a young and vigorous movement in contemporary letters. At the end of its second year, the paper was acquired by Charles Wentworth Dilke, the friend of Keats, continuator of Dodsley's *Old Plays*, and a contributor to several periodicals. Dilke at once took a stand against the then general practice of inserting paid puffs for the book trade. He reduced the price to fourpence, and changed the publishing time from Wednesday to Saturday.

Sterling and Maurice were co-editors of the *Athenaeum* from July to December 1828; Henry Stebbing acted as assistant editor almost from its founding; Dilke himself edited it, 1830-1846; Dilke's son followed him as proprietor; and later editors were J. K. Hervey, 1846-52; William Hepworth Dixon, 1853-69; John Doran, 1869-70; Norman MacColl, 1871-1900; Vernon Rendall, 1901-16; and Arthur Greenwood, 1916-1920. John Randall was press reader for thirty years under MacColl and Rendall, and continued as sub-editor under the latter. For a time Dilke's co-proprietors were J. H. Reynolds, Thomas Hood, and Allan Cunningham. He enlisted to his aid Charles Lamb, Barry Cornwall, George Darley, and even such foreign critics as Sainte-Beuve.[1]

In its earlier days, the *Athenaeum* exceeded, in circulation, any other similar paper. Its price was again reduced in 1862 to threepence, and it long held its own against increasing numbers of rivals. In the 1840's it assumed the format and physical appearance which were familiar to several generations of readers—the fine print and pages of small advertisements at beginning and end giving it an ultra-conservative appearance which belied its nature. In this general form it continued until the 1890's, gradually thereafter changing into the transformed journal of literature, science, art, etc., which it became under the editorship of H. J. Massingham and J. Middleton Murray, in 1920 and following.

Under various editors and varying fortunes, however, the *Athenaeum* has realized in every decade something, at least, of the high design of Buckingham, "to make it the resort of the most distinguished philosophers, historians, orators, and poets. . . ." It never, at any time after 1828, ceased to be an important journal of *belles-lettres*.

---

[1] See memoir of Dilke by his grandson in *The Papers of a Critic*, London 1875.

During the 1840's its literary merits were greatly enhanced by contributions from Thomas Carlyle, James Hogg, Thomas Hood, Leigh Hunt, Charles Lamb, Walter Savage Landor, and a little later, Robert Browning, J. C. Jeaffreson, Andrew Lang, Theodore Watts-Dunton, and Walter Pater. Dilke's valuable discussions of the authorship of the "Junius" letters, his defences of Wilkes and "Peter Pindar," and many of the results of his researches in the writings and career of Pope, appeared first in its pages. As the years passed, there were notes by Professor Walter Skeat, as well as valuable correspondence from G. M. Trevelyan, and many other English scholars, to give it weight. And a few years ago one could write, "There are middle-aged men who learnt almost all they know about poetry from Mr. Watts-Dunton's delightful and profound criticisms in the *Athenaeum*."[1]

Its volume gradually increased until, in 1905, we find the body of the *Athenaeum* made up of about twenty pages of articles and reviews, literary information, and various sections for special subjects of interest to the literary world, prefaced by six pages of advertisements, for books chiefly, and concluded by four pages of similar notices—a total of thirty pages. A distinct change of form and price came in 1920, soon after J. Middleton Murray took charge of it.[2] New features, now well known, such as the "Marginalia" by "Autolycus" (A. L. Huxley) appeared to lure its weekly readers. Its larger print and more attractive appearance made it a more popular publication—but more popular in aspect only. The high quality of its content is amply indicated by its

[1] *Poetry Review*, vol. V., p. 3.
Mr. A. W. Evans was literary editor under Greenwood, in 1916-20.
[2] From January 1916 to March 1919, the *Athenaeum* appeared as a 28-page monthly. It resumed its standard form on April 14, appearing thereafter weekly.

roster of contributors. A weekly story (a new element of interest) appeared each Saturday, of which the most notable contributor was Katherine Mansfield. Her work was in this way introduced to a discriminating public. Anton Tchehov, Max Beerbohm, Stella Benson, J. D. Beresford, W. M. Lodge, Virginia Woolf, Stephen Hudson, Arlo Williams, and Robert Nichols also contributed fiction. Poetry appeared from the pens of Hardy, Edwin Arlington Robinson, Edith Sitwell, Robert Graves, Laurence Binyon, Conrad Aiken, T. S. Eliot, Edmund Blunden, W. H. Davies, Eden Phillpotts, Wilfred Owen, Julian Huxley, and W. W. Gibson. Articles, mainly critical, represented the distinguished talents of H. M. Tomlinson (who was literary editor, 1917-23), R. W. Chapman, T. S. Eliot, George Santayana, W. J. Lawrence, Bonamy Dobrée, Logan Pearsall Smith, A. A. Milne, A. Clutton-Brock, George Saintsbury, J. T. Sheppard, Herbert Read, E. J. Dent, Edward Moore, W. E. Henley, Katherine Mansfield and Murray, himself.

Mr. Murray continued to edit the *Athenaeum* until, on February 11, 1921, it was merged with the *Nation*, a very similar weekly journal, which had been set up in 1907. The combined periodical now appears as *The Nation and the Athenaeum*, and is edited by H. D. Henderson.[1]

Before the birth of the *Athenaeum*, John Hunt had, on July 5, 1823, started a new weekly journal, *The Literary Examiner,* published like the *Examiner* on Saturdays, but unlike it, in that it was wholly devoted to the *belles-lettres*. It was another of the common sixteen-page periodicals. Leigh Hunt, who has been called the "editor," was really in Florence during the entire run of this

---

[1] *The Man of Letters*, an excellent but short-lived weekly journal should not be overlooked in this survey of the type. It was published in London by John Knight and Henry Lacey, and appeared as a fourpenny literary paper for eight numbers—from April 3 to May 22, 1824. In form it closely approximated the American *Saturday Review of Literature*, of a century later.

periodical, which lasted for only twenty-six numbers. He makes no further mention of it in his *Autobiography* than to say that his brother set it up and that he "contributed some articles" to it.[1] Each number contained an "Indicator" essay, evidently a continuation of the *Indicator* of 1819-1821 (an essay periodical which appeared on Thursdays for seventy-six weeks) since the first essay is numbered "LXXVII." This essay formed the first part of the two-part periodical; a "Review of Books" occupied the second. The last page or two was frequently devoted to miscellaneous literary materials—often poems. The *Literary Examiner* was brought to a close at the end of the year, with the number dated December 27.

The year 1828 seems to have been a fertile one for weekly periodic enterprises. One week after the initial number of the *Athenaeum* appeared, Leigh Hunt issued his *Companion*, an eight-page paper published on Wednesday, and selling for threepence. With the fifth number it became a sixteen-page journal, very similar to the *Athenaeum*; and, selling at fourpence, half the price of the latter, it was very obviously a throat-cutting competitor of Buckingham's enterprise. The early numbers contain excellent theatrical criticisms from the pen of Hunt, but otherwise the *Companion* had little to raise it above the general level of the weekly serials. Its end came with the 29th number, on July 23. Of slightly longer life was the *Literary Journal: a Weekly Review*, which began on January 5 and lasted until October 4, as an eight-page, unattractive, critical periodical. It ceased publication with the fortieth number, the editor dolefully lamenting that merit alone was not sufficient to give a periodical success.

Of more popular appeal was another competitor of these weekly journals, the *Spectator*, which has survived

---

[1] *Autobiography*, Ed. E. Blunden, Oxford 1928, p. 445.

to our own day. It was described on its title page as "a weekly journal of news, politics, literature, and science." Beginning in 1828, this periodical never ceased to be a mixture of politics and literature and science, although the news was later for some years dropped. This news element was, in the early *Spectator*, the most important component. Fifteen pages out of the twenty-four were given up to it. Obviously, the *Spectator* began as a newspaper with some popular and learned features. A Saturday publication, priced at one shilling, it offered, in each number, at least one review.

The belletristic matter in the early numbers of the *Spectator* occupied but a small percentage of the space. It consisted usually of only one weekly article—frequently a review of a book of fiction or travel, such as Bulwer's *Eugene Aram* or Borrow's *Gypsies in Wales*. By 1860 the periodical had acquired much more of a "literary" character, containing, among other things of interest, excellent reviews of Hawthorne, Lowell, and other American writers. By this time, also, it had been enlarged to thirty-two pages, the last six being entirely filled with advertising. Politics still had its place. News had been abandoned—to be re-introduced later, however. The "Spectator's Library" had become a department known as "Books." To-day, the *Spectator* exists as a Saturday journal of about thirty pages, consisting of news, politics, literature, music, art, correspondence, poetry, short articles on country life and sports, insurance matters, motoring, and almost anything else of human interest. The literary elements are chiefly to be found in the five or six pages of excellent reviews which appear each week.

The *Spectator* was established by Robert Stephen Rintoul, the printer and editor of the *Dundee Advertiser* (1811-25) who had come to London in 1826. He was the proprietor of the *Spectator* from 1828 to his death in 1858, with editorial assistance from Thornton Hunt; and under his directing hand the journal, neutral in politics but decided in its criticisms, took a prominent part in the discussion of all questions of social and political reform. Its "magisterial seriousness" under Rintoul's guidance, and under the subsequent joint-management of Richard Holt Hutton and that great journalist, Meredith Townsend, found expression in the somewhat opinionated treatment of men of letters; but the value of its later criticism is evident in its prompt recognition of such writers as Samuel Butler, W. E. Henley, Rudyard Kipling, Harriet Martineau, Walter Pater, R. L. Stevenson, George Moore, and Thomas Hardy. Its critics failed, however, to find the same merits that posterity has discovered in Tennyson, Arnold, Meredith, Dickens, and Charlotte Brontë. Carlyle, Leigh Hunt, Thomas Hughes, Edmund Gosse, Julian Hawthorne, H. D. Traill, W. E. H. Lecky, George Saintsbury, John Morley, John Buchan, E. V. Lucas, and Mrs. Oliphant are a few of the distinguished contributors of literary "copy," whose names are enumerated by the biographer of this famous journal.[1]

J. St. Loe Strachey, who began reviewing for the *Spectator* in 1885, continued to be a valuable member of its staff for more than ten years, before he finally became sole editor and proprietor. He quickly brought the *Spectator* to an unprecedented height of prosperity, with a circulation more than doubled. His right hand colleague was C. L. Graves, who had before worked with him on the *Liberal Unionist* and on the *Cornhill Magazine*, and who was and continued to be a contributor to *Punch*. Other helpers, who remain to this day upon the

---

[1] See W. B. Thomas, *The Story of the Spectator*, 1828-1928, London 1928; see also *Spectator*, Nov. 3, 10, 17, 1928.

staff, are J. B. Atkins and Stephen Gwynn. Sometime before his death, Strachey relinquished the editorship, in 1925, and for a few months J. B. Atkins acted as editor. Mr. Evelyn Wrench, who had already become the chief proprietor of the *Spectator*, then assumed the labor of the editorial office, which he continues to perform.

The policies of the *Spectator* have been singularly uniform throughout its long history. It was said of Rintoul that he endeavored to make his journal "a truthful and attractive record of all social movements, and of all that was accomplished in art, science, or literature, and he set himself to promote social and civil reforms irrespective of party." What Rintoul attempted, we find the *Spectator* still endeavoring to achieve to-day. Again, it was said in 1858,[1] and is probably still true, that "by far the greater part of the readers of the *Spectator* have always been of a class that is not affected by partisan spleen: its circulation being chiefly, as it must always aim to be, among the men of culture, who like to listen to all sides of controversies, provided the argument is conducted with fairness and moderation."

One other weekly paper of 1828 deserves more than casual mention. The *Edinburgh Literary Journal or Weekly Register of Criticism and Belles-Lettres*, appeared on Saturdays, its pages entirely devoted to the interests of writers and readers. It was first issued on November 15, and continued until December 1831. The first sixteen pages consisted of critical articles, reviews, and information valuable to students of literature in the period; pages 15 and 16 were regularly taken up with book and theatrical advertisements. The brevity of its career is not a recommendation for the support of literature in the Scotch capital. Alaric Watts, John Wilson, J. S. Knowles, Robert Chambers, Alexander Balfour,

[1] *Spectator*, May 1, 1858.

Henry G. Bell, Allan Cunningham, James Hogg, William Tennant, G. P. R. James, Lord Brougham, Thomas Campbell, and Robert Gilfillan were among the known contributors.[1]

Following in the wake of the *Examiner*, the *Literary Gazette*, the *Athenaeum*, and the *Spectator*, were several journals that deserve at least a passing comment. The *Censor*, a semi-weekly publication, appeared for sixteen numbers to rival the *Athenaeum* (which it attacked as "the most dull and pedantic periodical of the day"), on the one hand, and Leigh Hunt's publications on the other (see introductory address.) It continued from September 6, 1828 to April 4, 1829, including in its columns articles on Byron and Shelley, an "unpublished essay of Addison," and theatrical notices. The *Literary Guardian and Spectator of Books* (1831-1832) "by Messrs. Bookworm, Glow-Worm, and Silk-Worm," is really important for its reviews of contemporary works—chiefly novels and poems. In an article on the magazines of that time, it praises *Blackwood's* and, less warmly, the *Monthly*, regards the *New Monthly* as less meritorious than the *Monthly,* calls the *Metropolitan* "well furnished," and castigates *Fraser's* for its "indiscriminate habit of abuse and grumbling." *Chamber's Edinburgh Journal*, an eight-page Saturday[2] folio of 1832, was a work of William and Robert Chambers, publishers of Edinburgh. The long run of the *Edinburgh Journal* gives it a right to consideration, although its earlier material was often reprinted rather than original, and the writers who contributed their work to it were seldom of first rank. Poetry, fiction and biography made up most of its literary matter. After 1854, it was continued as *Chamber's Journal of Popular Literature, Science and Art.*

---

[1] The *Atlas*, "a general newspaper and journal of literature," of 1829, gave only one page of its weekly sixteen to the concerns of literature.
[2] The first number appeared on Friday, February 4.

The success of this venture in Edinburgh led to the establishment of a similar popular weekly in *Chamber's London Journal*, 1841-43, edited by Edward L. L. Blanchard, with some aid from William Henry Wills, who was later to be Dickens' assistant on the *Daily News*. It is still in progress, now a very "popular" monthly periodical of fiction and general articles.

Bell's Literary Intelligence, 1834, a short-lived Saturday, eight-page paper was almost completely literary, with current theatrical notices and other standard ingredients; *The Critic of Art*, 1844, continued as the *Critic; a Journal of British and Foreign Literature and the Arts*, 1844-63, was a well-intentioned but undistinguished weekly. *Hogg's Weekly Instructor or Titan*, 1845-53, continued as *Hogg's Instructor* until 1856, and then as a monthly magazine, *The Titan*, until 1859. Published at Edinburgh by James Hogg, it was, like the Chambers' work, largely made up of reprinted poetry and fiction of a generally inferior quality. It further showed the popularity of the Saturday journal of criticism, until it became a monthly magazine in 1856; and its biographical sketches of literary characters are noteworthy. A *Weekly Novelist* of 1858-59, was a variant of the type—a medium of highly romantic fiction. It was in the standard sixteen-page, folio form, and sold for the popular price of a penny. Its value, like that of its predecessors, *Bell's Weekly Magazine* of 1834 and the *Weekly Magazine* of 1838-39, lay in its helping to popularize fiction in a cheap form, and in further making acceptable the serial novel, as an ingredient of the periodical. These weekly journals and their like unquestionably prepared the way for the phenomenal popularity of periodical fiction at the present time.

Notes and Queries, "a medium of intercommunication for literary men, artists, antiquaries, genealogists, etc.," one of the most valuable, if unpretentious, of our weekly publications, began on Saturday, November 3, 1849, a sixteen-page pamphlet, selling for threepence. "When found, make a note of it," expressed the principle upon which it was conceived; its method—that of question and answer—takes us back to a similar periodical founded with much the same purpose, the *Athenian Mercury* of 1691-97. But while the oracular wisdom of the "Athenian Society" satisfied the readers of the late seventeenth century, the "curious" of to-day, find greater comfort in signed answers—in knowing the source of their information. This publication began with William John Thoms, as its founder and first editor. He was followed by Dr. John Doran and Joseph Knight. Vernon Rendall succeeded Knight in the editorial office until 1912, when the present editor, Miss Florence Hayllar, took charge. From the earliest days, *Notes and Queries* has served the interests of students, not only by answering questions but by publishing weekly bits of information that are too short or fragmentary to be included in the other journals of scholarship. Moreover, it has given lists of books issued by such publishing clubs and societies as the Roxburghe Club or *Der Literarische Verein* of Stuttgart. *Notes and Queries* remains with us to-day, an eighteen-page weekly, little different in appearance from the journal which appeared eighty years ago. It is now advertised as a work "for Readers, Writers, Collectors, and Librarians."[1]

No journalists of the century made greater efforts to develop the journal of *belles-lettres* than the brothers, John and Leigh Hunt. Leigh Hunt's *Tatler, A Daily Journal of Literature and the Stage* (September 4, 1830–March 31, 1832) is one of the most interesting periodicals

[1] The *Illustrated London News*, begun on May 14, 1842, has continued to our day as a weekly of great popularity. It now devotes three of its sixteen pages to books and authors. Its most notable feature is, of course, G. K. Chesterton's "Book Notes,"

of the century, in that it shows the failure of an attempt to issue a daily literary journal. This is the more interesting in view of the fact that in our own day, with many thousands of readers interested in matters of authorship and literature, not one such periodical exists. Hunt's effort to establish such a literary periodical is impressive when one remembers the comparatively small reading public of his generation. The *Tatler* was, while it lasted, a very noteworthy journal. Its motto, *veritas et varietas*, was suggestive of its nature and contents and the obvious ideal of its editor. It was written almost entirely by Hunt himself—an astounding display of literary fecundity. The "Play-Goer" department, "by the original theatrical critic in the Examiner," contains what were probably the most unprejudiced criticisms of contemporary performances and plays. The "Reader" department consisted of extracts from new books—a new application of an old critical method—with occasional illuminating comments. The *Tatler* was continued for 493 numbers, appearing every day of the week except Sunday, as a four-page folio publication, selling for twopence. It never became popular, so Hunt tells us, "beyond the coterie of play going readers."[1]

Another of Hunt's numerous literary periodicals was that known as *Leigh Hunt's London Journal*, which appeared on April 2, 1834, a sixteen-page folio, selling for a penny and a half. Always an experimenter in periodicals, Hunt planned this as a cheap Wednesday journal "entirely unconnected with politics," and announced that it would contain "a weekly abstract of some important book, after the fashion of *Johnston's Edinburgh Magazine*." Its miscellaneous materials of fiction, essays,

---

[1] *Autobiography*, Oxford 1928, p. 500. *The Chat of the Week*, 1830 another of Hunt's publications, practically non-literary, was stopped by the effort of the Government to stamp it.

poetry, etc., were "to assist the enquiring mind, animate the struggling, and sympathize with all." After sixty-two numbers had been issued, it absorbed the *Printing Machine*, and became *Leigh Hunt's London Journal and the Printing Machine*, selling for two-pence, as a Saturday journal, until its conclusion in December 1835. "The note which it had struck was of too aesthetical a nature for the cheap readers of those days," says Hunt, explaining its failure many years later in his *Autobiography*, in which he also pays tribute to Egerton Webbe, one of the chief contributors.[1] He points out that the *Journal* of 1850 (December 7–March 29) "a miscellany for the cultivation of the memorable, the progressive, and the beautiful," likewise a sixteen-page, penny-and-a-half paper, was the old *London Journal* revived; and that it failed after seventeen numbers were published "chiefly from the smallness of the means which the proposers had thought sufficient for its establishment." This revived periodical had some features to recommend it, such as the "weekly novelist" department, usually filled by Leigh Hunt. Many of the contributions were signed with the names of Charles Ollier, Walter Savage Landor, Vincent L. Hunt, R. H. Horne, William Allingham, and Henry Beauclerck.

Another *Hunt's Journal* appeared in 1844, on Saturdays (July 6–December 28), representing, in this case, the editorial activities of Frederick Knight Hunt. It appears to have been, for thirty-six numbers at least, a very original and successful variant of the standard type. In size and price it followed the previous works of Leigh Hunt. Its novelty lay in the effort of the editor "to describe the last new novel, the last new play, the last new book of travels, the last new poem, the last new music, and the

[1] *Autobiography*, Oxford Press, 1928, pp. 508-9, 540.

last new engraving." Its columns contained, also, original articles, fiction, a series of pen and ink sketches of London, and some other minor features.

The *Saturday Review*, one of the important periodicals of the century, began in 1855 as a twenty-four page journal containing little of literary value except a few reviews. By 1860, however, its reviews had become long and important. John St. Loe Strachey became an important contributor in the 'eighties. By 1890 almost half its thirty pages of contents were occupied with critical articles. At this point in its long and successful career, it was most belletristic in nature. In 1893 we find its contents broken up into sections suggestive of its later interests, and note that reviews have decreased in number. Editors of the *Saturday Review* in the last quarter century include Harold Hodge (1898-1913) Hon. Gervase Beckett and G. A. B. Dewar (1913-1916), Arthur A. Baumann (1916-1921), Sydney Brooks (1921), Filson Young (1921-24) and Gerald Barry (1924-30). It appears in its latest numbers as a miscellaneous publication with well-established sections—articles of general interest by T. Earl Welby, Vernon Rendall, J. B. Priestley, Gerald Gould, Ernest Betts, and Gordon Phillips; reviews of fiction supervised by L. P. Hartley, reviews of books by Edward Shanks, Robert Lynd and Humbert Wolfe; theatrical criticism by Ivor Brown; art by Walter Bayes; and poetry cared for by Gerald Bullett. The variety of its contents is shown by the sectional headings, "Broadcasting," "Letters to the Editor," "Acrostics," "Literary Competitions," "The City." The famous initials "G. B. S." appeared early in the career of the *Saturday Review*, and its popularity as a literary journal was enhanced by the arresting theatrical criticisms of the later dramatist. Not only Shaw, but H. G. Wells, Aubrey Beardsley, Arthur Symons, Max Beerbohm, and Cunninghame Graham were "discovered" by Frank Harris, while he was editor of the *Saturday Review*, between 1894 and 1898. Other chief contributors of literary matter have been Hardy, Hugh Walpole, Ernest Dimnet, Hillaire Belloc, Edward Davidson, Edmund Gosse, Stewart M. Ellis, Martin Armstrong, and H. J. Massingham.[1]

Unquestionably, one of the finest literary journals of the nineteenth century was the pretentious *Reader: A Review of Current Literature*, (1863-66). It first appeared on Saturday, January 3, a large folio of twenty-eight pages, selling for fourpence. The first four pages and the last six were taken up with book advertisements; pages 5 to 8 were usually devoted to short book notices, and the remaining fourteen pages consisted of longer reviews and articles. What was attempted by the founders is indicated in the preliminary announcement:

Each number contains a full and detailed list of all books and pamphlets published during the week, specifying their prices, size, number of pages, maps, etc., and, wherever it is desirable, each publication is accompanied by a short description notice. All works deserving further consideration are reviewed at length within a week or two of publication. The especial attention devoted by the READER to Foreign Literature, enables its readers to keep themselves acquainted with every work of interest published on the Continent or in America . . .

Correspondence on all literary and scientific topics from writers of note finds a place in the READER.

Like the *Monthly* and *Critical Reviews* of a century earlier, the *Reader* was a periodical designed to notice "all books." The fullness of this critical plan is important, in the light of later-day attempts and achievements. John Malcolm Ludlow, David Masson, John Dennis and Thomas Bendyshe were the editors, and through their

[1] Early in 1930, even as this account was being written, the editorial staff and most of the contributors, in consequence of a change of policy by the proprietor, abandoned the *Saturday Review*, and, under the leadership of Gerald Barry, set up a new journal, the *Week End Review*. Shaw and Bennett lent a hand in this latest undertaking.

efforts a galaxy of writers was added to the staff of the *Reader*, including Richard Garnett, Frederic Harrison, Thomas Hughes, F. D. Maurice, Mark Pattison, Wm. M. Rossetti, Leslie Stephen, R. H. Hutton, Mrs. Gaskell, Lowes Dickinson, Charles Kingsley, J. Norman Lockyer, and Laurence Oliphant. Bendyshe was proprietor, editor, and, to a large extent, the writer of this journal, which, if it failed to rival seriously the *Athenaeum*, deserves recognition as a worthy competitor. Bendyshe had a knack of dealing, in scholarly and original fashion, with literary subjects and persons of all periods. Fresh in approach and intolerant of the commonplace, the *Reader* probably affected favorably the literary journalism of the 'sixties and helped to bring about the great improvement that marked the next two or three decades.[1]

The prototype, in form at least, of the present *Times Literary Supplement* appeared in 1863 for eleven numbers. It was a sixteen-page, Saturday, penny periodical, issued from March 14 to May 23, called the *Literary Times*, "a critical journal of modern literature." The famous "*T. L. S.*" as we know it today, first appeared on January 17, 1902, as the *Times Literary Supplement*. It was issued on Thursdays. On March 17, 1914, it became a separate publication. The high quality of its contents has never varied. It reviews, with the utmost possible approximation of completeness, the scholarly output of the time. Thus, it rivals the so-called "scholarly" journals in the permanent value of its reviews and correspondence. Although, for the most part, it has preserved a consistent and discreet anonymity, its staff of discerning, well-informed critics have seldom abused their opportunities,

[1] See also the *Irish People*, 1863-5, Dublin, and the *Irish Book Lover*, 1909-16. The latter was a very valuable monthly magazine of 14-24 pages, wholly devoted to Irish literature and its contacts. It contained "editor's gossip," queries and replies, notices of books, Irish biographies and obituaries. It was published in London.

THE
Humours of a *Coffee-House* :
A
COMEDY.

As it is Dayly Acted by

Levy, *a Recruiting Officer.*	Venture, *a Merchant.*	Shuffle, *a Time-server.*
Hazard, *a Gamester.*	Talley, *a Stock-Jobber.*	Bays, *a Poet.*
Bite, *a Sharper.*	Querpo, *a Quack.*	Compass, *a Sailor.*
Nice, *a Beau.*	Trick, *a Lawyer.*	Harlem, *a News-writer.*
Blunt, *a Plain Dealer.*	Horoscope, *an Astrologer.*	Bohee, *the Coffee-man.*
Whim, *a Projector.*		

Note, These Persons are introduc'd only as occasion serves.

Wednesday, June 25th, 1707.

The PROLOGUE.

THE *various Humours that Divert the Age,*
In Pomp appear on This *frequented Stage :*
Soldier and Priest, each in their different ways,
Prophanely Curses, or Devoutly Prays :
The Doctor here, cries up his Cordial Pills,
Which some for Gain, but few for Conscience Sells.
The Parson, Gravely proves, from Writ Divine,
Coffee's a Christian Liquor, —— *after Wine ;*
Yet in his warmer Hours his Soul Unmasks,
And Bans the Heritick's Averse to Flasks,
But would more willingly a Turkish Faith approve,
Did but their Mufties Drink as well as Love.

The

AN IMPORTANT PREDECESSOR OF THE MODERN COMIC JOURNAL

and have made the *T. L. S.* to-day perhaps the most widely read and respected critical organ in the English-reading world.[1]

The *Academy*, "a monthly record of literature, learning, science and art," began on Saturday, October 9, 1869, as anything but the six-penny weekly journal of the last quarter of the nineteenth century. Mr. Charles E. C. B. Appleton set it up, and owned and edited it until his death in 1879. After 1871, it appeared as a distinctly literary journal; and it remained a most important organ of critical opinion until 1916, edited successively by C. E. Doble, J. S. Cotton, Lord Alfred Douglas, C. Cowper, and T. W. H. Crosland.

The *Academy* was not only a journal of the *belles-lettres* but a repository of learned fact—it combined the functions of the modern literary supplement and the scholarly periodical, such as the *Review of English Studies*.[2] During the last three decades of the nineteenth

[1] *The London Review and Weekly Journal of Politics, Literature, Art, and Society* (from July 7, 1860-December 31, 1864) was conducted by Charles Mackay. It consisted of a large twenty-four-page folio, issued on Saturdays for 3-4d, and running to a total of 235 numbers. Original poetry and reviews of books were regular features. It contained much excellent biography and criticism, although its "literary" features seldom occupied more than one fourth of the column space. In 1864 it published an important article on contemporary magazines, in which *Blackwood's, Fraser's, Macmillan's*, the *Cornhill*, the *Dublin University Magazine, London Society, Good Words*, the *Churchman's Family Magazine, Our Own Fireside, Christian Work*, and *The Month*, are mentioned as the outstanding miscellanies of the time. (Compare p. 315 n.)

The Book-Worm, 1866-71, of J. P. Berjeau, deserves passing notice. It was a sixteen-page monthly journal, selling for one shilling. Its contents were chiefly illustrated articles on manuscripts and on book-hunting, and notices of the sales of books.

The British Weekly, "a Journal of Social and Christian Progress," begun 1886, contains some competent criticism; but is mainly devoted to religious propaganda. It is now a two-penny journal of eighteen pages.

[2] *The Review of English Studies* was established in 1927 with R. B. McKerrow as editor, and most of the well-known English scholars in its "advisory panel." It is a quarterly of 128 pages. Equally well-known is the *Modern Language Review* published in Cambridge, and set up in 1905 by the *Modern Humanities Research Association*, with J. G. Robertson as its general editor. The *John Rylands Library Bulletin*, issued by the John Rylands Library of Manchester since 1903, is another publication of

century nearly every great scholar in the field of English literature contributed to its columns—Ernest Rhys, E. K. Chambers, Paget Toynbee, George Saintsbury, Henry Bradley, Walter Skeat, A. B. Grosart, Augustine Birrell, and David Masson are only a few of the names that may be found below its paragraphs. Critical contributors of the 'eighties were W. M. Conway, H. C. Beeching, John Owen, William Wallace, Matthew Arnold, Thomas Henry Huxley, A. W. Benn, Andrew Lang, and Mark Pattison. The next decade brought other names into prominence—William Sharp, Lionel Johnson, Campbell Dodgson, Arthur Galton, R. Brimley Johnson, W. L. Courtney, Richard Middleton, and Maurice Hewlett.

The last years of the century saw the prestige of the *Academy* at its highest, its literary influence unsurpassed by that of any other weekly journal. Unlike almost every other periodical of its age and type, the *Academy* has remained predominantly a journal of criticism and creative literature. It reviewed school books, books of general interest, and novels in large numbers; it found space for poetry, correspondence, obituary paragraphs, and notes on rare books; and it concluded usually with a summary of the "contents of the journals"—that is, other magazines, reviews, and weekly papers. Articles were signed, for the most part, from the beginning, until in 1900 or thereabout the *Academy* became for a time an almost completely anonymous publication.

In 1902, the *Academy* absorbed *Literature*, a large folio, thirty-two page, Saturday journal, published by the *Times*, and edited by H. D. Traill. *Literature*, which was issued from October 23, 1897, to January 11, 1902, was one of the most commendable journals of *belles-lettres*

---

great importance to the student of literature and philology. These highly specialized periodicals now publish much of the more serious scholarly writing formerly included in the weekly journals.

that had yet appeared, containing a leading article, correspondence, a French letter, an American letter, notes of book sales, and reviews; and its quality was assured by such names as those of Stanley Lane-Poole, Arthur Machen, Francis Thompson, Percy Fitzgerald, Leslie Stephen, Frederic Harrison, and Clement Shorter. Merged with the *Academy*, it carried over most of its talent to that publication.

Until the gray days of the Great War, the *Academy* continued as an important critical journal of thirty-two pages. Its last two years, however, were years of decline in size and prestige. By 1916 it had shrunk to sixteen pages—a penny publication, edited and apparently written for the most part by T. W. H. Crosland. Its end came during the most difficult days of the War.

Of high merit though short life was William Ernest Henley's *Scots Observer* of Edinburgh, 1889-90, continued as the *National Observer* of London, 1891. In contents and scope of interest it resembled the American *New Republic* or *Nation* of the present day. Three pages of political and social notes, in an average number, were followed by fifteen pages or less of articles and poems, some of them signed by the authors, a page of correspondence, about six pages of reviews, a list of books published during the week, and literary advertisements—a total of twenty-four pages to the number. Two literary supplements were issued each year, containing signed articles and reviews. For the brilliance of its staff of contributors one would have expected it to have a longer life. Among them were names that now lend magic to the files of this almost forgotten periodical. Rudyard Kipling, J. M. Barrie, Alice Meynell, Joseph Pennell, Frederick Pollock, Katherine Tynan, and W. B. Yeats, were among the authors of signed contributions, along with Robert Louis Stevenson, Richard Garnett, Edmund

Gosse, William Archer, Andrew Lang, H. F. Wilson, Charles and Leonard Whibley, and Henley himself.

A late scion of the weekly journal family, which began its career in the first year of our century, the *Sphere* of Clement K. Shorter, was described as "an illustrated newspaper for the home." In large folio form, with thirty-six pages of letterpress and pictures, it made a pretentious appearance, and promised literary material in abundance. Its promise has been well kept, even though it has never been primarily a journal of *belles-lettres*. Its early columns were filled with much matter of historical interest, chiefly, for the first few years, on the Boer War. It carried much fiction, however, from "the best living short story writers"—S. Baring Gould, Robert Buchanan, Shan F. Bullock, Hall Caine, Robert W. Chambers, Marie Corelli, F. Marion Crawford, George Gissing, Thomas Hardy, "Ouida," Mrs. Humphrey Ward, Max Pemberton, and Jerome K. Jerome—and from the beginning it always contained a certain amount of excellent critical writing, and biographical articles on men of letters.

Among the flourishing journals of the present day, the *New Statesman*, in spite of its title, ranks high as a weekly periodical of *belles-lettres*. Indeed, since its initial appearance in April 1913, it has been an important medium of criticism, some fifteen of its thirty-two pages being occupied with the concerns of literature. Edited from the beginning until February 1930 by Clifford Dyce Sharp, and since that date by Charles Mostyn Lloyd, it has claimed the critical talents of such writers as Harold Massingham, Sidney Webb, Gerald Gould, S. K. Ratcliffe, Osbert Burdett, J. C. Squire, Randall Davies, Desmond MacCarthy (the "Affable Hawk"), Arnold Bennett, Maurice Hewlett, W. H. Hudson, D. H. Lawrence, George Bernard Shaw, G. K. Chesterton, St. John

Ervine, Stephen Hawes, James Elroy Flecker, John Freeman, H. M. Tomlinson, Hugh Walpole, Rebecca West, and W. B. Yeats. It was started with professions of independence, "bound by no ties of party, class, or creed"—yet having, withal, a definite ideal, "to apply to social problems something of the detachment of the scientific spirit." The *New Statesman* has developed an enviable character as an organ of social opinion. But it has never lessened its interest in literature, art, and book matters; and carries to-day its departments called "Prose and Verse," "Music and Art," and "Correspondence." Published on Saturdays and selling for sixpence the copy, it faithfully carries on the tradition of the weekly journal begun a century ago by the *Literary Gazette* and its contemporaries. With poems by T. Sturge Moore, Hillaire Belloc, W. H. Davies, Henry Newbolt, Rupert Brooke, J. C. Squire, Edward L. Davidson, Francis Brett Young, Laurence Binyon, Robert Graves, and John Freeman; and with fiction from the pens of Evelyn Nesbit, Anton Tchekov (translated), Charles A. Bennett, St. John Ervine, Alice James, and others; with its pages of excellent criticism; and with an occasional Literary Supplement; the *New Statesman* has been, for nearly two decades, one of the foremost weekly journals.

John O'London's Weekly, another literary journal still in progress, was first published on April 12, 1919—a somewhat more popular and more specialized periodical than most of its predecessors. Its first editor was Wilfred Whitten ("John O'London") who was later joined by Sydney Dark, as acting editor. In 1924, Mr. Dark was followed by George Blake, and in 1928, Frank Whitaker was appointed associate editor. To-day *John O'London's* offers competent criticism, comment on educational matters, stories and anecdotes, biographies, gossip of books, authors, and actors, weekly letters to Gog and Magog, and book lists. Longer articles are from the pens of Robert Lynd, Edward Shanks, Lord Riddell, H. R. D. May, Frank Kendon, Hugh Walpole, Walter Grierson, Temple Thurston, Marjorie Bowen, Phyllis Bentley, L. P. Jacks, J. B. Priestley, Keighley Snowden, Matheson Lang and other well known writers. The "Book World" department of "F. H. K." offers the regular gossip of the publishers and authors, and another section called "New Books at a Glance" helps to keep the reader abreast with the literary flood. As a Saturday publication of forty pages, *John O'London's* is a useful, if somewhat popularized, descendant of the *Literary Gazette* of a century and a quarter ago.

If the magazine or miscellany has been the encourager of creative genius, and the Review has functioned as the arbiter of literary taste, the weekly journal has gone one step further by professionalizing periodical criticism. Once the avocation of the gentleman, as in the days of John Taylor Coleridge and Croker and Richard Monckton Milnes, or a by-product of creative writing as in the work of Goldsmith and Walter Scott, criticism of literary works has gradually become a definite department of journalism. Of course, there have been professional reviews for one hundred and fifty years—the work of men like Jeffrey, William Taylor of Norwich, or Robert Southey, who derived most of their incomes, for some part of their lives, at least, from the stipends they received for reviews. But these were not numerous, until the rise of the weekly literary journals, the *Literary Gazette, Athenaeum, Spectator*, and *Academy*, of the nineteenth century. To-day the majority of criticisms are written by professional critics and published in the weekly journals. But this "professional" criticism seems to have produced better-informed and fairer reviews; instead of resulting in those of the opposite sort. The "all

SIR WALTER SCOTT.

Published by T. Richardson, 98. High Holborn.

Scott, the Creator of the *Quarterly Review*—
Portrait from the *Literary Speculum*

gentleman and no pay" spirit has passed, along with its unpleasant concomitants—vituperation for party purposes and personal slander. If "log-rolling" continues in some quarters, it is of a comparatively innocuous sort, and with no lasting evil effects, in contrast with that carried on in the days of the *abiter elegantiarum* and the Tory critics. During the long and successful careers of the *Athenaeum* and the *Academy* and similar weekly journals, periodical criticism has out-lived the stigma put upon it by the malicious derogations of the Jeffreys and Lockharts and Crokers of a hundred years ago. Although this type of periodical has clung to the practice of publishing anonymous criticism, while the magazines and Reviews have practically abandoned it, there is little complaint in these later days. Critical manners have improved. The writer of a meritorious book may now look to the weekly journals, at least, for the usually honest and intelligent attempts of the "professional" reviewers to do it justice.

It seems to be a fact that the weekly journal of *belles-lettres* has become our most influential critical type. Its prestige now exceeds that of the Review or the magazine. The weekly frequency of its appearance and its large circulation have combined to enhance its value as an advertising medium for publishers. This, in turn, has brought it prosperity. Generations of competent writers have given it critical authority. Moreover, it acquires value from its immediacy and from its ability to cover well the field of its interests. The readers of the late eighteenth century once looked to the *Monthly Review* and the *Critical* for notices of *all* the important books; so we now read the *Times Literary Supplement* for a critical survey of published work, and in addition, for the literary announcements and news of the week. The present-day weekly journal of *belles-lettres* combines in itself the values of the seventeenth-century book catalog and the critical review. Among the products of two centuries and a half of critical journalism, this type is best adapted to the taste of modern readers.

XII

SOME MISCELLANEOUS TYPES OF LITERARY
PERIODICALS

i

THEATRICAL PERIODICALS

Before 1750, no English periodical was devoted wholly
to drama and the theatre, although many newspapers,
essay sheets, and miscellanies, from the 1690's on, gave
some of their space to such concerns. King William's
edicts against the corruption of the stage, in 1697 and
1698, were followed by increasing efforts to criticise and
evaluate stage productions. The *Moderator* of 1692, *Miscellaneous Letters* of 1694, and Tutchin's *Observator* of
1702 contained early observations on current plays.
Steele's *Theatre* of 1720 and the *Prompter* of 1734 were,
in spite of their titles, chiefly journals of general interest.
The *Grub Street Journal* of 1730-1737 contained a great
deal of dramatic criticism. But the theatrical periodical
as a specialized publication did not first appear until
1751, and then as a monthly miscellany.

One number only remains to show the pretentious beginning made in this year by the *Dramatic Censor*, "being
remarks on the conduct, characters and catastrophe of our
most celebrated plays." Dedicated fulsomely to Garrick,
its eighty pages were taken up with an article by Samuel
Derrick on *Venice Preserved* and observations on the
performances then to be seen on the London stage. A second number was promised, to contain *Richard III* as
altered by Cibber, but no second number has been preserved. Among succeeding miscellanies, the *Thespian*

Magazine and Literary Repository (1763-94) seems to have been most successful of all theatrical periodicals in the eighteenth century. This serial, a twenty-four-page miscellany of real importance to students of the drama, was imitated immediately by the *Theatrical Review* of 1763, which appears to have been a bitter rival. The *Thespian Magazine* was also attacked by the *Theatrical Monitor*, "or the Green Room laid open" (October 17-December 19, 1767), a six-page folio, carrying on well the essay-serial tradition, with its weekly essay, its letters, and its character of the "Monitor." Much of .its space was occupied with propaganda, attacking "Mr. Spatter" of "Thespis" (the *Thespian Magazine*). It reprinted one notable letter, that of Charles Macklin on his break with Garrick, dated December 5, 1743. Later imitations of the *Thespian* were the *Macaroni and Theatrical Magazine* of 1772, the *Prompter* of 1789, and the *Theatrical Guardian* of 1791.

The *Dramatic Censor or Critical Companion*, by Francis Gentleman, actor and playwright, is preserved in two bound volumes of 1770. None of the individual essays are dated, however, which makes it difficult to tell whether they preceded the *Theatrical Monitor*. It is possible that they were originally published as a department in some newspaper of the day. For information about the stage and players of this time, no periodical writings are more valuable. Accounts of the contemporary performances of *Hamlet, Richard III, Lear, Macbeth, Othello, The Merchant of Venice, Romeo and Juliet, Cymbeline, Henry IV, Julius Caesar, King John,* and *Much Ado About Nothing* are recorded in detail, although several of these were in the altered versions of Cibber and Garrick. Moreover, Gay's *Beggar's Opera*, Home's *Douglas*, Otway's *Venice Preserved*, Addison's *Cato*, Congreve's *Mourning Bride*, and a score of other plays by less prominent authors were discussed in these criticisms. In addition to such genuine theatrical periodicals in the eighteenth century, many other magazines and journals of the period carried departments of dramatic criticism—the *Universal Visitor* and the *Monthly Mirror*, for example. But stage matters became, toward the end of the century, an even more important element in newspapers. One of the best illustrations is to be found in the "Theatrical Review," a department which appeared regularly in the *Public Ledger* (September 21, 1771-June 10, 1772). Its sub-title was "New Companion to the Play-House." It was advertised as "By a Society of Gentlemen independent of managerial influences." Its expressed object was nothing less than "a critical and historical account of *every* Tragedy, Comedy, Opera, Farce, etc. . . . exhibited at the theatres . . . "and it may be mentioned here as a worthy ancestor of the departments of dramatic criticism in the newspapers of our day. The plays of Gay, Garrick, Foote, Cumberland, Congreve, Lillo, Steele, Addison, Southerne, Vanbrugh, Cibber, Moore, Otway, and Shakespeare—contemporary productions or revivals—were "covered" by this industrious criticism. Especially interesting to students are the accounts of *Hamlet* and *Cymbeline* as then presented, and —in view of its recent revival—the account of the *Beggar's Opera*.

Another genuine theatrical periodical was the *Prompter* (October 24-December 10, 1789). It began as a daily, with back-page notices of plays "this evening," then made an irregular appearance, thrice-a-week, until nineteen numbers had been issued. One department of this six-page serial was called "The Present State of the English Stage," another "The Present State of Dramatic Writers." There were also notes on managers and performers, of a sort valuable to students of the drama.

With No. 13, it began to furnish a three-page essay, well written and interesting, on some current play. *Hamlet* and *King Lear*, in contemporary performances, were among those discussed.

Independence of managerial influence was once more emphasized by the *Dramatic Censor, or Weekly Theatrical Report* of 1800-1801, edited by Thomas Dutton. Although it was issued weekly, this journal contained day-by-day accounts of the performances at local theatres, analytically describing the new plays, scene by scene. It contained also excellent criticism of a more general nature. A particular attack was made upon the *Morning Herald* for publishing "puffs" supplied by the theatrical managers; and, by way of illustration, the writer referred to the *Herald's* recent absurdity—extolling in an advance notice the skittle-ground scene in a new pantomime, when it was not included in the actual performance.[1]

The difficulties of independent and impartial criticism of theatrical productions at the beginning of the nineteenth century were again illustrated, when Col. Henry Greville and his little "Pic Nic" dinner group organized a "Pic Nic Club," and erected a little theatre for amateur performances. The Club was established in "Tottenham Street" in 1802, and in 1803 (January 8-April 9) a weekly periodical, not wholly theatrical, called the *Pic Nic*, was set up. Richard Cumberland was associated with it. Thomas Sheridan, son of Richard Brinsley Sheridan, was one of the patrons and managers of the little theatre. Drury Lane and Covent Garden interests were at stake, however, and soon the newspapers began, without exception, to attack the Club and its publication. The theatrical scheme and the *Pic Nic* were overwhelmed by

---

[1] The *Theatrical Register* of York (1788) and the *Townsman* of Manchester (1803-5) are evidences that the "provinces" were not without journals of theatrical criticism at this early date.

a flood of scurrilous opposition, which demonstrated the sinister power possessed by the established theatres. After fourteen numbers had been issued, the *Pic Nic* was merged with the *Cabinet*, a periodical then becoming popular.

Thomas Holcroft's *Theatrical Recorder* of 1805, a monthly journal of eighty pages, is of importance because of the large amount of space given to German and Italian drama. The translations were made by Holcroft's daughter, Fanny. It contained, moreover, essays on dramatic composition, on acting, and on the history of the stage, as well as short plays, anecdotes of the stage, and illustrations in color of actors and actresses. In spite of its brief career of six numbers, it was a remarkable periodical of and about the drama.

The most successful of such periodicals at the beginning of the nineteenth century was the *Theatrical Inquisitor and Literary Mirror* (1812-1821) a sixty-page monthly, "embellished with portraits," and varying its matter, which chiefly concerned the stage, with original poetry and literary reviews. Much of interest to the student of Byron, including his "Address" on the opening of the Drury Lane Theatre, appeared in its columns (several poems are addressed to him) ; there are memoirs of stage favorites, chat of the theatres, a letter from Paris, and the "Inquisitor" department—criticism of theatrical performances, both in London and the "provinces," and of individual performers. The *Theatrical Inquisitor* was by far the best dramatic periodical that had appeared at this date. After a career of nine years, it was combined with the *London Magazine* (1820-29).

The pressure of independent criticism apparently produced from the "monopoly," during the years 1816 and 1817, defense in the form of the *Drury Lane Theatrical Gazette* and the *Covent Garden Theatrical Gazette*. They were identical in form. Both were Tuesday-Thursday-Saturday serials of eight pages, selling for 3d. The first page of each consisted regularly of a play bill advertising a performance on the evening following publication. Each contained a detailed "descriptive analysis" of current plays. Whatever criticism one finds in them is, of course, "inspired" and valueless; but they are rich sources of information concerning the acting versions of plays of the day.

Thomas Kenrick's *British Stage and Literary Cabinet* of 1817 to 1820 rivalled in colorfulness, if not in size, the contemporary *Theatrical Inquisitor*, already mentioned, and attacked its older competitor with vindictiveness worthy of the quarterly reviews of this generation. To the usual theatrical matter in its twenty-four pages (monthly) it added Kenrick's "Reflector" essays, a "dramatic glossary," and "Shakespearean Comments Extraordinary."

Further competition, in this prolific period, was furnished in 1819 by the *Inspector*, "a weekly dramatic paper," of which the editor announced a plan "to visit every theatre every night," to give a "truthful report of the merits of every class of performance," and to supply a correct program of the amusements of every theatre for the coming week. The four numbers of this ephemeral publication contain many items of interest, but are chiefly distinguished by articles on the lectures of Hazlitt and Coleridge. A contemporary of the *Inspector* was *Drama* (1821-25) a tiny fifty-page monthly, described as a "theatrical pocket magazine." It contained a good deal of general criticism, and valuable comment on plays and actors. Of greater vitality was a penny daily, Nolan's *Theatrical Observer* (1821), which carried the brave motto, "Nothing extenuate nor set down in malice." The pungency and fearlessness of its criticism may have had much to do with the popularity of the *Theatrical Observer*. The accompanying excerpt on a performance of the *School for Scandal* (November 15, 1822) is an interesting example:

How great must be the unpopularity of the manager, how indifferent the feeling of the public, when *the best play that ever was written*, backed by *very tolerable acting*, was unable to draw a house, was in fact performed to empty benches. This at least is evidence that the public are in general discontented, and proves that the management of Mr. Farren is far from being satisfactory; and unsatisfactory it surely must be, so long as the system of favoritism is continued—so long as superior merit is postponed to the scenes behind the curtain—so long, in fine, as the "Rival Queens" shall "rule the roost." We thought we had said enough yesterday on the subject of thrusting Mrs. Simon and Miss Curtis into characters for which they are totally unsuited. We thought we had said enough on the *positive injustice* that was thus inflicted on Mesdames Jarman and Atkins. But no—the management would not be consistent if were not *obstinate, dogged*, and *stupid*— and accordingly we had last night the inexpressible mortification of seeing Mrs. Simon in *Lady Sneerwell*, and Miss Curtis in *Maria*; either of which characters Miss Atkins would play a million of times better than the persons who were pushed into them.

On the other hand, the *Observer* (April 7, 1823) could recommend quite as boldly:

On Saturday night Mr. Kean appeared as *Shylock* before the fullest and most fashionable audience that we have seen since his arrival. Shylock is one of those parts in which "a lodged hate" joined with the most determined inveteracy of purpose and a griping avarice are alone to be represented.—There is, it is true, in one scene the most poignant grief for the loss of his daughter, but this very natural and most commendable feeling soon gives place to the master passion, revenge. Hence it may be inferred that although it is no easy matter properly to conceive, and truly and perfectly to represent the Jew, yet that it is a much less difficult achievement than the personation of the conflicting congregation of passions which alternately arouse, agitate, inflame, as well as deform and degrade the wily and "hunch backed" tyrant. Reasoning on these *data* we conclude—whether rationally or no, we leave our readers to determine—that *Shylock* is a character in which Mr. Kean is less likely to be *wondered* at than any of the others which he has as yet appeared in. We use the word wonder because according to Dr. Young—"wonder is involuntary praise," and there is no man who so forcibly *extorts* praise and favor as Mr. Kean. In fact he pounces on your unsuspecting audience who have been accustomed to the same unvarying eternal sing-song for years, and dazzles them by a "coup de main" into the most determined approbation. This is alone the fire and the power of true genius than which there is nothing more despotic and sweeping in its way.

It has been objected to Mr. Kean that he has gone out of the beaten track. This (with great deference to those who raise the objection) we conceive to be this most gifted actor's great merit. It implies *prima facie* originality and strength of mind, and serves to convince those who are open to conviction that Kean is no imitator. He is not of the school of Garrick, or Cooke, or Kemble, for to all of these is he dissimilar— no, he is of the school of nature—she is the goddess of his idolatry—at her shrine has he worshipped, and from her presence has he caught the inspiration whose influence is all powerful. Among those excellencies which struck us the more forcibly on Saturday night was that in which Antonio solicits the loan of *Shylock*. The tone of pathetic earnestness mixed with the most irritable sensibility of wrong with which the retort "on such a day you spat on me, on such a day you called me knave," was given, was truly impressive. Again, on learning of his daughter's elopement, and her prodigality respecting the ring of his wife—nothing could be finer than the melancholy satisfaction with which he recounted the manner in which he had become possessed of the gift. It formed a fine contrast to the burst of indignation which followed—

"Would that she were hearsed here at my feet!" Again, in the trial scene when the passion rises to its *acme*, the effect was most appalling. The floating satisfaction with which he eyed his victim, and the demoniac pleasure with which he wheels the knife, were perfect specimens of the most exalted species of tragic excellence. Of the same order was the delivery in a tone of the most gratifying self-satisfaction of the words— "a Daniel—a second Daniel"—but the summit of perfection was reserved for the final award of the judge. The silent despair—the mental agony—the complete desperation and inward depressions with which the scales were dropped were indeed sublime—at the conclusion Mr. Kean was rewarded with three distinct cheers.

Such comment on the theatre of 1821 throws an interesting light on stage manners and conditions; but we can hardly expect to find in the *Theatrical Observer* any dramatic criticism of lasting value. The popularity of this modest enterprise, however, was astonishing. It began as a tiny four-page sheet, two pages occupied with play bills. Before the end of the first year it had "received the support of 1000 persons." After thirty-five pocket-size numbers had been run, it began a new and larger series, continuing in progress until 1876.

The success of this little periodical begot its legion of imitators, not only in London but elsewhere. Among these, the *Norwich Theatrical Observer*, a twice-a-week journal of 1827, is deserving of mention. It was edited for forty-two numbers by Dr. A. T. Fayerman, who proposed to make it the "best theatrical publication in England," and who declared a sale of 2000 copies in three weeks from the commencement of the work. Long reviews of the important plays on the stage, and short notices of others, tend to make this paper a really critical journal. While it lasted, it was a very good example of a serious dramatic publication.

A weekly serial of 1828 called *The Theatre* is distinguished by its mingling of humor and dramatic criticism. With the now conventional stage matters, it included a mock-epic entitled "The Stage," the "Reminiscences of a Strolling Player," and humorous poems such as "The Dramatic Poet and the Milk Man." Another weekly journal of the next year, *The Harlequin* of John Timbs, was, after nine numbers had been issued, killed by the imposition of the stamp duty (as if it were a newspaper). While it lasted, it was superior in point of style and interest to most theatrical papers. Timb's antiquarian leanings are apparent in the department of "Anecdotiana" and in the considerable matter about old English drama. An important monthly, the *Dramatic Magazine* (March 1829-April 1831) contains, among other matters of great interest, valuable biographical sketches and photographs of contemporary actors, such as Miss Kemble and Macready. Two weekly journals of 1839, *The Theatrical Journal* of H. P. Mills, and *The Theatrical Chronicle* of C. T. Fowler, rivaled each other for a year. The former survived the struggle, and continued publication until 1873. Both were cheap Saturday journals, and both are valuable to any student of the nineteenth-century stage.

Among the legion of theatrical periodicals in the latter half of the century, *The Theatre, a Monthly Review and Magazine* (1877-1897) is distinguished not only by its longer life but also by the scope of its design. A fifty-page shilling monthly, with an attractive format, it contained the usual survey of the London and "Provincial" theatres, an "Amateur Play-Box" department, art notes, musical notes, excellent photographs of actors, with much criticism and poetry and biography. It contained also novelettes, "echoes from the Green Room," and paragraphs devoted to the theatres of France, Germany, Austria, and America. Its "Portrait Gallery," a regular feature, is a "Who's Who" of the theatrical world, while the articles written by E. H. Sothern, Joseph Hatton, Kate Field, Percy Fitzgerald, H. J. Byron, Richard Mansfield, E. L. Blanchard, etc., gave earlier numbers an unusual substance. Among later contributors were F. J. Furnivall, John Hollingshead, Arthur Escott, W. J. Lawrence, Charles Dickens, Jr., Henry Irving, Henry Arthur Jones, Arthur W. Pinero, Moy Thomas, William Archer, F. C. Burnand, Arthur à Beckett and Joseph Knight. *The Theatre* carried eight to ten criticisms of theatrical performances to a number. Clement Scott, Bernard Capes, and Charles Eglington were editors at various periods of its career. In the 'eighties and 'nineties, *The Theatre* was unquestionably a periodical of dominating prestige and influence. In fact, not one among those which have flourished since seems to command quite the same respect from readers or support from the great actors of the age.

English periodicals devoted to the drama and the theatre are to-day represented by several publications. *The Stage* illustrates one phase of their development— an advertising medium, almost without "literary" values, beyond the brief notes on performances. Begun in 1880 as *The Stage Directory*, this publication became, in March 1881, *The Stage*. It is now a 32-page weekly, filled with "Publisher's Song Notes," "jottings" of theatrical folk, notices of the variety stage, "chit chat," occasional articles on copyright, etc., notices of the London theatres, provincial productions, and the American stage. Half the column space is occupied with advertising. Obviously, *The Stage* can hardly be classed as a literary periodical at all, except for the fact that it contains a record of performances that will sometime be of historical value.

Of somewhat more critical nature is the *Theatre World*, a monthly publication now in its fifth year. It is not above publishing "Exclusive Interviews," "Fashions Seen on the Stage" and a department called "Here and there (Round the Shops)." Yet the burden of its matter has time-honored and popular appeal—gossip of the stage and stage folk, announcements of future and present productions, popular "reviews" of current plays, profuse and excellent illustrations of actors and stage settings. Sheridan Bickers was the first editor of the *Theatre World*, in 1925. He was succeeded by Stanley Hale, who was responsible for the success of the enterprise until the present editor, David Fairweather, took charge in 1928. The purpose of the *Theatre World* is now stated thus: "to supply the intelligent playgoer with a frank and comprehensive summary of all new productions, together with articles from prominent figures in the theatrical world, illustrations from all the latest plays and films, caricatures, exclusive portraits, etc." Having recently incorporated *Theatre and Film Illustrated*, the *Theatre World* now appeals not only to theatre-goers but to film fans as well. "The Theatrical side of the paper will always be of paramount importance," says the editor (April 1930) and adds, "We realize that although there may be other film publications, there is no other monthly theatrical magazine of any real critical value." He further states that the *Theatre World* endeavours "to steer a middle course between what may be termed "high-browism" and exiguous gossip." Although its contents have little that may be termed "critical" in the literary sense, the *Theatre World* probably now represents, better than any other contemporary theatrical journal, the taste of the average theatre-goer. Its forty pages of monthly news, comment, and announcement, as well as its excellent illustrations, give it an historical value beyond its present utility.

Of much more serious purpose is *Drama*, first published July 1919, as a bi-monthly magazine, by the British Drama League. It contains an invaluable record of amateur theatrical activities. Now described as a "Monthly record of the theatre, in town and country, at home and abroad," and edited since its beginning by Mr. Geoffrey Whitworth, Secretary of the League, it attempts to comprehend all items and announcements of interest to lovers of the drama; and publishes also, in its sixteen pages, general articles upon the theatre and its concerns. Contributions from Professor Max Reinhardt, Mme. Karsavina, and Jaques Copeau, show that this periodical has more than national importance. Most of the important English writers on the theatre—Granville Barker, Ashley Dukes, Ivor Brown, Professor Gilbert Murray, Percy Allen, etc., have at one time or another helped to fill its columns. Recent books on the drama and volumes of plays are reviewed by Norman Marshall and others. Since November 1920, *Drama* has been issued as a monthly magazine, selling for sixpence. It is indispensable for English or American readers who wish to be in touch with the best thought and work on the contemporary stage.

The periodical mainly or wholly concerned with facts about the stage and stage folk, and with criticism of theatrical productions, past or present, has varied little in character since the appearance of the *Thespian Magazine* in 1763. The ingredients remain much the same from decade to decade—play-bills, announcements, comment on past productions, biographies of actors, gossip of managers and stage folk, descriptions of benefits, anecdotes humorous and otherwise, portraits of actors, sometimes poetry and theatrical news matter. During the last one hundred and fifty years, the number of such publications (usually of very brief career) has been astonishing; but their quality—especially in respect to their critical writing—has not been impressive. In the later years of the eighteenth century and the early years of the nineteenth, they recorded a bitter warfare between the independents and those who attempted to maintain a theatrical monopoly in London. And even in much later days the specialized periodicals of drama were greatly affected by the sinister power of managerial influence. From the beginning of the eighteenth century, much criticism of drama and news of the theatres appeared in the columns of newspapers and magazines of a general nature. To-day, it is probably true that the daily press supplies the most valuable information as well as the most vital criticism of stage productions.[1] But the specialized periodical of theatrical intelligence, as well as the dramatic critics' corner of the newspaper, may be looked upon as rich source material for the history of the stage and its people. This brief sketch of the development of theatrical journals can only suggest the value of such periodicals to students of English drama.

ii

MAGAZINES OF HUMOR

The humor magazine is an old periodical *genre*. Its lineage may be traced from the ribald and farcical half-sheet folios of the seventeenth century, through such forebears as Defoe's "Advice from the Scandal Club" in his *Review*, the *Tatler* and *Spectator*, Fielding's *Jacobite's Journal*, and Christopher Smart's *Midwife*. If we search out its remotest beginnings, we will find ourselves far back in the Restoration Period, among such half-sheet folios as the *Heraclitus Ridens* and *Mercurius Bifrons*. There one finds each periodical of amusement a servant of politics; and in every century since, the journal of humor has, with a few exceptions, been turned to social or partisan uses. The periodicals of Tom Brown and Ned Ward, at the end of the seventeenth century, might all be cited as forebears of the modern *Punch*.[2] The *Tatler*, *Spectator* and *Guardian*, and a score of their followers, contributed to the humor tradition. Smart's *Midwife* was purely comic, with no political or social purpose, as far as may be discerned. It differed in that way from most of the later humor magazines. The same may be said of the *Jester's Magazine or Monthly Merry-Maker* (October 1765–December 1766), which was not wholly humorous

---

[1] For example, see William Archer's dramatic criticisms in the London *World*, later reprinted in five volumes, 1893-97.

[2] See also such foreign periodicals as Jean Loret's riming *Gazette*, 1650-65, or *El Bufón de la Carte* of Madrid, circa, 1740.

in intention. But there can be no doubt regarding the purpose of the *Tomahawk or Censor General* of 1795-1796, a six-page, thrice-a-week paper, which in later numbers carried the slogan, "The King and the Constitution." It was an Administration paper, like the *Anti-Jacobin*, mentioned elsewhere in this survey. Its spirit is shown in the following verses—
("To the tune of Nancy Dawson")

I

Old England's glory I will boast,
Old England's health I still will toast;
And here's to him that vaunts the most
The glory of Old England.

II

French Democrats may boast their fill
And seek their Monarch's blood to spill;
I hope God's providence will still
Preserve great George of England!

III

I've been in Italy and Spain,
I've been in France and in Lorrain,
Yet none of these I will maintain,
Is like unto Old England.

IV

The fruitful Poland, frozen Russ,
Industrious Holland, warlike Pruss;
Yet none of all is like to us,
The freeborn sons of England.

V

It is not in wild anarchy,
Which Levellers call liberty;
But in a well-praised monarchy,
Consists the good of England.

VI

> Let's study in our fathers schools,
> Religion, morals, and good rules,
> And drink damnation to those fools
> Who'd breed Revolt in England.

The *Comick Magazine* of 1796, enriched with illustrations of Hogarth drawings, was for nine numbers an unimportant compendium of "mirth, humor, wit, gaiety, and entertainment," unscrupulously garnered from periodicals of the past and from the works of contemporary poets. It contained almost no original matter. The *Man in the Moon*, 1804, a tiny 64-page pocket magazine of crude burlesques, parodies and cartoons, contained perhaps the first comic strip; for each number began with a folded sheet containing a series of caricatures or "funnies." (A better *Man in the Moon*, issued 1847-9, and edited by Albert Smith and Angus B. Reach, to be "sold at every railway station in the Kingdom," contained plenty of amusement in its sixty-two pages.) The *John Bull Magazine* of 1824 was a periodical of perverted ingenuity and coarse personalities. "On my Wedding Night" (described as "The Obnoxious Chapter of Lord Byron's Memoirs") was a scurrilous contribution, called forth by the contemporary burning of Byron's *Memoirs* in Murray's grate. "Humbugs of the Age" included "The Opium Eater," Humphrey Davy, and other respected names. In fact, the *Magazine* ran amuck among the public figures of the day, dealing out insults and personal abuse to right and left. Its attitude toward the public is shown by a stanza from Number 1—

> We scribble doughty paragraphs
> A penny a line the price,
> To serve our English assery
> With many a rare device;
> To please our English assery

Our pains we freely show,
For we toil, and we moil,
While the type-fed cases go.

A very similar quality of humorous entertainment was supplied, in 1832, by the *Penny Comic Magazine* "or an amorous, clamorous, uproarious, and glorious society for the diffusion of broad grins." Like the *John Bull Magazine*, it was written for the "lower orders of society," and cannot be seriously regarded as a precursor of *Punch*.

Real humor, however, is to be found in the *Snob* (1829) of Cambridge (continued as the *Gownsman* 1829-30). Although a student publication, it merits passing notice, if only because it contained Thackeray's delightful parody, "Timbuctoo" (April 1829). Of better quality, also, was *Figaro in London*, edited by Gilbert à Beckett, 1831-39, a four- to eight-page Saturday weekly of liberal political tone.[1] In its combining of brilliant wit and social and political purposes, *Figaro in London* was a worthy precursor of *Punch*, which probably owed much to it. The later and greater periodical also owed something to Douglas Jerrold's *Punch in London*, 1832, a small, eight-page weekly miscellany, with humor sometimes unnecessarily broad, but with a political slant to much of its content, and with drawings and general appearance suggestive of *Punch*. Unquestionably, *Punch* was indebted somewhat to several annual publications, such as Hood's *Comic Annual* of 1830-39, George Cruikshank's *Comic Annual*, 1835-1853, and Louisa Sheridan's *Comic Offering or Ladies Melange of Literary Mirth* (1831-35), the last, a 350-page volume of nonsense and caricature. Probably, *Punch* derived also from Gilbert à Beckett's *Comic Magazine* of 1832, and the *Charivari* of Paris.

[1] See A. W. à Beckett, *The à Becketts of "Punch,"* N. Y. 1903, for an account of Gilbert à Beckett and his sons.

The oldest of our present-day humorous magazines, *Punch or the London Charivari*, was set up in 1841 by Ebenezer Landells, a wood engraver, Mark Lemon, a playwright and magazine writer, and Henry Mayhew. Lemon, who was a frequent contributor to periodicals after 1831, and is known to have been an editor of the *London Journal*, the *Family Herald, Once a Week*, and the *Field*, became the first editor of *Punch*, with assistance from Mayhew. From this time, Lemon's life was identified completely with this periodical. Henry Mayhew who helped Gilbert à Beckett with *Figaro in London* (1831-39) and in 1832 had started the *Thief*, earliest of the great crowd of paste-and-scissors journals, was one of the founders of that "philanthropic journalism" which was to take the poor of London for its theme. Horace Mayhew, the brother of Henry, and Joseph Stirling Coyne, writer of burlesque and farces, were also associated closely and vitally with the early years of this periodical. Landells, the engraver, claimed to have been the original projector, and declared that he gave the idea to Mayhew. But in view of the large number of humorous periodicals in the first half of the nineteenth century, the identity of the original projector is not important. Douglas Jerrold's *Punch in London*, 1832, a rival of *Figaro in London*, suggested the title as well as the character of the new venture in humor.

Punch was a humorous magazine with a difference. Part of the difference lay in its social purpose. It began as a radical and democratic organ, and resolute champion of the poor. The earlier volumes abound in eloquent references to the abuses and evils of the "Hungry Forties," and in burning pleas for reform of conditions. A second difference was in its tone. The humor of scurrility and personal abuse, or sheer slap-stick and horseplay, were abandoned for a quality of merriment that has individualized *Punch* beyond any other periodical. *Punch* developed a school of humorists with an individual manner—a good one. "They do not shout and they never need to whisper; their joking has the spontaneity of good table talk." What was recently said of the "code" of present-day *Punch* writers applies, with minor qualifications to those of the last half-century. It explains much of the unique quality of this dean of humor magazines—

> It has its code, and there are those who object that it is a narrow one. Among the jokes that "are not done" are the thirty-nine of the forty possible jokes that cannot—or could not in the days of the ingenuous Mark Twain—be told to ladies. On the other hand, the one possible joke is exquisitely turned out. The smallest detail of its clothing is carefully considered, and the attention paid to it is as carefully concealed. . . . Nonchalance is an essential of the code. As gentlemen— of either sex—writing for gentlemen, the writers can afford to admit their ignorance of those serious matters that experts and moralists and the rest of the lower orders live by. Invective, sarcasm, and the fiercer forms of satire are for professionals who excite laughter to serve some ulterior purpose, not for gentlemen who play the game for the sake of the game; and they are not used by *Punch* writers, who are like leaders in other branches of sport in contriving to turn their skill to account without comprising their amateur status.[1]

The first number of *Punch* was published by Bryant on July 17, 1841. It was owned in equal shares by Landells, Joseph Last, the printer, and Lemon and Mayhew, who edited it. At first its financial success was uncertain. Not until Bradbury and Evans purchased it, did prospects brighten. Mayhew retired from the sub-editorship early, but Lemon remained "the best of editors" until his death in 1870. Among his successors in the editorial chair were Shirley Brooks, 1874-80, and Sir F. C. Burnand, 1880-1904. During Lemon's career of twenty-nine years, as

[1] "Punch Writers" *Times Literary Supplement*, November 21, 1929, p. 963.

editor, and owing perhaps to the support of Douglas Jerrold, who contributed steadily from 1841 to 1857, *Punch* became a social power.[1]

At one time or another, virtually all the humorists of that generation contributed to this famous periodical. Notable among the earlier members of the staff were William Makepeace Thackeray, who wrote for it, 1842-1854, and contributed some 380 drawings; and Gilbert à Beckett, a leader writer on the *Times*, editor of earlier humor magazines, dramatist, Poor Law commissioner, and metropolitan magistrate. Douglas Jerrold, the life-long champion of the underdog, was the spear head of *Punch's* attacks on Protection, Bumbledom, unreformed corporations, cant and snobbery. He gave *Punch* its tone, and its trend toward liberalism in politics. Thomas Hood was another early contributor. His immortal "Song of the Shirt" was printed in the Christmas number of *Punch*, 1843—perhaps the most popular contribution this magazine ever published. But a high place among contributions must be reserved for Jerrold's "Caudle Lectures"; for "Jeames's Diary," the "Snobs of England," "*Punch's* Prize Novelists," and the "Bow Street Ballads" —the early works of Thackeray; not forgetting Tennyson's "New Timon and the Poets"—his answer to Bulwer-Lytton—the poet's single satire.

Among the other contributors to *Punch's* letterpress, a few deserve special mention—Horace and James Smith, Charles Lever, "Artemus Ward," E. J. Milliken, Ashby Sterry, George Augustus Sala, Andrew Lang, Stuart

---

[1] Douglas Jerrold must be numbered with Marchamont Nedham, Defoe, John Dunton, Swift, Cobbett, and Albany Fonblanque—the social and political reformers in journalism.

See Charles L. Graves, *Mr. Punch's History of Modern England*, London 1921, i, p. 5.

M. H. Spielmann, *History of Punch*, Lon. 1895.

Walter Jerrold, *Douglas Jerrold and 'Punch'*, London 1910. See bibliography of Jerrold's contributions to *Punch*, pp. 413-444.

W. B. Jerrold, *Life of Douglas Jerrold*, 2nd Ed., London, n. d., pp. 132-3.

Calverly, Barry Pain, St. John Hankin, R. C. Lehmann,
C. L. Graves, A. P. Herbert, E. V. Knox, A. A. Milne,
and Owen Seaman, who is the present editor.

It is obvious that the radical and humanitarian opinions expressed in the columns of *Punch* raise it far above
the ranks of most earlier comic magazines. Owing largely
to its excellent caricatures, this humorous periodical has
always been more or less a political weapon. There is
little relation, for example, between the social and political purposes of *Punch* and the frankly comic ends of
Smart's *Midwife*. In method, at least, there is likewise
little relation between Steele's *Spectator*, on the one hand,
and *Punch*, on the other. Both were social reformers, but
the former was always urbane, kindly, courteous, and
gentle; the latter has often been caustic and penetrating.
It is unquestionably true that *Punch* had an enormous
influence on subsequent ventures in periodical journalism.
All the important humorous magazines of the twentieth
century partake, in some degree, of *Punch's* humanitarian
and reforming purpose. And *Punch*, the pioneer, still
leads all the rest in prestige and popularity.

Among the later humorous magazines, a few should
be particularly noticed in this brief treatment. Hood's
Monthly Magazine and Comic Miscellany (1844-48)
was edited to the end of his life by Thomas Hood, who
had headed the staff of the *New Monthly Magazine*,
1841-43, and had contributed to *Punch*. F. O. Ward assisted Hood, and with others carried the magazine on
after the founder's death. *Hood's Magazine* was not
entirely comic in character, but contained poems, articles
and stories from such writers as Dickens, Samuel Lover,
G. H. Lewes, W. S. Landor, Leigh Hunt, Robert Browning, Richard Monckton Milnes, G. P. R. James, Bulwer-
Lytton, and "Barry Cornwall." Its merit as a magazine

of fiction perhaps exceeded its value as a "comic miscellany."

Fun, set up in 1861, and edited after 1865 by Tom Hood, the younger, was continued until 1901, when it was absorbed by *Sketchy Bits*, a periodical which had been begun in 1893. Ambrose Bierce, the American, who went to England in 1872, was for several years a member of the staff of *Fun*, and Bret Harte, another American, was "discovered" in its pages. Most of W. S. Gilbert's *Bab Ballads* first appeared in *Fun,* mingled with its *vers de sociètè* and cartoons.

Gilbert Arthur à Beckett, son of the first Gilbert, and also of the *Punch* staff, was the editor from 1867 to 1870 of another *Tomahawk*, "a Saturday Journal of Satire." In reality, it was a conservative organ, in opposition to Disraeli. It is interesting as a true follower of *Punch*, combining a good deal of genuine amusement with a zealous effort at social reform. It was succeeded in 1877-8 by *Mirth*, an imitator of *Fun*, a 36-page miscellany selling for a shilling, and edited by Henry J. Byron. This and many other competing periodicals in the years that have passed have failed to lessen the prestige of *Punch*, the greatest of English humor magazines. *Punch* remains, as it began, a periodical of amusement "with a difference." Alone among a legion of predecessors and imitators, it has consistently maintained literary quality and popularity. Primarily a periodical of entertainment, like the *Spectator* of two centuries ago, it is also an important influence in the reform of manners and the correction of public abuses.

iii

The Poetry Magazines

The periodical devoted exclusively to poetry has never thriven in England, although there have been such publi-

cations in almost all periods. From the days of the seventeenth-century half-sheet folios consisting of satirical
verse, periodicals made up wholly of poetry have been
short-lived and generally of low quality. On the other
hand, poetry as a component or ingredient of the miscellany has always had its value; and nearly every literary
periodical of note has had its section devoted to the muse.
The truth is, then, that poetry, like the essay, has always
appealed to a limited reading public. It is ill adapted to
be the entire substance of a periodical.

Be that as it may, there have been and still are journals
of poetry. From 1700 to 1930 they show little variation
or development, and to sketch their history is rather a
simple matter. The rare *Miscellanies over Claret* of 1697
appears to be the earliest example; it was followed by
an inconsequential *Poetical Observator* of 1702-3, the
Diverting Post (from 1705 consisted of poetry only), the
Poetical Courant of Samuel Phillips in 1706, a *Poetical
Entertainer* issued by Morphew in 1712-13, and the
Monitor of 1713 (Mar. 2–Apr. 24) designed for the "promotion of religion and virtue." After these early publications, with their sometimes not too respectable verse of
inferior quality, an interval of fifty years elapsed before
another similar publication was set on foot, although
during this time not only magazines and essay serials, but
even newspapers, carried regular departments filled with
poems. The *St. James Magazine* of Robert Lloyd, actor
and poet, marked the beginning of a real effort to make
poetry periodicals successful. Lloyd's publication survived for two years (1762-64), an eighty-page miscellany
devoted to poetry and criticism of poetry. It was followed
by a small (pocket-size) *Poetical Magazine or Muses
Monthly Companion* (January–June 1764) which appeared in six numbers, and was probably the work of
Charles Hanbury Williams. This contained many trans-

lations and a good proportion of verse that was obviously
not written for the *Magazine*, but rather borrowed, in
the predatory manner of the century, from other journals.
The *Poetical Register and Repository for Fugitive
Poetry* (1802-14) added little to the prestige of this type
of periodical. Nor did the *British Poetical Miscellany*
(1799) of Huddersfield, a courageous weekly undertaking, which was continued for thirty eight-page numbers.
It was almost entirely filled with reprinted verse.

Quite the most original and prosperous of poetry
journals at the beginning of the nineteenth century was
the *Poetical Magazine*, 1809-11, of Rudolph Ackermann, an art publisher of London. It was dedicated to
"lovers of the Muse," and profusely illustrated, with
extraordinary cartoons, done in color. The *Magazine*
numbered about fifty-six pages, and sold for two shillings.
Most of the poems were signed with the names of the
authors, their initials or pseudonyms. Some of the verses
are reprinted from other works. James B. Brown, W. L.
Bowles, J. Faulkner, John Hyde, John Morris Tindall,
S. B. Trome, Godfrey Wellwynn, and "Dr. Syntax," are
some of the names or pseudonyms one finds in its pages.
After the first six numbers of the *Poetical Magazine* were
issued, a sixty-page supplement was put out—a fact
which suggests that the editor did not at first lack for
contributors. The *Bard*, 1822, was an inconsequential
journal of verse put out, for eight monthly numbers, by
F. G. and G. Whiteson.

For the next forty or fifty years we find practically no
magazines of verse, a result, no doubt, of the rise of the
Annual, which flourished during the '20's and '30's, and
absorbed the production of poets up to and beyond the
middle of the century.[1] With the decline in the publica-

[1] The *Forget-me-not*, published in England in 1823, was undoubtedly
the first "literary annual." It was published by R. Ackermann, and edited
by Frederic Shoberl, who was influenced by the "Almanacs" and "Pocket-

tion of Annuals, there came an awakening of interest in the journal of poetry. From November 1860 to October 1861, John Bedford Leno edited a sixteen-page, monthly, twopenny miscellany, of and about poets and poetry. It was called the *Poetic Magazine*, and contained signed articles on poetical matters, as well as signed poems. In a second series, consisting of a thirty-two page journal, selling for sixpence, it continued from September 1862 to January 1863. The *Poetic Magazine* included within its three years contributed poems from John Blackman, William Young Grown, Edward Capman, C. S. Cheltnam, Thomas Field, George Giddings, Charles C. Harrison, J. Charles King, William Leighton, Robert L. Leighton, Peter Livingstone, G. H. Lovell, J. P. Robson, Laman Blanchard, William Catcott, Westby Gibson, James Reynolds Withers, J. C. Reid, William Sawyer, John S. Thompson, and J. C. Watts. The fact that not one of these is now remembered as a poet does not recommend either the discernment of the editor nor the reputation of the periodical. Nevertheless, the *Poetic Magazine* contains interesting articles—on Italian poetry by Thornton Hunt, on Paisley and its poets by Robert Leighton, on Cowper by John Blackman, on Newstead Abbey by Leno, on Chatterton by A. Langford, as well as "Miscellanea" concerning Kirke White and Leigh Hunt. At its conclusion, the *Poetic Magazine* was bound in cloth and sold for three shillings.

A *Poetical Magazine* (May-October 1870) appeared monthly for a few numbers, like its predecessor in that

---

books" that were appearing in Germany. Alaric A. Watts in 1824 edited the *Literary Souvenir*. These two were followed by the numerous tribe of annuals and pocket-books that appropriated much of the literary output of England during the next fifteen years. By 1832 as many as sixty-three of these "gift" books are said to have claimed shares of the public's patronage. The decline of this annual or gift book fad was as rapid as its rise, and by 1860 this phase of periodical publication in England was but a memory. For a full treatment of the subject, see F. W. Faxon, *Literary Annuals and Gift Books*, Boston, Massachusetts, 1912.

contributions were signed, and unfortunately like it also in that not a single poet of the lot is now numbered among the makers of Victorian literature. With the exception of a few lively parodies of Tennyson and some of his contemporaries, its contents are now forgotten. One may well ask, "Where are the poets of yesterday—these whose names filled the poetry journals of the 1860's and '70's?" Still another, the *Poets' Magazine*, appeared in August 1876, to continue until July 1877, as a monthly of sixty-four pages. Again we find contributions acknowledged; and once more it is true that they are, almost without exception, by poets too obscure to have been remembered even for half a century. But the *Poets' Magazine* has more to recommend it than its predecessors by reason of the numerous articles of a critical nature to be found in its pages. Articles on Tennyson, Elizabeth Barrett Browning, Hood, Swinburne, and Shelley, an "unpublished" poem of Barry Cornwall's, and contributions from Richard Hengist Horne, give it some mild interest to the reader of today.[1]

Before the opening of our century, the story of the magazine of poetry—that is, devoted exclusively to the concerns of verse—was a sorry one. Although many of the most famous poems of Coleridge, Byron, Tennyson, Rossetti, and Swinburne, and many poets of lesser rank in the nineteenth century, first appeared in print in the columns of newspapers or miscellaneous periodical publications, it is nearly true that no poem of importance was originally published in a poetry magazine. And it appears to be a fact—even more damning—that among the army of industrious scribblers who acknowledged their poetic offspring in the columns of the various journals of verse, not one became, in later years, a known poet.

With such evidence of the ephemeral nature of poetry

[1] See also the *Poets' Corner* (1899-1907).

journals before us, we cannot but approach the last quarter-century with diffidence and uncertainty. Perhaps the future historians of literary periodicals will view the poetry magazines since 1900 quite as we regard the *Poetic Magazine* of 1860. Yet if the critical feeling of our day is at all sound, two, at least, will have stood the test of time. The *Poetry Review* (1912-26) which had first appeared in 1909 as the *Poetical Gazette,* carried the legend

> Men of the world, mid hum and stir,
> Fret of anvil and throb of loom,
> Make for your souls a thoroughfare,
> Keep for your hearts a silent room.

Edited by Stephen Phillips, the *Poetry Review* was, during its earlier years, chiefly a journal of prose criticism about poetry and poets, containing some sixty pages monthly. Prose was supplied by Isadore G. Ascher, Darrel Figgis, David Lloyd George, James A. Mackereth, Ernest Rhys, Algernon Warren, Joyce Kilmer, Theodore Maynard, Israel Zangwill, A. C. Benson, and W. F. Rawnsley; poetry by Thomas Hardy, Mackereth, Florence Earle Coates, Richard Butler Glaenzer, Constance Skinner, Gilbert Thomas, Alice Meynell, F. Britton Austin, and others. After Phillips' death in 1915, with Galloway Kyle as editor, this periodical became much more of a medium for original verse. Its criticism included much French literature, and more American work was welcomed to its columns. As the official organ of the Poetry Society of England, it was continued until 1926. By 1918 it was referred to as the "leading poetry magazine of the world." The *Poetry Review* is an invaluable record of a late generation of poets, many of them "war poets" like Victor Ratcliffe, Charles Hamilton Sorley, Julian Grenfell, and John William Street. Contrary to the usual rule, its contributors seem destined, in many cases, to be known to future generations.

Possibly the finest periodical of verse ever published in England was *New Numbers*, a quarterly publication of sixty pages of poetry. It was a joint-production of John Drinkwater, Lascelles Abercrombie, Wilfred Wilson Gibson, and Rupert Brooke, whose work filled its pages. The first copies were issued in February 1914, from Ryton, Dymock, in Gloucestershire. The beginning of the Great War wrecked the small enterprise, and the fourth and last number came out in December of that year. Of its contents, one need only note that they include Brooke's famous five sonnets, his "Great Lover," his "Retrospect," and "Tiare Tahiti." Brooke's contributions above all else gave *New Numbers* a poetic quality never surpassed by an English journal of poetry.

iv

THE RISE OF PROVINCIAL PERIODICALS

The rise of the provincial newspaper press in the first twenty years of the eighteenth century inevitably brought with it later the literary periodical. Some of the more exceptional magazines, reviews, and essay serials published outside of London have been mentioned in the preceding pages. But as a class they possessed little distinction or originality. They counted among their contributors few writers whose names are now well known. They were, for the most part, of brief life and inferior merit. Taken together, however, their presence is significant; the rise of the provincial literary journal—indicating the spread of the reading habit and the growing interest in *belles-lettres*—is one of the most illuminating phenomena of the early eighteenth century.

From 1700, the increased number of printing presses in Norwich,[1] Oxford, Cambridge, Bristol, Exeter, New-

---

[1] See W. H. Allnutt, "English Provincial Presses," *Bibliographica*, ii (1896), 276-308.

castle, Glasgow, Manchester, and York—to say nothing of Edinburgh and Dublin, which had been for centuries the literary capitols of Scotland and Ireland, and were, therefore, somewhat earlier in developing their periodical literature—led to a corresponding increase in the number of local newspapers. It later led gradually to the founding of local magazines and reviews, also. Of these, the first important miscellany was Raikes and Dicey's *Northampton Miscellany* (1721) already mentioned. Another was the *Miscellaneæ Curiosæ* of York (1734-35). These were soon followed by the *Dublin Literary Journal* of 1734, The *Scots Magazine* of 1739 (Edinburgh), *The Curiosity; or, Gentleman's and Ladies' Repository* (1740) of Lynn, the *Bath Miscellany* of 1741, *Exshaw's Magazine* (1741-93) of Dublin, and the *Agreeable Miscellany* (1745) of Kendal. Only the *Scots Magazine* and *Exshaw's Magazine* (the *London Magazine* reprinted) had long and apparently successful careers, and these pioneer provincial enterprises were uniformly unoriginal, almost invariably appropriating the contents of London magazines, and serving this material up to their readers, interlarded with occasional local contributions.

Three causes contributed to set on foot the country newspaper press—the strength of the Jacobite party in the country, the commencement (with the *Daily Courant*, 1702) of the London daily papers, and the Stamp Acts.[1] With some modifications, these causes effected also the rise of the provincial miscellanies, reviews, and essay serials. Unquestionably, the establishment of Cave's *Gentleman's Magazine* had its influence, although this did not appear immediately in the nature and content of country magazines, except in the case of the *Scots Maga-*

[1] See (J. G. Muddiman) *Tercentenary Handlist of English and Welsh Newspapers*, London 1920, p. 216.

zine of Edinburgh. The middle of the eighteenth century saw a comparatively few provincial periodicals of a literary nature, like the *Highland Gentleman's Magazine* of Edinburgh (1751), the *Limerick Magazine* of 1752, the *Newcastle General Magazine* of 1747-60, or the *Student* of Oxford (1750-51). For the most part, the "literary" field was still dominated by a single enterprise in Edinburgh, the *Scots Magazine*, and by the great London periodicals, the *Gentleman's*, the *London*, and the newly established *Monthly Review*.

Whatever its cause, a signal increase in the provincial literary periodicals (most of them were of the magazine type) came after 1750. The *Edinburgh Magazine* (1757) competed with the *Scots Magazine* until 1762. The *Dublin Repository* of 1763, the *Literary Register* of Newcastle (1769-71), the *Bath and Bristol Magazine* of 1776, the *Dundee Magazine* of 1775, the *Dumfries Magazine* of 1777—these showed the gradual diffusion of literary interests throughout Great Britain. This is further illustrated before the end of the century by such widely separated publishing enterprises as the *Caledonian Magazine and Review* of Perth (1783), the *Magazin de l'Isle de Jersey* (1784), the *Berwick Museum* of 1785-87, the notably successful *County Magazine* of Salisbury (1786-92), the *Yorkshire Magazine* of 1786, the *Kentish Register* (1793-5) of Canterbury, the *Berkshire Repository* (1797) of Maidenhead, the *Alston Miscellany* (1799) of Aldstone, and the *Arbroath Magazine* and *Ipswich Magazine* of the same year.[1]

These are by no means all, but they are enough to indicate the widespread interest in literary periodicals by the end of the eighteenth century. In many cases the

---

[1] See J. M. M'Bain, *Bibliography of Arbroath Periodical Literature*, Arbroath, 1839, for a description of typical provincial conditions, and the literary periodicals arising therefrom, during the late eighteenth and early nineteenth centuries.

individual publication indicated the presence of a literary clique—in Arbroath or Salisbury, in Exeter or Limerick. It cannot be said that the purer stream of English literature received many notable contributions from this periodical activity. The contents of the provincial magazines (with a few notable exceptions, of course) remained derivative and uninspired to a degree that induces a settled melancholy in the mind of him who now has the courage to turn their dusty pages. The nineteenth century brought some small improvement in the quality of the country magazines; but as the publications issuing from the three great centers—London, Edinburgh, and Dublin—have increased in quality and circulation, they have cut into the always narrow and unstable resources of the provincial magazines. Unfortunately for them, the tendency of the last fifty years, with rapidly improving means of communication, has been always towards increase in the power and prestige of the few at the expense of the many. Success in periodical enterprises of a literary nature—like success in many other things—appears to operate on the "to him that hath" principle.[1]

[1] The really distinguished literary journals published outside of London are mentioned elsewhere in this work.

XIII

PERIODICAL LITERATURE AND THE NEWSPAPER

It is conceivable that the periodical of literature and entertainment might have developed from the newspaper —an evolution of the features used to fill up pages or attract readers. But such does not seem to have been the case. On the contrary, a study of the newspaper press makes it evident that the early journal of news nearly always borrowed its "literary" features from the serials of learning or entertainment. The earliest news sheet of importance which showed a deliberate aim to entertain readers was the *Mercurius Bifrons* (1681) with its page of serious news matter balanced by its page of "jocular intelligence." A few other seventeenth-century news sheets need to be included in the same category. The first really good example of a newspaper with features was John Dunton's *Pegasus, with News, an Observator, and a Jacobite Courant.* It was a thrice-a-week half-sheet folio, "written in a different method from all other newspapers." It was begun June 15 and stopped September 14, 1696, after forty numbers had been issued. The "Observator" department was a palpable anticipation of the "observators" of Dunton's monthly *Post Angel*; while the "Jacobite Courant" was designed "to correct the insolences of the Government's enemies and divert its friends." The last department was written in verse at first, and changed to prose on June 29. Articles included "A short character of Ambition," an essay in the manner of Bacon, Old Tredskin's "new ark of novelties," and dialogues between a Williamite and a Jacobite. Dunton closed the first volume with the thirtieth number, and thereafter the *Jacobite Courant* was abandoned. Distinguished neither as a newspaper or a periodical of amusement, the *Pegasus* is noteworthy as an early combination of the two.

Except for occasional verse in the *Post-Boy* of 1695 and the *London News Letter* of 1696 (frequently used because of the lack of news), almost no other "literary" features are to be found in newspapers until the appearance of Defoe's *Review* in 1704. In spite of Defoe's utterances to the effect that he saw value in giving readers entertainment along with their news, few or none of his contemporaries seem to have profited by his example.[1] In fact, nothing worthy of record follcwed Defoe in the newspaper field until the *Tatler* appeared, although the *Tatler* cannot be regarded as a genuine newspaper any more than the *Gentleman's Journal* of 1692 or the *Diverting Post* of 1704, which likewise included news in their columns. In truth, after Defoe's *Review* there was almost no effort made by newspaper publishers to entertain readers, until the half-sheet folio form was abandoned generally for the four- or six-page newspaper.

Although the *Tatler* and *Spectator* did not immediately influence newspapers to include entertaining features, such as verse, letters, and essays, these elements, which later became commonly mingled with news matter, gained slowly in acceptance. The *Flying Post; or the Post Master* (*cir.* 1710), the *Protestant Post-Boy* (1711), Mist's *Weekly Journal; or Saturday Post* (1716 ff), and

---

[1] . . . He (Defoe) was the first to notice and to help forward the growing assimilation by the daily newspaper of the most attractive and therefore profitable features previously regarded as exclusively proper to literary miscellanies having for their object less current information than general entertainment" (T. H. S. Escott, *Masters of English Journalism*, Lon. 1911, p. 52). The author of this suggestive observation fails to take into account the fact that the daily newspaper was rare in Defoe's day. Moreover, it is misleading to say that anything had been "exclusively proper" to the few miscellanies which had at that time appeared. See *Gentleman's Journal, Diverting Post*, etc., above.

Read's *Weekly Journal; or British Gazeteer* (1715 ff),
printed verses or essays calculated to entertain as well as
inform readers. Applebee's *Original Weekly Journal*
(1720 ff.) was started with an expressed purpose: "For
the diversion of readers we shall always insert at the end
of the news, poems entirely new, serious, humorous and
comical, performed by the greatest wits of the age."
Defoe's *Robinson Crusoe* (reprinted) captivated readers
of Harris's *London Post* in 1719 (nos. 125 to 389). The
Churchman's Last Shift; or, Loyalist's Weekly Journal,
1720-21, published serially the *Voyages of Sinbad the
Sailor*, giving it always first-column space. Other news
serials, between 1712 and 1725, such as the *Orphan Reviv'd, or, Powell's Weekly Journal* in 1719, the *Caledonian Mercury of* 1720, and the *St. James's Journal, with
Memoirs of Literature*, 1722, leavened their news with
original features, from ribald verse to moral essays, until
by 1725, most of the newspapers (they were by this time
nearly all six-page serials) had resorted to these entertaining features.

At this date, Mist's prosperous *Weekly Journal* had
outstripped all its rivals in the range and quality of its
entertainment, and contained considerable criticism of
contemporary literary works. Parker's *Penny Post*, a
small four-page thrice-a-week, begun in this year, published the *Arabian Night's Entertainments*, in installments which ran through eighty-nine numbers; and followed up the success of this feature with other narratives,
including the "Story of Lady Cornelia" and the "Liberal
Lover"—Spanish "novels." The *London Journal* of the
same date contained the letters of "Momus." Two years
later, the *British Journal* was enlivening its columns with
ballads and very disreputable poems, while the *Flying
Post* (in French and English) printed a large percentage
of entertaining matter. By 1728 a notable tendency is

observable—for papers like the *London Journal, Craftsman*, Fog's *Weekly Journal*, and Read's *Weekly Journal* to reserve the first column, or even the first page, for an essay or other diverting feature.

Thus, a survey of the newspapers with literary contents leads us, in 1728, to the *Universal Spectator,* which has already been discussed in an earlier chapter. Practically every newspaper published at this time was resorting to such devices to attract and hold readers. Notable among them was the *Craftsman* of "Caleb D' Anvers" (Nicholas Amhurst) with its tales, fables, dreams, allegories, and occasional criticism.[1]

The *Grub Street Journal* was the first of a number of news serials which made no pretence of gathering news, but with malicious intent borrowed their information on domestic or foreign affairs from the columns of other journals. This practice seems to have had its effect on the legitimate newspapers, which appear, in the next few years, to take more pains with their entertaining elements than with their news matter. Read's *Weekly Journal* on January 1, 1732, appeared with its entire first page devoted to poems, and two years later published among many other attractions an abridgement of Bishop Burnet's *History of His Own Times.* In 1735 a "novel" usually occupied the first two or three columns of space in Applebee's *Weekly Journal*; in the same year a regular three-column essay by "R. Freeman" appeared on the front page of the *London Journal*; the *Weekly Miscellany* gave the position of honor to essays, poems, letters, and other diverting forms; even the *Corn-Cutter's Journal* in 1735 reserved its first column for an essay or letter; the *Weekly Register* (1730 ff.) had a two-column leader in the form of a moral essay, poem, or criticism, with such themes as

[1] See the long discussion of Spenser, Nov. 15, 1735. Swift called Gay the "chief author" of the *Craftsman.* Bolingbroke and Pulteney were also contributors.

"A Critique of Milton," "On Contempt of Snobs," and "A Dialogue between the Sexes"; *Common-Sense* (1737-41) contained essays by Chesterfield and Lyttelton, of more than passing or political value, as well as letters, poetry and epitaphs; while the *Weekly Oracle* (1734-37) relieved its newsmatter by epigrams, essays, and dialogues, in pursuance of a plan set forth in the first number —"It is proposed that the first page of this sheet shall always contain some moral or instructive essay, in prose or verse, either original or extracted from the best authors; so the following is taken from the works of a late eminent writer" (an essay entitled "Of Impudent Delight in Wickedness").

The *Champion; or, British Mercury* (1739-40) was a four-page, thrice-a-week Whiggish newspaper, edited by Fielding and James Ralph. Because of its relation to the *Tatler* and *Spectator*, it has been rather fully discussed in preceding pages. Nothing further need be said of it, except that it was a distinguished example of the newspaper with features, i.e., containing a leading essay, along with verse, parody, etc. Important, however, is the certain influence of such serials as the *Universal Spectator* and *Champion* on subsequent newspaper methods. The success of these papers did not go unnoticed by rival journalists. Moreover, the forms of amusement provided in the journals multiplied. Sentimental novels, published in installments, occupied more and more space. Biography and court memoirs increased the variety of diversion. Toward the end of the half-century nearly all the newspapers gave the best columns—the first page in an average four- or six-page paper—to entertaining and instructive features. Of all these sorts of diversion, the serial essay was the most important. Although in many cases the essays were of political nature, although articles on morals and manners often sugared the special pleading

of the party scribe, yet this practice—beginning thus—
gradually lifted the essay of Addison and Steele out of
the reckoning as a separate periodical, and gave it the
status it has most frequently to-day—that of an interesting
and vital part of many a newspaper.

When one is considering the features in newspapers in
the later eighteenth century, his mind naturally leaps to
Johnson's *Idler*. As a matter of fact, several important
examples of this sort are to be found before 1758, the date
when the *Idler* essays appeared. The *London Daily Advertiser* carried the *Inspector* essays of John Hill, by
which the author attacked Smart, Garrick, and Fielding,
in the famous "Paper War." These essays occupied most
of the first page of this daily newspaper, and were published for two years (1751-53), Hill being frequently
assisted by William Popple, a mediocre playwright of
the day, or by Eustace Budgell. At the same time, Read's
and several other weekly journals were using verse and
other entertaining matter to fill their columns.

The year 1758 found Owen's *New Weekly Chronicle;
or Universal Journal* giving much of its eight-page space
to literary features—reprinted poems of Shenstone and
Parnell, letters on Dodsley's *Cleone*, on contemporary
periodicals, etc. Like the *Grub Street Journal* and the
Gentleman's Magazine, the *Weekly Chronicle* borrowed
essays and news from other weekly serials, especially the
Monitor; or, British Freeholder (1755-65) which was
quoted more frequently than any other paper of the time.
But we look to the great rival of Owen's paper for the
outstanding example of literary entertainment in eighteenth-century newspapers. In Payne's *Universal Chronicle; or, Weekly Gazette*, which began April 8, 1758,
appeared (April 15, 1758-April 5, 1760) Johnson's *Idler*
essays. They were printed on the first page, filling two
columns, and were set in type one point larger than the

news matter. Johnson, like many of his predecessors, had an eye on the book value of the work, when he entered into an agreement with Payne to supply such an essay as would elevate the *Universal Chronicle* above its contemporaries. When a sufficient number had been printed to make two good volumes, the *Idler* essays were deliberately discontinued. Of the 103 essays, twelve were by friends of Johnson—Bennet Langdon, Thomas Warton the younger, Sir Joshua Reynolds, and others. The rest were from the prolific pen of Johnson himself, and covered a range of subjects almost as wide as the matter of the *Tatler* and *Spectator*. It is now determined beyond doubt that Warton's contributions were numbers 33, 93, and 96. Langdon wrote 67, and Reynolds 76, 79, and 82.

The contents of the *Idler* had literary merit—merit fully attested by time and many critics. They were as fresh and diversified as the contents of the *Spectator*. Like Steele and Addison, Johnson purified the journalistic atmosphere. More than any other serial essay published as a department in a newspaper, the *Idler* dealt with literature and writers. Numbers 36, 59, 60, 61, 63, 65, 66, 68, 69, 70, 77, 84, 85, 90, 91, and 97 were chiefly critical. Of these, 60 and 61 on "Minim the Critick" showed Johnson's low opinion of criticism in general. The fate of posthumous works, the loss of ancient writings, the history of translations, "easy writing," and "hard words defended" are among his characteristic themes. Numbers 7, 30, and 55 dealt with hardships of the literary life as Johnson saw them, in the days which followed the decline of political patronage.

The *Universal Chronicle* quoted news and opinion from other papers, according to the fashion of the time, and frequently contained short book reviews and much verse, indicating that the editor did not depend upon Johnson's essays alone to attract a large public. A feature called the "Occasional Querist" is curiously reminiscent of Dunton's reforming *Night Walker* of 1696-7.

The *London Chronicle*, from 1757 had much verse and other entertainment, reprinted poems and good critical notices of the older authors—Wycherley, Congreve, Sidney, Spenser, Shakespeare, Milton, Dryden, and others. During the two years, 1760-62, the "Schemer" essays were published weekly, as the work of another descendant of Bickerstaff—the great philosopher "Helter van Skelter." James Boswell gave the Chronicle many contributions between 1766 and 1790. He was writing at the same time for the *Public Advertiser*, the *Edinburgh Advertiser*, the *Caledonian Mercury*, the *St. James Chronicle*, as well as the *Evening Courant, Weekly Journal*, and *Chronicle* of Edinburgh. Goldsmith's "Chinese Letters" appeared in the *Public Ledger*, from January 1760. The *St. James Chronicle* reserved the first column on the last page for the "Poets' Corner," and during the period, June 1761–January 1762, published the *Genius* essays of George Colman, which in point of style are superior to his work in the *Connoisseur*. The *Cambridge Chronicle* (1762) contained more of literary value than most of its contemporaries, including Mason's elegies, Richardson's essays, and poems (reprinted) from many authors. Lloyd's *Evening Post* and the *Westminster Journal* employed the usual features; theatrical reviews relieved the pages of the *Whitehall Evening Post* of this period. Felix Farley's *Bristol Journal* was made notable by the poems of Chatterton; while the "Gentleman" (July 10-December 4, 1775) an essay department in the *London Packet*, was another of Colman's efforts to render the newspapers vehicles for "rational amusement." Finally, the *Public Advertiser* contained the poems of William Cowper.

The criticisms of the *Rolliad*, which appeared in the *Morning Herald* in 1784, have always been regarded as "literature," in spite of their political object, and well they may be, for few of the serious critical writings of the century show more wit and brilliant creative genius. They were the work of Whig satirists—Richard Fitzpatrick, the intimate of Fox, Lord John Townshend, Joseph Richardson, Richard Tickell, French Laurence, and George Ellis, who was later concerned in the *Anti-Jacobin* and in the *Quarterly Review*. The *Rolliad*, subject of the mock criticism, was the suppositional work of John Rolle, M.P. for Devonshire, a stolid Tory. These mock criticisms of a mock epic became very popular, and when collected in 1785 ran through twenty-two editions. The young wits discontinued this form of raillery before they had overdone it, and transferred their efforts to *Political Eclogues* and then to a series of *Probationary Odes* for the laureateship, vacant by the death of Whitehead in 1785.

The closing years of the eighteenth century found the newspapers generally employing original or borrowed literary matter to enliven their pages and attract readers. A few illustrations will suffice. Hoey's *Dublin Mercury* of 1770 contained some poetry, a serial novel called "The Little Gypsey," on the last page, as well as the "Speculations of Geoffrey Wagstaffe, Esq.," a series of essays. Johnson's *Original Star and Grand Weekly Advertiser* (1778) offered "poetical beauties," theatricals, and "literature" in a series of departments. The *Aurora and Universal Advertiser* (1781) carried a back page of verse. The *Edinburgh Herald* of 1790 had its literary features, as is shown by its first printing of Burns' *Tam O'Shanter* (March 18). Mitchell's *Sunday London Gazette and Weekly Monitor* of 1790 anticipated the modern Sunday newspaper with its essays, poems, and other diverting matter. The *Oracle and Public Advertiser* had in 1797 an occasional department of "Dramatic Ana," and like the *Times*, its contemporary, had theatrical news and advertisements. Scott and Ballantyne's *Edinburgh Weekly Journal*, 1798-1848, contained John Ballantyne's brilliant dramatic criticisms, as well as letters by Scott, and many "fugitive pieces," Lockhart's work and that of Thomas Aird and James Browne. The *General Evening Post, General Advertiser, World, Morning Herald, Morning Chronicle*, and *London Evening Post*, all carried theatrical matter during the last decade of the century, showing that news for playgoers and theatrical folk had, by the beginning of the nineteenth century, become a regular ingredient of the newspaper.

In the nineteenth century, a few outstanding newspapers must serve as examples of the prevailing tendency. The *Times* (1788 ff.) a continuation of John Walter's *Daily Universal Register* of 1785, owned and managed by three generations of Walters, was never without its literary matter. The present weekly edition began publication January 5, 1877. From the first it contained exceptional elements of interest to men of letters. It has always been quite distinct from the *Times Literary Supplement*. The *Sunday Times* has been edited since 1901 by Leonard Rees. Within our century, its chief contributors of literary matter have been Sir Edmund Gosse, Desmond MacCarthy, and E. V. Lucas. The *Manchester Guardian*, established in 1821 by John Edward Taylor, and edited by him and Russell Scott Taylor until 1848, was begun as a Saturday four-page journal, and included from the first its literary matter—poems by Thomas Moore, Byron, and others, a defence of the "Manchester Poets" against the strictures of *Blackwood's*, and articles on the authorship of *Waverley*, on Byron, and other matters of contemporary interest to the literati. Not infrequently it published long reviews. In fact, the proportion of space given to such materials corresponds very well to the proportion of space given to similar matter in the *Guardian* to-day. Like the *Times*, the *Manchester Guardian* is still with us, and is still regarded as a critical voice that cannot be ignored. Finally, a third newspaper which still survives is the *Observer*, which began in 1791. It further illustrates the service of the newspaper to pure literature. Piloted in later years by Edward J. S. Dicey (1870-89), Austin Harrison (1890-1908) and J. L. Garvin (the present editor), the *Observer* has secured contributions of literary matter from practically every critic or authority on current thought. Along with editorial discussion of international peace and national well-being, the reader of the *Sunday Observer* may regale himself with belletristic matter of a high quality, including some of the most discerning reviews of the day.

The newspaper has thus been a medium of poetry, essays and fiction, although in a limited way, since its major purposes have always been the publishing of news and the moulding of public opinion on political or social lines. It has offered early opportunity to many writers of "literary" quality. It has served them for the promotion of cherished theories, for the dissemination of social propaganda. In the 1790's, Perry's *Morning Chronicle* gave to the world the early revolutionary poems of Coleridge. Later it claimed the efforts of Lamb, Richard Brinsley Sheridan, Hazlitt, and Thomas Moore; and still later, of Thackeray and Dickens. The *Morning Post* and the *Courier* of Daniel Stuart were contributed to by Lamb, Mackintosh, Wordsworth, Praed, Southey, and Coleridge.[1] Thomas Barnes, later a famous editor of the *Times*, contributed a brilliant series of criticisms, on English poets from Milton to Campbell, and on novelists like Miss Edgeworth, to the *Champion* of 1814-22.

[1] For Coleridge as journalist, see Escott, *Masters of English Journalism*, Lon. 1911, pp. 166-7.

Hazlitt was dramatic critic for the *Morning Chronicle*, and wrote reviews for the *Scotsman*; DeQuincey was editor of the *Westmorland Gazette* before he produced the best known of his works. The young Thackeray served a kind of author's apprenticeship on his own *National Standard* (1833), an unfortunate newspaper venture in which he dissipated a considerable part of his patrimony. Henry Crabb Robinson, the diarist and friend of genius, was the earliest of nineteenth-century special correspondents. Theodore Hook conducted *John Bull*, long before he made his fame as novelist, and was editor of the *New Monthly Magazine*.[1] Thomas Love Peacock and R. H. Barham wrote during the 1830's for the *Globe*. Benjamin Disraeli in the *Times*, the *Representative* and the *Press* made good his boast to be a "gentleman of the press." Alfred Austin, later Poet Laureate, edited successively the *Daily Telegraph* and the *Standard*. Dickens began

[1] According to Richard Garnett (see DNB) Walter Scott may have been connected with the establishment of *John Bull*, a political paper, set up in 1820, with Theodore Hook as editor. Barham, however, in his *Life of Theodore Hook* (i, 198) expresses the opinion that Scott had nothing to do with it. Lockhart wrote for the *Quarterly Review* in May 1843 (LXXII, 53-108) an essay on Theodore Hook, based on an examination of Hook's diary and papers. He said that Scott meeting Hook in April 1820, liked him so well that he recommended him to a nobleman who was about to establish a paper. Lockhart implied that the nobleman was Wellington and the paper *John Bull*. Barham, and Myron Brightfield (*Theodore Hook and his Novels*, Cambridge 1928, pp. 133 ff.) think it improbable that Scott or Wellington had anything to do with this paper, although Scott unquestionably helped to found the *Beacon*, a Tory journal of the next year (See Lockhart, *Life of Scott*, v. 152-153). *John Bull* now and then commented upon authors of merit, usually with sweeping condemnation. The following epigram from it is reprinted in *Sweepings from Parnassus*:

> Shelley styles his new poem "Prometheus Unbound,"
> And 'tis like to remain so while time circles around;
> For surely an age could be spent in the finding
> A reader so weak as to pay for the binding.

Of *John Bull*, 3739 numbers were published, the last July 16, 1892. It was revived in 1903 and again in 1906. The last resurgence of this periodical was under the editorship of Horatio Bottomley. It is still in progress, but contains nothing of literary interest. The *Beacon* was issued in 1822, for seven numbers, April 12 to June 2.

his career as reporter on the *True Sun* and *Morning Chronicle*; and later, because of pique against the latter newspaper, set up his *Daily News*. George Borrow, even while gathering materials for his *Bible in Spain*, was an occasional correspondent for the *Times*. Frederick Greenwood, co-founder and editor, made his *Pall Mall Gazette* the literary, as well as the political, leader of the cultured class, and attached to his staff such writers as "George Eliot," Charles Reade, Anthony Trollope, and Thomas Hughes. Coventry Patmore's delightful and discriminating criticism appeared regularly in the *St. James Gazette*. Barrie began his literary career in 1882-3, as dramatic critic on the Edinburgh *Evening Courant*.

Such examples—and many more could be shown—sufficiently reveal the later relation of the newspaper to creative literature, and the debt of literary men to journalism. The daily or weekly periodical of news has gradually become dissociated from literature of a high order. No longer do we look to its columns for the best writing of our day—for such contributions as the "Idler" essays of Johnson or the poems of Coleridge. Yet it is still the preparatory school of literature, in many cases; and scores of the most famous authors of to-day have learned their craft, like Dickens, in the toil and hurry of journalism. Others return to it occasionally to advocate a cause or advance a cherished principle.

It may be said, in conclusion, that the late tendency toward specialization has left its mark on the newspaper, as well as on the miscellaneous periodical. Thirty-five years ago the evening journalism of London, represented by the *Pall Mall Gazette*—to use only one illustration—was notable for the quality and intensity of its interest in letters as well as in politics. Now, the "*P. M. G.*" and its kind of newspaper are gone—swallowed up in a super-syndicated and popularized press. The weekly critical journals and the literary supplements have taken over the functions and most of the influence of the newspaper with literary features. Literary interest may still be present in the reviews and essays and occasional verse of the daily newspaper, but "literary quality" in the newspaper press is very nearly extinct.

IN CONCLUSION

The periodical literature of the English people contains a living record of their esthetic and intellectual progress. Half sheets, essays, magazines, reviews—these afford an opportunity for the examination and appraisement of the cultural progress of Great Britain, from the seventeenth century to our own time. The periodicals, are, in effect, the "score keepers"; from generation to generation they have marked the steps forward. More than this, they have rendered immense service to literature, both by direct contribution, and by the essential support they have given men and women in their younger days—who, perhaps through the very training they were thus able to obtain, achieved literary eminence.

A main purpose of this work has been to show clearly the importance of the growth of English periodicals on the development of English authors, and to sketch the relations of the chief writers with periodicals from the seventeenth century to our own day. This effort has made it necessary, on the one hand, to show the development of periodical types, and on the other, to describe to some extent the most important individual serials of a literary character. Such a descriptive survey has comprehended the gradual emergence of the modern critical periodical from seventeenth century news sheets, book catalogues and journals of abstracts; the development of types such as the "learned" periodical and miscellany of entertainment before 1700, and the single-essay serial, magazine, and review, in the years following. It has related the half sheet folio of 1690, designed "to lie for common chat and entertainment on every coffee-house board," to the "magazine" of 1740, perused at his leisure by the English squire in his library. It has revealed, by the multiplication and popularity of journals, a growing public, as education increases. It has shown the essay serial specialized to a score of uses—reform, humor, criticism, fiction—the magazine adapted to a hundred concerns of men—husbandry, trade, industry, history, biography, business, travel, politics, social reform, evangelism, besides the literary concerns of poetry, fiction, and the more perishable commodity, criticism. It finds the first invitation to contributors in the *Universal Historical Bibliotheque of 1687*, the first timid criticism, about the same time, the rise and decay of the essay serial as a *genre*, the gradual elimination of news from the columns of the magazines, the beginning of the critical journals, the vagaries of political reviewing, the breaking up of universal anonymity. It shows periodical writing, at first ignoble, made respectable, the gradual crystallization of periodical types in the early eighteenth century and the dissolving of these traditional classifications in the nineteenth, the spread of education followed by the rise of provincial magazines between 1720 and 1750, the significant beginning and growing vogue of the weekly journal of *belles-lettres* in the nineteenth century—the latest and now the most important of our critical periodicals.

The bewildering heterogeneity of periodical enterprises has now become almost appalling. Every business, industry, sport, trade, profession, artistic leaning, intellectual interest, ethical tendency or religious faith, has its magazines and journals. But the most important fact—and the one that concerns us here—is that literature has, since the death of Queen Anne, claimed the periodical as its handmaiden. By a thousand individual forms and methods, the periodic publication has served during the last two centuries the interests of English writers. One finds it impossible to conceive of a world without it.

Nothing is more certain than that its development has enormously increased the volume of writing and has raised the average quality. It has produced no Chaucer nor Shakespeare nor Milton; but that the journey-work of literature is far more competently done than it was a century or two ago, may safely be laid to the credit of the periodical. Against the inevitable journalistic tendency to half-work and haste, and the temptation to crop the soil too frequently, may be placed the undoubted truth that the magazines and other literary journals have been the means of calling into being some works which have the stamp of the highest genius and many more that the world would now regret to lose. Without the literary periodical we should have had no *Mercure Scandale, London Spy, Tatler, Spectator*, and *Rambler* essays, no Boswell nor Johnson, nor Goldsmith, perhaps (who knows?) ; no Scott, Macaulay, Dickens, and Thackeray. Without the opportunity and incentive that the periodical has given to struggling authors, how many hundreds of those "contributions" which now gladden and inspire the hearts of men would never have seen the light?

The present day *Bookman*, the *Times Literary Supplement*, the *Criterion*, the *London Mercury*, the *New Adelphi*, and *Life and Letters*, represent the final, specialized development—the most advanced forms—of the English literary periodical. Although they have evolved from somewhat various lines of growth, they contain much the same elements of literary interest. Only the *Times Literary Supplement* contains no fiction or poetry; a weekly journal of *belles-lettres*, it is specialized even more highly than the others. The other periodicals, although differing in form and price and in the precise appeal which they make to the reading public, offer—

each in its own manner—the same variety of literary entertainment.

To exaggerate the value of the periodical in the making of English literature is both easy and absurd. It was, in the final analysis, a late development. All the work of Chaucer, Shakespeare, Spenser, Milton, and Dryden had been done before the "literary" journal became a factor of importance. Defoe, Swift, Pope and Gay used it; but not for their best writing. Steele discovered the essay's possibilities and revealed them to Addison. The decline of political patronage led to an enlargement of the magazine's usefulness and its service to authors. Since the death of Queen Anne, the influence of the periodical has been hard to estimate, but of obviously increasing importance. Now, its prestige with the reading public and its influence on authorship are supreme. Just as the reign of Anne was the Golden Age of political patronage, so our own time is the Golden Age of periodical publication. The medium of literary expression which was once despised and rejected has now become of paramount importance to men of letters.

BIBLIOGRAPHY

No comprehensive treatment of English literary periodicals, as distinguished from newspapers, has heretofore existed; a fact which furnishes the chief reason for the present study. Much information may be found, however, in the following books and articles.

Agnew, D. C. A., *Protestant Exiles from France*, Edinburgh 1871, 2 vols.

Aitken, Geo. A., *Life of Richard Steele*, London 1899, 2 vols.

Allnutt, W. H., "English Provincial Presses, Part III," *Bibliographica*, II (1896), 276-308.

Ames, J. G., *English Literary Periodicals of Morals and Manners*, Mt. Vernon, Ohio 1904.

Andrews, A., *A History of British Journalism*, London 1859, 2 vols.

Anonymous, "Essay on the Causes of the Declining Popularity of the British Essayists," Constable's *Edinburgh Magazine*, March 1819.

Anonymous, *The Battle of the Reviews*, 1760 (Pamphlet).

Anonymous, "The Centenary of the 'Quarterly Review'", *Quarterly Review*, CCX (April 1909), 731-784, and CCXI (July 1909), 279-324.

Anonymous, "The *Edinburgh Review* (1802-1902)", *Edinburgh Review*, CXLV (July 1902), 275-318.

Arber, Edward (Ed.), *The Term Catalogue*, London 1903-1906, 3 vols.

Arnot, Hugo, *History of Edinburgh*, Edinburgh 1779.

Bain, Alexander, *James Mill, A Biography*, London 1882.

Baldwin, E. C., "The Relation of the Seventeenth Century Character to the Periodical Essay," *Pub. Mod. Lang. Assoc.*, XIX (1904), 75-114.

Baldwin, E. C., "La Bruyère's Influence upon Addison," *Pub. Mod. Lang. Assoc.*, XIX (1904), 479-495.

Barham, R. H., *Life and Remains of Theodore Hook*, London 1848.

Barwick, G. F., "Some Magazines of the Eighteenth Century," *Trans. of the Bibliographical Society*, X (1908-9), 109-40.

Bateson, F. W., "The *Errata* in the *Tatler*," *Review of English Studies*, V (April 1929), 155-166.

Beattie, William, *Life and Letters of Thomas Campbell*, London 1850, 3 vols.

à Beckett, A. W., *The à Becketts of "Punch,"* New York 1903.

Betz, L. P., *Pierre Bayle und die "Nouvelles de la République des Lettres,"* Zurich 1896.

Bodleian Library, *Catalogue of Periodicals*, Oxford.

Bond, R. P., "A Fragment by Addison" (in the *Universal Spectator*), *Review of English Studies*, V (April 1929), 203-4.

Boswell, James, *Life of Samuel Johnson*, Ed. G. B. Hill, Oxford 1887, 6 vols.

Bourne, H. R. Fox, *English Newspapers*, London 1887, 2 vols.

Brewster, Dorothy, *Aaron Hill, Poet, Dramatist, Projector*, New York 1913.

British Museum, *British Museum Catalogue of Printed Books: Periodical Publications*, London 1899-1900.

Burn, J. H., *Catalogue of a Collection of Early English Newspapers and Essayists, formed by the Late John Thomas Hope, Esq.*, Oxford 1865.

Carlisle, H. E. (Ed.), *A Selection from the Correspondence of Abraham Hayward, 1834-1884*, London 1886, 2 vols.

Carver, P. L., "Hazlitt's Contributions to *The Edinburgh Review,"* *Review of English Studies*, IV (October 1928), 375-393.

Caskey, J. Homer, *Life and Works of Edward Moore*, New Haven 1927.

Chalmers, George, *Life of Thomas Ruddiman*, London 1794.

Cockburn, Lord, *Life of Francis Jeffrey*, Philadelphia 1853.

Colby, Elbridge, *A Bibliography of Thomas Holcroft*, New York 1922.

Collins, A. S., "Growth of the Reading Public during the Eighteenth Century," *Review of English Studies*, II (1926), 284-294; 428-438.

Collins, A. S., *Authorship in the Days of Johnson*, London 1927.

Constable, Thomas, *Archibald Constable*, Edinburgh 1873, 3 vols.

Cook, E. T., "The Jubilee of the *Cornhill,"* *Cornhill Magazine*, CI (January 1910), 8-27.

Copinger, W. A., *On the Authorship of the First Hundred Numbers of the Edinburgh Review,"* Manchester 1895.

Couper, W. J., *The Edinburgh Periodical Press*, Stirling 1908, 2 vols.

Courtney, W. P. and Smith, D. N., *A Bibliography of Samuel Johnson*, Oxford 1915.

Crane, R. S. and Kaye, F. B., *A Census of British Newspapers and Periodicals, 1665-1800*, Durham, North Carolina 1927.

Cross, Wilbur L., *The History of Henry Fielding*, New Haven 1918, 3 vols.

Curwen, Henry, *A History of Booksellers, the Old and the New*, London 1873.

Dibdin, Thomas F., *Bibliomania*, London 1809.

Dibdin, Thomas F., *Reminiscences of a Literary Life*, London 1836, 2 vols.

Dickens, Charles, *Works* (Chapman and Hall Edition), London 1908.

Diesch, Carl, *Bibliographie der germanistischen zeitschriften*, Leipzig 1927.

Dilke, C. W., *The Papers of a Critic*, London 1875.

D'Israeli, Isaac, *Curiosities of Literature*, London 1871.

D'Israeli, Isaac, *Calamities of Authors*, London 1812-13.

Dix, E. R. M'C., "The Earliest Periodical *Journals* Published in Dublin," *Proceedings of the Royal Irish Academy*, 3rd series, VI, 33-35 (1900-2).

Drake, Nathan, *Essays Biographical, Critical and Historical, Illustrative of the Tatler, Spectator, and Guardian*, London 1805, 3 vols.

Drake, Nathan, *Essays . . . Illustrative of the Rambler, Adventurer*, etc., London 1809, 2 vols.

Dunton, John, *The Life and Errors of John Dunton*, London 1818, 2 vols.

Edmonds, Charles, *Poetry of the Anti-Jacobin*, 2nd Ed., London 1854.

Ellis, Stewart M., *Mainly Victorian*, London 1924.

Escott, T. H. S., *Masters of English Journalism*, London 1911.

Faxon, F. W., *Literary Annuals and Gift Books*, Boston, Massachusetts, 1912.

Fitzpatrick, W. J., *Life of Charles Lever*, London 1879.

Forster, John, *Historical and Biographical Essays*, London 1858.

Forster, John, *Life of Charles Dickens*, London 1904.

Foster, Dorothy, "The Earliest Precursor of Our Present-Day Monthly Miscellanies," *Pub. Mod. Lang. Assoc.*, XXXII (1917), 22-58.

Francis, J. Collins, *John Francis, publisher of the "Athenaeum,"* London 1888.

Frost, W. A., "A List of the Works of G. P. R. James," *Notes and Queries*, 12th series, II (August 26, 1916), 167-168.

Gates, L. E., (Ed.) *Selections from the Essays of Francis Jeffrey*, Boston 1894.

Gildon, Chas., *History of the Athenian Society*, London 1691.

Gillies, R. P., *Memoirs of a Literary Veteran*, London 1851.

Gordon, Mrs. Mary M., *Christopher North, a Memoir of John Wilson*, Edinburgh 1862.

Gordon, Mrs. M. M., *The Home Life of Sir David Brewster*, Edinburgh 1869.

Graham, Walter, *The Beginnings of English Literary Periodicals*, New York 1926.

Graham, Walter, "Shelley's Debt to Leigh Hunt and the *Examiner*," *Pub. Mod. Lang. Assoc.*, XL (1925), 185-192.

Graham, Walter, "Contemporary Critics of Coleridge, the Poet," *Pub. Mod. Lang. Assoc.*, XXXVIII (1923), 278-289.

Graham, Walter, "Robert Southey as Tory Reviewer," *Philological Quarterly*, II (1923), 97-111.

Graham, Walter, "Some Predecessors of the *Tatler*," *Journal of English and Germanic Philology*, XXIV (1925), 548-54.

Graham, Walter, *Tory Criticism in the "Quarterly Review*," New York 1921.

Grant, James, *The Newspaper Press*, London 1871-2, 2 vols.

Graves, Charles L., *Mr. Punch's History of Modern England*, London 1921.

Greenough, C. N., "The Development of the *Tatler*, Particularly in Regard to News," *Pub. Mod. Lang. Assoc.*, XXXI (1916), 633-663.

Gregory, Winifred, *Union List of Serials*, New York 1927.

Grosart, A. B., *Robert Fergusson*, Edinburgh 1898.

Halkett, S. and Laing, J., *Dictionary of Anonymous and Pseudonymous English Literature*, Edinburgh 1927.

Haller, William, *The Early Life of Robert Southey*, 1774-1803, New York 1917.

Haney, John Louis, *Early Reviews of the English Poets*, Philadelphia 1904.

Haney, John Louis, *Seventeenth and Eighteenth Century Periodicals*, (MS. copy) Newberry Library, Chicago.

Hatin, E., *Bibliographie historique et critique de la presse périodique française*, Paris 1866.

Hatin, E., *Histoire politique et littéraire de la presse en France*, Paris 1859-61, 8 vols.

Hayley, William, *The Life and Letters of William Cowper*, Chichester 1809.

Hayward, Abraham, *Biographical and Critical Essays*, London 1858-74, 5 vols.

(Hazlitt, William,) "The Periodical Press," *Edinburgh Review*, XXXVIII (May 1823), 349-378.

Hazlitt, William, *The Spirit of the Age*, London 1825.

Head, Francis B., *Essays*, London 1857.

Herzfeld, Georg, *William Taylor von Norwich*, Halle 1897.

Hillhouse, J. T., *The Grub Street Journal*, Durham, North Carolina 1928.

Horner, Leonard, *Memoirs and Correspondence of Francis Horner*, London 1853, 2 vols.

Hughes, T. R., "John Scott: Editor, Author, and Critic," *London Mercury*, XXI, (April 1930), 518-528.

Hunt, Leigh, *Autobiography*, Oxford 1928.

Hutton, R. H., (Ed.) *Poems and Essays of William C. Roscoe*, London 1860.

Jensen, Gerard E. (Ed.), *Covent Garden Journal* (reprint) New Haven 1915, 2 vols., Introduction.

Jerdan, William, *Autobiography*, London 1852-1853, 4 vols.

Jerrold, Walter, *Douglas Jerrold and "Punch,"* London 1910.

Jerrold, Walter, *Life of Douglas Jerrold*, London, n. d.

Jerrold, Walter, *Thomas Hood, his Life and Times*, London 1907.

Johnson, Samuel, "An Account of the Life of the late Mr. Cave," *Gentleman's Magazine*, XXIV (February 1754), 55-58.

Johnstone, G. H., *The Ruddimans in Scotland*, Edinburgh 1901.

Jones, R. F., *Lewis Theobald*, New York 1919.

Kebbel, T. E., "John Wilson Croker," *Fortnightly Review*, (July 1884), 688-702.

Kerr, Robert, *Memoirs of the Life, Writings, and Correspondence of William Smellie*, Edinburgh 1811, 2 vols.

Kinnear, J. Boyd, "Anonymous Journalism," *Contemporary Review*, V (July 1867), 324-339.

King, R. W., *The Translator of Dante; the Life, Work and Friendships of Henry Francis Cary*, London 1925.

Kippis, Andrew, *Biographia Britannica*, 2nd ed., London 1778-93, 6 vols. (Incomplete).

Kitchin, Geo., *Sir Roger L'Estrange*, London 1913.

Kluge, J., *Henry Mackenzie, sein Leben und seine Werke*, Halle A. S. 1910.

Knight, Charles, *Passages in the Life of Charles Knight*, New York 1874.

Lane-Poole, S., *The Life of the Right Honourable Stratford Canning*, London 1888, 2 vols.

Lang, Andrew, *Life and Letters of John Gibson Lockhart*, London 1897, 2 vols.

Laughton, J. K., *Memoirs of the Life and Correspondence of Henry Reeve*, London 1898, 2 vols.

Lee, William, "Forgotten Periodical Publications," *Notes and Queries*, 3rd series, IX (January-June 1866), 53-54.

Lee, William, "Periodical Publications during the twenty years, 1712 to 1732." *Notes and Queries*, 3rd series, IX (January-June 1866), 72-75; 92-95; also IX, 164, 268, and X (July-December 1866), 134.

Lehmann, R. C., *Charles Dickens as Editor*, London 1912.

Lockhart, J. G., *Life of Sir Walter Scott*, Edinburgh 1837-38, 7 vols.

Lockhart, J. G., "Remarks on the Periodical Criticism of England," *Blackwood's Magazine*, II (March 1818), 670-679.

M'Bain, J. M., *Bibliography of Arbroath Periodical Literature*, Arbroath 1839.

McCutcheon, R. P., "The Beginnings of Book-reviewing in English Periodicals," *Pub. of the Mod. Lang. Assoc.*, XXXVII (1922), 691-706.

McCutcheon, R. P., "John Dunton's Connection with Book-Reviewing," *Studies in Philology*, XXV (July 1928), 3.

McCutcheon, R. P., "John Houghton, a Seventeenth-century Editor and Book-Reviewer," *Modern Philology*, XX (1922-23), 255-260.

MacFarlane, Charles, *Reminiscences of a Literary Life*, New York 1917.

Mackenzie, Henry, *Works*, Edinburgh 1808.

Madden, Richard R., *The History of Irish Periodical Literature*, London 1867, 2 vols.

Marr, George S., *The Periodical Essayists of the 18th Century*, New York 1924.

Marston, E., *Sketches of Some London Booksellers of the Time of Dr. Samuel Johnson*, London 1902.

Matz, B. W., "Dickens as a Journalist," *Fortnightly Review*, LXXXIII, N. S. (May 1, 1908), 817-832.

Matz, B. W., "George Meredith as Publisher's Reader," *Fortnightly Review*, LXXXVI, N. S. (August 2, 1909), 282-298.

Mill, J. S., *Autobiography*, Ed., J. J. Coss, New York 1924.

Millar, J. H. A., *A Literary History of Scotland*, London 1903.

Muddiman, J. G., *The King's Journalist*, 1659-1689, London 1923.

(Muddiman, J. G.,) *Tercentenary Handlist of English and Welsh Newspapers, Magazines and Reviews*, London 1920.

Mumby, Frank A., *The Romance of Bookselling*, Boston 1911.

"Myops", "Charles Lamb as a Journalist," *Notes and Queries*, 9th series, VIII (July-December 1901), 125-6.

Napier, Macvey, (Jr.) *Selections from the Correspondence of the late Macvey Napier*, London 1879.

Nichols, John, *Literary Anecdotes of the Eighteenth Century*, 1812-1815, 9 vols.

Nichols, John, *Illustrations of the Literary History of the Eighteenth Century*, 1817-1858, 8 vols.

Nichols, John, "Rise and Progress of the (*Gentleman's*) *Magazine*," *Index of Gentleman's Magazine*, 1787-1818, London 1821.

Niven, G. W., "The Authorship of the *British Apollo*," *Notes and Queries*, 9th series, VIII (July-December 1901), 97-8; 158-9.

North, Roger, *Examen*, London 1740.

Oliphant, Mrs. Margaret, *William Blackwood and His Sons*, Edinburgh 1897.

"Paston, George," "The Monthly Review in the 18th Century," *Monthly Review*, VIII (August 1902), 123-137.

Plomer, H. R., *A Dictionary of the Printers and Booksellers who were at work in England, Scotland and Ireland from 1668 to 1725*, Oxford 1922.

Pope, Alexander, *Letters*, Elwin and Courthope Ed., II, 417, London 1871.

Pottle, F. A., *The Literary Career of James Boswell*, New York 1929.

Powell, L. F., "Johnson's Part in *The Adventurer*," in *Review of English Studies*, III (1927), 420-429.

Procter, Bryan Waller ("Barry Cornwall") *An Autobiographical Fragment*, London 1877.

"Rawlinson Manuscript," Bodleian Library, "Rawlinson Mss.," vol. 72, no. 65.

Redding, Cyrus, *Personal Reminiscences of Eminent Men*, London 1867, 3 vols.

Robberds, J. W., *Memoir of the Life and Writing of the Late William Taylor of Norwich*, London 1843, 2 vols.

Roberts, William, "The *Gentleman's Magazine* and its Rivals," *Athenaeum*, No. 3235, (October 26, 1889), p. 560.

Robinson, Henry Crabb, *Diary, Reminiscences, and Correspondence*, London 1869, 3 vols.

Roscoe, E. S., "Letters of Dr. Johnson to Sir Robert Chambers," *Cornhill Mag.*, CXI (1929), 407-421.

Saintsbury, George, *Collected Essays and Papers*, London 1923.

(Scott, John), "Lord Byron: his French Critics: the Newspapers; and the Magazines," *London Magazine*, I, 492-497.

Scott, John, "Blackwood's Magazine," *London Magazine*, II (July-December 1820), 509-521.

Scott, John, "The Mohock Magazine," *London Magazine*, II, 666-685.

Scott, John, "Cockney Writers and the Quarterly Review," *London Magazine* III, (January-June 1821) 69-73.

Scott, Sir Walter, *Familiar Letters*, Edinburgh 1894.

Scott, Sir Walter, *Journal of Sir Walter Scott*, Edinburgh 1891.

Seitz, R. W., "Goldsmith and the *Literary Magazine*," *Review of English Studies*, V, 410-430.

Sherburn, George, "Edward Young and Book Advertising," *Review of English Studies*, IV (1928), 414-417.

Shorter, Clement K., "Newspapers," *Encyclopedia Britannica*, 11th Edition, New York 1911, XIX, 544-565.

(Skelton, Sir John,) *Nugae Criticae*, Edinburgh 1862.

Smiles, Samuel, *A Publisher and His Friends*, London 1891, 2 vols.

Smiles, Samuel, *Brief Biographies*, Boston 1861.

Smith, D. N., Chapman, R. W. and Powell, L. F., *Johnson and Boswell Revised*, Oxford 1928.

Smith, H. Jewett, *Oliver Goldsmith's "The Citizen of the World,"* New Haven 1926.

Smith, Sydney, *Memoirs*, London 1869.

Smollett, Tobias, *Letters*, Ed. Noyes, Cambridge, Massachusetts 1926.

Southey, Cuthbert C., *The Life and Correspondence of Robert Southey*, London 1850.

Southey, Robert (Ed.), *The Works of William Cowper*, London 1836-7.

Spence, Joseph, *Anecdotes, Observations, and Characters, of Books and Men*, London 1820.

Spielmann, M. H., *The History of Punch*, London 1895.

Stearns, Bertha, "The First English Periodical for Women," *Mod. Phil.*, Aug. 1930, pp. 45-59.

Stokes, Francis Griffin, (Ed.) *An Essay Written in a Country Churchyard*, (by Thomas Gray), Oxford 1929.

Straus, Ralph, *The Unspeakable Curll*, London 1927.

Straus, Ralph, *Robert Dodsley*, London 1910.

Tedder, Henry Richard, "Periodicals," *Encyclopedia Britannica*, 11th Edition, New York 1911, xxi, 151-157.

Thomas, W. B., *The Story of the Spectator*, 1828-1928, London 1928.

Thoresby, Ralph, *The Diary of Ralph Thoresby* . . . (1677-1724) London 1830.

Timperley, C. H., *Encyclopedia of Literary and Typographical Anecdote*, 2nd edition, London 1842.

Towers, C. M. D., "John Stuart Mill and the *London and Westminster Review*," *Atlantic Monthly* LXIX, (January 1892), 57-74.

Townsend, C., *et al.*, "The Centenary of the *Spectator*," *Spectator*, CXLI (November 3, 1928), Supp. pp. 1-48.

Tupper, Caroline F., "Goldsmith and 'The Gentleman who Signs D'," *Modern Language Notes*, XLV (1930), 71-77.

Walpole, Horace, *A Catalogue of the Royal and Noble Authors of England*, Twickenham 1758.

Ward, A. W. and Waller, A. R. (Ed.), *Cambridge History of English Literature*, Cambridge 1907-1916, vii, 389-416; ix, 1-28, 29-72; xii, 154-180; xiv, 184-225, 226-233, 258-264, and bibliographies.

Warter, J. W. (ed.), *Selections from the Letters of Robert Southey*, London 1856, 4 vols.

Waugh, Arthur, "The Biography of a Periodical," *Fortnightly Review*, CXXVI, N. S. (October 1, 1929), 512-524.

Welby, T. Earle, *The Victorian Romantics*, 1850-1872, London 1929.

"Williams, J. B.", (J. G. Muddiman) *History of English Journalism to the Foundation of the "Gazette,"* London 1908.

Wilson, Walter, *Memoirs of the Life and Times of Daniel Defoe*, London 1830.

Yates, Edmund, *Recollections and Experiences*, London 1884.

Yeowell, James (Ed.), *A Literary Antiquary, Memoir of William Oldys*, London 1862.

Zeitlin, Jacob, "The Editor of the *London Magazine*," *Journ. Eng. Ger. Phil.* XX (1921), 328-354.

INDEX

This index contains the titles of periodicals mentioned in the foregoing pages, names of authors, editors, and contributors, and the names of the more important writers, like Dryden or Wordsworth, who wrote little or nothing for serial publication. Titles of English periodicals are followed by the dates of initial publication. If the title used in the body of this work is not the original title, the latter is given below in parentheses.

DATE DUE

JA30'73			